Living Gluten-Free

FOR

DUMMIES®

by Sue Baic, Nigel Denby, and Danna Korn

BICENTENNIAL
1807
WILEY
2007
BICENTENNIAL

John Wiley & Sons, Ltd

Living Gluten-Free For Dummies®

Published by
John Wiley & Sons, Ltd
The Atrium
Southern Gate
Chichester
West Sussex
PO19 8SQ
England

E-mail (for orders and customer service enquires): cs-books@wiley.co.uk

Visit our Home Page on www.wiley.com

Copyright © 2007 John Wiley & Sons, Ltd, Chichester, West Sussex, England

Published by John Wiley & Sons, Ltd, Chichester, West Sussex

All Rights Reserved. No part of this publication may be reproduced, stored in a retrieval system or transmitted in any form or by any means, electronic, mechanical, photocopying, recording, scanning or otherwise, except under the terms of the Copyright, Designs and Patents Act 1988 or under the terms of a licence issued by the Copyright Licensing Agency Ltd, 90 Tottenham Court Road, London, W1T 4LP, UK, without the permission in writing of the Publisher. Requests to the Publisher for permission should be addressed to the Permissions Department, John Wiley & Sons, Ltd, The Atrium, Southern Gate, Chichester, West Sussex, PO19 8SQ, England, or emailed to permreq@wiley.co.uk, or faxed to (44) 1243 770620.

Trademarks: Wiley, the Wiley Publishing logo, For Dummies, the Dummies Man logo, A Reference for the Rest of Us!, The Dummies Way, Dummies Daily, The Fun and Easy Way, Dummies.com and related trade dress are trademarks or registered trademarks of John Wiley & Sons, Inc. and/or its affiliates in the United States and other countries, and may not be used without written permission. All other trademarks are the property of their respective owners. Wiley Publishing, Inc., is not associated with any product or vendor mentioned in this book.

LIMIT OF LIABILITY/DISCLAIMER OF WARRANTY: THE PUBLISHER, THE AUTHOR, AND ANYONE ELSE INVOLVED IN PREPARING THIS WORK MAKE NO REPRESENTATIONS OR WARRANTIES WITH RESPECT TO THE ACCURACY OR COMPLETENESS OF THE CONTENTS OF THIS WORK AND SPECIFICALLY DISCLAIM ALL WARRANTIES, INCLUDING WITHOUT LIMITATION WARRANTIES OF FITNESS FOR A PARTICULAR PURPOSE. NO WARRANTY MAY BE CREATED OR EXTENDED BY SALES OR PROMOTIONAL MATERIALS. THE ADVICE AND STRATEGIES CONTAINED HEREIN MAY NOT BE SUITABLE FOR EVERY SITUATION. THIS WORK IS SOLD WITH THE UNDERSTANDING THAT THE PUBLISHER IS NOT ENGAGED IN RENDERING LEGAL, ACCOUNTING, OR OTHER PROFESSIONAL SERVICES. IF PROFESSIONAL ASSISTANCE IS REQUIRED, THE SERVICES OF A COMPETENT PROFESSIONAL PERSON SHOULD BE SOUGHT. NEITHER THE PUBLISHER NOR THE AUTHOR SHALL BE LIABLE FOR DAMAGES ARISING HEREFROM. THE FACT THAT AN ORGANIZATION OR WEBSITE IS REFERRED TO IN THIS WORK AS A CITATION AND/OR A POTENTIAL SOURCE OF FURTHER INFORMATION DOES NOT MEAN THAT THE AUTHOR OR THE PUBLISHER ENDORSES THE INFORMATION THE ORGANIZATION OR WEBSITE MAY PROVIDE OR RECOMMENDATIONS IT MAY MAKE. FURTHER, READERS SHOULD BE AWARE THAT INTERNET WEBSITES LISTED IN THIS WORK MAY HAVE CHANGED OR DISAPPEARED BETWEEN WHEN THIS WORK WAS WRITTEN AND WHEN IT IS READ. SOME OF THE EXERCISES AND DIETARY SUGGESTIONS CONTAINED IN THIS WORK MAY NOT BE APPROPRIATE FOR ALL INDIVIDUALS, AND READERS SHOULD CONSULT WITH A PHYSICIAN BEFORE COMMENCING ANY EXERCISE OR DIETARY PROGRAM.

For general information on our other products and services, please contact our Customer Care Department within the U.S. at 800-762-2974, outside the U.S. at 317-572-3993, or fax 317-572-4002.

For technical support, please visit www.wiley.com/techsupport.

Wiley also publishes its books in a variety of electronic formats. Some content that appears in print may not be available in electronic books.

British Library Cataloguing in Publication Data: A catalogue record for this book is available from the British Library

ISBN: 978-0-470-31910-9

Printed and bound in Great Britain by Bell & Bain, Ltd., Glasgow

10 9 8 7 6

WILEY

About the Authors

Nigel Denby trained as a dietitian at Glasgow Caledonian University, following an established career in the catering industry. He is also a qualified chef and previously owned his own restaurant.

His dietetic career began as a Research Dietitian at the Human Nutrition Research Centre in Newcastle upon Tyne. After a period working as a Community Dietitian, Nigel left the NHS to join Boots Health and Beauty Experience where he led the delivery and training of Nutrition and Weight Management services.

In 2003 Nigel set up his own Nutrition consultancy, delivering a clinical service to Hammersmith and Queen Charlotte's Hospital Women's Health Clinic and the International Eating Disorders Centre in Buckinghamshire, as well as acting as Nutrition Consultant for the Childbase Children's Nursery Group.

Nigel also runs his own private practice in Harley Street, specialising in Weight Management, PMS/Menopause and Irritable Bowel Syndrome.

Nigel works extensively with the media, writing for the *Sunday Telegraph Magazine*, *Zest*, *Essentials*, and various other consumer magazines. His work in radio and television includes BBC and ITN news programmes, Channel 4's *Fit Farm*, BBC *Breakfast*, and BBC *Real Story*. He is the co-author, with Sue Baic, of *Nutrition For Dummies* and *The GL Diet For Dummies*.

Sue Baic is a Lecturer in Nutrition and Public Health in the Department of Exercise and Health Sciences at Bristol University. She has a first degree from Bristol University followed by a Master of Science in Human Nutrition from London University. Sue is a Registered Dietitian (RD) with over 15 years' experience in the field of nutrition and health in the NHS and as a freelance consultant. She feels strongly about providing nutrition information to the public that is evidence-based, up-to-date, unbiased, and reliable.

As a member of the public relations committee of the British Dietetic Association she has written for the media on a variety of nutrition-related health issues. Sue lives in Bristol and spends her spare time running up and down hills in the Cotswolds in an attempt to get fit.

She is the co-author, with Nigel Denby, of *Nutrition For Dummies* and *The GL Diet For Dummies*.

Danna Korn is also the author *of Wheat-Free, Worry-Free: The Art of Happy, Healthy, Gluten-Free Living* and *Kids with Celiac Disease: A Family Guide to Raising Happy, Healthy Gluten-Free Children*. Respected as one of the leading authorities on the gluten-free diet and the medical conditions that benefit from it, she speaks frequently to health care professionals, celiacs, parents of celiacs, parents of autistic kids involved in a gluten-free/casein-free dietary intervention program, and others on or considering a gluten-free diet. She has been invited twice to be a presenter at the International Symposium on Celiac Disease.

Danna has been researching celiac disease since her son, Tyler, was diagnosed with the condition in 1991. That same year, she founded R.O.C.K. (Raising Our Celiac Kids), a support group for families of children on a gluten-free diet. Today, Danna leads more than 100 chapters of R.O.C.K. worldwide. She is a consultant to retailers, manufacturers, testing companies, dietitians, nutritionists, and people newly diagnosed with gluten intolerance and celiac disease. She also coordinates the International Walk/Run for Celiac Disease each May in San Diego.

Dedication

This book is dedicated to the people who have patiently supported my sometimes-over-zealous-and-usually-over-the-top efforts as The Glutenator, singing the praises of a gluten-free lifestyle throughout the land. Most importantly, to my family and friends, who encourage, inspire, and energise me. Your support means more to me than you could ever know, and I couldn't have written a word without you. And to those of you who embrace or are planning to embrace the gluten-free lifestyle, I hope I can make a difference, if only a small one, in your lives by inspiring you to love the gluten-free way of life.

— **Danna**

Authors' Acknowledgements

Thanks to John and Rosie and close friends for their interest and encouragement whilst I've been writing this book, and it's been a pleasure, as ever, to work with my co-author Nigel.

— **Sue**

Thanks as always to my writing partner Sue, for keeping me focused and to our schedule. My part in writing this book is dedicated to a dear friend Denise Helmn who was always so encouraging and supportive in everything I did. Denise passed away whilst I was working on this book, and I miss her very much.

We would both like to thank the excellent team at Wiley, especially Alison Yates and Simon Bell, for their part in bringing this book to fruition. Thank you too to Lynne Garton and Claire Loades for their valuable contributions.

— **Nigel**

A huge thank-you to the hard-working team at Wiley Publishing. First, thank you to Mikal Belicove, the acquisitions editor who came up with and promoted the idea of doing a *For Dummies* book about the gluten-free lifestyle, and then held my hand as I learned the ropes of writing in the *For Dummies* format. To senior project editor Tim Gallan, thank you for keeping me on track and for your attention to organization and detail. To both Tim and copy editor Danielle Voirol, thank you for tolerating my sometimes quirky sense of humor and my many made-up words. It must have driven your spell-checker crazy. Danielle, your speedy grasp of the subject, in-depth research, and clever questions were amazing. Can't get anything by you, that's for sure!

I'd like to thank Emily Nolan for testing all of the recipes, and for her tactful and humorous comments when the dishes I had invented were outrageous flops (don't worry, we fixed 'em!). And thank you to Patty Santelli for nutritional analysis of the recipes.

I'm extremely grateful to my friends and colleagues, Michelle Pietzak, M.D. and Cynthia Kupper, R.D., for their careful technical review of the book. Both of you go far and above the 'call of duty' in helping the gluten-free community each and every day.

To the entire gluten-free community, thank you for your steadfast encouragement. You motivate me to be passionate.

And last, but by no means least, I'm incredibly grateful to my family and friends. After I finished the book before this one, I asked you to slip cyanide in my coffee if I ever thought about writing another book. Thanks for not doing that. Seriously, without your patience, encouragement, support, optimism, love and inspiration, I couldn't have written a word.

— **Danna**

Publisher's Acknowledgements

We're proud of this book; please send us your comments through our Dummies online registration form located at www.dummies.com/register/.

Some of the people who helped bring this book to market include the following:

Acquisitions, Editorial, and Media Development

Project Editor: Simon Bell

Acquistions Editor: Alison Yates

Copy Editor: Juliet Booker

Proofreader: Andy Finch

Technical Editor: Lynne Garton, Registered Nutritionist and Dietitian, www.alimenta.co.uk

Executive Editor: Jason Dunne

Executive Project Editor: Martin Tribe

Content Editor: Steve Edwards

Recipe Tester: Emily Nolan

Cover Photo: GettyImages/Diana Miller

Cartoons: Ed McLachlan

Composition Services

Project Coordinator: Jennifer Theriot

Layout and Graphics: Stephanie D. Jumper, Alicia B. South

Proofreaders: Jessica Kramer, Susan Moritz

Indexer: Aptara

Special Help

Brand Reviewer: Jennifer Bingham

Publishing and Editorial for Consumer Dummies

Diane Graves Steele, Vice President and Publisher, Consumer Dummies

Joyce Pepple, Acquisitions Director, Consumer Dummies

Kristin A. Cocks, Product Development Director, Consumer Dummies

Michael Spring, Vice President and Publisher, Travel

Kelly Regan, Editorial Director, Travel

Publishing for Technology Dummies

Andy Cummings, Vice President and Publisher, Dummies Technology/General User

Composition Services

Gerry Fahey, Vice President of Production Services

Debbie Stailey, Director of Composition Services

Contents at a Glance

Table of Contents

Introduction

· ·

*N*ot so many years ago, the gluten-free lifestyle was reserved for a small cluster of people who were forced to settle for foods that often looked like cardboard but didn't taste as good.

Today, with improved diagnostic tools, and with many people simply choosing to give up gluten, the gluten-free lifestyle is far more common. Attractive and palatable gluten-free products abound (and are a far cry from the only foods that used to be available), food labelling is far less ambiguous, and people no longer look at you as if you have four heads when you ask for a burger without the bun.

Being gluten-free isn't about being on a diet. It's about living a lifestyle. Whether you've been gluten-free for decades or are only considering the idea of giving up gluten, this book is packed with information that can impact on every aspect of your life, from the obvious – your health and how you shop, cook, and eat – to more subtle facets, like finances, socialising, and eating with friends and family.

We have no supplements to sell you and no gluten-free food products that we endorse but between us we hope we have a wealth of experience, having worked with many people to help them make the transition to a gluten-free lifestyle.

This book is the reference guide you need to help you with all those aspects. It's your reference for living – and loving – a gluten-free lifestyle.

About This Book

Living Gluten-Free For Dummies, like all *For Dummies* books, is divided up so you don't have to read it all at once, or even from the front to the back, if you don't want to. You can skip from B to R to A and even reread B if you want to. You can read it sideways and standing on your head if you like; all you have to do is find a section you're interested in and dip in. We suggest you peruse the Table of Contents and see whether any particular chapter or subject in particular appeals and start there. Or you can flip through the book and see whether any of the headings catch your interest.

If you're new to the gluten-free lifestyle and have plenty of questions, you're probably best off starting at Chapter 1 and working your way through most of the book in order.

If you've been gluten-free for years, do yourself a favour and take a look at Chapter 4. You may be surprised at some of the foods that are allowed on the gluten-free diet that used to be considered no-nos. You may find this chapter opens a lot of cupboard doors that you once thought were closed!

Conventions Used in This Book

To keep things consistent and easy to follow, here are some of the basic ground rules and conventions this book uses:

- ✔ All Web addresses appear in monofont, which looks like `this`.

- ✔ When this book was printed, some Web addresses may have needed to break across two lines of text. If that happened, rest assured that we haven't put in any extra characters (such as hyphens) to indicate the break. So when using one of these Web addresses, just type in exactly what you see in this book, pretending as though the line break doesn't exist.

- ✔ Feel free to tinker with the recipes. If you don't have an ingredient a recipe calls for, don't worry – make a substitution. You may find your swap is a huge improvement. And don't worry if you don't want to measure. We estimated the measurements, anyway, because we're not sure we even own measuring spoons and cups!

- ☺ If you want a vegetarian recipe, just look for the tomato icons.

Here are some conventions for the ingredients themselves:

- ✔ If an ingredient appears in a recipe, it's assumed to be gluten-free. For instance, we don't specify 'gluten-free vanilla', because all vanilla is gluten-free. And soy sauce usually has gluten, but when we call for soy sauce in a recipe, we're assuming you'll use a gluten-free version.

- ✔ Baking with gluten-free flours works best if you use a mixture of flours. Chapter 8 goes into detail about how to mix gluten-free flours to get the best results.

- ✔ Milk substitutes can be used in place of milk in most recipes.

- ✔ Eggs are large.

- ✔ Butter and margarine are interchangeable.

What You're Not to Read

You won't get in trouble if you *do* read everything, but if you're a skimmer, you can skip some parts and not miss anything important. In other words, there won't be a test on the following:

- **Anything that has a Technical Stuff icon:** The Technical Stuff icon represents information that's interesting but not crucial to your understanding of the subject matter.

- **Sidebars:** These are the stories and snippets of information in shaded boxes scattered throughout the chapters. Just like the Technical Stuff, you may find the information interesting, but you won't be missing critical information if you skip them.

- **Recipes:** Unless you're actually using them to cook or to decide what to make for dinner, recipes aren't the best late-night reading material. Feel free to skip them until you're ready to whip up some gluten-free goodies.

Foolish Assumptions

You spent your hard-earned dosh on this book, and that means either you want to learn more about the gluten-free lifestyle or you're related to us. Because our family members have already heard far more about gluten than any human should have to endure, we've written this book with you in mind – and we've taken the liberty of making a few assumptions about you. One or more of the following should apply:

- You're considering going gluten-free and will use this book to determine whether to take the plunge.

- You love someone who's gluten-free, and you're so nice that you want to learn about the lifestyle so you can be supportive.

- You're new to the diet and are looking for the "manual" that can tell you how to live a gluten-free lifestyle.

- You've been gluten-free for years and want the latest, greatest information about dietary guidelines and state-of-the-art research.

- You're a professional who has gluten-free clients, customers, or patients, and you want to learn more about the gluten-free lifestyle and the medical conditions that benefit from it.

At the same time, you can make a few assumptions about us and what we tell you in this book:

✔ We generally know what we're talking about. Danna, our American co-author, lives a gluten-free life and has raised her son on a gluten-free diet. As Registered Dietitians in the UK, both Sue and Nigel have worked for many years with patients who have coeliac disease or gluten intolerance and seen them through the whole transition from gluten eaters to living gluten free lifestyles. Between us we all have the experience to help you too.

✔ To the best of our knowledge, the information in this book is correct and the contents have been reviewed by our technical editor, another UK dietitian who is also an expert in the field.

✔ This book is intended to supplement but not replace medical advice from your healthcare team, so you're not allowed to sue us for anything! Always consult your healthcare team for clarification if you are unclear about anything we've said – don't forget, medical follow-up and monitoring is vital to staying in tip top health on a gluten-free diet. There. Our backs are covered!

How This Book Is Organised

Living Gluten-Free For Dummies is organised so that all the related material goes together. So we don't repeat too much information, we sometimes include cross-references to related topics. This book has six parts. Each part has several chapters, and each chapter is divided into sections. In the following sections, we explain how the parts are divided up.

Part 1: Going Gluten-Free: Who, What, Why, and How?

As the name implies, this part delves into the big-picture basics of being gluten-free. Chapter 1 is an overview. If you read nothing else in this book, read Chapter 1, because then you'll at least sound like you know what you're talking about. The rest of this part talks about who may want to consider going gluten-free and why, what gluten intolerance means for you, and the ins and outs of coeliac disease – who gets it, why, and what it does.

Part II: Digging Deeper into Eating Gluten Free

This part covers what you can and can't eat on the gluten-free diet, and how to dig a little deeper so you're *sure* the foods you're eating are really safe for you. If you want the inside track on substitutes for glutenous foods, how to come to terms with labelling, and the nutritional thinking behind the gluten-free diet, this is the part for you.

Part III: Planning and Preparing: The Preludes to Cooking

Part III takes you to the next level: getting ready to eat. It starts with some guidance on choosing the most nutritious approach to the gluten-free lifestyle and then helps you with preparing your kitchen, planning menus, shopping, and developing the techniques unique to gluten-free cooking that you'll want to know before you cook.

Part IV: From Menus to Meals: Recipes for the Gluten-Free Gastronome

You can find 65 recipes in this part submitted by non-cookbook authors: us. Okay, we admit we made 'em up. And we admit we don't measure, nor is any one recipe ever the same the second time around. But our publisher has a real-live tester on hand to make sure the recipes work, and much to our surprise, they do! So go ahead, get stewing – or baking – or whatever it is you want to do in the kitchen. Whether you're a culinary fledgling or a Delia Smith protégé, you'll find these recipes to be simple, delicious, sometimes impressive, and most definitely gluten-free.

Part V: Living – and Loving – the Gluten-Free Lifestyle

For some people, the gluten-free lifestyle presents unique social, practical, and emotional challenges. In this part, we help you work out ways to deal with some of the practical issues like social events; eating at restaurants;

travelling; talking with friends and loved ones about your lifestyle; and raising happy, healthy, gluten-free kids. We also help you deal with some of the emotional challenges that sometimes come up so you can truly learn to love the gluten-free lifestyle.

Part VI: The Part of Tens

What would a *For Dummies* book be without a Part of Tens? Incomplete, that's what, because nearly all *For Dummies* books have them, and this one's no exception. The Part of Tens is a few short chapters, each with (cleverly enough) *ten* tips, questions and answers, factoids, and nuggets of information about the gluten-free lifestyle.

Icons Used in This Book

Some people are more visual than others. That's why icons are helpful. This book uses several icons, and each has a little snippet of information associated with it. Here's what each icon means:

Cleverly designated as Tips, these are, well, *tips* that can help you live (and love!) the gluten-free lifestyle. They include info to help you save time or cut down on frustration.

Everyone can use a friendly little reminder. The Remember icon is a quick and easy way to identify some of the more important points that you may want to make note of throughout the book.

Text flagged with the Warning icon can keep you out of trouble.

Sometimes we get really into the juicy, technical, and scientific stuff. Some of you will love it; others will be bored to tears. That's why we put it in its own area, marked by a Technical Stuff icon, so you can skip it (if you want to) without missing the gist of what's going on in that chapter or section.

Where to Go from Here

What we suggest you do at this point is curl up in your comfiest chair and dip into the book. If you find the section you start with boring (heaven forbid!) or for whatever reason it doesn't hit the spot then skip it and move on to a part which does.

If you're feeling a little down about going gluten-free, we hope our sincere passion for the gluten-free lifestyle and the healthy benefits that go along with it helps you by offering positive, practical advice, support, and inspiration.

Part I
Ready, Set, Going Gluten-Free

'Abdominal Bloating? Let me introduce you to Weight Loss, Skin Rash, Chronic Diarrhea, Intestinal Infection, Muscle Cramps, and Apthous Ulcers.'

In this part . . .

We cover the basics to help get you off and running on the gluten-free lifestyle. We start by taking a look at the many medical and psychological conditions that improve on a gluten-free diet so you can decide whether this lifestyle can benefit you and can set realistic expectations for how your health may improve. So what are you waiting for? Today may be the first day of the rest of your new lifestyle.

Chapter 1

Getting Started: The Basics of Being Gluten-Free

....

In This Chapter

▶ Coming to grips with gluten

▶ Discovering the advantages of a gluten-free lifestyle

▶ Making the most of meals

▶ Going from gluten-gorger to gluten-free forager – and loving it

....

*Y*ou may be wondering why this book needs three authors. Discovering that you need to live a gluten-free life can be a big shock for some people. You need to take in a whole load of information, and as you try to get your head round what you can and can't eat you may start to think that life is never going to be the same again. Because living gluten-free has a lot to do with food, dietitians are responsible for giving you all the practical information, and so that's why two of your authors are dietitians who have experience of working with gluten-free diets. Danna is someone who has been on the receiving end of all that information and applied the recommendations on a daily basis. Better than that, she has discovered that living gluten-free just becomes a way of life and is pretty easy once you know what to look out for. You can read Danna and her son Tyler's story at the end of this chapter. We think that our combined experience is just right to help you make the move to a gluten-free life smooth and easy as pie – gluten-free pie, of course!

At first, Danna thought the doctor had made a mistake. 'You mean *glucose*,' she corrected him with a tinge of exasperation at his clumsy blunder. 'You must mean my son can't eat *glucose*.' Goodness this was going to be tough. No more dolly mixtures.

'No, I mean *gluten*,' he insisted. 'And to be honest, I really don't know much about the gluten-free diet. You can see our practice nurse, but she may not have much on the diet, either. You're going to have to do some homework of your own.'

All Danna could muster was a blank stare. What on earth was *gluten*? Keep in mind that this was 1991, when she knew as much about gluten as she did about piezoelectric polymers: approximately, nothing.

Stranded on some figurative island located somewhere between Terror Bay and the Dread Sea, Danna decided that she had two options: Her son, Tyler, could starve to death, or she could get busy trying to work out what exactly gluten was all about. People probably frown on mums who let children starve to death.

The Internet hadn't been discovered yet, and she couldn't find any books or support groups; the time had come to get resourceful and creative. Danna was determined to find out everything she could – and then share her discovery with the world.

Little did she know that gluten intolerance would explode into what it is today – one of the fastest-growing diagnoses in the world – and that this mission of hers would become all-consuming. This chapter gives you a basic rundown of what living gluten-free is all about.

What Is Gluten, Anyway?

Gluten has a couple of definitions; one is technically correct but not commonly used, and the other is commonly used but not technically correct. We give you more details on both definitions in Chapter 4, but to get you started and for the purposes of most of this book, here's the common definition: *Gluten* is a mixture of proteins found in wheat, rye, and barley. Oats don't have gluten but may be contaminated with other cereals during processing or storage, so they should be avoided, too. Experts are still uncertain whether or not oats should be included in the gluten-free diet. If you are considering including oats in your gluten-free diet always check with a suitably qualified health professional that doing so is okay.

Some people with gluten intolerance are also sensitive to pure, uncontaminated oats. Some clinicians allow pure oats to be included as part of a gluten-free diet but because individual variations exist, the inclusion should always be monitored under medical supervision. The support charity Coeliac UK advises patients to refer to their healthcare team, and check for sources of pure oats using appropriate food directories.

Common foods that contain gluten

You can find lots of information about what you can and can't eat in Chapter 4, as well as more information on safe and forbidden ingredients by visiting the home page of the UK's only patient support charity, Coeliac UK, www.coeliac.co.uk. In Chapter 4, we even tell you about some of the gluten-free foods that are available to certain people on prescription. But you need to have a general idea of what kinds of foods have gluten in them so you know what to avoid. Things with flour in them (white or wholegrain) are the most common culprits when you're avoiding gluten. The following are obvious gluten-rich foods:

- ✔ Bread and similar products, such as pitta, crumpets, bagels, and muffins
- ✔ Biscuits, cakes, and most other baked goods
- ✔ Crackers and crisp breads
- ✔ Pasta
- ✔ Pizza
- ✔ Wheat-based snacks, such as pretzels

But you find many not-so-obvious suspects, too, like liquorice, breakfast cereals, and some food additives including flavourings and fillers. When you're gluten-free, you get used to reading labels and digging a little deeper to know for sure what you can and can't eat (more on that in Chapter 5).

You have to do without those foods, and yet you really don't have to do *without*. Food manufacturers make delicious gluten-free versions of just about every food imaginable these days. We talk more about those and where to buy them in Chapter 8.

Wheat-free doesn't mean gluten-free

You may see lots of labels proudly declaring a product to be wheat-free (some of which, like spelt and triticale, aren't really wheat-free at all). That doesn't mean the food's gluten-free.

You need to be aware of some hot labelling terms as they all guarantee that a substantial dose of gluten is lurking inside the packaging somewhere:

- ✔ Wheat starch
- ✔ Wheat flour
- ✔ Wheat rusk
- ✔ Wheat bran
- ✔ Wheat germ
- ✔ Barley malt

> ✔ Barley flour
>
> ✔ Oat bran
>
> ✔ Rye flour

Gluten is in wheat, but it's also in rye and barley – and most people don't eat oats on the gluten-free diet, either. So, something can be wheat-free but still have other gluten-containing ingredients, like malt, which is usually derived from barley. In that case, the product's wheat-free, but it's not gluten-free.

Since November 2005, labels have had to comply with a new EU regulation that states that any food containing gluten has to clearly indicate the fact on the packet. The labelling can be shown in a box format (*allergy advice*), or the list of ingredients can detail the information, so check both. Remember that you need to check not only for gluten, but also for wheat, rye, and barley. Some manufacturers use 'contains gluten' but others may just list the grains that contain the gluten.

Discovering the Benefits of a Gluten-Free Lifestyle

A gluten-free lifestyle isn't just about your diet. Yes, this book talks about food, but the diet itself takes up only a few pages. Being gluten-free involves a lot more than just cutting gluten out of your diet. Following this method can affect many aspects of your life, from how you handle ordering food at restaurants, to attending social functions, and dealing with emotional challenges.

We believe that the key is to take control of the diet rather than the diet taking control of you. If your children are gluten-free, you need to help them gain control. Going gluten-free also gives you an opportunity to help others who may be embarking upon the wonderful world of gluten freedom, as well as a chance to discover more about nutrition and what you're actually putting into your body on a daily basis. If that sounds like a lot of work, relax. We guide you through the path to being gluten-free. And not only can you feel physically better, you can also feel emotionally better about yourself, too!

You're in good company. The gluten-free population is growing for lots of reasons, but the one that stands out is that when people who are intolerant to gluten give it up, they often feel better. This section tells you what the gluten-free diet can do for your body, and whether going gluten-free can help you – as well as the benefits you can enjoy. People today live in a panacea-pursuing, pill-popping, make-me-better-fast society, and if they see the promise of a quick fix, they want it. Changing both your diet and lifestyle isn't quick or easy, but when you need to do so, the benefits of going gluten-free can be fantastic – no surgery or medication required!

If you have a problem with consuming gluten then following a gluten-free diet is a great idea. If you don't, it isn't. Gluten-free living is not a quick fix, a fashion accessory, or a nutritional nirvana. It's a therapeutic diet for people with specific conditions.

Eating isn't supposed to hurt

Food is supposed to give you energy and make you feel good, not make you ill. But when you eat things that your body doesn't like for one reason or another, it has a sometimes not-so-subtle way of telling you to cut it out. Food to which your body objects can cause the following:

- Fatigue
- Gastrointestinal distress (wind, bloating, diarrhoea, constipation, vomiting, heartburn, and acid reflux)
- Headaches (including migraines)
- Inability to concentrate
- Weight gain or weight loss
- Infertility
- Joint, bone, or muscle pain
- Depression

The list's impressive, isn't it? The idea that eliminating one thing from your diet – gluten – can improve so many different conditions is almost hard to believe. Yet, it's true – and changing to gluten-free really makes sense when you realise that if the food you're eating is toxic to your body or stopping you from absorbing nutrients then your body's going to complain in lots of different ways.

So no matter how your symptoms manifest as an intolerance to gluten, the only thing that's likely to make you feel any better is a gluten-free diet.

The great thing about this method is that when you work out which food or foods your body doesn't approve of, you can stop eating them, and your body soon stops acting stroppy. In fact, feed it right, and it can make you feel great in lots of different ways.

Making nutrition your mission: Head-to-toe health benefits

The 12th-century physician Maimonides said, 'Man should strive to have his intestines relaxed all the days of his life.' No kidding! When your intestines aren't relaxed – or when they're downright edgy or uptight – they affect all your other parts, too. You can compare the situation to when you're in a really good mood and your best friend is grumpy – the atmosphere can make you grumpy, too; a cantankerous intestine can be a downer for the entire body.

In a way, the body's reaction to gluten doesn't seem logical. Some signs of gluten intolerance include headaches, fatigue, bone or joint pain, depression, or infertility; at first, these types of symptoms may seem unrelated to something going on in your gut, let alone to something you eat – something as common as wheat in your diet.

But those symptoms – and many others – can be signs of coeliac disease and gluten intolerance. To get the low down on coeliac disease and gluten intolerance jump over to Chapter 2. People with coeliac disease or gluten intolerance do sometimes have gastrointestinal symptoms, but more often the symptoms are *extraintestinal*, meaning that they take place outside the intestinal tract.

If your body has problems with gluten, the gluten-free diet may help relieve lots of the symptoms.

Abstinence makes the gut grow stronger

When gluten is making you feel ill, the exact nature of your symptoms doesn't matter; even if your symptoms don't seem to be related to your gastrointestinal tract, nasty battles are going on inside your gut.

Hair-like structures called *villi* are situated on the lining of your small intestine. The job of the villi is to increase the surface area of the small intestine (to the same surface area as a football pitch) so that it can absorb more nutrients.

For people who have gluten intolerance, the body sees gluten as the enemy and attacks it. In doing so, it also accidentally attacks the villi, which get blunted and shortened, sometimes to the extreme of becoming completely flat; thus reducing the surface area.

What happens? The flat villi can no longer absorb stuff, so those good-for-you nutrients just slide right by and you don't get enough of the important vitamins, minerals, and other elements that are vital for good physical and emotional health. You develop what's called *malabsorption* and become poorly nourished.

Don't worry! This story has a happy ending. Your villi are tenacious little things, and when you stop eating gluten, they begin to heal straightaway. Before you know it, your villi grow back and absorb nutrients again, and your health is fully restored. That's why we say abstinence makes the gut grow stronger.

By the way, lactase, which is the enzyme that breaks down milk sugar or lactose, is produced in the tip of the villi. When the villi get blunted, sometimes your ability to digest lactose decreases and you become lactose intolerant. When you stop eating gluten and the villi heal, you're usually able to tolerate dairy foods again.

Grading the grain: So, is wheat good or bad for you?

We've all been barraged with messages hailing the virtues of wheat – especially in its wholegrain form! Along with other grains it hogs the biggest section of the healthy plate food model (see Figure 1-1), and those of us who have no problem eating wheat can and should consume mountains of the stuff. Wholegrain, unrefined wheat is a good source of fibre and nutrients and provides plenty of health benefits, but, if you need to, you can get them from other food sources instead. For people with gluten intolerance the presence of gluten provokes an immune response that undoes all this benefit, meaning they're better off cutting out gluten-containing cereals altogether.

During the immune response the body treats the gluten like an 'attacker' and uses special immune cells called *antibodies* to try and neutralise the effects of the 'attacker'.

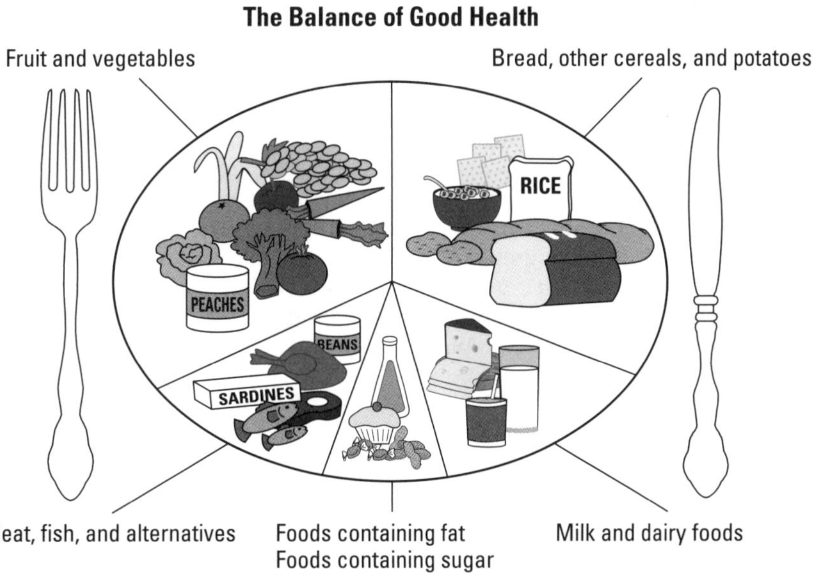

The Balance of Good Health

Fruit and vegetables

Bread, other cereals, and potatoes

RICE

PEACHES

BEANS

SARDINES

Figure 1-1:
The 'healthy plate' food model.

Meat, fish, and alternatives

Foods containing fat
Foods containing sugar

Milk and dairy foods

Mastering the Meals

Living Gluten-Free For Dummies is really about a lifestyle, not a diet. But no matter where that lifestyle takes you – eating in, eating out, social events, choosing, planning, shopping, preparing – being gluten-free all comes down to one thing: food.

If you're a culinary catastrophe and you're afraid that you're going to have to wake up at 4 a.m. to bake gluten-free bread and make fresh pasta, turn off the alarm and go back to sleep. You can find plenty of gluten-free foods available to take the place of all your old favourites, and you don't have to go to specialty shops to buy them. Most are available in your local supermarket and some are even available on prescription if you have a diagnosis of coeliac disease (see Chapter 2).

Whether you're a kitchenphobe or a foodie, living a gluten-free lifestyle and modern food shopping offers you an enormous selection of foods and ingredients to choose from.

Planning and preparing

Putting together delicious and healthy gluten-free meals is a lot easier if you plan ahead. Walking through a supermarket, perusing restaurant menus, or (gasp!) sitting in a café with a growling tummy isn't exactly conducive to making good food choices.

Give yourself a healthy advantage by planning and preparing meals in advance, especially if your busy schedule means you're eating away from home frequently. If you know you're pressed for time at breakfast or lunch, make your meals the night before, and carry healthy gluten-free snacks with you.

One of the best things about adopting a new dietary lifestyle is exploring new and sometimes unusual foods. You may never have heard of lots of the gluten-free foods and ingredients, many of which are not only gluten-free and delicious but are also nutritional powerhouses. With the new perspective on food that the gluten-free lifestyle can offer, you may find yourself inspired to think outside the typical menu plan, exploring unique and nutritious alternatives.

Shopping shrewdly

The healthiest way to enjoy a gluten-free lifestyle is to eat things you can find at any supermarket or farmer's market: meat, fish, seafood, fruits, and a variety of fresh vegetables (but resist the temptation to load up your shopping basket with potatoes – check out Chapter 6). If you want to add canned, processed, and even junk foods to your shopping list, you can still do most of your shopping at a regular supermarket, and you can even buy own-label brands.

If you hope to enjoy the delicious gluten-free specialty products that are available these days, you can find them in 'free-from' aisles or at health food or specialty shops. Or you can shop in your pjs on one of the many Internet sites specialising in gluten-free products (if you're using your library's Internet or an Internet café to shop online, we suggest you change out of the pjs first, though!).

Some people worry about the cost of the gluten-free lifestyle, but eating this way doesn't have to be more expensive. We talk about eating gluten-free affordably in Chapter 7.

Rearranging the kitchen

For the most part, a gluten-free kitchen looks the same as any other kitchen – without the gluten, of course. You don't need to go out and buy special gadgets and tools, and with only a couple of exceptions, which we cover in Chapter 8, you don't need two sets of pots, pans, utensils, or storage containers, either.

If you're sharing a kitchen where food with gluten is prepared, you need to be aware of some contamination issues so that you don't inadvertently *glutenate* (contaminate with gluten) a perfectly good gluten-free meal. Keeping your crumbs to yourself isn't just a matter of hygiene but can mean the difference between a meal you can eat and one you can't.

Some people find having separate areas in the pantry, cupboards, and fridge for their gluten-free products helpful. This idea is especially good if you have gluten-free children in the house, because they can easily see that lots of things are available for them to eat and can quickly grab their favourite gluten-free goodies from their special area.

Cooking outside the recipe box

We believe that if you give someone a regular recipe, you feed that person for one meal. Show them how to make *anything* gluten-free, and you feed them for a lifetime. The point is, you can make anything gluten-free, and you're not constrained by recipes or the fact that you can't use regular flour or bread-crumbs. All you need is a little creativity and some basic guidelines for using gluten-free substitutions, which you can find in Chapter 8.

If you're a die-hard recipe fan, never fear – we give you recipes in Chapters 9 to 14. Most of them are really simple to follow but leave your guests with the impression that you spent all day in the kitchen (and being thus indebted, they may volunteer to do the dishes).

Getting Excited about the Gluten-Free Lifestyle

Most people who embark on a gluten-free lifestyle are doing so because of health issues – and that means they have little or no choice in the matter. When people are forced to make changes in their routine, especially changes that affect what they can and can't eat, they're not always so quick to see the joy in the adjustments.

If you're a little gloomy about going from a gluten-glutton to a gluten-free zone, we understand. But prepare yourself to read about the scores of reasons why you should be excited about a gluten-free lifestyle (for you impatient types like us, feel free to skip to Chapter 18 for a jump-start on the positive, fluffy side of being gluten-free).

Adapting your perspective on food

If you've been eating gluten (we believe that would make you a *glutenivore*) for a long time – say, for most of your life – then giving up foods as you know them may seem like a difficult transition at first. Besides the obvious practical challenges of discovering how to ferret out gluten where it may be hidden, you have to deal with the emotional, physical, social, and even financial challenges of the condition.

You have to do only one thing in order to love the gluten-free lifestyle, and that's to adjust your perspective on food just a tad. You really don't have to give anything up; you just have to make some modifications. The foods that used to be your favourites can still be your favourites if you want them to be, just in a slightly different form.

Or you may want to consider the change to be a new and superhealthy approach for you: eating leaner meats, fresh fruits, and a variety of fresh, non-starchy vegetables. Again, you may have to tweak your perspective a bit before the diet feels natural to you, but it is, in fact, natural, nutritious, and naturally nutritious. We talk more about this approach in Chapter 6.

Savouring gluten-free flavours

People who are new to the concept of being gluten-free sometimes comment that the diet is boring. When we ask what they're eating, their cuisine routine usually centres on carrots and rice cakes. Who wouldn't be bored with that? That type of a diet is appalling, not appealing.

We *love* food. We love the flavour, the feeling of being full, and the nutritional value it provides. Most of all, we love to explore foods we've never tried before – as long as they're gluten-free, of course. We'd never encourage you to endure a diet of blandiose foods that can double up as cardboard.

A healthy, gluten-free diet doesn't have to be boring or restrictive. If you enjoy bland foods, good for you. But if you think gluten-free has to be flavour-free, you're in for a pleasant surprise.

Getting out and about

You don't have to let the gluten-free lifestyle hold you back from doing anything you want to do. Well, okay, you can't do some things – like eat a pizza from the place around the corner or devour a stack of gluten-laden donuts. But as far as your activities and lifestyle are concerned, you can – and should – get out and about as you always have.

In the majority of cases, ordering out isn't as easy as walking into a restaurant and asking for a gluten-free menu. But eating at restaurants is definitely possible and easier to do than a few years ago; you just need to start to ask for what you want and be alert to contamination concerns. Travelling is a doddle after you master eating at restaurants (and get your head around language considerations if you're travelling abroad – resources are even available to help translate common gluten-free speak into various languages). Going to social events just requires a little advance planning, and holidays may barely faze you – after you get the hang of getting out and about gluten-free style. Chapter 15 gives you more information on this aspect.

Before you travel check out www.coeliac.co.uk for some great resources to help translate common gluten-free food speak into a variety of different languages.

Bringing up your children to love the lifestyle

When Danna heard that Tyler would have to be gluten-free for the rest of his life, she was flooded with a bunch of emotions, most of which weren't very pleasant. At first, she felt burdened and overcome with grief and frustration, and longed for the perfectly healthy little baby she thought she was entitled to. Focusing on what she'd lost and all that she'd have to change in their lives was all too easy. But making adjustments didn't take long, and soon she discovered not just to live the gluten-free lifestyle – but to *love* the gluten-free lifestyle.

Most importantly, Danna wanted Tyler to love the lifestyle. After all, it was his diet, his life, and his future that would be most impacted. Thankfully, Tyler does love the gluten-free lifestyle, and your children can, too.

Trying out lots of ideas is key to raising happy, healthy, gluten-free children. Some of the highlights include giving them control of their diet from day one; always having tasty gluten-free treats on hand; reinforcing the benefits of the gluten-free lifestyle (if you need some crib notes, head to Chapter 19); and always remembering that they're finding out how to feel about the lifestyle from *you*. Promoting an optimistic outlook can instill a positive approach in them. Chapter 16 deals in detail with raising children to love the gluten-free lifestyle, and for even more inspiration and practical advice, visit the 'For Families' pages at the www.coeliac.co.uk Web site.

Children are flexible and resilient. Adopting a new lifestyle is usually harder for the parents than for the child.

Setting realistic expectations

Some people have nicknamed Danna as PollyDanna because they think she has an unrealistically optimistic view of the gluten-free lifestyle. Her outlook may be optimistic, but it's not unrealistic.

Setting reasonable expectations for what things are going to be like when you adopt a gluten-free lifestyle is important, because you *will* encounter challenges, and you need to prepare to handle them well. Friends, family, and loved ones may not understand. They may not accommodate your diet when you hope or expect them to do so. You may find social events to be overwhelming at first; or you may get confused or frustrated and feel like giving up on the diet. You can overcome these trials and come out the other side stronger for them, and being prepared is the best way to get through the transition time.

This book is the resource you need to guide you through – so make your way through it, and bookmark the pages you want to come back to when you need some practical or emotional reminders for how to deal with difficult issues. If you have an optimistic but realistic approach, you'll encounter fewer obstacles along the way.

Arming yourself with good information

The good news is that because the gluten-free diet is better understood and more commonly followed now than a few years back, you can find lots of information about it. The bad news is that not all that information is accurate.

Be wary of what you hear and read, and check the reliability of the source on everything. If you find conflicting information – and you will – dig deeper until you find out which source is right.

We cite a few good sources of information in Chapter 5, and we're sure that you can find more on your own. Just remember to keep a sceptical eye out for the good, the bad, and the completely ludicrous.

Danna and Tyler's story

I didn't aspire to do any of this. I was deeply involved in a successful career, and was a mum first and foremost. But today I'm an accidental author, researcher, and support group founder who was pushed into the deep end of the gluten-free pool and realised that I needed to find out how to swim. Fast.

Until 1991, my family and I ate a fairly typical diet. I tried to keep it nutritious (extra Parmesan cheese on the spaghetti to add protein), and I was aware of the need to limit fat and calories (forget the extra cheese), but we didn't spend a lot of time worrying about what we ate or the long-term effects food may have on our bodies. We pretty much took eating for granted.

All that changed when my first child, Tyler, was about 9 months old and developed what seemed to be chronic diarrhoea. The paediatrician put it down to the antibiotics Ty was taking for ear infections and told me to call if it hadn't cleared up in a few weeks. Three weeks later, I was back in the paediatrician's surgery. 'Yep, he still has diarrhoea,' the doctor declared with confidence. 'Yes, I know. That's why I'm here,' I mumbled with self-restraint worthy of the Nobel Peace Prize. 'Give him foods that plug him up like stodgy white bread – and call me if it hasn't cleared up in a few weeks,' said the doctor.

I waited. Not patiently (patience isn't my greatest strength), but I waited. Three weeks later, after another perfunctory examination of Tyler's ears, nose, and throat, the doctor made that 'mmhhhmmm' noise that doctors make when they work out the problem. Yippee! We were finally going to get some answers! 'Yes. He still has diarrhoea.' All those years of medical school had really paid off. 'Don't worry about it. He's not dehydrated, and he's in the 75th percentile for height and weight. It's nothing to be concerned about.' I wonder whether the fact that I practically infuse him with liquids has anything to do with the fact that he wasn't dehydrated? And whether the fact that he started off in the 99th percentile and has *dropped* to the 75th means anything? Apparently not. I was instructed not to bring him back for diarrhoea because there was nothing to be concerned about. If I insisted on bringing him back, I'd be kicked out of that paediatric clinic. I think they meant it.

Doctor number two agreed with doctor number one. After a quick look in the ears, nose, and throat, he declared that we had a healthy baby boy. 'But what about the diarrhoea?' I eeked. 'Really, it's nothing to worry about. He's a healthy height and weight, he's not dehydrated, and he looks fine to me,' he chirped as he raced to his next 4-minute appointment. I considered offering to give Doctor Do-Nothing a close look at the 22 diarrhoea nappies a day that I was changing but somehow managed to control myself.

(continued)

(continued)

In desperation, we consulted another doctor, and – long story short – a quick look in the ears, nose, and throat turned up – you guessed it – nothing. By this time, Tyler's tummy had grown hugely distended, his arms and legs had wasted to skinny little limbs, his willy had disappeared completely, and his personality had changed. He had transformed from a lively, energetic toddler to a listless, irritable, clingy, and quiet little boy. Nearly a year had passed since the diarrhoea first started, and we decided that we were just neurotic first-time parents with a quiet child who pooed a lot.

Eventually, we ended up in the hands of doctor number four. By this time, 'realising' that there was nothing wrong with Tyler, I thought nothing of dragging a lifeless baby with a swollen belly into the paediatrician's clinic. After looking in Tyler's ears, nose, and throat, he laid Tyler down on his back and thumped on his tummy like you may thump a honeydew melon to see whether it's ripe. 'My goodness,' he said with that I'm-alarmed-but-I'm-a-doctor-and-don't-want-to-freak-you-out tone. 'What's going on with his tummy? It's very distended.' I couldn't answer through the tears of relief.

After testing for cystic fibrosis, blood diseases, and cancer, we finally got the bittersweet diagnosis. 'Your son has coeliac disease.' *Huh?* Is that anything like the flu? Surely a few weeks of antibiotics will wipe it out. 'He'll need to be on a gluten-free diet for the rest of his life.'

I don't have room here to give the details of the rest of the story. Suffice to say that the words 'for the rest of his life' had a huge impact, and we realised that it was time to step up to the challenge and do some research and lifestyle and attitude adjustments to help ourselves – and others.

When we heard that Tyler would have to lead a gluten-free lifestyle, we had come to a fork in the road. At first, we were devastated, confused, frustrated, and grief-stricken. But we knew we could choose an alternative path – a path that would have a more positive effect on Tyler's life. As we found out how to live with the diet and its ramifications, we worked hard to find a way to turn the adversity into a positive force in our lives. More than a decade later, I realise that what we once interpreted as misfortune has actually been a huge blessing in our lives – and most importantly, Tyler agrees.

Chapter 2

Going Gluten-Free:
Who's Doing It and Why

So you or a loved one have given up – or are considering giving up – gluten. If you're like most people, this action is for one of three reasons:

✔ A medical professional has diagnosed you with coeliac disease and advised a gluten-free diet in order to safeguard your health.

✔ You haven't had a diagnosis of coeliac disease but you suspect you're going to feel better on a gluten-free diet. However, before you do cut out gluten altogether, consider that a diagnosis of gluten intolerance is much easier and more reliable if you stay on gluten until you can be properly tested.

✔ Every celebrity in town says gluten-free is the way to go!

Which group you fall into doesn't matter – you may be right on all counts (except maybe the last reason).

And you're definitely not alone. Millions of people live gluten-free for a variety of reasons, and some are seeing dramatic improvements in their health. The bottom line is that gluten doesn't sit well with some people if they have a form of gluten intolerance. So you're thinking, 'What exactly does that mean, and can or can't I eat pizza?' Ah, you want to get right to the point! The problem is, though, you won't always find an easy answer to either of those questions.

This chapter explains what gluten intolerance is, how gluten can affect your body and in some cases even your behaviour, and what tests can help you decide whether you need to go gluten-free.

Shedding Light on the Gluten-Intolerance Spectrum

Gluten intolerance is a physical intolerance to the presence of gluten in the gut – hence the clever name! It's not a true food allergy but as with most allergies, intolerance reactions can vary enormously from one person to another. However, intolerance reactions commonly take longer to show themselves than allergic reactions, making the task of identifying the culprit food more tricky.

Gluten intolerance can come in many forms. Think of sensitivity to gluten as running along a spectrum ranging from 'no noticeable symptoms at all' to 'full-blown coeliac disease' (which can make you really quite unwell), and a whole range in between:

- ✔ **Full-blown or classical coeliac disease:** Many people with gluten intolerance have coeliac disease formally diagnosed following testing. This group of people is the easiest to treat because coeliac disease is well-defined. Others may actually have it, but they fail to test positive if the testing is improperly done or is insufficient to yield conclusive results (for an explanation of these instances, see the later section 'Testing positive: Now what?'). Sometimes people remove gluten from their diet before they have a test and this can also lead to inaccurate results.

- ✔ **Subclinical coeliac disease:** Some people may not have classical coeliac disease – yet – but if they continue to eat gluten, they may develop a tendency towards it, as a previously untriggered condition (the condition in its early stages is sometimes referred to as *subclinical* or *latent* coeliac disease).

- ✔ **Atypical coeliac disease:** Other people may not have coeliac disease and may never get it. But they do have an intolerance to gluten, and their health improves on a gluten-free diet. People with this condition are sometimes called *atypical* coeliacs.

- ✔ **Silent coeliac disease:** Still others never show any obvious signs or symptoms, which makes the whole thing even more muddled. This group are sometimes called *silent coeliacs*. Latent, silent, and atypical gluten intolerance is often only discovered because you were tested or *screened* after a family member developed full-blown coeliac disease.

The diagnosis you receive is largely determined by the results of a combination of tests, which we describe in the later section 'Getting Tested for Coeliac Disease and Gluten Intolerance'. The bottom line for any of these conditions is that you and your health are probably going to benefit significantly from following a gluten-free diet.

Symptoms, or the lack of them, can be the same for gluten intolerance as for coeliac disease, and as with coeliac disease, they usually go away on a gluten-free diet. The testing is what helps clarify whether you have coeliac disease or gluten intolerance. If you test positive for coeliac disease, that's what you have. But if you're negative for coeliac disease, and yet your symptoms go away on a gluten-free diet, you probably have another less specific form of gluten intolerance. Sadly, because protocol for defining and diagnosing gluten intolerance isn't yet fully established and insufficient awareness of gluten intolerance exists in the medical community, patients are often told to ignore inconclusive or confusing test results and to go back to eating their bread and pizza. Sometimes this approach can have serious and long-term health complications (see the later section in this chapter 'Considering the Risks If You Don't Give Up Gluten').

Crossing the Line: Full-Blown Coeliac Disease

Coeliac disease is a relatively common (yet often misdiagnosed) genetic intolerance to gluten. When someone with this level of intolerance eats food that contains gluten, the immune system responds by attacking the gluten molecule, and in so doing also attacks your body cells. This response, called an *autoimmune response*, leads to inflammation of the gut and can develop at any age and in people of any ethnicity. It results in damage to the small intestine, which can cause poor absorption of nutrients. Although the damage occurs in the gastrointestinal tract, not all symptoms are gastrointestinal in nature. In fact, symptoms are vast and varied, and they sometimes come and go, which makes diagnosis difficult.

Coeliac UK, an organisation working with coeliac sufferers in Britain, estimates that around 125,000 people have been diagnosed with coeliac disease. However, recent studies suggest this figure may just be the tip of the iceberg. Estimates are that 1 in 100 people in the UK have coeliac disease, which means that almost another 500,000 people have as yet undiagnosed coeliac disease. These figures estimate the number of people wandering around who don't even have a clue that anything is wrong. Even more alarming estimated figures exist for people who go along to their doctor because they feel unwell, but get an incorrect diagnosis.

What's the difference between wheat allergy and gluten intolerance?

No such thing as an allergy to gluten exists, but someone can have an allergy to the things that contain gluten: wheat, rye, and barley. In fact, wheat is one of the most common allergens, affecting millions of people.

These allergies are just like other typical food allergies – the same as an allergy to strawberries or shellfish, for example. They're all responses to a food allergen, and the reaction that someone has to those foods varies from person to person and from one food to another.

Many food allergies are called *IgE-mediated responses* (IgE is an abbreviation for immunoglobulin type E) to foods. Basically, this means that the immune system is overreacting to a food, treating it as a foreign 'invader'. IgE just designates a class of immunoglobulin. *Immunoglobulin* are proteins that the body makes to help fight against things it perceives to be threats. IgE's main evolutionary role has been to protect the body against parasites, but it also fights other 'bad guys', which is what it's doing when you have an allergic reaction to food. The body creates a specific variation of IgE antibody for each allergen it encounters.

Allergic symptoms can be respiratory, causing coughing, nasal congestion, sneezing, throat tightness, and even asthma. Acute allergic reactions to food usually start in the mouth, with tingling, itching, a metallic taste, and swelling of the tongue and throat. Sometimes symptoms are further down the intestinal tract, causing abdominal pain, muscle spasms, vomiting, and diarrhoea. Any severe and acute allergic reaction also has the potential to be life threatening, causing anaphylaxis. *Anaphylaxis* – or *anaphylactic shock* – affects different organs, and symptoms can include a tingling sensation, swelling in the mouth or throat, and a metallic taste. Other symptoms can include a feeling of agitation, hives, breathing problems, a drop in blood pressure, and fainting. Anaphylaxis can sometimes be fatal unless the person having the allergic reaction receives an epinephrine (adrenaline) injection.

Identifying Symptoms of Gluten Intolerance and Coeliac Disease

The symptoms that we describe in this section are accepted as symptoms of coeliac disease, but they're also symptoms of gluten intolerance. Notice that the symptoms affect all different parts of the body. That's because coeliac disease is *multisystemic*; although the actual damage is occurring in the gastrointestinal tract – specifically in the small intestine – the symptoms manifest in many different ways.

Gluten intolerance and coeliac disease have hundreds of symptoms, so we can't list them all. The following sections give some of the more common ones, starting with the symptoms that are gastrointestinal in nature. You can talk to a hundred people with coeliac disease or gluten intolerance and each one tells you about a different set of symptoms.

Symptoms are as varied as people themselves, but ignoring *your* symptoms means you may be one of the estimated half million UK people who go undiagnosed.

Going for the gut: Gastrointestinal symptoms

Many people think the most common symptoms of coeliac disease are gastrointestinal in nature – diarrhoea, constipation, wind, bloating, reflux, and even vomiting. The following are some of the 'classic' – though not the most common – symptoms of coeliac disease:

- ✔ Abdominal pain and distension
- ✔ Acid reflux
- ✔ Bloating
- ✔ Constipation
- ✔ Diarrhoea
- ✔ Greasy, foul-smelling, floating stools
- ✔ Nausea
- ✔ Vomiting
- ✔ Weight loss or weight gain
- ✔ Wind and flatulence

Introducing the best of the rest: Non-gastrointestinal symptoms

Interestingly, although gluten intolerance and coeliac disease affect the gut, many people's symptoms are not gastrointestinal in nature. Many of the non-gastrointestinal symptoms are as a result of poor nutrient absorption, which in turn upsets the balance of another body system. People more commonly have what are called *extraintestinal* symptoms, and the list of those is extensive, topping over 250. The following list is only partial and includes some of the more commonly reported symptoms:

- ✔ Fatigue and weakness (due to iron-deficiency anaemia)
- ✔ Vitamin and/or mineral deficiencies

- Headaches (including migraines)
- Joint/bone pain
- Depression, irritability, listlessness, and low mood
- 'Fuzzy brain' or an inability to concentrate
- Infertility
- Abnormal menstrual cycles
- Dental enamel deficiencies and irregularities
- Seizures
- Clumsiness (ataxia)
- Nerve damage (peripheral neuropathy)
- Respiratory problems
- Mouth ulcers
- Lactose intolerance
- Eczema/psoriasis (skin conditions; not to be confused with dermatitis herpetiformis, which we talk about in Chapter 3)
- Rosacea (a skin disorder)
- Acne
- Hashimoto's disease, Sjögren's syndrome, lupus erythematosus, and other autoimmune disorders
- Early onset osteoporosis
- Hair loss (alopoecia)
- Bruising easily
- Low blood sugar (hypoglycaemia)
- Muscle cramping
- Nosebleeds
- Swelling and inflammation
- Night blindness

Studies have shown that the prevalence of unrecognised coeliac disease (as a cause of low fertility) in women presenting to fertility clinics is in the range of 2.7–3 per cent, significantly higher than that found in the general population (1.06 per cent). Researchers found that *menarche* (the beginning of menstruation) was significantly delayed among untreated patients with coeliac disease and an earlier age of menopause has also been seen in women with undiagnosed coeliac disease. Undiagnosed coeliac disease is also associated with a

When no symptoms *are* a symptom

Some people have no noticeable symptoms whatsoever – these people are called *silent coeliacs* or *asymptomatic*. (Truly, though, if they read the list of 250+ symptoms, we're wondering whether they can honestly say they have *none* of them!) Even though they don't feel any symptoms, gluten is damaging their small intestine in the same way it does in a coeliac who has multiple symptoms and can result in the same nutritional deficiencies and associated conditions. These people have it tough, in terms of both diagnosis and treatment. They usually get diagnosed because they have a relative who has coeliac disease and they're clever enough to know that this means they should be tested, too. As for treatment, they need to be gluten-free in order to stay healthy. But staying motivated to give up some of your favourite foods is tough when those foods don't seem to make you feel ill!

poorer outcome for the foetus. A Danish study found that babies of patients with untreated coeliac disease had lower birth weights than controls. The prevalence of low birth weight before and after a gluten-free diet prescribed to coeliac mothers fell from 29 per cent to 0 per cent.

An increased incidence of miscarriage among patients with untreated coeliac disease has also been reported. Following a gluten-free diet, the miscarriage rate among patients with untreated coeliac disease was similar to that of the non-coeliac population.

Spotting symptoms in kids

Children who have coeliac disease tend to have the 'classic' gastrointestinal symptoms of diarrhoea and weight loss. They may also have some of the following symptoms:

- Inability to concentrate
- Irritability
- Failure to thrive (in infants and toddlers)
- Short stature or delayed growth
- Delayed onset of puberty
- Weak bones or bone pain
- Abdominal pain and distension
- Nosebleeds

Recognising common misdiagnoses and missed diagnoses

Doctors now know that coeliac disease affects far more people than previously thought, with large-scale screening studies suggesting that the average prevalence across Europe is 1 per cent. This discovery makes coeliac disease one of the most common chronic autoimmune disorders and is the most common cause of nutrient malabsorption in the United Kingdom.

Due to the genetic nature of coeliac disease the prevalence is increased to 1 in 10 in families where coeliac disease exists.

Whether or not screening should be carried out for coeliac disease is still a matter for debate, but many people find themselves in favour of screening when they consider how often diagnosis is missed.

A *Reader's Digest* article titled '10 Diseases Doctors Miss' cited coeliac disease as one of the top ten misdiagnosed diseases. For every person diagnosed with coeliac disease, 140 go undiagnosed. Thankfully, as awareness of coeliac disease and gluten intolerance is increasing, diagnoses are on the rise, and sufferers are discovering improved health on a gluten-free diet.

But in the meantime, under-diagnosis (when not enough clinical evidence exists to give an accurate diagnosis or an incorrect diagnosis is given) is still a big problem. Patients are often misdiagnosed with a variety of conditions before finding out that they really have coeliac disease – easily cured by diet. Common misdiagnoses include

- Irritable bowel syndrome (IBS) or spastic colon
- Chronic fatigue syndrome (CFS) or fibromyalgia
- Lupus (an autoimmune disease)
- Unexplained anaemia
- Migraines or unexplained headaches
- Unexplained infertility
- Psychological issues (hypochondria, depression, anxiety, or neurosis)
- Inflammatory bowel disease (IBD), such as Crohn's disease or ulcerative colitis
- Cancer
- Viral infections (viral gastroenteritis)
- Food allergies or lactose intolerance
- Parasites or other infections

- Gall bladder disease
- Thyroid disease
- Cystic fibrosis (a genetic respiratory disorder)
- Acid reflux
- Diverticulosis (small pouches in the colon where food gets trapped)
- Diabetes
- Eczema or psoriasis (skin conditions)

Missing the point of diagnosis

Gluten intolerance and coeliac disease are common. They can cause severe problems if undiagnosed. Yet many people with gluten intolerance or coeliac disease go undiagnosed or are misdiagnosed. So why does a common condition not always get picked up? Some ideas as to how they slip through the net are as follows:

- **Doctor's aren't exposed to the condition enough in medical training.** Time spent at medical school is influential in forming doctors' opinions and future practices. If they don't hear enough about the disease during their period of training, they're not likely to look for it after they graduate.

- **Some doctors get 'continuing medical information' from drug reps, journal articles, and conferences.** Right now, no drugs are available to treat coeliac disease, so drug reps aren't strolling into doctors' offices and talking about it. Conferences and journal articles on the subject are scarce so the format for bringing coeliac disease to the forefront of testing and raise awareness is limited.

- **Symptoms are considerable, variable, and sometimes even absent.** Symptoms of gluten intolerance and coeliac disease are often quite varied, affecting many different parts of the body, sometimes all at once. Some people don't seem to have any symptoms, which makes pinpointing a cause difficult.

- **Doctors may think that patients are exaggerating or just plain 'crazy.'** More than one person with coeliac disease has been called neurotic or a hypochondriac because of the many and sometimes dramatic symptoms involved. The long list of symptoms may come across as being exaggeration or hysteria.

- **Routine blood tests don't pick it up.** *Full blood counts* (FBC) and routine biochemical tests don't test specifically for coeliac disease or gluten intolerance. So although a physician is likely to order FBC and biochemical tests for patients with coeliac symptoms, the results don't offer any hints that a patient may have coeliac disease. An astute doctor, though, sees signs in the following results: Anaemia, low potassium, low bicarbonate, low albumin (protein) levels, and high liver enzymes are red flags for gluten intolerance and coeliac disease.

- **Routine endoscopies don't detect coeliac disease.** Some patients think they've been tested for coeliac disease because they've had an *endoscopy* – a test where you swallow a long flexible tube that has a camera and light inside it, which is used to look at the inside of your digestive system. But an endoscopy without a biopsy doesn't detect coeliac disease. (Jump forward to the later section 'Biopsy' for more.)

Blaming the Bread: Does Gluten Affect Behaviour?

Some people blame gluten as a major culprit for wreaking havoc on mood and behaviour. You may well assume that if you're feeling lousy and not absorbing your full quota of nutrients from your food, you may also feel emotionally low, find concentrating difficult, and even be a little tetchy with your nearest and dearest.

However, this theory is at full stretch when it links gluten intolerance or coeliac disease to schizophrenia, attention deficit disorder, autism, clinical depression, and bipolar disorder. The trend for gluten-free diets as the answer to many emotional and psychological disorders and illnesses is on the up, but much of the evidence to support the trend is *anecdotal* – that is, currently not supported by validated clinical trials. As a result, adopting a gluten-free diet to help with these conditions remains very much a trend or even a fashion, rather than the basis of conventional medical treatment of these serious conditions.

Gluten-free diets: A treatment for autism?

Autism is a lifelong condition affecting social, cognitive, and imaginative abilities. A great deal of controversy prevails over the choice of treatment, with complementary and alternative treatments often being self-prescribed. Gluten-free and casein (cows milk protein)-free diets are one of those treatments.

Treatment with gluten-free and casein-free diets centres on the opioid-excess theory of autism. *The opioid-excess theory* is based on the idea that autism is the result of a metabolic disorder. Foods that contain gluten and casein are high in peptides (proteins) with opioid (a compound resembling opium) activity. These peptides are able to pass through the intestinal membrane, which is thought to be abnormally permeable, and enter the central nervous system. This occurrence has an effect on neurotransmission (nerve function) and can produce other physiological symptoms associated with autism. Abnormal levels of urinary peptides have been reported in people with autism and

this finding had lead to the theory that removal of casein and gluten from the diet should reduce the symptoms associated with autism.

The majority of research in this area is anecdotal, and studies have been done on a very small scale. Therefore, very little clinical evidence is available to support using such a restrictive diet in the treatment of people with autism. Children with autism often have selective eating and may already be habitually self-limiting their diet, so careful thought needs to be given before even considering a diet that further restricts what they eat and increases the risk of nutritional deficiency. This method is a contentious issue but the current state of play is that The British Dietetic Association and Coeliac UK do not support the routine use of this dietary approach in treating people with autism. We strongly recommend that you consult with a specialist paediatric dietitian before even considering a gluten-free diet for your child – whatever the reason.

Getting Tested for Coeliac Disease and Gluten Intolerance

Testing for coeliac disease and gluten intolerance isn't an exact science – and scientists don't agree on protocol for some of the testing procedures available today. The most widely accepted testing protocol for coeliac disease includes a simple, blood test, often just a finger prick, which if positive is followed by a more invasive intestinal biopsy to confirm diagnosis.

Blood tests

A blood test is the first step to a diagnosis of gluten intolerance or coeliac disease, but as we mentioned before, a standard blood count is not what's needed. A more specific blood test that looks for specific antibodies when gluten is present is the only effective test. A positive result – which shows that antibodies are present – takes you to the next step of diagnosis if coeliac disease is suspected: the biopsy.

Two types of antibodies can be uncovered by this more specific blood test, which can determine whether you have an intolerance to gluten or coeliac disease.

- **tTGA (tissue transglutaminase antibodies)-IgA(Ig = Immumoglobulin Antibody, A = type A):** This antibody is very specific to coeliac disease, meaning that if you have a positive tTGA, it's very likely that you have coeliac disease. The tTGA blood test is a very useful as an initial screening test. This test can have a number of different names including tTGA, tTG, or TG-IgA- but they are essentially the same.

- **EMA (endomysial antibodies)-IgA:** This test is also specific to coeliac disease. It's the initial screening test of choice but may be negative in 2 per cent of people with coeliac disease who are IgA-deficient. When you test positive, especially if tTGA is positive too, you are extremely likely to have coeliac disease. However, for a definitive diagnosis you will probably be referred for a biopsy of the small intestine, too (see the next section 'Biopsy').

Both antibodies only show up in your blood test if you have been exposed to gluten. Therefore, do not remove gluten from your diet before you get tested, as its presence is essential for achieving an accurate result. The amount of gluten you need to eat before a test varies from person to person, but as a rough guide about four slices of bread per day or the equivalent amount of pasta, wheat based cereal, or other wheat based food should be eaten for around three weeks before you're tested.

Current research suggests that blood tests that look for both of these antibodies together are between 80–95 per cent accurate, but the possibility of getting a negative result and still having coeliac disease does crop up. So, what if you have strong coeliac symptoms but get a negative test result? That's where the biopsy comes into its own.

Biopsy

A biopsy involves a flexible viewing tube, known as an endoscope, being passed via your mouth down into the small intestine (this procedure can be done using local anaesthetic on the throat together with sedation). A small tissue sample is collected then examined under a microscope to check for abnormalities.

A biopsy is the gold standard for the diagnosis of coeliac disease. Coeliac disease is recognisable from damage done to the hair-like structures, called *villi*, which are situated on the lining of your small intestine (the mucosa). The villi increase the surface area of the small intestine so it can absorb more nutrients, but the body's system can sometimes interpret gluten as the enemy, attacking it and the villi at the same time (accidentally!), which then get flattened over time, upsetting the function of the intestine (malabsorption).

In the past, the damage to the villi in the gut lining had to be almost total for the coeliac diagnosis to be given. Nowadays technological advances in the way biopsy is taken, stained, and examined under the microscope mean less extreme, earlier grades of damage or villous atrophy (destruction of the villi) can be spotted. These tests can still give the diagnosis but are useful for detecting less symptomatic cases, defining the degree of damage caused by gluten, and monitoring the effectiveness of the one, and only, treatment – the gluten-free diet. The most commonly used of the tests is the four stage Marsh classification which takes into account the extent of flattening of the villi and the degree to which antibodies have invaded the lining of these villi.

Other blood tests the doctor may carry out

Your doctor may also want to run some other blood tests to see if malabsorption from your coeliac disease has had any other effects on your nutrient status. This may feel like a lot of tests, but they provide important information to help you on the road to recovery.

These tests include:

- ✔ **Haemoglobin (Hb) level:** This test shows the amount of oxygen-carrying pigment in your red blood cells. If the result is lower than normal, you may be suffering from anaemia. This test is often combined with a *serum ferritin* test that shows whether your iron stores have been depleted as a result of anaemia.

✔ **Red cell folate:** This substance (made from the B vitamin folic acid) is another important constituent of red blood cells that may be lower than normal if you're suffering from malabsorption.

✔ **Serum albumin:** This plasma protein count can be low if you've not been absorbing protein properly.

✔ **Alkaline phosphatase:** The amount of this enzyme in the sample can be raised if you're suffering from a shortage of vitamin D or calcium through malabsorption, or any damage to your bones.

✔ **B12 and vitamin D status:** These two vitamins are often badly absorbed in coeliac disease. Abnormally raised levels are therefore a marker of coeliac disease.

Finding the missing 500,000 undiagnosed coeliacs

With so many people out there who may have coeliac disease without knowing it, some exciting developments are happening right now, as we write this book, which may make things easier to find out who needs to follow a gluten-free diet.

A home-testing kit for coeliac disease is now available in the UK. The test involves a simple pinprick blood sample taken from the finger, and tests for the same antibodies for which your doctor would look. Of course, you do have some issues to consider before you undertake this test.

People who have a close relative with diagnosed coeliac disease are probably the best candidates for home testing because they are more at risk of having silent coeliac disease (the condition with no symptoms).

You still need to make sure that you're eating foods containing gluten for at least three months before you take the test to make sure that you have enough gluten circulating in your blood for the antibodies to be present in the first place.

Importantly, if you get a positive test result you must get the right dietary advice from a registered dietitian.

As with the test that your doctor would perform, you can still get a false negative result. This may mean that you're less likely to consult with your doctor about any symptoms you're experiencing and may remain a silent coeliac for even longer, missing out on the advice that a gluten diet will improve your long-term health!

Coeliac UK say that home testing kits are not a substitute for an official diagnosis for coeliac disease from a blood test and biopsy.

Remember:

✔ A home testing kit can only act as an indicator that you may have coeliac disease; it is not a diagnosis tool.

✔ If you're considering trying a home testing kit you must have been eating foods containing gluten for at least three months before you take the test or the results are meaningless.

✔ If the result of a home testing kit is positive you still need to see your doctor to have further tests, which will lead to an accurate diagnosis.

Ascertaining food allergy

The use of complementary and alternative medicine (CAM) for the diagnosis of food allergy and intolerance is growing fast. You can find many types of 'tests' available on the high street and on the Internet. With so much information available, knowing what is what is difficult. Many CAM tests have little clinical evidence to validate them and so are unhelpful. Other, more validated tests, have good evidence to support them for diagnosing food allergy and some food intolerances but are not appropriate for diagnosing coeliac disease This is because many different types of immune responses take place in the body but only one is involved in coeliac disease – you have to use the right for test for the immune response connected with the condition you suspect. Otherwise it can be like looking for a needle in a haystack.

The following tests for food allergy are all performed by qualified health professionals:

✔ **Skin prick test:** A minute amount of the suspect food is placed on the skin. The skin is then pricked. If a small red swollen weal occurs, this indicates an allergy to that specific food. This test is only performed under medical supervision.

✔ **Blood test also known as RAST (radioallergosorbent test) or MAST (multi-allergen screening test):** These tests measure the amount of IgE (immunoglobulin type E) antibodies to the suspect food in the blood. Commercial companies are out there offering this type of blood test direct to the general public, but it's important to check that the service is CE marked (meets the requirement of the European IVD Directive).

✔ **Open food challenges:** Minute amounts of the suspect food are given orally and symptoms are observed. Clearly, because a true food allergy can result on sudden severe and even fatal reactions, only experienced health professionals in a specialist allergy centre should carry out this test.

Food intolerance is much harder to diagnosis than food allergy. Many commercially available tests claim that they can diagnose food intolerance, and you can find a whole host of unqualified people who are only too happy to take your money and give you inaccurate results and very little advice about what to do with them. A list of such tests – some worthwhile, some not so – follows:

✔ **Gold standard test:** In this test, the suspected food is excluded for a period of time and a medical professional observes the patient's symptoms. If symptoms improve then the suspect food is reintroduced. If symptoms return then this change indicates that the patient has an intolerance to that particular food. This test can be very time-consuming. It's best carried out under the supervision of a registered dietitian, especially if children are involved, as you need to ensure that a well-balanced nutritional intake is adhered to.

✔ **IgG blood test:** This test measures IgG antibodies present in the blood. Doctors think that an increase in IgG to a certain food indicates an intolerance to that specific food. Some commercial companies offer this type of blood test direct to the general public, but you must check that the service is 'CE marked' (that it meets the quality and clinical evidence requirements of the European In Vitro (IVD) Directive concerning lab-based medical diagnostic devices carried out in test tube). At the moment, only one company meets this requirement, providing clinical evidence that their test is effective in detecting food intolerances. Check out Allergy UK at www.allergy uk.org for further details.

✔ **Kinesiology:** Some practitioners believe that certain foods cause an energy imbalance in the body. This imbalance is detected by testing the response of the muscle. The client holds the suspect food and the therapist tests the muscle response. The result can lead to many foods being eliminated from the diet. Research studies show that this test is no better than chance and is not recognised as valid.

✔ **Hair analysis:** A small sample of hair is sent off to a laboratory and analysed for heavy metals such as lead and mercury. The thinking is that these heavy metals cause food intolerances. No rational scientific basis for this test exists at present.

✔ **Cytotoxic testing:** This is a blood test where the white blood cells are mixed with the suspect food and if they swell this indicates a problem with that food. No rational scientific basis lies behind this test and any results would not be recognised as a true diagnosis of a food intolerance.

✔ **Pulse test:** The pulse is taken before eating the suspect food and then 15 minutes afterwards. An increase of 10 beats per minute indicates a food intolerance. Research shows that no connection is warranted between an increase in pulse rate and food intolerance. We think the increase in pulse rate may be more to do with the bill you get for the test!

✔ **Electrodermal (Vega) test:** This test measures the electromagnetic conductivity in the body. The person being tested holds a brass tube in one hand that is connected by a wire to the Vega Machine. An offending food is supposed to show a dip in the electromagnetic conductivity. Research studies show that this test only has a 50 per cent chance of diagnosing you correctly, and so you are just as likely to get a false result.

If you're looking at getting a commercial test for food allergy or intolerance you can find plenty more tests on the market with little or no science behind them. So before you hand over your cash always ask the following questions:

✔ How is your test validated, and what sort of clinical trials have been carried out to get that validation?

✔ What kind of support and advice do I get if I need to change my diet?

✔ Does this test comply with European diagnostic regulations?

Testing positive: Now what?

If you test positive your next step depends on what you've tested positive for. Where you go from here also depends on whether you've undergone the complete set of tests. Read on.

You're positive for gluten intolerance

If you actually have gluten intolerance and not coeliac disease, you may be able to get away with eating gluten from time to time. We can hear you now: *Yeah, I reckon I have a gluten intolerance, not coeliac disease. Pass the pizza and beer, please!* You may want to rethink that strategy unless you know for sure that you're really negative for coeliac disease, because sometimes people are told they're gluten sensitive when, in fact, they have coeliac disease. If that's the case and you do go back to eating gluten, you may be doing some hefty damage every time you indulge. Ask yourself and your doctor:

- ✔ **Were all the tests for coeliac disease done?** Sometimes doctors don't do any of the tests that are specific to coeliac disease; they just test for gluten intolerance. Other times, they only do a blood test for coeliac disease, which may not be enough when a biopsy would provide the true diagnosis.

- ✔ **If a child's being tested, is the child old enough to show an antibody response from a blood test?** The blood tests that are specific to coeliac disease may not show accurate results in children under 2 years old because their immune systems aren't strong enough to produce antibodies. In that case, a child may appear to be positive for gluten intolerance but not coeliac disease – when in fact, he or she actually has coeliac disease.

- ✔ **Were the results 'inconclusive', or were they definitive?** Sometimes someone's coeliac-specific antibodies are considered 'inconclusive' because the results from blood tests are insufficient. Sometimes, these people are told they don't have coeliac disease, but they do have gluten intolerance. If they went on to have a biopsy these people may then be given the correct diagnosis of coeliac disease.

If you aren't sure that a valid and reliable test has been done or you can trust your test results, you may want to be tested again somewhere down the line. Unfortunately it means that sometimes you have to be persistent and get a second opinion or gently persuade your doctor to investigate you again. Because diagnosis can be easily missed and does have implications it may be a good idea to take a copy of the information regarding diagnosis from Coeliac UK when you see your GP.

You're positive for coeliac disease

If you've been diagnosed with coeliac disease you know the key towards your better health: a gluten-free lifestyle. Going gluten-free right away is important. You may make mistakes at first, and that's okay. Take the positives from them, and move on.

Coeliac disease is a genetic condition. If you've been diagnosed, your family members need to be tested, too.

You're positive for wheat allergies

Although the conditions are different, you may have an allergy *and* a gluten intolerance or coeliac disease. So if you're diagnosed with wheat allergies from a skin prick test for instance (refer to the earlier sidebar 'What's the difference between wheat allergy and gluten intolerance?'), make sure that you're also tested for the more global conditions, gluten intolerance, and coeliac disease to know just what dietary restrictions you need to follow.

If you're not positive for those conditions but have only a wheat allergy, you need to avoid wheat but can still eat rye and barley which is different from following a gluten-free diet. If you suspect that you may have an anaphylactic response, you should consider carrying an EpiPen or other brand of epinephrine (a drug that stops the anaphylactic response) shot that allows you to inject yourself, in case you accidentally eat wheat. Anaphylactic shock is an extreme allergic reaction, which is more commonly seen in people who have an allergy to bee stings or foods like nuts. Someone with a gluten intolerance doesn't have an allergic response to gluten, they have an intolerance – eating gluten is not good news for them, but it doesn't cause an anaphylactic reaction.

Considering the Risks If You Don't Give Up Gluten

Invariably, at least four groups of people decide that they're going to continue to eat gluten even if they have problems with it:

- ✔ People who feel that the diet is too restrictive, and so they're not going to bother trying.

- ✔ People who don't feel any symptoms or were never properly diagnosed and decide that cheating from time to time is okay.

- ✔ People who feel symptoms but decide that the discomfort is worth the chance to enjoy a few beers (or other glutenous favourites) from time to time.

- ✔ People with persuasive relatives who refuse to hear anything about gluten: 'One little bit of cake won't hurt!'

If you fall into one of these categories and refuse to give up gluten even though you have or suspect that you may have gluten intolerance or coeliac disease, there's not much anyone can do. But before you finish your doughnut, at least read the next two sections, which talk about the conditions that are associated with coeliac disease – and the serious complications that can arise if you continue to eat gluten.

Looking at associated conditions

Certain conditions are associated with coeliac disease, meaning that someone who has one is more likely to have the other. Doctors aren't always sure which one developed first (except, for instance, Down's syndrome, which people are born with), but if you don't give up gluten, your chances of developing some of these conditions may increase.

Also, if you have one of these conditions but haven't been tested for gluten intolerance or coeliac disease, you should be tested, because the two go hand in hand; the fact that you have one of these diseases is a red flag that you may also have gluten intolerance or coeliac disease.

Autoimmune diseases

Several autoimmune diseases are associated with coeliac disease, including

- Addison's disease (hypoadrenocorticism)
- Autoimmune chronic active hepatitis
- Crohn's disease
- Insulin-dependent diabetes mellitus (Type 1)
- Myesthenia gravis
- Raynaud's phenomenon
- Scleroderma
- Sjögren's syndrome
- Systemic lupus erythematosus
- Thyroid disease (Graves' disease and Hashimoto's disease)
- Ulcerative colitis

Nutritional deficiencies

Because gluten intolerance and coeliac disease affect the small intestine, nutritional deficiencies are associated. In addition to specific vitamin and mineral deficiencies, people may have

- Anaemia
- Osteoporosis, osteopenia, or osteomalacia

Some people who are diagnosed with coeliac disease suffer from a secondary lactose intolerance, caused by the gut damage. Usually, this condition is a temporary problem and resolves when the gut begins to heal.

Other conditions

Several other conditions are commonly associated with coeliac disease. Cancer (especially intestinal lymphoma) can be a 'side effect' of poorly controlled coeliac disease, but once the gluten-free diet is followed closely for 3–5 years the risk is reduced back to that of the general population.

Type 1 diabetes and coeliac disease often go hand in hand and are both autoimmune disorders (explained at the beginning of this section). About 6–10 per cent of people with Type 1 diabetes have coeliac disease, but many don't know they have it. People with coeliac disease and Type 1 diabetes combined often find that managing blood-sugar levels is much easier on the gluten-free diet. Some doctors suggest that everyone with Type 1 diabetes should also be tested for coeliac disease, but as yet this is not mandatory in the UK.

Living with compromised health

You may feel perfectly healthy. You may be *asymptomatic* (have no apparent symptoms) or have mild symptoms that you barely notice. But if you have gluten intolerance or coeliac disease and you continue to eat gluten, you're undoubtedly compromising your health. Your body is being robbed of important nutrients that it needs to function properly and stay strong.

Many people say that they didn't realise how bad they felt until they went gluten-free. Then they enjoy such improved and even optimal health that they realise that eating gluten compromised their health, and they didn't even know it.

Healing Begins Right Away

One of the best things about going gluten-free when you have gluten intolerance or coeliac disease is that you often start to get better the minute you start on the diet.

Most people begin feeling better immediately; some take months to improve; and some feel better initially but then take a nosedive a few months into the diet. All these responses are normal to your body's healing process, and in the long run, you can look forward to improved health in ways that you may not have even expected.

Although most, if not all, of the intestinal damage caused by gluten is reversible, some of the prolonged malnutrition and malabsorption issues, such as short stature and weakened bones, may have long-lasting, if not permanent effects. That's one of the reasons catching gluten intolerance or coeliac disease early is important – so you can start skipping down the road to recovery.

Eating Gluten-Free Is for Life

Coeliac disease is quite unique in that it's a disease where the only available treatment is a gluten-free diet. The word *diet* can suggest that living gluten-free may be a little like a weight-loss diet, where you can be careful about what you eat most of the time, and then relax at the weekend or when you go on holiday. That is absolutely and completely *not* the case with a gluten-free diet for coeliac disease.

If a drug was available to cure your coeliac disease (which there isn't), you'd probably take it every day, right? Especially if that drug (which doesn't exist, remember) can help protect you from some really nasty complications of untreated coeliac disease. Your gluten-free diet works exactly like that non-existent drug – it's your passport to staying fit and well and the most important tool you can use to protect you from nutrient malabsorption, osteoporosis, and even cancer, as well as a whole host of possible complications.

Of course, the good news is that living a gluten-free life is easier now than it's ever been, and of course now that you've discovered *Living Gluten-Free For Dummies*, you have everything you need at your fingertips to make the change and get on with your life!

Chapter 3

Taking a Closer Look at Coeliac Disease

. . . .

In This Chapter

▶ Examining the prevalence of coeliac disease

▶ Understanding the causes and effects of coeliac disease on your bowel

▶ Exploring dermatitis herpetiformis, another form of coeliac disease

▶ Recognising the importance of maintaining strong bones when you have coeliac disease

▶ Monitoring your progress after diagnosis

. . . .

Coeliac disease is a common but much under-diagnosed condition. Contrary to popular belief, the condition is not an allergy but an autoimmune disease in which the body produces antibodies that attack its own tissues in response to the presence of gluten in the gut. Coeliac disease is intriguing. If undiagnosed it can result in severely compromised health but the good news is that it's fully treatable by a gluten-free diet. So just how common is it? Well, since you asked. . . .

Coeliac disease has a variety of other names that all mean the same thing, including *sprue*, *coeliac sprue*, *non-tropical sprue*, and persistent *gluten-sensitive enteropathy*.

Exposing One of the Most Common Genetic Diseases of Humankind

Doctors now know that coeliac disease is much more common than previously thought. Indeed, the condition is arguably one of the most common genetic diseases affecting humans. When we first qualified as dietitians, back in the Dark Ages, our lecture notes told us that the prevalence was 1 in 1000 people. However in recent years, since diagnosis has become easier, screening has become more widespread. Large-scale surveys across several countries, such as the European Cluster Project, suggest that the average prevalence is as high as 1 in 100 (or 1 per cent) of the population. Due to the strong genetic predisposition, this number goes up to 10 per cent or 1 in 10 in families where another member is affected. Anyone who has a relative, especially a first-degree relative such as a parent or sibling, may be at increased risk.

The diagnosis rate has increased massively since the 1970s – 10-fold in some coeliac clinics around the UK. Coeliac UK, an organisation working with sufferers of coeliac disease, estimates that 125,000 people in the UK have been diagnosed with coeliac disease. However, this discovery is probably only the tip of the iceberg with at least another 500,000 who have undiagnosed coeliac disease.

To put these numbers in perspective, coeliac disease is more common than Crohn's disease, ulcerative colitis, multiple sclerosis, Parkinson's disease, and cystic fibrosis. Take a look at Table 3-1 to see how coeliac disease measures up.

Table 3-1	Prevalence of Common Diseases in the UK
Disease	*Estimated Number of People Diagnosed in the UK*
Coeliac disease	125,000 (Coeliac UK)
Epilepsy	160,000 (National Society for Epilepsy)
Parkinson's disease	120,000 (Parkinson's Disease Society)
Ulcerative colitis	120,000 (National Association of Colitis and Crohn's Disease)
Crohn's disease	60,000 (National Association of Colitis and Crohn's Disease)
Multiple sclerosis	85,000 (Multiple Sclerosis Society)
Cystic fibrosis	7,500 (Cystic Fibrosis Trust)

People often wonder: If coeliac disease is so common, why don't more people have it? They do! They just don't know it yet (and may never know it).

Myths and misconceptions

Some of the things that we hear about coeliac disease have about as much truth as the Loch Ness Monster legend, (no, it isn't catching). Here are some of the more common myths:

Myth: Coeliac disease is rare.

Fact: Coeliac disease is one of the world's most common genetic diseases, affecting about 1 per cent of the population in Europe and North America.

Myth: Coeliac disease is a childhood condition.

Fact: Actually, if you inherit the genes, the symptoms can be triggered at any time in your life – for example during illness or stress. Coeliac disease diagnosed in childhood is now much less common. In fact the majority of cases are diagnosed in adulthood. Data from Coeliac UK suggest that more over 60s are diagnosed each year than under 16s. In 2001, 89 per cent of newly diagnosed members were adults and the average age at diagnosis was around 45 years. Most people are diagnosed between 30–45 but about 25 per cent of people with coeliac disease are diagnosed over the age of 60 years.

Myth: Severe gastrointestinal problems, like nausea, wind, bloating, and diarrhoea are the most common symptoms.

Fact: Many people with coeliac disease don't have any classic gastrointestinal symptoms, much less severe ones – their symptoms are outside the bowel. They can range from headaches, chronic tiredness, bone or joint pain, anaemia, persistent mouth ulcers, neurological problems, and hair loss through to fertility problems including spontaneous miscarriage, and depression. Adults may show signs of weight loss or indeed be overweight. Children with coeliac disease can experience the same symptoms but if left untreated can suffer from weight loss and faltering growth.

Pinpointing Who Develops Coeliac Disease and Why

Doctors have no way of knowing who is going to develop coeliac disease. What we *do* know is that you need at least three things in order to develop the condition:

- ✔ A genetic predisposition
- ✔ A diet that includes gluten
- ✔ An environmental trigger

Even if you have all three, you may never develop coeliac disease. We do know, however, that if you're missing one of these three things, you aren't going to develop coeliac disease.

Coeliac disease is a non-discriminatory condition, found in all races and nationalities. Occurrence is commonly thought to be more prevalent in people with Northern European ancestry, but that distinction is diminishing as populations are becoming more intermingled.

Some people think that civilisations that developed between the Tigris and Euphrates in the Middle East, where grain was first cultivated, have had longer to evolve to cope successfully with gluten-containing grains; that's why the prevalence of gluten sensitivity among these people is lower. Other groups, like the Germans, Scandinavians, and Celts of England, Scotland, and Ireland, began cultivating wheat only in limited amounts in the post-Roman era. They were mostly hunter-gatherers until the Middle Ages, and so those populations have had less time to adjust to gluten-containing grains.

Finding the key genes

No one has yet discovered all the genes involved in developing coeliac disease, but researchers do know, largely from studies of twins, two of the key players involved. These genes are located on chromosome 6 in the body. Both are forms of the human leukocyte antigen (HLA) genes known to their friends as HLA DQ2 and HLA DQ8. You don't have to have both – just one will do – and DQ2 is the one seen in 95 per cent of people with coeliac disease.

Interestingly, about 20–30 per cent of the general population has these genes yet doesn't develop coeliac disease. In other words, if you have the genes, you may or may not develop coeliac disease. But if you don't have either gene, you are very unlikely to ever develop it.

Coeliac disease isn't a single dominant or recessive genetic condition – unlike, for example, cystic fibrosis, colour blindness, or haemophilia. It's a complex *multifactorial* or *polygenic disease*, meaning several different types of genes play a part in the full manifestation of the condition in combination with lifestyle and environmental factors.

Triggering coeliac disease: What turns it on?

People use the word *trigger* in two ways when they talk about coeliac disease. The first refers to gluten being the trigger for initiating a response of the body's immune system. The type of trigger we're talking about here is an environmental trigger that 'turns on the switch', so to speak, launching coeliac disease into an active mode.

Most people have a pretty clear idea of when their coeliac disease was triggered, because in many cases they're relatively healthy, and then *boom!* Their symptoms appear out of the blue, and they have no idea why.

Common triggers include:

- ✔ Pregnancy
- ✔ Surgery
- ✔ Car accident or other physical injury
- ✔ Emotional stress – for example following divorce, redundancy, bereavement, or another emotional trauma
- ✔ Illness or infection

Understanding Coeliac Disease and What It Does to the Body

Coeliac disease is an *autoimmune disease* (a disease in which the immune system attacks the body) that gets activated when a susceptible individual eats gluten. To help you understand exactly what damage is being done, we review just a bit of basic human anatomy of the gastrointestinal tract. Bear with us – we promise to keep it brief!

Some people think that because coeliac disease is an autoimmune disease, someone with coeliac disease has a compromised immune system. Not at all! In fact, the opposite is true: The immune system is working overtime to fight what it perceives to be the enemy – gluten.

How your small intestine is supposed to work

Open your hand and put it flat against your belly button, with your thumb pointing up to your waist and your little finger pointing down. Your hand is now covering most of the relatively small space into which your small intestine – nearly seven metres of it – is neatly coiled.

By the time it gets here, your food has already been chewed, swallowed, passed through the stomach, and broken down by enzymes into nutrients that the body needs to absorb to nourish itself.

To help it do this, the lining or *mucosa* of the small intestine is made up of a series of folds covered with finger-like projections. The technical name for these small fingers is *villi* (singular: villus). The purpose of the villi, shown in Figure 3-1, is to increase the surface area of the intestine so that they have more room to absorb important nutrients. Each villus is covered with smaller projections called *microvilli*, and every villus and microvillus is programmed to accept a specific nutrient – and no other.

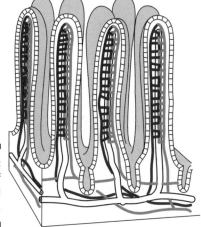

Figure 3-1:
The villi of your small intestine.

How your small intestine works with coeliac disease

When someone with coeliac disease eats gluten, everything's going along just fine until it reaches the upper small intestine. In these people the presence of gluten interacts with their particular genes to provoke an immune-mediated inflammatory response and stimulate release of immune cells (T-lymphocytes). These cells themselves invade the gut lining or mucosa and in turn release protein-based chemicals known as cytokines, which over time damage the gut wall and promote inflammation and subsequent flattening of the villi (*villous atrophy*), as shown in Figure 3-2. This flattens the lining of the intestine, leading to a decreased surface area for absorption of nutrients from food.

Villi   Villi

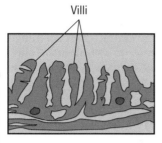 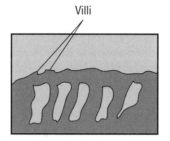

Figure 3-2:
Villi
flattened in
coeliac
disease.

Villi in a healthy intestine   Flattened villi in an intestine
with coeliac disease

An *autoimmune disease* is one in which the body's immune system produces antibodies that react against normal, healthy tissue (rather than against bacteria or viruses), causing inflammation and damage. Other examples include Type 1 diabetes, rheumatoid arthritis, pernicious anaemia, and autoimmune thyroid disease. Coeliac disease is unique, because it's the only autoimmune disease for which people know the trigger that sets off the response. Families may inherit the predisposition to autoimmunity, which can manifest itself differently in different members. If a family has a history of autoimmune disease, getting other members screened for coeliac disease is worthwhile. A survey in the USA found that 45 per cent of people eventually diagnosed with an autoimmune disease were initially labelled as hypochondriacs because doctors thought that they were imagining their symptoms! Doctors believe that people with untreated coeliac disease are more at risk of developing other autoimmune disorders.

Specifically, the body attacks the villi on the lining of the small intestine. As the villi get chopped down – *blunted* is the technical term – they can no longer be as effective in absorbing nutrients. That's why you see *malabsorption* (poor nutrient absorption) and nutritional deficiencies in people with coeliac disease who still eat gluten.

Because the food is just passing through without being absorbed the way it's supposed to be, diarrhoea is also a symptom. But think about this: The small intestine is nearly seven metres long, and damage from coeliac disease starts at the upper part – so you've got a *lot* of small intestine to compensate for the damaged part that's not able to do its job. This helps explains why some people have few or no bowel symptoms. This fact also means that by the time you have diarrhoea, the coeliac disease may have been around a long time and you may be quite unwell.

On a gluten-free diet the gut starts to heal immediately. You may feel better within a few weeks but it can take between six months to two years for the villi to recover fully. The reaction to eating gluten again can range from an immediate triggering of bowel symptoms to no symptoms at all. However, whether or not you notice any symptoms, damage to the bowel will occur.

Scratching the Surface of Dermatitis Herpetiformis

Dermatitis herpetiformis (or *DH* as we refer to it from now on) is another manifestation of coeliac disease resulting from gluten sensitivity. Although first described as long ago as 1884, the link between DH and coeliac disease was not made until 1968. DH is much less common than coeliac disease, with a prevalence of about 1 in 10,000, but also has tendency to be inherited. It can occur at any age but is rare in childhood and usually first appears in young to middle-aged adults, although it can occur for the first time at any age. The occurrence is slightly more common in men than women, with 60 per cent of adult sufferers being male.

The symptoms of DH are mainly external – on the skin – and include:

- A rash that may occur on the elbows, upper forearms, knees, back of the neck, buttocks, or scalp but can also be on the face, trunk, and other parts of the arms and legs – in fact almost anywhere apart from the soles of the feet.
- Persistent raised red-coloured bumps.
- Watery blisters on the surface that are easily scratched away and scab over.
- Intense itching or stinging.

Everyone with DH has coeliac disease, but not everyone with coeliac disease has DH. In DH the coeliac disease may be mild and not cause any symptoms although most people actually have some gut inflammation and villous flattening, which would be visible on biopsy. Fewer than 10 per cent of people with DH have the classic bowel symptoms of coeliac disease.

To diagnose DH, a dermatologist takes a biopsy of the skin *near* (but not in) the lesion. The process isn't painful, because they can use a local anaesthetic to numb the site. They're looking for an antibody called IgA (we talk more about IgA in Chapter 2), and if they see it, they make a diagnosis of DH. Antibody blood screenings can confirm the diagnosis and help doctors monitor progress on a gluten-free diet, but a small intestinal biopsy may be necessary in some cases.

Reducing the chance of your baby developing coeliac disease

New studies show that you may be able to protect your baby from developing coeliac disease later in life. University of Colorado scientists have published information indicating that exposing babies to gluten in the first three months of a baby's life increases the risk of coeliac disease fivefold. Their studies indicate that waiting until the baby is at least six months old decreases the risk but that waiting beyond seven months increases the risk again. In other words, the best time to introduce gluten, according to this study, is at about six months old.

Another factor that seems to have an effect on the development of coeliac disease is breast-feeding. Studies show that breastfeeding for longer than three months may delay the onset of coeliac symptoms and decrease the risk of developing coeliac disease. Gradual introduction of gluten-containing foods and continuing to breastfeed while those foods are introduced also seem to reduce the risk of developing coeliac disease.

The cornerstone of treatment of DH is a strict gluten-free diet, but the diet usually takes some time to become effective. To reduce the rash more quickly patients are put on medication, such as dapsone, but carefully monitored for side effects. The intense itchiness reduces within a few days but continued medication may be needed for up to two years. If medication is stopped before the gluten-free diet has become effective the rash may return. Ideally, patients can be advised to begin to decrease their use of medications after about six months as they start to improve on the gluten-free diet.

If the gluten-free diet doesn't help, patients may be advised to avoid other chemicals as well. Iodine is involved in the rash formation and so excess intake can present a problem. It's concentrated in iodised table salt, sea-weeds such as kelp (found in some toothpastes and in some oriental foods), and potassium iodide (used in some mineral supplements, salt substitutes, and in cough medications), so patients should be advised check with their doctor if this substance may be the cause. Iodine is not usually a problem once the rash has disappeared.

The name for DH comes from *dermatitis*, meaning inflammation of the skin, and *herpetiformis*, because it looks similar to herpes, which involves clusters of lesions. Some people have made the erroneous assumption that DH is caused by the herpes virus, but no relationship to the herpes virus exists at all.

Maintaining Healthy Bones with Coeliac Disease

Our bones are living tissues and the whole skeleton is replenished about every 7–10 years in adults, and more frequently in children. Our bodies contain about 1 kilogram of calcium and 99 per cent of this amount is found in our bones. We need a regular dietary supply of calcium, along with vitamin D to help absorb it, to help rebuild new bones. In the UK alone, three million people have osteoporosis or a porous, brittle bone structure that is more prone to fracture. As many as one in three women and one in five men over the age of 50 suffer from it. Osteoporosis is even particularly common in people with coeliac disease, especially those diagnosed later in life, and up to 75 per cent of adults with untreated coeliac disease will suffer from it at some stage. Because the bones become more fragile, osteoporosis can lead to an increased risk of fractures, mainly of the wrist, hip, or spine. For those diagnosed at a young age, osteoporosis is less of a problem as bone density improves on a gluten-free diet.

What can happen to your bones in coeliac disease?

Anyone, whether they have coeliac disease or not, can develop *osteoporosis* (defined in the previous section). However, in coeliac disease bone metabolism can be disrupted mainly due to prior or persistent malabsorption of calcium and vitamin D. Low bone mineral density can lead to osteoporosis in later life. If you have coeliac disease you may be at higher risk of having reduced bone strength. Nearly half of all people diagnosed with coeliac disease have some reduction in bone mineral density; indeed, sometimes this finding is the only clinical sign of coeliac disease. No cure for osteoporosis has been developed but studies on adults suggest that after about one year on a strict gluten-free diet, bone density improves considerably and the risk of continued mineral loss with age is reduced.

Low bone density can usually be detected by a simple and painless scan by means of *dual-energy X-ray absorptiometry* (DEXA). This scan can be carried out as soon as coeliac disease is diagnosed, or as part of ongoing follow-up.

Adopting lifestyle strategies to help keep your bones strong

Strategies to prevent osteoporosis are especially important in people with coeliac disease. These include:

✔ **Following a diet rich in calcium.** Some people with coeliac disease have been found to have low calcium intake, and they benefit from specific advice to increase their calcium intake above that recommended for the rest of the population. The goal is to get a total of at least 1200 milligrams of calcium a day. To get this you need at least four servings of dairy products per day, which can include milk, hard cheese, or yogurt. Lower-fat varieties are just as good.

Some people with coeliac disease may be temporarily unable to tolerate the sugar in milk (a condition called *lactose intolerance*) until the villi in the gut return to normal and produce sufficient quantities of the enzyme *lactase* to digest it. They may benefit from dietary advice, and from the reduction of all foods with hidden milk. Often, however, they can tolerate yogurt or hard cheese better than fresh milk; if not, fortified soya milk and yogurt are valuable.

Other sources of calcium include tofu, sesame seeds, canned oily fish (where you eat the bones), green leafy vegetables, nuts, some dried fruits and fortified fruit juices, and some bottled waters (check the label). Very usefully, some prescribable gluten-free mixes and breads are also fortified with calcium to a level three times above that found in normal bread – check the label for actual levels. However, for all alternatives to dairy, you do need to eat reasonable portions regularly to ensure adequate intake. Table 3-2 shows a list of dietary sources of calcium.

Table 3-2	Some Dietary Sources of Calcium, Each Providing Approximately 250 Milligrams
Food	*Portion Size*
Milk	1/3 pint (200 ml)
Cheese	Small chunk (30 g)
Yogurt	1 small carton (150 g)
Cottage cheese	1 large carton (200 g)
Soya milk fortified with calcium	1/3 pint (200 ml)

(continued)

Table 3-2 *(continued)*

Food	Portion Size
Soya yogurt fortified with calcium	1.5 small cartons (200 g)
Tofu (soybean curd)	1 serving (50 g)
Fish where the bones can be safely eaten (such as canned salmon, sardines and pilchards, or whitebait)	1 serving (60 g)
Fortified gluten-free bread	2–3 slices or 1 roll
Green leafy vegetables (such as broccoli, curly kale, or watercress)	5 servings (400 g)
Baked beans	3 servings (500 g)
Mixed nuts	2 large bags (300 g)
Sesame seeds	3 tablespoons (35 g)
Dried figs	5 figs

✔ **Increasing your vitamin D intake**: Vitamin D is mostly made from the action of UV sunlight on the skin but dietary sources include margarine, egg yolks, fortified milks, cereals, and oily fish. If dietary sources prove impractical, your doctor can prescribe a supplement that contains calcium, vitamin D, or both. This prescription is usually given to housebound people who don't get much exposure to sunlight. This should normally be taken at meal times, but depending on dose it may be split across two meals to ensure optimal absorption.

✔ **Taking regular physical activity**: Exercise is important, especially where you bear the weight of your body, as when walking, jogging, dancing, or playing tennis.

✔ **Avoiding smoking, excess alcohol, and salt**: All these actions can inhibit normal bone construction.

✔ **Ensuring adequate intake of fruit and vegetables**: Recent studies show that the alkaline nature of the minerals left after we digest fruit and vegetables helps to prevent maintain the chemical balance in our bodies and reduce calcium loss from our bones caused by the over production of acidic urine.

For more information visit www.nos.org.uk, the Web site of the National Osteoporosis Society (NOS), which is the UK's only national charity dedicated to osteoporosis.

Following-Up after a Positive Diagnosis: What to Expect from Your Healthcare Team

Coeliac disease is a permanent, lifelong condition and successful treatment depends on your ability to follow a continuous and strict gluten-free diet. Complete gluten freedom is essential in order to resolve symptoms and reduce the risk of complications even if you had only vague (or even no) symptoms in the first place.

As a minimum, you should be reviewed by a healthcare professional (such as your dietitian or doctor) at three months, six months, and one-year intervals following diagnosis to check that you understand the need for – and have responded to – a gluten-free diet, and to monitor your return to full health. This may involve further blood antibody tests or a small intestinal biopsy. Children and teenagers may need to be monitored more frequently to check adequate growth and to encourage compliance.

In the longer term, you may benefit from continued, regular follow-up by a healthcare professional to monitor overall health, weight, check nutritional status, and ensure that complications are avoided or treated. The policy on long-term follow-up may vary locally, but for the most effective outcome you should continue under the care of a specialist gastroenterologist or your GP.

Occasionally, long-term compliance with the diet can be poor, or unintentional lapses can occur. Patients with non-bowel complications, such as anaemia, infertility, or low bone density, are more likely to lapse, because they're less likely to notice the effects of these lapses. One study found that one in four of patients who believed that they were on a strict gluten-free diet were actually consuming up to 10 grams of gluten per day.

Continued support from a Registered Dietitian once or twice a year is useful in helping to avoid these problems and to keep you up to date with products and advances. Dietitians can ensure that your diet is varied and well balanced, containing adequate energy (especially from carbohydrate), fibre, calcium, iron, and B vitamins, and that you're obtaining sufficient amounts of gluten-free foods on prescription. (More information on these foods is given in Chapter 4.) For this reason, more and more patients receive their follow-ups at specialist dietitian-led clinics. Whether follow-up is managed by your dietitian or by your GP, they're still likely to refer you back to a gastroenterologist if you respond poorly to the diet, or suffer weight loss, a change in bowel habits, abdominal pain, abnormal blood test results, or other medical symptoms of concern.

Even if you are coping fine with your coeliac disease it is a good idea to attend at least an annual review. This ensures that you remain aware of all the latest developments in the field. Your care can also be tailored to your circumstances if they change – for example during illness, pregnancy, or after the menopause in women. A recent study showed that current follow-up arrangements can be variable, with 38 per cent of the respondents receiving no follow-up care. Of those who did, nearly all found the visit had a positive impact and was useful. The preferred method of follow-up was with a dietitian, with a doctor being available if required.

Part II
Digging Deeper into Eating Gluten-Free

'I just hope it's gluten-free, that's all!'

In this part . . .

We spell out the nitty-gritty of the gluten-free diet and introduce you to foods you may never have even heard of before, some of which are far more nutritious than gluten ever wished it could be. We also give you a run-down of the relatively few foods you can't touch. We tell you how to think outside the ingredients box so you know what hidden sources of gluten to look for and how to make *sure* products are, in fact, gluten-free.

Chapter 4

Grasping the Ground Rules of the Gluten-Free Diet

*W*hether you're brand new to the world of gluten-freedom or an old hand who's been gluten-free for years, we hope this chapter tells you things about the gluten-free diet that may surprise you.

The essence of the diet sounds so easy: Gluten is in wheat, rye, and barley – so just avoid those foods, right? If the diet were that simple, we'd feel happy signing off right now, and this chapter would be finished. Unfortunately, the principle isn't quite that straightforward, thanks to the complexities of food manufacture and the presence of flavour enhancers, fillers, binders, and other ingredients, which can turn out to be names for 'stuff that may have gluten hidden in it.'

The good news is that the list of things you can eat is a lot longer than the list of things you can't. Yes, you're going to have to say goodbye to gluten-containing pizza, along with your usual bread, biscuits, cakes, pasta, and – yes – beer, but – and we stress this point – only in the gluten-loaded brands that you're currently used to.

You'll come to know the world of incredible gluten-free foods that can take the place of your old favourites, many of which are easily available to you on prescription if a diagnosis of coeliac disease is confirmed. You can also enjoy a whole range of naturally gluten-free cereals – some of which you may never have heard of before. If you think *buckwheat* is a type of wheat or *sorghum* is what you get when you break in a new toothbrush, now's the time to find out more about some of the other grains and starches available to you on a gluten-free diet.

Don't be discouraged if you find the diet a little confusing at first. For some people, discovering what's allowed and what isn't on a gluten-free diet requires an entirely different mindset, but experience comes with time. Whether you're a one or a ten on the 'I'm-totally-confused-by-this-diet' scale, this chapter is vital reading, because it establishes basic gluten-free guidelines. We outline what is and isn't gluten-free and why you sometimes have to question a product. We introduce you to gluten-free alternatives and talk about non-food items that you may or may not need to be concerned about, such as alcoholic drinks, medication, and non-consumable products like toothpaste and lipstick.

When In Doubt, Leave It Out

We can say unequivocally that at some point you are sure to have occasion to wonder whether a product is gluten-free; you're at a restaurant or party and you have no idea what's in the food, no list of ingredients is provided, or if one is, you don't recognise half the words on the label. And if you don't have your handy copy of *Living Gluten-Free For Dummies* nearby, you may be tempted to make assumptions that can cause problems. If something looks really delicious you may be tempted to assume that it's safe to eat when you really don't know. Please don't risk eating it. If you need a reminder of what you're doing to your body when you eat gluten, take a look at Chapter 2, which talks about associated conditions and serious complications that can develop if you have gluten sensitivity or coeliac disease and eat gluten, even from time to time.

Even if your symptoms are mild or absent, the damage gluten causes – even tiny amounts of gluten – can be severe. You're a lot better off being safe rather than sorry, and so follow our common-sense rule: When in doubt, leave it out.

Defining Gluten So You Can Avoid It

You need to know what gluten is – and not just so you can be the life and soul of the party, opening tantalising conversations with lines such as, 'So, which do you find hardest to avoid: gliadin, hordein, or secalin?' No, you need to know about gluten so you can avoid it. The definition of this term is so convoluted that offering a technically correct definition of gluten is difficult, but we're going to try.

Gluten is a storage protein found in the *endosperm* – or food supply of a seed – of wheat. Technically, it comes from wheat and only wheat. Gluten is what gives wheat flour, especially 'strong' flour, its elastic qualities when dough is kneaded. This elastic property traps the carbon dioxide gas that's released when yeast ferments or baking powder is activated, allowing bread and cakes to rise. Gluten also gives the chewy texture to baked goods such as bagels.

At some point in our not-so-distant past, someone made the association between wheat (specifically gluten) and coeliac disease. People widely accepted that gluten makes people with coeliac disease ill, which is true. Soon, doctors realised that barley and rye make people with coeliac disease ill, too, and people started saying, 'Coeliacs can't eat gluten. They can't eat wheat, barley, or rye, either; therefore, wheat, barley, and rye all have gluten.' Right? Well that's nearly right, but not quite! One of the types of proteins in gluten is also in barley and rye.

Prolamins is the collective name for the group of storage proteins present in a variety of grains, and they're what cause problems for people who can't eat 'gluten'.

Technically, gluten is made up of the proteins glutenin and alpha-*gliadin*, a specific type of prolamin in wheat. However, gluten has become a general term for any kind of potentially harmful prolamins. The prolamins that cause damage to people with coeliac disease include alpha-*gliadins* (in wheat), *secalins* (in rye), and *hordeins* (in barley). Prolamins are found in other grains, too – *zeins* (in maize or corn), *avenins* (in oats), and *orzenins* (in rice) – but these prolamins aren't toxic to people with coeliac disease probably as a result of the different amounts of amino acids, specifically the proline content.

The avenins in oats are now thought to be OK for many people with coeliac disease, however some with severe sensitivity to gluten may also be sensitive to oats themselves or to the gluten in oats contaminated during storage with other cereals.

The 'wheat, barley, and rye all have gluten' idea stuck, and even though this notion isn't technically correct, it *is* widely accepted today. For the purposes of this book, we stick with it, too.

Wheat-free doesn't mean *gluten-free*. Something can be wheat-free and still contain, for instance, malt (derived from barley). So that means it's not gluten-free. Similarly, some gluten-free foods contain wheat starch but the toxic fraction in coeliac disease – the gluten – has been removed so as to be below an agreed safe standard. (See the section 'Gluten-Free Foods at a Glance'.)

Gluten-Free Foods at a Glance

Keep in mind that you may have to check ingredient lists when you're discovering the intricacies of the gluten-free diet.

The reason the gluten-free diet can seem cumbersome at first is that *derivatives* of gluten-containing cereals, such as pasta, also contain gluten. Additionally, many processed foods can contain ingredients, seasonings, and additives that raise questions.

But breaking foods down into those that usually have gluten and those that don't isn't too difficult. Bear in mind that the lists we provide in this chapter are only intended to get you started. *The Food and Drink Directory* produced by Coeliac UK is really the gluten-free bible. This annually produced booklet is sent free to members of the society each year, and lists over 11,000 safe products verified to be gluten-free. Always use an up-to-date version as manufacturers have an annoying habit of changing the ingredients in their products. If you're thinking that surely things can't change that often, read on. As we like to be thorough with our researchers, we checked. We selected a month at random and found 35 new products that met with the gluten-free standard, and 15 modified products that no longer did! It pays to check! Monthly updates can be accessed via the Coeliac UK Web site, or can be e-mailed to you in the monthly newsletter. They can also be sourced on BBC 2 Ceefax, via a telephone hotline, or even via good old Royal Mail (if you send a self-addressed envelope to Coeliac UK). Visit www.coeliac.co.uk for full details.

Forbidden grains

We're not starting with the forbidden grains just to be negative – we're starting with them because the list is a lot shorter than the list of grains you can eat. Here are the grains you need to avoid on a gluten-free diet:

- ✔ Barley
- ✔ Oats (because of contamination issues during storage and manufacturing)
- ✔ Rye
- ✔ Triticale (a hybrid of wheat and rye)
- ✔ Wheat

You need to double-check any product with the word *wheat* in it. This includes hydrolysed wheat protein, wheat starch, wheatgerm, and so on. Wheatgrass, however, like all grasses, is gluten-free. (But see the nearby side-bar 'Grasses, sprouted grains, and grass berries' to make sure that you're not dealing with contamination. Hey, we know it's confusing; don't shoot the messenger!) Here are a few additional details to consider:

- Wheat starch is actually wheat that's had the gluten thoroughly washed out. In the UK, a special type of wheat starch called, rather fancily, Codex Alimentarius Standard wheat starch (or Codex Standard, from now on) is allowed in the manufacture of gluten-free foods. (See Chapter 5 for more on the Codex Standard.) It enables these products to resemble standard foods closely in both texture and taste, making compliance with the diet easier. The Codex Standard is internationally recognised to mean that the gluten content has been reduced to a trace level so as not to cause problems in the majority of people with coeliac disease.

- Triticale is a hybrid grain – produced by crossing wheat and rye. Biologists developed it to combine the productivity of wheat with the ruggedness of rye, not just to add another grain to your list of forbidden foods. And relatively speaking, it's fairly nutritious but only for people who can eat gluten.

- Wheat has several names and varieties. Beware of aliases such as *bulgur*, *semolina*, *spelt*, *durum*, *kamut*, *farina*, *couscous*, and *bran*.

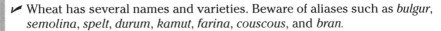

  Often marketed as a 'wheat alternative', *spelt* is a member of the wheat family, and not even remotely gluten-free.

- Derivatives of gluten-containing grains aren't allowed on the gluten-free diet. One derivative that you need to avoid is *malt*, which is usually made from barley. You find it in malted milk drinks and concentrated malt extract. In addition, malt extract and malt flavouring are found in small amounts in a range of processed foods and in malt vinegar. The level of gluten in these varies and small amounts are generally tolerated. However, some items, such as cornflakes, have been found to have levels that do not comply with the Codex Standard. For this reason they are not listed in Coeliac UK's *The Food and Drink Directory*. Other foods where malt extract does meet this standard are listed.

So you want to sow your oats. . .

Whether to include oats in the gluten-free diet has been debated for years, and still no clear-cut answer exists – yet. We know that people desperately want to include them in their gluten-free diet. However, commercially available oats aren't usually guaranteed to be pure, and so they're still on the 'forbidden' or 'questionable' list because of contamination from other gluten-containing cereals. They may be harvested in fields adjacent to wheat or contaminated with wheat during commercial processing, milling, or storage.

A recent five-year clinical trial in Finland involving 45 adults with coeliac disease eating 50 grams of pure oats on a daily basis, suggested that oats do not damage the gut lining (tested by biopsy) or aggravate other symptoms (blood antibodies) of coeliac disease. Some people argue that the risk of contamination is extremely low – but you need to assess whether you're willing to take that risk. If you can find pure, uncontaminated oats, they may not present a problem – certainly at levels of up to 50 grams day – but you're safer avoiding them altogether if you can't. Discussing this subject on an individual basis with an informed healthcare professional is always worthwhile. If you do decide to eat oats you should at least do so with support and monitoring.

Grains and starches you can safely eat

You can include a large choice of gluten-free grains and starches in your diet (some of these are explained in more detail in the later section 'Exploring Alternative Grains'). Even if you've been gluten-free for years, we're guessing some of these may be new to you:

Amaranth

Arrowroot

Buckwheat (groats/kasha)

Carob

Corn or maize (cornflour, polenta, cornstarch, cornmeal)

Gram (chickpeas or chana dahl)

Millet

Potato (potato flour, potato starch)

Quinoa

Rice (rice flour, ground rice, rice bran)

Sago

Sorghum

Sweet potato

Tapioca (cassava, manioc)

Yams

Other foods that are usually gluten-free

In general, these foods are usually gluten-free at least in their plain and unprocessed forms:

Beans and pulses, dried or canned (such as lentils, chick peas, aduki, cannellini, and red kidney beans)

Dairy products, including milk, cheese, yogurt, and fresh cream (and dried milk powder)

Eggs

Fats, including butter, margarine, and oils

Fish

Fruit

Meat

Nuts and seeds

Poultry

Quorn (a meat substitute made from mycoprotein)

Salt and pepper (sea salt, pepper corns)

Seafood

Soya, soya bean curd, soya bran, textured vegetable protein

Sugar, jam, marmalade, honey

Tea, coffee (fresh or instant), herbal teas

Vegetables

Yeast

Grasses, sprouted grains, and wheat berries

Grasses such as wheatgrass and barley grass, frequently sold in health-food stores and at juice bars, are gluten-free. The grass hasn't yet formed the gluten-containing storage proteins that cause problems in people with coeliac disease. Be careful, though, of grasses that are an ingredient in a product. They may be contaminated with cereal seeds, and because you don't know for sure, you can risk ingesting gluten.

You should avoid sprouted grains because you don't know how much of the storage gluten has been used for growth and how much remains in the plant. Eating the sprouts may be okay, but it may not be. Wheat berries are the wheatgrass seed kernels often found as bulgur wheat (wheat kernels that are partially boiled then dried) and are definitely not safe. Remember the common-sense rule we refer to in this chapter: *When in doubt, leave it out.*

Foods that usually contain gluten

A huge range of bread, crackers, cakes, biscuits, and pasta are available made from gluten-free ingredients, many on prescription. We explore them later in this chapter. Meanwhile, you should assume that the following foods contain gluten unless otherwise identified:

Bagels

Barley water and cloudy fizzy drinks

Batter

Beer, lager, and stout, including Guinness

Bran

Bread and rolls, including white, brown, wholemeal, mixed grain, rye, pitta

Breadcrumbs

Biscuits and cookies

Breakfast cereal

Bulgur/bulgur wheat

Cakes, including sponges, doughnuts, muffins, scones, brownies, and other baked goods; cake decorations

Confectionery

Couscous

Crackers, crispbreads, and prawn crackers

Croissants

Croutons

Crumpets

Flour, including white, plain, self-raising, wholemeal, barley flour, rye flour

Frozen chips and potato wedges (with savoury coating)

Ice cream cones and cornets

Imitation seafood sticks (for example crab sticks)

Indian breads, including naan, chapattis, paratha, and poppadoms

Lemon curd

Liquorice (contains wheat flour)

Marinades and thickened sauces

Mashed potato (instant)

Mayonnaise, salad cream

Mincemeat

Miso paste and miso soup

Muesli and muesli products, such as bars or yogurt

Mustard, pickles, and chutneys

Oats, oatcakes, and oat-meal if contaminated by other grains during storage. Check label. Always consult a suitably qualified health profes-sional before introducing oats into your diet

Pasta and noodles (dried, fresh, and canned)

Pastry products (all types, pies both savoury and sweet, crumbles)

Pearl barley

Pizza base

Pretzels, flavoured crisps, dry roasted nuts

Ready meals and manu-factured foods

Sauces and sauce mixes, gravy

Sausages and other manu-factured meat products, such as rissoles, haggis, faggots

Seasoning, stock cubes/bouillon, and spice mixes

Semolina

Soups

Soy sauce

Stuffing mix

Suet

Vending machine hot chocolate, malted milk drinks, coffee essence, and coffee substitutes made from barley

Wafers (communion and ice cream)

Waffles

Worcestershire sauce

Exploring Alternative Grains

When people come to consider grains beyond wheat and rice, many of us don't know our amaranth from our arrowroot. Actually, you can find a huge range of gluten-free grains out there, many of which are delicious and nutri-tious. Now's your chance to try some of these alternative grains and discover an entirely new world of gluten-free foods.

We've called them 'alternative grains', but many aren't grains at all. Instead, they come from a range of other plants or plant parts. For years, rumours have spread that some of these alternative grains aren't gluten-free. Although some people may have had reactions to these grains (as they would to corn, soya, or other allergens or foods to which they may have a sensitivity), it's not a gluten reaction. But regardless of whether a food contains gluten, if it makes you ill, don't eat it!

Amaranth

Amaranth isn't a true cereal grain at all but a relative of the ornamental flower called *cockscomb* or *plume plant*. Loaded with fibre, iron, calcium, and other vitamins and minerals, amaranth is also high in essential amino acids and so is an excellent source of protein. A small bead-like grain, the seeds of amaranth are not only good for you but also delicious, with a pleasant peppery and hearty nutty flavour. Amaranth can be milled or toasted, which gives it extra flavour. You can even 'pop' whole seed varieties like popcorn to add crunchiness to homemade bread, salads, soup, and muesli. You can boil the seeds and eat them like breakfast cereal, or as a side dish. Amaranth flour also makes a nice thickener for gravies, soups, and stews. Sprouted Amaranth goes well in salads or prepared cereals.

You should always cook amaranth before eating it, because like some other edible seeds, it contains compounds that can inhibit the proper absorption of certain nutrients.

For centuries, the Aztec culture depended on amaranth and believed it had mystical powers that brought strength and power even to the weakest of men. The name means 'not withering', or more literally, 'immortal'. Although amaranth may not make you immortal, it's extremely nutritious – and gluten-free.

Arrowroot

Once revered by the ancient Mayans and other inhabitants of Central America as an antidote to poison arrows, arrowroot is now used to soothe the stomach and has an antidiarrhoeal effect. People also use it in cooking as a thickener for soups, sauces, and desserts.

Arrowroot is a fine, white powder with a look and texture similar to that of cornstarch. The translucent paste has no flavour and sets to an almost clear gel. You can use arrowroot in gluten-free cooking or as a thickening agent, although it thickens at a lower temperature than cornstarch or wheat and its consistency doesn't hold as long after cooking. The superfine grains are easy to digest, making arrowroot a perfect 'invalid' food. In fact, arrowroot biscuits are one of the first solid foods that babies can safely eat (but beware – manufacturers usually add wheat flour to arrowroot biscuits, and so they're not gluten-free).

Buckwheat

The fact that buckwheat is gluten-free often confuses people; after all, buck-wheat has the word 'wheat' right there in the name. But *buckwheat* isn't even related to wheat; in fact, it's not even a true cereal grain. Buckwheat is a fruit, a member of the rhubarb family. High in lysine, which is an amino acid lacking in many traditional grains, buckwheat contains several other amino acids. In fact, this grain has a high proportion of all eight essential amino acids, which the body doesn't make but still needs in order to keep functioning. In that way, buckwheat is closer to being a complete protein than many other plant sources. It's also high in many of the B vitamins, as well as the minerals phosphorus, magnesium, iron, copper, manganese, and zinc. And buck-wheat's a good source of linoleic acid, an essential fatty acid.

Whole white buckwheat is naturally dried and has a delicate nutty flavour that makes it a good stand-in for rice or pasta. Buckwheat seed has a pale kernel and may be sold crushed and hulled under the name of groats or Saracen corn. When the hulled buckwheat kernels are roasted, they're called *kasha*, which has a deep tan colour, nutty flavour, and a slightly scorched smell. Cooks often use buckwheat in pancakes, biscuits, and muffins – but be aware that manufacturers often combine buckwheat with wheat in those products, and so you have to read the labels carefully before buying buck-wheat products. In Japan, people often make buckwheat into *soba*, or noodles, which sometimes – but not always – have wheat flour as well.

Carob

Carob comes from a Mediterranean tree, a member of the pea and bean family. The trees may be male, female, or both at once but only female trees produce fruit, known as pods. These begin life as bright green pods and ripen to a dark brown. The pods can be roasted and ground to produce flour, which is rich in fibre, natural sugars, vitamins, and minerals. Carob is used in baking alongside other gluten-free flours.

Gram flour

Gram flour is pale yellow fine flour milled from *gram* or *chana dal*, a lentil-like member of the chickpea family. It is commonly used in Middle Eastern and Indian cooking and is rich in protein and fibre. It has a rich earthy flavour making it most suitable for savoury dishes such as falafels, bhajis, pakoras (fritters), and pancakes.

A-maize-ing grains

Maize originated in North America and dates back thousands of years. The cultivation was a remarkable feat. Native Americans (Hopi) developed as many as 24 different kinds of maize to accommodate the length of growing season, altitude, rain, sunlight, and soil type. To ensure a full season's yield, the people grew both early and late ripening crops, and all the corn came in a variety of colours. Christopher Columbus and Sir Walter Raleigh first brought maize to Europe.

Maize has played an important role socially, as well. A Hopi bride-to-be would grind corn for three days at her future husband's house to prove she had 'wifely skills'. When a Hopi child was born, he or she received a special blanket and a perfect ear of corn as a welcome into the world. And early American settlers quickly came to depend on corn, which is easy to grow and store and needs little maintenance. Maize-based dishes became a backbone of early frontier dining for rugged settlers who were busy fending off grumpy Native Americans (undoubtedly more than a bit annoyed that their cornfields were being taken over) and cantankerous outlaws.

Maize or corn

You may run across different names or forms of maize (or corn) that are gluten-free. They include grits, hominy, polenta, cornstarch, cornflour, corn bran, and cornmeal.

Cornflour is a fine white power used to thicken sauces and custards, and bind ingredients. It is used in gluten-free flour mixes.

Millet

Millet is another member of the grass family with small, round, yellow kernels, similar in appearance to mustard seed, which swell when cooked. Millet is packed with B-complex vitamins and iron, magnesium, phosphorus, and potassium; it's also loaded with fibre and protein. Millet is easier to digest than many traditional grains.

Millet has been a staple food in Africa and India for thousands of years, and people grew it as early as 2,700 B.C. in China, where it was the prevalent grain before rice became the dominant staple. Today, millet is still a significant part of the diet in northern China, Japan, and various areas of the former Soviet Union, Africa, India, and Egypt. Grown today in Western countries mostly for cattle and bird feed, millet is also gaining popularity as part of the human diet.

Potatoes, potato flour, and potato starch

Potatoes are edible underground tubers and were originally native to the Peruvian Andes, probably first taken to Europe in the 16th century by Spanish explorers. The popularity of the potato spread quickly in temperate climates where it grew well. A huge variety of potatoes can be used as staples in the gluten-free diet. In addition, potato flour can be made from cooked, whole potatoes dried and ground. Potato flour has quite a strong flavour and heavy texture and its ability to absorb and retain moisture means that it's not appropriate on its own in baking. However, potato flour is useful in a mix with other gluten-free flours, such as maize or rice, where the moisture retaining properties are a bonus, such as in cakes, bread, and pizza bases.

Potato starch is a fine flavourless powder made from dehydrated raw potato. It absorbs moisture on cooking making it useful as a thickening agent in soups, sauces, and gravies.

Quinoa

Quinoa (pronounced *keen*-wa) is yet another of the grains that isn't really a grain; it's actually a fruit and a relative of the common weed known in the UK as Fat Hen. The American National Academy of Science describes quinoa as 'the most nearly perfect source of protein from the vegetable kingdom.'

Like other alternative grains, quinoa is packed with lysine and other amino acids that make it a good quality protein. It's also high in phosphorus, calcium, iron, vitamin E, and assorted B vitamins, as well as fibre. Quinoa is usually pale yellow in colour but also comes in pink, orange, red, purple, and black.

Because the uncooked grains are coated with *saponins* – sticky, bitter-tasting stuff that acts as a natural insect repellent – you should rinse quinoa thoroughly before cooking. Most quinoa that you buy has already been rinsed.

People in the South American Andes have cultivated quinoa since at least 3,000 B.C. Ancient Incas called this annual plant 'the mother grain' because it was self-perpetuating and ever-bearing. They honoured it as a sacred food product, because a steady diet appeared to ensure a full, long life; and the Inca ruler himself planted the first row of quinoa each season with a golden spade.

Rice and rice flour

Rice is believed to be the oldest cultivated grain and is a staple of many cultures throughout the world. Indeed, it's grown on every continent. All types of rice are gluten-free including wild rice. Even the so-called *'glutinous'* rice doesn't contain gluten! Manufacturers make glutinous rice, or *sweet sticky rice*, by grinding high-starch, short-grain rice. Glutinous rice thickens sauces and desserts in Asian cooking and is often the rice that's used in sushi.

Most rice flour is finely ground from polished white rice, but if you try you can find brown rice flour with some of germ left. Rice flour is easy to digest and is commonly used in Indian cooking for puddings, biscuits, and the dough or batter for the Southern Indian pancakes known as idlis and dosas. Flour made from glutinous rice is also used to make Chinese dumplings. Rice flour is commonly used in gluten-free mixes. Rice bran or rice polish is a useful source of gluten-free fibre and originates from the outer layer of the rice seed, which is removed to make wholegrain rice into white rice.

Sago

Sago is extracted from the pith inside the trunk of the Sago Palm tree, *Metroxylon sagu*, also known as the Tree of a Thousand Uses – 1001 if you count providing another food for a gluten-free diet. It's a staple in the diet of many people around the Pacific and Indian oceans. Sago is high in carbohydrate and a reasonable source of fibre, vitamins, and minerals. Locals bake the flour into bread, pancakes, and even noodles, but we're more familiar seeing it as the coarse pearls, rather like tapioca, used in milk puddings or in dishes such as sago plum pudding.

Sorghum

Sorghum is another of the oldest known grains – though again, it's not a true cereal grain – and it's been a major staple of nutrition in Africa and India for centuries. Sorghum is generating excitement as a gluten-free insoluble fibre. The protein and starch in sorghum are more slowly digested than that of other cereals and it's high in iron, calcium, and potassium.

Sorghum fans boast of its bland flavour and light colour, which don't alter the taste or look of foods when you use sorghum in place of wheat flour. Many cooks suggest combining sorghum with soybean flour.

Sorghum and millet are both rich in a group of compounds called nitrilosides. Some people notice a correlation between high nitriloside intake and low cancer rates, leading some to speculate that nitrilosides may actually help fight or prevent cancer. For instance, in Africa, where as much as 80 per cent of the diet consists of high-nitriloside-yielding foods, the cancer incidence is very low.

Getting into gums

Gums, such as *xanthan* (pronounced 'zanthan') *gum* and *guar gum*, contain no gluten. They're used frequently in processed foods, such as sauces and salad dressings, as emulsifiers and stabilisers. They're also really useful in home-cooked gluten-free baked goods, offering the elastic texture, softness, and volume in baking that you usually get from gluten. Gums are also added to some commercially available gluten-free mixes. Xanthan is made during the fermentation of sugar with a friendly bacterium, *Xanthomonas campestris*. The gum is later pasteurised to kill the bacteria. Guar is extracted from the seeds of the locust bean, a leguminous shrub that normally grows in India. Many health-food shops stock these gums as powders, which dissolve in water and can be added to your flour mix, but where they've been added already to a commercial mix you don't need to add extra when baking. Many excellent cookery books are available that give you a seemingly endless variety of recipes using gums in bread, cakes, and pastry.

Be warned: For some people guar gum may have a slight laxative effect.

Sugar beet fibre

As the name suggests, *sugar beet fibre* is the fibre extracted from sugar beet pulp once the sugar has been removed. It's free from gluten and provides an excellent source of fibre for those with coeliac disease. Sugar beet fibre is an especially good balance of insoluble fibre, which helps alleviate constipation, and soluble fibre, which can help lower cholesterol levels.

Tapioca

Tapioca is the dried and treated starch extracted from the inner root of the *cassava* or *manioc* plant. Cassava is used widely grown as a staple crop throughout Central and South America, Africa, and the West Indies, because it produces a high crop yield even in relatively poor soils. Tapioca is available as flakes, flour, or white pearls. The flour is used in flour mixes along with other gluten-free flours such as rice and potato. The pearls are virtually flavourless and so combine well with a range of other cooking flavours. Generally, they need soaking, but on cooking they swell and become transparent – anyone remember frogspawn at school lunch? Tapioca can be used in puddings, soups, and casseroles to give texture and body.

Checking Up on Added Ingredients

The diet gets a little trickier when you don't know whether a food meets the Codex Standard. (Check out Chapter 5 for more on the Codex.) In this section, we look at the ingredients that can commonly be added to processed foods. We explore those you definitely need to avoid, and those you need to question. Finally, we discuss some of the foods that people used to question but we now know are gluten-free.

Knowing which ingredients to avoid

Ingredients that are not gluten-free include:

- Barley malt, malt, or malt extract (unless complying with the Codex Standard)
- Flour: wheat, rye, and barley
- Wheat bran, oat bran
- Wheat rusk
- Wheat starch, modified wheat starch, or fillers (unless complying with the Codex Standard)

Knowing which ingredients to question

Some ingredients in processed foods *may* contain gluten, including:

- Baking powder
- Blended seasonings and curry powder blends
- Gravy mix and browning
- Mayonnaise, salad cream
- Mustard/mustard powder
- Soy sauce
- Stock and bouillon
- Worcestershire sauce

Thanks to new labelling laws, far fewer 'questionable' ingredients are included in foods and manufacturers have to indicate clearly if a product has a gluten-containing cereal in it, or even if an ingredient has been derived from a gluten-containing cereal. The Codex Standard ensures that a product contains less than 200 parts of gluten per million parts of product. This trace level can be tolerated by the majority of people with coeliac disease and can be applied to products containing ingredients from wheat, rye, or barley such as barley malt or wheat starch. (See Chapter 5 for more details on the new laws.)

Putting an end to the controversy over certain foods

People used to question certain ingredients, and they were on the 'have-to-dig-deeper-to-make-sure-this-is-gluten-free' list. They were questioned because of rumours, misinformation and misunderstanding, or even ambiguous labelling laws. But today, thanks to new laws and more definitive research, the following ingredients are no longer in question – we know they are gluten-free:

Alcohol (distilled)	Fish sauce
Artificial sweeteners, including aspartame, sorbitol, and malitol	Gelatin
	Hydrolysed vegetable protein (HVP)
Balsamic vinegar	
	Isomalt
Bicarbonate of soda	
	Maize, modified maize starch, modified starch
Caramel	
Citric acid	Mixed herbs, mixed spices
Coconut cream/ coconut milk	Mono- and diglycerides
Cream of tartar	Monosodium glutamate
Dextrin, dextrose, glucose syrup, and maltodextrin (may be derived from wheat refined to contain negligible gluten)	Potato or rice starch
	Rice malt or corn malt
	Rice rusk

Textured vegetable protein	Wheatgrass
Vanilla and vanilla extract	Xanthan gum
Vinegar	Yeast

The gluten-free status of these ingredients applies to ingredients produced in the European Union. Countries outside the EU may have different manufacturing processes.

Thinking about wheat starch

Starch including food starch, edible starch, and modified starch, are often found on the ingredients list of manufactured foods. Generally, they're used as fillers or thickeners and may come from a variety of cereals. Normal grade wheat, barley, or rye starch contains gluten and should be avoided. If the origin of the starch is listed is as potato, rice, or cornstarch you know that it's safe. If the modified starch comes from a cereal containing gluten it says so – for example, modified wheat starch. If the label simply states 'modified starch', it should gluten-free. To double-check, consult the gluten-free bible, *The Food and Drink Directory*, from Coeliac UK. All products listed containing starch have been verified with the manufacturers to establish gluten-free status. If all else fails, remember, and we're sorry if we're repeating ourselves: When in doubt, leave it out.

Codex Standard wheat starch is produced by thoroughly washing the gluten out of wheat starch until it meets an agreed international standard. In practice, this means that it has less than 200 parts of gluten per million parts of product. The majority of people with coeliac disease can tolerate this trace level, and so Codex wheat starch is used in the manufacture of many gluten-free foods to give an acceptable texture and taste.

Unfortunately, life's never that simple is it? A minority of people with coeliac disease do not recover fully on a diet that includes Codex wheat starch and may be advised by their doctor or dietitian to exclude both gluten and wheat starch as a precaution to avoid all risk of bowel damage. They still have many suitable manufactured gluten-free foods available to them.

The facts on flavourings and flavour enhancers

Most flavourings and flavour extracts found in foods in the UK are gluten-free. Malt is made from germinated barley and is not gluten-free. As a result, malt in concentrated amounts, such as in pure malt extracts and malted milk drinks, is not suitable. Malt extract and malt flavouring are widely used, although in small amounts, as flavour enhancers in foods such as breakfast cereal, ready meals, soups, and snacks. Both malt extract and malt flavouring may still contain small amounts of protein in the form of gluten. Some items with trace amounts, including certain processed foods and malt vinegar, are generally tolerated by people with coeliac disease. However, with more sensitive measuring tools, it has become apparent that some foods contain higher levels of malt extract – and therefore gluten – than previously realised and do not meet the Codex Standard. Only products containing malt extract or flavouring that are also listed in the current edition of *The Food and Drink Directory* produced by Coeliac UK should be considered suitable.

Liquorice flavouring (but not solid liquorice) used in the making of some sweets is gluten-free. Monosodium glutamate (MSG) used to enhance the flavour of many foods is manufactured from wheat. However, the final product is so refined as to be perfectly safe for people with coeliac disease. When cooking at home always check that seasonings and spice blends are gluten-free. Be wary of those bought abroad, as they may have been contaminated or contain cereal fillers.

Qualifying for Gluten-Free Foods on Prescription

Once a diagnosis of coeliac disease, or the closely related condition dermatitis herpetiformis (DH), has been confirmed, a large range of gluten-free alternatives to your everyday staple foods are easily available to you on prescription from your GP. This range includes items such as bread, flour, crispbreads, crackers, biscuits, and pasta. The range in the UK is excellent and has greatly improved the ability of people with coeliac disease to follow a strict gluten-free diet. A recent study of over 1,000 adults in the UK shows that those who receive regular gluten-free products on prescription from their GP lapse much less frequently than those who don't. Getting these products on prescription may help you stick to your diet and is certainly cheaper than buying them individually. Prescription foods are intended for use only by the patient and not for other family members.

Knowing how to obtain gluten-free products on prescription

Surveys show that about 90 per cent of people with coeliac disease do obtain their staple foods on prescription from their GP surgery. Most people find that putting an order in on a monthly basis is easiest. Some surgeries require notice for any repeat prescriptions or changes to a prescription, and so forward planning helps. Your local pharmacist may be able to deal with repeat prescriptions by getting the order sent direct to them, but once again they may need notice especially if you're requesting something new.

Generally, you pay a prescription fee for each item – an item is classed as a multiple case of an identical product, for example six loaves of bread or four packets of biscuits. Many people in the UK are entitled to free prescriptions. This includes children under 16 and adults over 60, pregnant women, and those on certain benefits, such as income support. People with coeliac disease are not automatically exempt from prescription charges. If you do pay for prescriptions, the cheapest way to get gluten-free products may be to use a pre-payment certificate (FP95). This can be purchased annually for a fixed fee and works out cheaper if you have more than 14 prescriptions in a year (not just for gluten-free foods). Ask your pharmacist for details, or visit the Department of Health's Web site at www.dh.gov.uk to pre-pay online.

Appreciating the range of prescribable products

The range of gluten-free foods on prescription is listed in full at the front of *The Food and Drink Directory* produced by Coeliac UK. The range is enormous and growing all the time – at last count it ran to over nine pages of the directory!

The range includes:

Bread, bread rolls, baguettes. These may be fresh, part baked, or vacuum packed; white, brown, high fibre, multi-grain, or wheat-free. Loaves are generally about half the size and standard weight of UK loaves

Crackers and crispbreads, including plain, flavoured, and high fibre

Flour, including plain, white, self-raising, brown, high fibre

Pasta, including tagliatelle, macaroni, lasagne, penne, spaghetti

Pizza mix or bases

Savoury biscuits

Speciality mixes for making pastry, cakes, and bread

Sweet biscuits, including cookies, tea biscuits, and digestives

Most of the manufacturers offer taster packs or samples of their products so you can try them before you decide which ones to order on a regular basis. Products vary considerably from brand to brand, and so experimenting to find the ones you like is worthwhile.

The availability of fresh bread delivered directly to the pharmacist has revolutionised the gluten-free diet and led to the improved dietary intake for many people with coeliac disease. In one recent survey of adults who switched from packaged to fresh gluten-free bread, over two thirds said that they had increased their consumption of bread, and 65 per cent of them were eating eight or more loaves a month.

Many people may want to vary their prescription to avoid boredom or because of a change in the seasons or their lifestyle. Changing your order is generally straightforward, but depending on your GP you may need to make the request by letter, consultation, or telephone. Check in advance with your GP practice on their procedure.

Deciding how much gluten-free product you need

Patients vary considerably in their need for gluten-free products depending on age, sex, and activity level. Nevertheless, guidelines have been produced for the recommended *minimum* monthly amounts of gluten-free foods required for different age and sex groups, including pregnant and breastfeeding women. These guidelines are based on typical food patterns and recommendations for a balanced diet where prescribable foods would make up about 15 per cent of the total energy intake. Table 4-1 gives the minimum amounts you should be entitled to on prescription on a monthly basis. When ordering think about storage as some have a short shelf life. Freezing them can be useful. Table 4-2 shows what constitutes a unit in Table 4-1.

Table 4-1	Recommended Minimum Monthly Allowance of Prescribable Gluten-Free Items
Sex/Age	*Suggested Minimum Number of Units Per Month*
Child 1–3 years	10
Child 4–6 years	11
Child 7–10 years	13
Child 11–14 years	15
Child 15–18 years	18
Male 19–59 years	18
Male 60–74 years	16
Male 75+ years	14
Female 19–74 years	14
Female 75+ years	12
Breastfeeding	Add 4
Third trimester of pregnancy	Add 1
High level of physical activity	Add 4

Table 4-2	What Constitutes A Unit?
Food Item	*Number of Units*
400 g bread/roll/baguette	1
500 g flour mix	2
200 g biscuits/crackers	1
250 g pasta	1
2 pizza bases	1

How does this information translate into a monthly allowance? For a female 19–74 years old the minimum level is 14 units. This allowance can be made up of the following:

- 8 loaves of bread (8 units)
- 1 pack of pizza bases (1 unit)
- 500 g pasta (2 units)
- 2 boxes crackers (2 units)
- 1 box sweet biscuits (1 unit)

Indulging in Some Non-Prescription Products

Many other non-prescription gluten-free foods are available. Often the same suppliers who make the prescribable items produce these foods, but they are considered to be luxury items rather staples. They can be purchased directly from your pharmacist or, increasingly, online or by mail order. Some can be bought at health-food shops or even from the health-food aisle of your local supermarket. At last count, we estimated that there were 15 suppliers of Codex Standard gluten-free products in the UK alone. Manufacturers' details are listed in *The Food and Drink Directory* from Coeliac UK.

Some non-prescription gluten-free items that took our fancy are as follows:

Almond croissants	Custard creams
Blueberry muffins	Fruit buns
Brownies	Ginger snaps
Carrot cake	Madeira cake
Cheese and bacon pasties	Muesli
Chicken and mushroom pie	Naan bread
Chocolate-chip cookies	Oat flakes
Chocolate digestive biscuits	Short bread
	Suet
Crumpets	

Knowing that you can purchase several other useful gluten-free products to make life easier is also worthwhile. These include:

Celebration cakes suitable for birthdays

Cereal bars

Christmas pudding and mince pies

Cornish pasties, sausage rolls, and quiches

Hot-cross buns

Ice cream cones and wafers

Pretzels

Ready made pastry

Ready meals, including pasta and pizza dishes

Stuffing mix

Sweet pancakes

Teacakes

Bakers often sell cakes such as meringues or macaroons that don't contain gluten, but these do run the risk of being contaminated by other foods during baking, storage, or even by particles of flour in the air. They are best avoided.

Getting the Buzz on Booze: Choosing Alcoholic Beverages

We cover food and soft drinks in this chapter, but now we take a look at something a little stronger – alcohol. Many alcoholic drinks are gluten-free – and if you try, you can even find gluten-free beer.

Booze you can use

The choice of gluten-free alcoholic drinks is far longer than the list off-limits. This list covers the basics of the booze you can use:

Most alcopops such as Bacardi breezer and Smirnoff ice

Brandy

Cider

Cognac

Gin

Liqueurs

Perry

Port

Rum

Schnapps	Vodka
Sherry	Whisky and malt whisky
Tequila	Wine (red, white, rose), sparkling wine, and champagne
Vermouth, such as Martini	

Knowing what kinds of spirits you can consume can be confusing, because some, for example malt whisky, are distilled from gluten-containing grains such as barley. However, because these products are distilled and the grains aren't added back into the gluten-containing mash, the drinks remain gluten-free.

Step away from the bottle

A few types of alcoholic beverages aren't allowed on the gluten-free diet. Technological advances show that measurable amounts of barley protein are found in all beers traditionally brewed from barley, and so you're safer excluding all types. This includes (but may not be limited to):

Beer, including bitter	Low-alcohol beers and lagers
Home brewed beers	
Lager	Real ale
	Stout, including Guinness

The distillation process completely eliminates any traces of gluten, which is why you can safely eat distilled vinegar and many alcoholic beverages made from distilled alcohol. If you're still not sure that your favourite tipple is gluten-free, check the gluten-free alcoholic beverages list in *The Food and Drink Directory* or get confirmation from the manufacturer.

Making Sure Your Medicines Are Safe

Remember, anything you eat can cause problems if it's not gluten-free – even a tiny pill. Be sure to check the label first, because some products actually say 'gluten-free' on the label.

Three cheers for gluten-free beers!

Most beer contains gluten but a few enterprising brewers have started to manufacture gluten-free specialty beers. They include Green's (www.glutenfreebeers.co.uk) and Hambleton Ales (www.hambleton ales.co.uk), both of whom brew gluten-free beer, stout, and lager. Heron Foods (www.glutenfreedirect.com) also produce a gluten-free beer. All these beers can be purchased online or at some larger supermarkets (see the brewers' Web sites for stockists). If you like to make your own home brew, recipes usually involving rice or buckwheat are available on the Internet. A quick search should turn up several options.

 In the UK the huge majority of drugs, medicines, and nutritional supplements, whether bought over the counter or prescribed, are gluten-free. Only a handful of medications, mostly no longer in general use, employ wheat as a filler. We recommend that you double-check that any over-the-counter products you commonly use are gluten-free. This may include painkillers, fever reducers, cold medications, and anti-inflammatories.

 Sometimes a drug may cause adverse effects on the gut, such as abdominal pain or diarrhoea. This can be confused with a return of coeliac disease symptoms causing you to wonder if the drug contained gluten. If you do get a reaction, or if you're unsure about a prescription drug, ask your GP or pharmacist to check that the product is gluten-free. If the pharmacist doesn't know, ask him or her to check in their drugs bible, the *British National Formulary*, or with the manufacturer in question. Ask your GP or pharmacist to make a note in the computer for use in the future.

Using Non-Food Products: What You Need to Know

You can get lots of conflicting information about non-food products and whether you need to be concerned. You may hear that you need to beware of plastic storage containers, pots and pans, lotions, shampoos, envelopes, stamps, glues, and so on . . . what are you supposed to do?

The biggest question is that if you're not eating it, does it really matter? The answer is sometimes yes, and sometimes no!

Not many people know this, but play dough is 40 per cent wheat flour. We know you're not supposed to eat play dough, but really – who can resist a nibble or two? Children should be supervised so that they don't eat it. Alternatively, a recipe for gluten-free play dough is as follows:

> 340 g of gluten-free white flour mix
>
> 225 g salt
>
> 30 ml vegetable oil
>
> 30 ml cream of tartar
>
> 360 ml water
>
> Food colouring, as desired

1. Place all the dry ingredients in a non-stick pan and gradually mix in the oil, water, and food colouring.

2. Stir until smooth.

3. Place over a low heat for about 5 minutes, stirring well, until the mixture thickens.

4. Remove from the heat and knead the dough to get rid of any lumps, and then allow to cool.

5. Roll into a ball and wrap in cling film to store.

You don't have to worry about plastic storage containers, pots, and pans. In the UK, the glue on stamps and envelopes is gluten-free and safe.

Make-up matters

Sometimes make-up matters, and sometimes it doesn't. The make-up that matters is make-up that you're likely to get in your mouth (or someone else's), such as lipstick, lip gloss, lip balm, and anything else that goes on or near your lips. Lipstick contains only very small amounts of gluten, but as with so many other products, you can check with the manufacturer. Foundation, eye make-up, powder, and other make-up products shouldn't matter unless you get them close to your mouth and may possibly ingest them. Sensitivity to a brand of make-up is unlikely to be related to the presence of gluten in the product.

Lotions and potions

Gluten molecules are too large to pass through hair or skin, and so any lotions, shampoos, conditioners, and other external products such as wheat germ oil shouldn't be a problem.

Sometimes lotion from your hands or arms can get on the food you're eating or preparing, which can cause a problem. Be sure to wash your hands well (along with any other area that may touch food) so that you don't end up eating your lotion.

Dental products

We know that you're really not supposed to eat toothpaste or drink your mouthwash – but you're undoubtedly going to swallow a little from time to time. If that swallow contains gluten, it can potentially cause a problem. Coeliac UK, along with the British Dental Association, has confirmed with major manufacturers that no toothpaste or mouthwash in the UK contains gluten.

Most products used by your dentist, such as fixatives, polish, fluoride, and other dental agents, are gluten-free. But it doesn't hurt to ask your dentist to double-check the products for you.

Chapter 5

Scrutinising the Evidence: Making Sure It's Gluten-Free

. . . .

In This Chapter

▶ Finding out why 'gluten-free' isn't always straightforward

▶ Understanding labelling laws

▶ Using product listings and ingredients labels to find suitable foods

▶ Getting help from food manufacturers

▶ Searching for other sources of reliable information

. . . .

A product is gluten-free or it isn't, right? End of story. Well, no.

We generally like things to be straightforward, and so we understand if the lack of a simple answer is driving you mad. The good news is that a lot less ambiguity exists about foods containing gluten than in the past, and clarity is improving all the time. The bad news is that sometimes you still have to take an extra step (or two) before you know for sure whether a product really is gluten-free.

In this chapter, we show you ways to help ensure that the food you're eating is as gluten-free as possible. We take you through the art of reading labels, explain why 100 per cent gluten-free may not really mean 100 per cent gluten-free, and offer a crash course in double- and triple-checking products.

Putting Gluten-Free Advice into Perspective

You: Does your product contain gluten?

Polite lady on phone: We don't add any gluten to our products.

> **You:** (heavy sigh of relief) Oh, terrific. Then it's gluten-free?
>
> **Polite lady on phone:** Oh, no, I didn't say that, but thanks for calling!

You may feel like you're being fobbed off. Customer service managers seem to specialise in beating around the bush when you ask the seemingly simple question, 'Is this product gluten-free?'

The truth is they're not messing you around just for fun. Questions, and doubts about the correct answers, arise for a variety of reasons. The most common reasons are unclear food labelling, uncertainty about the origin of ingredients, and contamination concerns.

Tackling ambiguous food labelling

Wouldn't it be great if you could just know which types of processed foods contain gluten and which don't? Well unfortunately, some food items and ingredients aren't consistent; sometimes they contain gluten, and sometimes they don't, and sometimes you just can't tell from the label. Until recently, when an ingredient only constituted a small part of the product it didn't have to be included in the ingredients list. Now this rule no longer applies and all ingredients have to be listed. This regulation covers all types of ingredients, including additives and flavourings. That's why reading labels is such a useful skill in gluten-free shopping.

New labelling regulations

In November 2005, things got even better for people on a gluten-free diet. A new European Union (EU) Directive on allergen labelling became mandatory. This ruling is amazing progress for the consumer because it makes the identification of foods that can cause food intolerances so much easier. The Directive states that the presence of 12 major allergens, including milk, egg, soya, fish, shellfish, and peanut, must be highlighted clearly on food labels. It also covers wheat and 'other cereals containing gluten and products thereof' whenever they are used. This includes minute amounts in foods or drinks, including alcoholic beverages that do not necessarily have an ingredients list. The presence may be indicated as 'CONTAINS GLUTEN' in a separate box on the label or on the ingredients list, for example as 'malt extract from barley' or 'malt extract (contains gluten)'. Products that don't comply with the Directive should no longer be available for sale within the EU.

This Directive applies to foods released on to the market after November 2005. Some products with a long shelf life may possibly have been labelled before this law took effect. In addition, the provision of allergen information for food that is sold loose or non-pre-packed is still under review. You may need to double-check these products with the supplier.

Ingredients exempt from labelling

Just when you thought it was getting too easy along come a few items that are exempt from labelling as allergens. In practice, this exemption is not a problem: The products are only excluded because they're so processed as to remove any gluten toxicity. The exemption includes ingredients derived from wheat or barley, such as glucose syrup, dextrose, maltodextrin, and cereal-based ingredients used in distilled products including spirits, wine, cider, and balsamic vinegar.

Other ingredients known to be gluten-free

A whole range of other ingredients have caused confusion in the past. Fortunately, we now know that many of them are safe. The following can all now be confirmed as gluten-free when used within the UK:

- Artificial sweeteners, including aspartame, sorbitol, and maltitol
- Caramel
- Dextrose
- Isomalt
- Maize starch
- Modified maize starch
- Modified starch
- Textured vegetable protein (but check no gluten-containing cereals have been added to products using it)
- Xanthan gum

Being aware of contamination risks

Although the presence of wheat and other gluten-containing grains (barley and rye, for example) and their derivatives are highlighted on labels, you may need to be aware of the possibility of trace amounts of gluten that arise from contamination. Even if a product is made without any gluten-containing ingredients, contamination can occur at several points during processing. (Contamination is a risk when you're preparing and cooking your own foods, and when manufacturers are dealing with food on a much larger scale. You can see more about how to avoid contamination in the kitchen in Chapter 8.)

Grain processing

Commercially grown grains can contain trace amounts of other grains, because preventing cross-contamination is nearly impossible. The cross-contamination starts at the farm, where crops are often rotated between fields each year, and crops from previous years can pop up where they're least expected. Contamination can also occur in grain storage, transportation, and during milling.

So if the product you're eating contains a grain – even a non-gluten-containing grain – a risk of contamination exists. Usually, the amount of contamination is minuscule and doesn't pose a health threat. The only time you know that no cross-contamination exists is when the grains are from suppliers who grow, harvest, mill, and package only one (gluten-free) grain.

Oats are a good example of a grain that often undergoes cross-contamination. Frequently rotated with fields where wheat is grown, oats – naturally gluten-free – can be contaminated in the fields as well as in the transportation and milling processes. Oats are more likely to be contaminated (and at greater levels) than other grains, which is one of the reasons why many oat products are on the forbidden list but other grains are still considered safe. (For further discussion on the role of oats in the gluten-free diet, see Chapter 4.)

Shared equipment or facilities

Many companies produce several different products on one production line. For instance, a company that produces several types of cereal may run them all on the same equipment. Although the UK and many other countries have strict laws about cleaning lines between products, sometimes traces of gluten remain on the lines – or in the facility – and contaminate the gluten-free products that are made there. This reason is why some foods with no obvious source of gluten don't make it into gluten-free listings. Some people eat only products made in dedicated gluten-free facilities.

For a variety of reasons, usually concerning cross-contamination, even foods that are inherently gluten-free sometimes turn out to contain gluten. Of course, this doesn't mean that you can cheat on the assumption that you're going to get glutenated anyway. Quite the opposite. You need to be even more diligent to make sure that you're doing everything you can to be safely gluten-free – as gluten-free as you can be.

Defining Safe Amounts of Gluten

We unequivocally stress the need to be strictly gluten-free at all times – we admonish you for even thinking about smelling freshly baked bread, just in case some crumbs jump off and force their way into your mouth. However in reality, something that's gluten-free isn't necessarily 100 per cent gluten-free, but may contain *safe amounts of gluten*. We may seem to be contradicting ourselves, but what we mean is really, really minute amounts of gluten.

Understanding the role of the Codex Alimentarius Commission

The Codex Alimentarius Commission was set up in 1963 by the Food and Agriculture Organisation (FAO) of the United Nations and the World Health Organisation (WHO) to develop food standards to protect the health of consumers and encourage their use worldwide. These standards are based on scientific principles, and for gluten content the International Codex Standard safe threshold is less than 200 ppm. But safe thresholds for gluten content vary around the world and not every country accepts the Codex Standard. A draft international standard has been proposed for foods using the term gluten-free as less than 20 ppm for naturally gluten-free foods and less than 200 ppm for foods containing Codex wheat starch. This is the standard we use in the UK, but it has yet to be accepted by every country as an international standard.

Codex standards can be very helpful to the consumer. For example, normal wheat starch is not gluten-free. However, Codex Standards wheat starch is a specially prepared form of wheat starch where the gluten has been removed to less than 200 ppm. Many people with coeliac disease can tolerate Codex wheat starch and it's used in several gluten-free products. Be aware that foods containing Codex wheat starch are labelled as containing wheat even when they are gluten-free.

Occasionally people with coeliac disease can't even tolerate the levels of gluten found in Codex Standards foods, including wheat starch and malt extract, and their coeliac disease continues to cause problems until these foods are also removed from the diet. They may benefit from specific guidance from their healthcare teams regarding their individual level of tolerance.

As long as those traces are truly small, a product may still be called gluten-free and be safe for everyone – regardless of the degree of gluten intolerance.

People measure gluten in *parts per million (ppm)*. One ppm denotes one particle of a given substance for every 999,999 other particles. No internationally agreed standards have been agreed for what's gluten-free, but guidelines do exist. Some countries, including the UK, use 200 ppm as a limit, meaning anything that has less than 200 ppm of gluten can be considered gluten-free. But the standards vary from country to country: For example, in Finland they use 100 ppm.

What does parts per million mean, anyway? Well, it's the number of parts of gluten in a million parts of a food. Take bread that contains 200 ppm of gluten as an example. Cut that slice of bread into 5,000 pieces, and you have 5,000 crumbs. One of those crumbs is equivalent to 200 out of a million parts – equal to the amount of gluten in that piece of bread. That fraction of the bread weighs about 0.006 grams, or about 0.0002 ounces.

Using Product Listings to Find Gluten-Free Foods

Several product listings, such as Coeliac UK's *The Food and Drink Directory*, are available, which cover everything from gluten-free baby foods to ready meals and soups. These are great references because all the hard work has been done for you. You just need to remember to bring it with you when you go shopping!

Always use an up-to-date listing because manufacturers sometimes have an annoying habit of changing the ingredients in their products. Although it's not that common, an item can be gluten-free one day, appearing on the list, and the next thing you know the ingredients have been modified and the product's off the list. Any product listing is only up-to-date at the time of printing. However, if you do want to use product listings, you have several choices.

The Food and Drink Directory

The Food and Drink Directory produced by Coeliac UK is the gluten-free bible and is invaluable. Produced annually, the booklet is sent free to members of Coeliac UK each year or non-members can buy it from their online shop. The booklet is small enough to fit into your pocket but manages to lists over 11,000 safe products verified to be gluten-free. This includes the whole range of prescribable products and lists of own-label products from nine of the major supermarkets. What we particularly like about the directory (apart from its compact size) is that it's so easy to keep up-to-date. Monthly updates to product changes can be accessed via the Coeliac UK Web site or e-mailed to you in the monthly newsletter. They can also be sourced on BBC 2 Ceefax, via a telephone hot line, or even via post (if you send a self-addressed envelope to Coeliac UK). Full details are available at www.coeliac.co.uk.

Requesting safe product lists from a company

Many of the large supermarkets and fast-food outlets produce lists of own-brand items that are gluten-free, covering everything from breakfast cereals to yogurts. These organisations are usually happy to send you a list on request, and increasingly are making examples available for download from store Web sites. These can be useful if you always shop in the same place but once again you need to make sure that you're shopping with the most current list.

Keeping an eye for gluten-free symbols

If gluten is not present, a product isn't necessarily labelled as gluten-free. However, some manufacturers have chosen to label gluten-free foods more positively in this way, for example by using the Crossed Grain symbol to highlight the fact (see the figure in this sidebar). The Crossed Grain is known globally as a symbol of gluten-free food and is useful for people on a gluten-free diet. Coeliac UK own the trademark symbol in the UK and the European Community, and license the symbol to manufacturers, distributors, and retailers to use on their gluten-free products. Currently, more than 45 companies in the UK have adopted the symbol and the list continues to grow. This gluten-free verification symbol can be a real bonus to you, making shopping even easier.

As with all product listings, bear in mind that if a product isn't on the list, that doesn't mean it's not gluten-free. A company may have chosen not to provide information or it may not have supplied it in time to be included in the publication. Recently, someone we know received a listing of gluten-free items from a fast-food chain. She quickly passed on news to her local support group that a particular item was not gluten-free, causing panic to guilt-ridden mums who'd been feeding it to their kids for weeks. Another mum double-checked and found out the product was, in fact, gluten-free but hadn't been listed due to publication deadlines.

Testing for Gluten in Foods

With so many questions about what does and doesn't have gluten, you'd think there'd be a test that tells you for certain. And there is!

Several types of laboratory based gluten tests are available commercially. Many manufacturers use them to make sure that their foods comply with gluten-free status. Some rapid response immunological tests are also available for domestic use, going by the friendly sounding name of ELISAs (enzyme-linked immunosorbent assays). These take about 15 minutes to carry out and are highly sensitive to wheat, triticale, rye, and some amounts of barley, with some able to detect less than 100 ppm (parts per million). Gluten home tests can be used on cooked, raw, or processed foods. They work a lot like a home pregnancy test. You mix some of the food with a special liquid in a test tube, place a few drops on a testing pad, and after a short wait a series of coloured dots or lines, depending on the make of kit you're using, appears if gluten is present. The depth of colour gives you a measure of how much gluten is in the food. Kits cost around £7 a go (about the cost of buying a copy of *The Food and Drink Directory*), and so they're not intended for foods where the job of testing has already been done and confirmed by the manufacturer for you.

Making Sense of Labels

The good news is that now every ingredient has to appear in the ingredients list, you don't have to look for the words 'gluten-free' (or even check in your gluten-free product listing for that matter) to find suitable foods. You just need to know how to read food labels!

Reading labels on food products can be informative, enlightening, question-provoking, confusing, frustrating, and time-consuming – all at the same time. Sometimes, seeing what's in the foods you eat is pretty scary. But for people who are living gluten-free, reading the ingredients list is essential.

In fact, reading the list of ingredients is almost an art – if you've been reading them for a while, you know what we mean. You grab a product, and with a fancy flick of the wrist, you turn to the ingredients list and scan for forbidden items. Spot one, and the product goes back on the shelf. This becomes such a habit that you may find yourself scanning the label on products you don't even eat!

Labels can be intimidating at first, because many processed foods contain all sorts of multisyllabic ingredients (many of which are chemicals and are on your safe ingredients list). But you soon become familiar with the many ingredients you can eat, and before you know it, you've mastered label reading.

Bear in mind that not all gluten-free foods necessarily say 'gluten-free' on the label. However, if a product does contain gluten it should be indicated on the packaging.

Reading Glutenese: Knowing what to look for

The key to efficient label-reading is knowing what to look for. Of course, if you happen to spot the words 'gluten-free' or see the Crossed Grain symbol on the label, you may find yourself wanting to crack open the champagne. Go ahead, finding them on a label is worthy of celebration. But usually, label-reading is more complex than that.

 If you want to check out additives or ingredients that you've never heard of before, the safe and forbidden ingredients and additives lists provided at www.coeliac.co.uk and in Chapter 4 of this book are good guides. Any up-to-date gluten-free product listing should confirm whether ingredients are safe but some people like to print out a copy of the list to take with them when they shop. When you encounter ingredients that are unfamiliar to you, you can check your lists before confidently deciding whether the product goes back on the shelf or into your trolley.

 As with product listings you need to keep up-to-date with what's been newly released on to the market and check labels often. Ingredients change, and a product that may have been gluten-free at one time may not necessarily still be gluten-free. If you are thinking 'surely things can't change that often?' read on. We cross-checked a month at random with Coeliac UK's *The Food and Drink Directory* and found 15 modified products that no longer met the gluten-free standard! It pays to check.

 The gluten-containing status of some ingredients is not entirely black and white. Most flavourings and flavour extracts found in foods in the UK are gluten-free. However, more sensitive gluten testing methods have raised some concerns. For example, malt extract and malt flavouring derived from barley, which are used in breakfast cereals, ready meals, soups, and snacks, may still contain levels of gluten above the Codex Standard. For this reason, some products containing larger amounts of malt extract or malt flavouring, in particular breakfast cereals, have been removed from recent gluten-free product listings. Foods that contain malt extract and malt flavouring should be cross-checked in an up-to-date product listing, such as *The Food and Drink Directory*. Only those listed meet with the Codex Standard and can be considered gluten-free.

 Some processed ingredients derived from wheat or barley are considered safe for people with coeliac disease because the level of remaining gluten is so low. This includes ingredients such as Codex Standard malt extract or Codex wheat starch or glucose syrup derived from wheat. These items are gluten-free even though they are labelled as containing wheat or barley.

Avoiding tempting marketing claims

Labels can be cluttered with tempting enticements offering all sorts of benefits like *organic*, *natural*, *GMO-free*, *healthy*, *low-fat*, and the dreaded *new and improved*. None of these claims say anything about the gluten-free status of a product. In fact, 'new and improved' is just another way of saying 'now you definitely have to double-check – because we've changed our product formulation.'

People sometimes make the false assumption that if a product is healthy, it's more likely to be gluten-free. Not true. In fact, if you see the words *wholegrain* emblazoned on a label, step away from the product. Chances are it's not gluten-free.

Even if a product says *wheat-free* on the label, that doesn't mean it's gluten-free. You still need to watch for barley, rye, and oats – as well as their derivatives.

Being Sure It's Gluten-Free

Today, finding gluten-free foods is pretty easy. Within the UK, the vast majority of items can be found in a reliable product listing, such as Coeliac UK's *The Food and Drink Directory*. If you're in the EU and a product is not given on your listing, you should still be able to tell if it contains gluten from the label. However, if you're in doubt you can double-check with the manufacturer.

Some products have a free help line number listed on the package. Sometimes all you have to say when you call is, 'I'd like to speak to the Customer Service Manager to find out whether your product is gluten-free,' and the friendly person on the other end knows exactly what you're talking about.

More often though, being specific is helpful and even necessary. Say, 'I'm calling to see whether this product is gluten-free, which means it doesn't contain wheat, rye, barley, or oats.' When you call the help line number, you often get connected with someone who actually knows what you're talking about. However, you can get confusing answers to your questions. If you can't get a straight answer from anyone, play it safe and leave the product out of your shopping basket.

Understanding the replies from manufacturers

Fortunately, as a result of concerted campaigns by various consumer support organisations, most customer service departments for food suppliers and manufacturers now know what 'gluten-free' means. However, occasionally they may not have a clue what you're talking about. If so, you can politely try to explain what types of ingredients you're concerned about in their products. If they still can't help, ask to speak someone who knows for sure, such as a company nutritionist. If in doubt as to the reliability of the information leave the product on the shelf.

For completeness we've listed several other responses you may get from customer services and their possible interpretations.

'We can't guarantee our product is gluten-free'

This comment may be translated as, 'Our product is gluten-free, but our legal department asks that we cover our backs by telling you we can't guarantee it.'

Aside from legal considerations, the 'we can't guarantee our product is gluten-free' reply – the most common reply you'll hear – may be because the company suspects that other products produced in the facility may cause contamination.

'Our product is not gluten-free'

Sometimes the 'no, our product is not gluten-free' response is really what the customer service manager means. But don't make the mistake of interpreting this one as always being 'our product is not gluten-free.' You need to probe a little deeper. On one occasion, when we told the customer service manager that we didn't see anything in the ingredients that appeared to contain gluten, we were told that it was the whey. We pointed out that whey doesn't contain gluten. She quickly replied, 'Well, then, it must be the rapeseed oil.' We quickly lost faith in this woman's credibility.

'Yes, our product is gluten-free'

You have to judge for yourself whether the person on the other end of the phone truly understands the concept. Did he or she really understand what you were talking about? Or did he or she then say, 'Of course we don't put gluten in our products . . . sugar isn't good for you, anyway'?

Sometimes they follow-up the gluten-free claim with, 'There are no sources of wheat, rye, barley, or oats, and there are no questionable additives. Therefore it's safe for someone with gluten intolerance, or coeliac disease.' The ideal reply: How great does that sound?

Getting the most out of your calls to manufacturers

If you're going to go to the length of contacting manufacturers, you may as well get the most out of your calls. When you make your call, bear these things in mind:

- ✔ **Tune in.** Really listen to the person on the other end of the phone. Do they understand what you're saying, or are they pretending to? Are they giving you conflicting information or taking wild guesses? Do they sound confident and knowledgeable? You need to assess these things before you know for sure that you can trust what the person is saying.

- ✔ **Don't be afraid to channel your query upwards.** Asking to speak to a supervisor isn't offensive or rude. If you feel the person you're talking to isn't giving you credible answers, ask to speak with a supervisor or, better still, the company nutritionist.

- ✔ **Learn from the answers.** If you see an ingredient on a package you've never heard of before and you can't find it on any of the available lists, call the manufacturer. If customer service tells you that the product is definitely gluten-free, take note. That means the ingredient is gluten-free, too. Feel free to question the specific ingredient to make sure, and you may find that the customer service's person is especially knowledgeable and can tell you the exact source.

- ✔ **Acknowledge the customer service department's knowledge.** You need customer service managers, and the fact that they're becoming more knowledgeable about the gluten-free status of the company's products is immensely helpful. If they're friendly and knowledgeable, let them know how much you appreciate their help. Maybe even take the time to write a letter to the company thanking it for supporting the gluten-free community by having such knowledgeable staff and gluten-free products.

Searching for Information: The Good, The Bad, and the Completely Ludicrous

The good news is that tons of information on gluten, gluten intolerance, coeliac disease, and the gluten-free diet is available. The bad news is that some of the information is rubbish.

No matter what the source, always question the credibility of the authors, and remember that even seemingly credible sources can give false or misleading information.

Unless you're using reliable sources, you may get information that's conflicting. A few tips are listed here to help sort out the reality from the ridiculous:

- **Check the publication date.** Information on the Internet and in books and magazines can become outdated very quickly, and so make sure that what you're reading is current.

- **Look for credentials.** Are the authors qualified to give advice, or are they just sharing personal experiences and opinions? Where do they get their information? Not all writers are reliable: You don't need a licence to publish, and some writers don't let the facts get in the way of a good story.

- **Compare the information to what you find from other sources.** Some of the information out there is conflicting, and so compare all the sources and decide which source stands up to closer scrutiny. The sources of information that we cite in this chapter are reputable and reliable.

The Internet, for better and for worse

The Internet's very convenient. You can be in your pyjamas, cup of coffee in hand, before the sun even rises and find out more about gluten than you ever knew you didn't know. The problem is that you can't always trust what you read online, and checking credibility can be difficult. Furthermore, people publish information to the Web and sometimes forget about it or don't take the time to update it. What you're looking at may be several years old – and a lot has changed in the past several years in the gluten-free world.

Nevertheless Web sites can be invaluable if you know you can trust the information they deliver. What we look for in a health-related Web site is accurate and up-to-date information, written and edited by qualified health professionals or others with relevant practical experience in the field. The following section covers some of our favourites.

Health-related Web sites

- ✔ **www.coeliac.co.uk:** You've probably realised by now that we're big supporters of the patient support charity Coeliac UK. In fact, we devote the whole of Chapter 20 to ten reasons why you should become a member (not least of which is that it's free to people with coeliac disease and to the parents of children with the condition). This resource is their fantastic Web site. It covers a huge range of reliable and up-to-date information on healthcare, diet, families, shopping, cooking, research, and support groups. We could go on and on. Why not take a browse yourself?

- ✔ **www.gluten-free-onthego.com:** This site is also run by Coeliac UK and is the answer to managing a gluten-free diet when you're out and about. It guides you to gluten-friendly hotels, restaurants, pubs, fast-food outlets, and even coffee shops by geographical region, including some in the US and mainland Europe. Venues listed have signed up to the gluten-free code of practice covering ingredients, preparation techniques, avoidance of cross-contamination, training, and customer service. The site allows you to search for menus, price bands, directions, and contact details.

- ✔ **www.pcsg.org.uk:** This resource is the site of the Primary Care Society for Gastroenterology but don't let the name put you off! It offers an online medical information resource, which although primarily designed for use by health professionals, has several areas of use to the general public (including links to patient information leaflets). The site also contains an interesting set of downloadable recommendations for the follow-up care that people with coeliac disease should receive in primary care settings.

- ✔ **www.nos.org.uk:** The National Osteoporosis Society is the only national charity dedicated to improving the prevention, diagnosis, and treatment of fragile bone disease. This dedicated Web site resource is packed with useful information that you can download on all aspects of treatment and prevention.

- ✔ **www.coeliachelp.me.uk:** This is the Web site of the local Sheffield Group of Coeliac UK, which is clear, well-written, and easy to navigate. All the usual information on health and diet are covered, including a great section designed just for children. It also provides useful information for holidays, including gluten-friendly guesthouses in the local area and a list of international organisations for coeliac disease.

✔ **www.cdrc.org.uk/en/home.asp:** This site is intended primarily as a support resource for heath professionals working in the field of coeliac disease. However, it does have some useful information and if you're interested in viewing medical images of coeliac disease and dermatitis herpetiformis (DH), including a normal and flat biopsy of the small intestine, have a look at the image library at this site.

Web sites for manufactures and suppliers of gluten-free foods

Most of the main manufacturers and suppliers within the UK have their own Web sites providing information on their product range, including prescribable products, new product developments, recipes suggestions, and even events such as product tastings or cookery demonstrations held across the UK. Some have dedicated customer care lines or leaflets and videos that you can order. Contacting the manufacturers can be useful for people newly diagnosed with coeliac disease because they often provide free sample packs of products enabling you to taste the products before ordering them. The best sites we've found include:

✔ www.glutafin.co.uk

✔ www.juvela.co.uk

✔ www.gfree.co.uk

✔ www.glutenfree-foods.co.uk

✔ www.ok-foods.co.uk

✔ www.trufree.co.uk

International Web sites

Within the international community you find several Web sites that can provide a useful exchange of information on areas such as recipes or coping with a gluten-friendly family life. Two sites that we found helpful are

✔ **www.celiac.com:** A North American gluten-free diet support site, which includes general information, research, products, a message board, news, and dietary resources for coeliac sufferers.

✔ **www.glutenfreemd.com:** Another very educational North American site, which addresses the medical issues associated with gluten intolerance and coeliac disease.

Carrying out a quick Internet search also turns up several discussion boards or chat rooms for people living a gluten-free lifestyle.

Always remember that different countries have different healthcare systems and food labelling regulations. Information on international Web sites may not necessarily be applicable in the UK.

Discovering the truth about conflicting information

How come so much of the information you find about gluten is conflicting? Good question. (Thanks, we thought of it ourselves.) For one thing, a lot has changed in the gluten-free world during the last few years. Ingredients that were once questionable because they were thought to possibly contain gluten were found rarely, if ever, to actually contain gluten. Modified food starch is a good example. The new allergen labelling laws that require manufacturers to list gluten on labels mean that just about all the once-questioned 'questionable' ingredients are no longer questionable at all – yet on many lists you still see these ingredients listed as doubtful.

Another reason for conflicting information is that old rumours are hard to squash. The best example is that of distilled wine or spirit vinegar including balsamic vinegar, which has always been gluten-free. Yet information has been published for years (and continues to be published) claiming that balsamic vinegar may contain gluten – so the misinformation lives on.

Similarly, remember that although malt extract is found in very small amounts in malt vinegar, it is generally safely tolerated by most coeliacs.

Rapeseed oil fell victim to rumour in the United States a few years ago when someone said it made him feel ill and naively concluded that rapeseed oil has gluten in it (it doesn't). People began spreading the 'fact' that rapeseed oil has gluten in it (it doesn't), and soon enough, rapeseed oil was listed as a questionable ingredient, even by some very reputable sources.

Magazines and newsletters

Some outstanding magazines and newsletters are targeted to the gluten-free community. They're some of the best places to find current, accurate information about gluten-free products and health guidelines. In particular, we recommend:

- ✔ *Crossed Grain:* The magazine produced by Coeliac UK, and sent out free of charge three times a year to all Coeliac UK members. It's a lively, vibrant magazine packed full of practical advice and inspirational features written by experts. Non-members can buy copies from the online shop, and the magazine is also available on audio tape.

- ✔ *eXG:* A free monthly online newsletter, also from Coeliac UK, containing news, medical updates, new cooking products, and *The Food and Drink Directory* updates. You can subscribe to receive a copy via their Web site.

Some of the manufacturers of gluten-free foods also produce informative newsletters. You can sign up by contacting them directly or via their Web sites (check out the section 'Web sites for manufacturers and suppliers of gluten-free foods' earlier in this chapter).

Books

Several other superb books about gluten-free living (in addition to *Living Gluten-Free for Dummies* of course!) are available online, at bookshops, or via the Coeliac UK online shop. Some of our favourites include:

- ✔ *Totally Flour-Free Baking* **by Dinah Alison:** A step-by-step guide to baking over 100 recipes from simple breads to delicious celebration cakes.

- ✔ *Gluten-Free Cooking* **by Lyndel Costain and Joanna Farrow:** Provides expert advice from a Registered Dietitian on maintaining a balanced diet alongside delicious recipes for anything from a family dinner to alternatives to problem foods, such as pasta, bread, pastry, and cakes.

- ✔ *Healthy Gluten-Free Eating: 100 Recipes for Anyone Who Loves to Cook* **by Darina Allen:** Contains recipes for everything from cakes to gourmet dishes, including plenty of advice on breakfasts, snacks, soups, salads, light meals, main courses, and desserts.

- ✔ *Kids with Celiac Disease: A Family Guide to Raising Happy, Healthy Gluten-Free Children* **by Danna Korn:** Written by one of your expert author team, this survival guide for parents or carers does exactly what it says on the tin. The book is full of practical advice to help families of children and teenagers cope with coeliac disease and their diet.

- ✔ *Real Food: Gluten-Free Bread and Cakes from Your Breadmaker* **by Carolyn Humphries**: Offers a whole host of ideas for using this handy kitchen accessory, the gluten-free way.

- ✔ *The Ultimate Gluten-Free Diet: The Complete Guide to Coeliac Disease and Gluten-Free Cookery* **by Peter Rawcliffe and Ruth James:** A reassuring and practical guide to understanding coeliac disease, discussing symptoms and diagnosis, and introducing the gluten-free diet. Written in conjunction with a Registered Dietitian the book includes sound nutritional advice, hints, and tips on adapting to a gluten-free lifestyle, and a wealth of recipes.

International support groups

If you're planning to travel abroad you can find some useful information by looking up the international gluten-free patient support group serving the local community before you go. Argentina, Australia, Canada, Israel, South Africa, and the USA all have their own organisations. Within Europe similar groups can be found in Austria, Croatia, the Czech Republic, Denmark, Finland, Germany, Holland, Hungary, Ireland, Italy, Portugal, Slovenia, Spain, Sweden, and Switzerland. You can find contact details by searching on the Internet or via Coeliac UK's Web site.

Chapter 6

Acquiring a Taste for Nutritious Gluten-Free Health

*W*hether you're a salad-dodger or suffering from orthorexia (an extreme desire to eat only healthy foods), eating a gluten-free diet that's nutritious is simple, but not unappetising. You don't have to weigh portions, keep a food diary, or count calories – and you're not limited to deprivation dining.

We have more than just a passing passion for nutrition, after all, two of us are dietitians, and our interest extends far beyond whether something is gluten-free or not. We love to eat, and we believe food is to be respected and revered – partly for the diversity of flavours, textures, and consistencies; partly for the buzz you get from enjoying a delicious, nutritious meal; partly for the energy it gives you; and most definitely as a way to nourish your mind, body, and soul.

In this chapter, we share our quest for promoting food as being more than just something that satisfies your hunger pangs. We explain why gluten-free doesn't always mean guilt-free and why paying attention to the glycaemic load is crucial to a healthy lifestyle. And with a few gentle nudges, we hope to help steer you – ever-so-gently – down the path to eating gluten-free, nutritiously.

If the subject of nutrition seems intimidating or overly complex, don't worry. We boil it down to the raw ingredients and make this a lesson in nutrition that's easy to digest.

Appreciating Your Food

We may be preaching to the converted, because if you've been following a gluten-free diet for a while you probably already pay attention to what you eat, whether by choice or necessity – faithfully reading labels and scrutinising the ingredients, acutely aware of where gluten can be lurking, and avoiding it like the plague. But if you want to be healthy and gluten-free, you have to modify your thinking about what you're eating. The food you choose to eat has a lot more to offer you and your body than just being gluten-free.

People tend to think that *gluten-free* automatically means *healthy*. After all, gluten-free foods are usually available only at 'health-food' shops and special aisles in the supermarket, right? They can cost considerably more than 'normal' foods, too. And more importantly, they're often packaged to suggest that they're *the* healthy alternative. So does that mean you should trust the marketing claims and take the manufacturers' word for it? In a word – no; well, not always.

Most people focus on their gluten-free diet with one thing in mind – keeping it gluten-free! And of course that's the most important thing, so they deserve a pat on the back from that aspect.

Another way to approach your diet, though, is ensuring that it's both gluten-free and nutritious. Food can fuel your body, help prevent disease, improve your skin's appearance, help you to manage your weight, decrease symptoms of premenstrual syndrome (PMS) and the menopause, and maybe even help you live longer! It can keep you feeling great on the inside and looking fantastic on the outside. You can be gluten-free – nutritiously! (For a quick rundown of the health benefits of being gluten-free, check out Chapter 18.)

Food is obviously essential – without it, you'd starve. But the *type* of food you eat has powerful effects on preventing disease and on maintaining proper organ function, energy levels, moods, appearance, keeping you strong, fit, and active, and can even improve your longevity. Almost everything about how you look and feel is related in some way to the food you eat.

Weighing Up Carbohydrates: Introducing the Glycaemic Index and Glycaemic Load

Hey! Put down that remote control! We know you're tempted to skip this section because this sounds complicated, tedious, boring, or all the above. Please don't! This section is really important, because it forms the basis of what we talk about in this chapter, so bear with us.

To start, here's a quick quiz: True or false – a potato is worse for you than a chocolate bar? Surprisingly, the answer is *true*, at least it is if you're talking about a large, floury white baked potato versus a bar of high-cocoa solids chocolate, and the effect that these can have on your blood sugars. Now have we got your attention? Read on. . . .

Understanding the importance of blood-sugar levels

You may now be wondering what blood-sugar levels have to do with eating a gluten-free nutritious diet. The answer is, lots. Your blood-sugar levels can have a profound effect on your health in many ways: disease risk and prevention, weight loss and weight gain, moods, and energy levels.

In order to keep your gluten-free diet well-balanced you need to consume a wide range of non-gluten-containing foods, many of which are high in carbohydrates (flick to Chapter 4 to find out more on alternative grains and the foods you can safely eat). Foods that contain *carbohydrate* (*carbs* for short) aren't all composed in the same way, and so they don't all have the same effect when your body breaks them down. When you eat carbohydrates (whether they're gluten-free or not), the digestive process breaks them down into the sugar *glucose*, which is what gives your body the energy it needs to function. Because glucose is a sugar, it raises your blood-sugar levels when it enters your bloodstream.

The underlying principle is simple: What goes up must come down. When you eat certain foods – such as white bread, pasta, bagels, pizza, biscuits, and cakes (gluten-free or not) – your blood sugar spikes. The sorts of foods that cause this spike are classified as *high-glycaemic*, which means they don't take long to digest and quickly release sugar into your blood stream (see the later section 'Measuring the sugar rush with the glycaemic index (GI)'). When your blood-sugar levels rise dramatically (spike), they immediately cause your body to release *insulin*, a hormone produced by the pancreas. Insulin's job is to get nutrients from the blood and make them available to various tissues in the body.

Glucose is the fuel that your body uses to function. Insulin is in charge of getting the glucose into the cells where they can use it for energy. Think of insulin as the delivery person – bringing glucose to the cells, opening the door, and depositing the glucose inside.

When insulin shuttles the glucose from the bloodstream into the cells, the insulin *lowers* your blood-sugar level (the sugar isn't in the blood anymore; it's in the cells).

When your blood-sugar level is high, your body makes bigger batches of insulin to try to bring that level down. The problem is that insulin is sometimes a little *too* good at its job.

Feeling the high cost of high insulin

When you eat a lot of high-glycaemic-load foods (see the later section 'Taking stock of the glycaemic load (GL)'), your blood sugar spikes and the pancreas has to work really hard to pump out enough insulin to bring your blood-sugar level down to normal. And the process works well – your blood sugar drops, fast. Too fast, and so you crash. You get fatigued, sometimes a little dizzy – and hungry.

When high-glycaemic-load foods cause your blood-sugar levels to spike and then drop quickly, your hormones are at the forefront of this roller-coaster ride, wreaking havoc on your energy levels, and even your moods.

People who eat high-glycaemic-load foods for years can develop a condition called insulin resistance. *Insulin resistance* is when the body has so much insulin all the time that it doesn't respond as it should. Usually, just releasing a little insulin can bring blood sugar down, but in someone who's insulin resistant, this doesn't happen. So in an effort to lower blood-sugar levels, the body keeps producing insulin, resulting in a constant elevated level at all times. This state can be very hard on the body.

Syndrome X, or *metabolic syndrome*, is a cluster of conditions and symptoms caused by insulin resistance. These conditions include:

- Raised blood glucose or blood sugar levels (hyperglycaemia)
- High blood pressure
- A high level of bad or *low-density lipoprotein* (LDL) cholesterol and a low level of good or *high-density lipoprotein* (HDL) cholesterol
- Central weight gain and obesity
- An excess of triglycerides (fat in the bloodstream)

Excess insulin is also blamed for nutrient deficiencies, including deficiencies in calcium, magnesium, zinc, vitamin E, vitamin C, B complex vitamins, and essential fatty acids.

Measuring the sugar rush with the glycaemic index (GI)

The *glycaemic index* (GI) is a measurement of how much your blood sugar increases in the two hours after you eat. Foods that are high in fat and protein don't have a significant effect on your blood-sugar levels (if anything, they stabilise it), and so we concentrate on using the glycaemic index for foods that are high in carbohydrates (refer to the earlier section 'Understanding the importance of blood-sugar levels'). However, all food types have a value on the glycaemic index.

To measure the glycaemic index of food, you need a reference point. To determine that reference point, someone had to find a food that had a super-high glycaemic index – one of the common culprits you can eat in terms of turning to sugar the minute you eat it. And the winner was . . . white bread! The glycaemic index of white bread was set at 100, and subsequently all foods are compared to it.

A food's glycaemic index is how much that food increases your blood-sugar level compared to how much that same amount of white bread would increase it. (The amount of food is measured in grams (g) of carbohydrates, not by the weight or volume of the food.) Whether foods contain gluten or are gluten-free doesn't necessarily help you predict where they fall on the index.

Some GI charts use pure glucose as the reference point instead of white bread. In the white bread index, glucose has a glycaemic index of 140, and so different charts have different glycaemic indices for a particular food, depending on whether they use the white bread or the glucose scale. Charts should tell you which food they use as a reference point. To convert to a white bread scale, multiply the score on the glucose scale by 1.4.

The lower a food's glycaemic index, the slower the effect on blood-glucose levels. Obviously, the higher a food's glycaemic index, the more it causes a spike rapid in blood sugar.

The glycaemic effect of foods depends on a number of factors, including the type of starch it contains, whether that starch is cooked, how much fat is present, and the acidity. For example, adding vinegar or lemon juice (acidic) to a food actually lowers the glycaemic index. And fat or dietary fibre can help inhibit the absorption of the carbohydrates, which also lowers the glycaemic index. That, by the way, is why a chocolate bar – which has fat in it – has a lower glycaemic index than a big white baked potato. Processing affects the glycaemic index of a food, too. The more highly processed a grain such as rice, corn, or wheat is, the higher its glycaemic index and the more quickly your blood sugar rises; the same principle applies when foods are overcooked.

People with diabetes used to think they had to avoid sugar – as in granulated sugar. But eating ordinary sugar doesn't make your blood-glucose level rise any faster than some complex carbohydrates do. That's why the glycaemic index is a more valuable tool for controlling your blood-sugar levels than cutting down on your sugar intake.

Comparing the glycaemic indices

Take a look at the glycaemic indices of some grains and starches. Remember, lower is 'better', because a lower score means the food doesn't cause a rapid rise in your blood sugar. You may find variations from one chart to another. This glycaemic index is based on the glucose scale, where glucose = 100. Note: glucose has a figure of 140 when white bread is the reference point, if glucose is the reference point it has a figure of 100

Glycaemic Index of Selected Starchy Foods

Food	Average Glycaemic Index	Food	Average Glycaemic Index
Rice (white)	88 high	Rice (brown)	57 moderate
Potato (jacket or baked)	85 high	Potato new	57 moderate
Corn flakes	83 high	Sweetcorn	55 moderate
Rice Crispies	82 high	Buckwheat	54 moderate
Rice cakes	77 high	Sweet potato	54 moderate
French fries	75 high	Quinoa	51 moderate
Corn Maize	75 high	Spaghetti white	<50 low
Millet	75 high	Porridge	49 low
Tortilla chips	74 high	Baked beans	48 low
White bread	73 high	Wholewheat pasta	45 low
Potato (mashed)	70 moderate	Chickpeas	42 low
Refined flour	70 moderate	Butter beans	31 low
Wholemeal bread	69 moderate	Kidney beans/ lentils	29 low
Rice (Basmati)	58 moderate	Pearl barley	25 low

Many gluten-free, starchy foods have a low to moderate GI. The presence of gluten can affect the slow speed of digestion of a starchy food cereal but in practice this has little effect. A study carried out by dietitians at the Hammersmith Hospital in London in 2001 compared the GI of gluten-free products including breads, flours, crackers, and pasta and found they were similar or only marginally higher than those containing gluten.

The glycaemic index value tells you how fast a carbohydrate turns into glucose, but it doesn't tell you how much of that carbohydrate is in a particular food. That's where the glycaemic load comes in. And as luck would have it, that's what we discuss in the next section (head to 'Taking stock of the glycaemic load (GL)').

Check out www.weightlossresources.co.uk and www.glycaemicindex.com for more extensive GI ratings.

Taking stock of the glycaemic load (GL)

Using the glycaemic index alone can be misleading. Watermelon, for example, has a high glycaemic index, but because watermelon's mostly water, you have to eat a lot of it to raise your blood sugar significantly. The glycaemic load (GL) measurement is actually a lot more valuable. *Glycaemic load* looks at how many grams of available carbohydrates a food provides. The *available carbohydrates* are the ones that provide energy, like starch and sugar, but not fibre.

The key to this method is that glycaemic load is measured by serving size, which not only standardises the numbers so that you can compare one food to another, but also allows you to add up your total glycaemic load for each meal. Less than 80 glycaemic load units per day is a low-glycaemic-load diet; more than 120 is high.

Importantly, you can further lower the overall GL of your meal, especially if you're eating relatively high-GL foods, by combining them with other foods, such as sprinkling Parmesan cheese on your pasta, including beans in your soup, or drizzling olive oil on your salad. For more on the intricacies of GL, check out our book *The GL Diet For Dummies*.

The reason we don't include a chart of foods and their glycaemic loads is that the portion size is subjective (our portion may be half as big again as yours). So a small portion of white bread, for instance, may end up with a lower glycaemic load than a large portion of buckwheat, which suggests that white bread was a better choice than buckwheat – not so, glycaemically or in terms of gluten.

The GL gives you an accurate and sensible picture of what real effect carbohydrates have on your blood sugars (carbs).

1. **Take the GI rating of the food.**

2. **Divide that number by 100.** For example, carrots have a high GI of 75 (75 ÷ 100 = 0.75).

3. **Multiply that number by the actual carbs in an average portion.** For example, 100 grams of carrots contains around 7 grams of carbs (0.75 × 7 = GL of 5.25). 100 grams of carrots is a normal portion, but to get 50 grams of those crucial useable carbs (the carbohydrates that affect your blood sugars) from carrots for GI testing you need about

750 grams or 1½ pounds of carrots, which may be normal if you're a donkey, but is probably a bit on the heavy side for the likes of us humans.

The basic principle of calculating the GL of carrots (and many other gluten-free foods for that matter) is that a normal serving of carrots with a GL of 5.25 is considered low-GL, which means that we can continue to enjoy carrots as part of a well-balanced healthy diet. As far as the glycaemic ratings go – don't get too hung up on them, though – most of the carb-based foods we refer to in this book and use in our recipes (find out more in Chapters 9–14) have a perfectly acceptable GL when eaten in normal portion sizes.

	Glycaemic Index	*Glycaemic Load*
Low	Below 56	Below 11
Medium	56 to 69	11 to 19
High	70 and above	20 and above

Adopting a Healthy Approach to Gluten-Free Eating

Being gluten-free is a great start to improving your health! White rice, some potatoes, and other high-glycaemic-load foods are gluten-free, but although they have some good nutritional attributes they are not good news for your blood sugars (they're not slow-releasing energy foods). They can, as we discuss in the preceding section, unbalance your blood-sugar levels and eventually cause some health concerns when eaten in high quantities over a long time period.

Over the last 500 generations or so, the human body has had to adapt to digesting a variety of cereal grains, high-sugar content products, and convenience foods, because they've become dietary staples in the modern world. But by forcing our bodies to adapt, humans have interfered with Mother Nature – resulting in a whole host of digestive problems.

One approach to the gluten-free lifestyle – or *any* lifestyle, for that matter – is to eat what your body was designed to eat: meats, fish, seafood, fruits, vegetables, nuts, and berries – all freshly prepared from scratch (not out of a packet).

Looking to the past for healthy eating ideas: The Paleolithic diet

We weren't actually around at the time, but we think we can safely say that rarely, if ever, did cave dwellers – even French cave dwellers – eat croissants. Do you know why? Because early humans were hunter-gatherers, eating what they were able to hunt – and gather.

They ate what their bodies were designed to eat and what was naturally available – lean meats, fresh fruits, and predominantly vegetables. The practice of cultivating the soil or rearing livestock hadn't been developed, and so cave dwellers had no farm animals or crops: Meaning that all their food was gluten-free – because gluten didn't exist. The approach we outline in this section is simply provided as a starting point to giving you a better understanding of what constitutes a healthy gluten-free diet, and where the principle stems from in human development. Therefore, we're not specifically recommending that you follow this diet as presented, but encourage you to look to it for influence when making adjustments to your own eating habits. If you're considering trying this sort of diet, we suggest that you discuss the pros and cons with your dietitian.

You may be thinking that with some scary (and hairy) exceptions, today's humans don't really resemble cave dwellers, and so this stuff isn't relevant – but you'd be mistaken. Deoxyribonucleic acid (or DNA, as it's more commonly known) evidence shows that, genetically, humans have hardly changed at all in the last 40,000 years.

Because the hunter-gatherers we're referring to lived in the Paleolithic era, their diet is cleverly known as the *Paleolithic diet*, which follows these basic guidelines:

- ✔ **Lean meat, fish, and seafood:** *Lean* meat was a key staple in the Paleolithic diet. During that time, they didn't have the intensively farmed, plump livestock that people eat today. The animals they hunted were lean, mean, fighting machines – as were the hunters who ate them.

  We realise that a good woolly mammoth steak is hard to find these days. But you can find a good selection of lean meats at your local butcher or supermarket – you can even try something different with lean game meats, such as venison or ostrich.

- ✔ **Fruits and vegetables:** You have a large choice of great fruits to eat, including apples, figs, kiwis, mangos, cherries, and avocados. Just about any vegetable is a good bet (although watch out for the high-GL varieties, such as floury white potatoes and parsnips). Artichokes, cucumber, broccoli, cabbage, spinach, sweet potatoes, and mushrooms offer lots of nutritional value.

✔ **Nuts and seeds:** These foods play an important role in the Paleolithic diet because they're a great source of monounsaturated fats, which tend to lower cholesterol and decrease the risk of heart disease. Nuts and seeds include almonds, cashews, Macadamia nuts, pecans, pistachios, pumpkin seeds, sesame seeds, and sunflower seeds.

✔ **No cereal grains:** Grains weren't part of the human diet until about 10,000 years ago. That's *yesterday*, evolutionarily speaking. Interestingly, when grains were introduced, health problems began to increase. Although no scientific evidence is available to make a correlation, plenty of other coincidental influences can be found. Some fans of the Paleolithic diet suggest – very contentiously – that the average height of humans has decreased and people now have more infectious diseases than compared to their ancestors, with an increase in childhood mortality, and in some cases shorter lifespans. Modern humans also have more osteoporosis, rickets, and other bone-mineral disorders, as well as vitamin and mineral deficiencies that caused diseases like scurvy, beriberi, pellagra, and iron-deficiency anaemia.

✔ **No legumes:** Off-limit legumes include all beans, peas, peanuts, and soybeans.

✔ **No dairy:** Figuring out why cave dwellers didn't do milk is pretty easy. Picture them catching a wild ox – what then? It raises the question, 'How many cave dwellers does it take to *milk* a wild ox?' We believe that dairy products are the best provider of absorbed calcium in the diet, but if you do cut them out you can get your calcium intake from other sources; you just need to eat rather a lot of them (refer to Chapter 3 for more on calcium in your diet). Eating plenty of fish with soft bones is also a good source – such as tinned sardines and pilchards. You may even consider taking a supplement of calcium with vitamin D if you choose to cut out dairy from your diet.

✔ **No processed foods:** (Of course.)

As a general rule, you can probably simplify the Paleolithic approach to the following principle: If humans made it, don't eat it.

You have to choose a lifestyle that you're comfortable with and that satisfies *and* nourishes you – and this may be a modified version of this diet. But overall, this approach offers complete nutrition, is comprised of foods that have a low-glycaemic-load, and best of all, is gluten-free.

Find your own balance. Everyone is different – maybe you don't want or need that much protein. Maybe you're a vegetarian and prefer to get your protein from other sources.

You can find lots of detailed, and at times wacky, information about the Paleolithic diet when you do a quick search on the Internet. So, you should be prepared to treat this information on the Internet with scepticism and, if in doubt, get it double-checked by a professional.

If you want to know about nutrition, ask a dietitian!

Examining the differences between sensible versus restrictive low-carb diets

Diet trends come and go faster than celebrity marriages. Within a matter of weeks, the absolutely-guaranteed-to-make-you-lose-two-stone-in-20-minutes diet is replaced with an approach that doesn't even remotely resemble it. So how can they all be right? They can't.

And we want to point out that although the cave dweller approach we outline in the preceding section ('Looking to the past for eating ideas: The Paleolithic diet') may help you with weight management, our objective isn't to talk about weight loss; we want to talk about achieving optimal health through nutrition – and in this case that just happens to involve a gluten-free diet.

You're probably gathering by now (that's a pun, in case you missed it) that the hunter-gatherer diet is naturally low in carbohydrates. But this principle isn't like other no-carb or low-carb diets. The important distinctions are as follows:

- ✔ **The Paleolithic approach isn't a low-carb or no-carb lifestyle – it's a** *slow*-**carb lifestyle (a diet with a naturally low-glycaemic effect on your blood sugars).** A healthy diet needs to include essential carbohydrate foods that slowly release energy to keep your blood sugars stable and your body functioning properly.

- ✔ **By eliminating all carbs, as some diets recommend, you cut out eating foods like fruits and vegetables.** That means you're missing out on important vitamins, minerals, fibre, antioxidants, and other nutrients.

- ✔ **Some low-carb diets suggest eating high-fat foods like cheese, butter, and bacon.** These are high in saturated fat and can cause cholesterol levels to rocket.

- ✔ **Most popular low-carb, high-fat diet plans don't make a distinction between good fats and bad fats.** Monounsaturated fats are good; saturated fats are mostly bad. Polyunsaturated fats are a little of each, depending on the ratio in which you eat them. (Check out Table 6-1 for the different categories of fat.)

Table 6-1	Fat Categories	
Saturated Fats	*Monounsaturated Fats*	*Polyunsaturated Fats*
Meat and meat with visible fat	Olives and olive oil	Fish oils
Cream, butter, and cheese	Rapeseed oil	Sunflower seeds and oil
Coconut and coconut oil	Peanut oil	Sesame seeds and oil
Cakes, biscuits, and pastry	Margarines made from olive oil and rapeseed oil	Nuts

✔ **Most low-carb, high-fat diets don't talk about the dangers of salt.**
People do need salt, or sodium chloride, in their diets to help regulate
fluid balance, but if you get too much of it, sodium can cause high blood
pressure, which can lead to heart disease and other health problems.
High levels of salt can also upset the body's ability to absorb calcium,
which can eventually lead to bone loss and osteoporosis.

Even if you don't add salt to your food, you may be getting far too much salt
in your diet. The sodium that's found naturally in foods like shellfish and
some cheeses isn't usually a problem. But processed foods are often loaded
with hidden sodium in the form of flavour enhancers and preservatives.

Sodium or *sodium chloride* is the chemical name for common table salt, but
sodium is often how salt is shown on nutrition tables of food labels. You can
easily work out the salt equivalent of sodium by simply multiplying the
sodium figure by 2.5:

Example: 780 milligrams of sodium × 2.5 = 1875 milligrams or 1.88 grams
of salt

Studies estimate that in the UK we eat up to 12 grams of salt (2 teaspoons) a
day, but we should be trying to half this amount to just 6 grams (1 teaspoon).
Statistics also show that up to 75 per cent of our salt intake comes from
processed foods and savoury snacks, and so eating fewer of these products
and enjoying fresh foods in their 'natural' state is one of the best ways to
keep your salt intake in line with health guidelines.

We give you a lot of technical information about how carbohydrates are graded
and given values according to their glycaemic index and glycaemic load. But
we're not into obsessive counting and don't expect you to be either, and so
don't get hung up on keeping tabs on your carbs' GI values. Simply follow the
guidelines that we give you for choosing the best gluten-free grains, cereals,
flours, and thickeners (Chapter 4 recommends which gluten-free foods to use).
We use low-GL carbs in our recipes, too (head to Chapters 9 to 14 to find out
more).

Differentiating between gluten-free and low-carb

People get confused because some low-carb diets tend to be gluten-free, or at least gluten-light, and so they think gluten-free automatically means low-carb – but that's not how it works.

In fact, gluten-free can still be very high-carb. Frequently, when people give up gluten they choose gluten-free replacements, like gluten-free breads, bagels, pastas, pizzas, biscuits, and cakes. These foods often register very badly on GI charts due to their high glycaemic effect. However a study by dietitians at the Hammersmith Hospital in 2001 compared the glycaemic effects of gluten-free foods with similar gluten-containing foods. They had expected that the glycaemic index of gluten-free carbohydrate foods would be higher due to disruption of the starch–protein interaction that occurs on removal of gluten. However, they found no significant difference between the glycaemic index of the gluten-free foods used, including bread, pasta, and biscuits, and their gluten-containing equivalents.

Gluten-free pasta produced the lowest glycaemic response, which was similar to gluten-containing pasta, and gluten-free white bread had a similar high GI to its gluten rich equivalent.

The practical message we can take from this report is that whether you're eating gluten-free foods or not you can't make assumptions about the glycaemic effects of foods; but as a general rule, if a gluten-containing food has a high GI or GL, its gluten-free alternative probably has a similar effect.

Be warned: The confusion between low-carb diets and a gluten-free diet can be a dangerous misconception. On many low-carb programmes, small amounts of gluten are allowed back into the diet after the initial phases. For people who need to be gluten-free, reintroducing gluten to the diet is not acceptable. Ensure that you review any change to your diet in advance with your dietitian or doctor.

Remembering to keep gluten-free eating healthy and simple

In this chapter, we discuss many techniques to help you ensure your gluten-free diet is well-balanced and nutritious – the glycaemic index, glycaemic load, the Paleolithic diet, and clarifications on the low-carb/no-carb, good-carb/bad-carb controversies. However, the primary message of this information is simple. We've taken all the best bits from the various diets we've already looked at and summarised them into some easy to follow principles for your own personal healthy gluten-free diet.

The best approach for a healthier gluten-free lifestyle is for you to:

- ✔ Keep your diet absolutely and completely gluten-free.
- ✔ Ensure that you include plenty of slow energy releasing carbohydrates such as fruits and vegetables, including pulses and gluten-free whole grains.

✔ Try to select low-glycaemic-load foods, which raise your blood sugar levels gradually, without the roller-coaster effect of high-glycaemic foods.

✔ Make sure that the foods you eat offer nutritional value. Don't rely on foods that are basically empty calories.

✔ Adopt a Paleolithic style approach – eating seafood, lean meats, fruits, and non-starchy vegetables – which provides you with a healthy basis to your diet. However, in the real world you probably need to modify the diet to meet your personal preferences and practical needs.

✔ Remain realistic. Staying gluten-free is the most important aspect of your diet. Occasionally indulging in your favourite gluten-free chocolate sponge pudding is a good thing – and is all part of enjoying life's little pleasures.

Good food is food that goes bad quickly. That means fresh produce and other foods without many preservatives.

Being Healthy, Stealthy, and Wise

Writing and reading about nutritious foods is one thing, but actually *eating* them is another. Some people want the nutrients that good foods offer, but they (or the people they're feeding) don't like the taste (or texture, consistency, colour, density, or idea) of nutritious foods. Don't worry. You don't have to love brussels sprouts to eat well. You just have to be creative about how you hide nutrient-rich foods in your meals. Most of the time, people don't even notice. A few ideas for quietly introducing fruit and vegetables into your meals follow:

✔ Hide fruit, and even vegetables, in smoothies; cut them into small pieces and blend well.

✔ Sneak broccoli, courgettes, and other vegetables into lasagne or pasta sauce. Grating vegetables makes them harder for people to recognise but they still retain all their nutrients.

✔ Homemade soups and sauces are another good way to get extra vegetables in your diet without having to wade through bowls of steaming cabbage. Cut vegetables into tiny pieces or alternatively blend the mixture until smooth.

Avoiding nutritional pitfalls on the gluten-free diet

People often ask whether nutritional deficiencies arise as a result of being gluten-free. The answer is maybe yes, and maybe no.

If you choose the healthy approach to gluten-free living that we outline in this chapter, you shouldn't need to worry about nutritional deficiencies. You'll be as healthy as, or healthier than, most people who eat gluten.

If, however, you eat a gluten-free diet that consists mostly white or refined gluten-free 'replacement' foods like bread, pizza, pasta, biscuits, and cakes – and if your 'vegetables' consist of white rice, corn, potatoes, and tomatoes in pasta sauce – then you may have some nutritional concerns. The same is true if your diet consists of similar foods on a non-gluten-free diet.

When adopting a gluten-free lifestyle, people tend to turn to starchy stand-bys, like rice, corn, and potatoes. You gravitate toward these foods partly because they're easily available and filling, just like the bread and pasta that you were accustomed to eating when you included gluten in your diet. Ironically, the same foods that you crave because they fill you up and give you that satisfied feeling also make you hungrier. We talk more about this problem in the later section 'Losing weight on the gluten-free diet'.

Unfortunately, refined rice, cornflour, potatoes, and other starchy foods don't offer a complete nutritional package – especially when you consider the high calorie count you incur. Not much nutritional punch for your caloric pound, so to speak.

You have plenty of other gluten-free foods to choose from that can provide you with that 'I'm full feeling', many of which provide far more nutritional value and diversity than rice, corn, potatoes, or wheat. They include:

✔ Amaranth

✔ Buckwheat

✔ Millet

✔ Quinoa

✔ Sago

✔ Sorghum

✔ Tapioca

Often these alternative grains provide you with greater quantities of protein, fibre, and vitamins and minerals. (If you want to read more about the nutritional value of these wheat alternatives, check out Chapter 4.)

The most common concerns focusing on nutrient deficiencies in a gluten-free diet revolve around folate or folic acid, iron, fibre, and B vitamins. The B vitamins specifically lacking in some gluten-free flours include vitamin B1 (thiamine) and B3 (niacin) as well as the mineral calcium. Choosing the healthier approach we discuss is the best way to make up for any nutritional deficiencies. Supplements may work, too, but make sure that they don't contain any gluten, and consult your doctor first.

Deficiencies in B-complex vitamins, calcium, and iron may arise because people eating gluten tend to consume a lot of products containing flour, which in the UK is fortified by law with calcium, iron, niacin, and thiamine. Gluten-free flours aren't enriched with these elements. People who suffer gastrointestinal symptoms of coeliac disease and gluten intolerance can experience some 'hangover' deficiencies due to malabsorption, which can be rectified by eating a *balanced* gluten-free diet.

Getting the fibre you need on a gluten-free diet

Fibre is an important part of a healthy diet for many reasons. The best-known benefit of fibre is that it helps keep the gastrointestinal system moving smoothly (that's right, fibre keeps you regular), and that's good for the whole gastrointestinal tract. Fibre can help reduce blood cholesterol levels and lower your chance of heart disease and some cancers.

People who give up gluten and eat a diet consisting mostly of gluten-free flours, such as rice and potato or tapioca flours, are sometimes at risk of consuming too little fibre. If you use flours, try to incorporate alternative flours made from pulses, such as chickpea or gram and amaranth flours, into your cooking. They contain much more fibre than white or even brown rice. Fruit, vegetables, pulses, and naturally gluten-free whole grains, such as brown rice, buckwheat, and millet, are all good fibre providers. Another way to increase fibre is to choose products such as gluten-free muesli, gluten-free porridge, soya, rice bran, and high-fibre multigrain gluten-free breads and crackers.

The most healthy diet that ensures you have an adequate intake of fibre is the approach that most closely resembles the diet your ancestors ate, which is high in fruits and non-starchy vegetables – all of which are good fibre providers whether fresh, canned, dried, or juiced. Whether it's gluten-free or not, the healthiest diet is the one that's nutritiously varied and well-balanced.

Knowing the whole truth (and nothing but) about whole grains

If you're going for grains, the goal is whole. A grain has three parts: the germ, the endosperm, and the bran. *Wholegrain* foods contain all three parts:

- **Germ:** A new plant spouts from this part of the grain, and it's where you can find a lot of niacin, thiamine, riboflavin, vitamin E, magnesium, phosphorus, iron, and zinc. The germ also has a little protein and some unsaturated fat.

Chewing the fat with mega omegas

Saying 'fat is bad' is like saying politicians are honest: Some are – some aren't – but you certainly can't label them all the same. Some fats are good and some are bad. The *saturated* kind, like you find in fatty meats and cheeses, are bad, at least in excess. So are the *trans fats* you find in hydrogenated oils and many fast-foods and manufactured biscuits, cakes, and pastries. Most people know these fats increase the bad cholesterol and can contribute to heart disease.

Some fats are good, though — like monounsaturated fats and polyunsaturated fats. Omega-3 fatty acids – like the ones found in fresh and canned salmon, mackerel, pilchards, sardines, and fresh tuna – are super-beneficial. Not only do they keep your arteries clear, but they also affect your *neurotransmitters* – the chemical messengers in your brain – which are linked to reducing depression and improving your moods. Most of us don't eat nearly enough fish and the guide to aim for is at least two portions a week with one of those being an oily fish rich in omega-3s.

 ✔ **Endosperm:** The kernel of the grain, the endosperm is the bulk of the seed. Because the seed stores its energy in the endosperm, it has most of the protein and carbohydrates, as well as some vitamins and minerals.

 ✔ **Bran:** This part contains most of the fibre, and forms a protective coat around the other parts of the grain.

Refined grains have been stripped of their bran and germ layers during processing, so all that's left is the endosperm. They contain a little protein and fat, and some fibre and nutritional value may be present, but most of the good stuff gets thrown out during the refining process.

The individual components of whole grains – vitamins, minerals, fibre, and other nutrients – work together to help protect against chronic diseases, such as Type 2 diabetes, heart disease, and certain cancers. Grain components are *synergistic*, meaning that each individual component is important but the value of the whole grain is greater than the sum of its parts.

Quinoa, buckwheat, and some of the other alternative grains we talk about in Chapter 4 are whole grains, and they provide all the value that makes whole grains so nutritious.

Refined grains usually have nutrients added back into them after processing, but they're not as nutritious as wholegrain products would be, and they lack the fibre that whole grain provides. (If the food were really nutritious, why would it need to be fortified?)

A healthy, well-balanced diet is one that has a good mix of *soluble fibre* (the type that helps control blood cholesterol levels) from fruits and non-starchy vegetables and pulses as well as *insoluble fibre* (the bran type for keeping you regular) from gluten-free whole grains.

Winning the Weight Wars

The gluten-free diet is paradoxical – if you're too heavy, it can help you lose weight. If you're too thin, it can help you gain weight. We know, even the miracle pills on TV don't claim to swing both ways, helping you lose *or* gain weight. But trust us . . . it's true!

Losing weight on the gluten-free diet

If you're fighting the battle of the bulge, you're obviously not alone. The UK is now officially the heaviest nation in Europe! In today's world of globesity, whether you're a baby boomer, a war baby, or still at school, it makes no difference: More and more of us are getting heavier each year.

The good news is that the gluten-free diet may be the key to losing extra pounds and maintaining a healthy weight. Unfortunately, gorging on gluten-free cakes and biscuits isn't part of this weight-loss plan; the key to weight control is that you adhere to a low-glycaemic-load, nutrient-dense diet with a healthy dose of good quality lean protein. (For more info take a look at the sections entitled 'Looking to the past for healthy eating ideas: The Paleolithic diet' and 'Weighing Up Carbohydrates: Introducing the Glycaemic Index and Glycaemic Load'.)

Battling hunger and cravings

Your blood-sugar levels affect hunger and cravings. Gluten-containing foods like bread, crackers, and biscuits are most likely to send you into the roller-coaster effect of peaks and falls in blood sugars. Those foods – and their gluten-free counterparts – cause a rapid rise in blood sugar, which sends signals to your body to produce insulin.

Insulin does its job to bring down your blood-sugar level, but it can bring it down so low that you get hungry, and in fact, crave more of the same kind of foods that made it rise in the first place. Insulin also tells your body to store fat.

On the other hand, when your body absorbs sugars slowly, as when you eat low-glycaemic-load foods and proteins, the rise in blood sugar is gradual, and so is its descent after insulin begins doing its job. The gentle decline in blood sugar means your cravings are less.

Making too much insulin causes you to store fat and stimulates the liver to make more cholesterol, increasing blood cholesterol levels. Excess insulin also inhibits the breakdown of fat that's already stored in your body, so even if you're working out like a fiend, losing those extra pounds is extra hard.

Utilising the power of protein

Eating protein makes you feel fuller than fats or carbs do, and so you tend to eat less than if your meal consists mostly of carbs and fats. Try to include some lean meat, fish, poultry, egg, pulses, or nuts with your meals.

Protein also plays a critical part in the production of new cells, and so is important for the process of healing the villi (which line your gut to absorb nutrients) as you recover from the effects of coeliac disease and gluten intolerance. (Refer to Chapter 3 for more on how coeliac disease affects the villi.)

If you've been reading up on protein, you may have heard that eating too much protein is bad for the bones. Too much protein can cause your body to get rid of calcium instead of absorbing it as your body's supposed to do (to make strong bones). So eating too much protein can cause calcium to leach from your bones, and causes a whole host of problems for people with liver and kidney diseases. However, you have to eat an enormous amount of protein to make that happen, and so you don't have cause for concern. Most people can get all the protein they need from eating a balanced diet, although special protein supplements are available for anyone who has a specific clinical reason to need them. For example, people recovering from surgery or people with poor appetites.

Gaining weight on the gluten-free diet

Some people who have suffered malabsorption as a result of being gluten sensitive or having coeliac disease are underweight and actually need to gain a few pounds.

When these people go gluten-free, their gut usually heals quickly, and they begin to absorb nutrients and calories. Their weight is usually normalised quickly as a result of being gluten-free.

Sometimes when people go gluten-free, they inadvertently cut calories by cutting out things like bread and butter. If you're already underweight, you may need to supplement eating the healthy diet we outline in this chapter with some high-unsaturated fat foods, such as seeds, avocados, olives, and olive oil.

Gaining unwanted weight on the gluten-free diet

Lots of people gain weight when they go gluten-free, sometimes causing a weight problem that they didn't have before. This gain usually happens for two reasons:

✔ People suffering from gluten intolerance often aren't absorbing all their nutrients – or all their calories – before they embark on a gluten-free lifestyle. After they go gluten-free, their health begins to improve, and they're able to absorb nutrients – and calories – again. But they're usually still eating the same number of calories – often too many to maintain their pre-gluten-free figure.

✔ Some people gain weight because they're eating lots of rice, corn, and potatoes, which are high-glycaemic-load foods that immediately turn to sugar. They may also be eating more than their fair share of gluten-free treats, such as biscuits and cakes, in an effort to stave off feelings of deprivation.

If you've packed on a few unwanted pounds since going gluten-free, stick to a low-glycaemic-load approach, and you should have an easier time controlling your weight. You should also feel a little more energetic now that you are absorbing your nutrients properly so this is a good time get out and get active.

Understanding Other Special Dietary Considerations

Sometimes when you're gluten intolerant, your stores of certain vitamins and minerals can remain low even after you've been following a gluten-free diet for a while. Wheat and wheat-based foods are naturally good sources of vitamins and minerals, and regulations ensure that manufacturers have to add them to any refined wheat flour as well. But here's the problem: Very few gluten-free foods are enriched or fortified with vitamins or minerals. However, we're pleased to say that the situation is changing because, increasingly, forward-thinking companies are fortifying not only bread, but also rolls and even pizza bases, with key nutrients – just check the label to find suitable brands.

The general lack of fortified gluten-free cereals doesn't cause so much of a problem because you can find other sources of these nutrients. However, if you're trying to juggle being gluten-free with other dietary considerations this requirement can become a bit of a nightmare. In this section we give you the low-down on some other common dietary factors that you may need to combine with eating a gluten-free diet, and supply you with top tips on how to keep all those nutritional balls in the air at once.

I'm pregnant and planning to breastfeed my baby

Producing a little bundle of joy can put quite a strain on the body, and so you may not be surprised to hear that the physical stress of pregnancy can cause a slight worsening of your symptoms in coeliac disease. Receiving regular health checks, monitoring, and support through pregnancy becomes particularly important.

Just as in any pregnancy, a balanced and varied diet for both baby and mum is important, but you don't need to heed the old chestnut about eating for two. Strangely, your actual energy requirement only increases slightly and not until the last three months of pregnancy (and afterwards if you decide to breastfeed). This increased need is taken into account, and you quality for an extra allowance of gluten-free foods on prescription during this time. Check out Chapter 4 for more details on obtaining foods on prescription.

 Folic acid is needed for the healthy development of your baby's brain and spinal cord and helps reduce the risk of problems such as spina bifida. The UK Department of Health recommends that women trying for a baby should start taking a daily 400 microgram supplement of folic acid as soon as they stop using contraception right up until the 12th week of pregnancy. This dosage is over and above the usual daily recommended intake of 200 micrograms, which you can get from your diet. This requirement becomes especially important on a gluten-free diet because few gluten-free cereal products are fortified with folic acid. So, unlike gluten-containing counterparts, you can't rely on these foods to supply your needs. Some gluten-free sources of folic acid include:

- ✔ Dark green leafy vegetables, such as broccoli and spinach

- ✔ Brown rice

- ✔ Yeast extract

- ✔ Oranges

- ✔ Orange juice

- ✔ Potatoes

- ✔ Fortified gluten-free bread, rolls, and pizza bases (check the label to find suitable brands)

Depending on your own nutritional status, your healthcare team may also advise you to take additional supplements of key nutrients, such as calcium, vitamin D, iron, or vitamin B12, during pregnancy if they have any doubt about you getting an adequate intake.

We don't want to be alarmist but we now know that if you have coeliac disease, you have an increased chance that your baby is going to develop an intolerance to gluten. However, the good news is that if you're able to breastfeed, especially for longer than three months, you can decrease the risk of your child developing coeliac disease. The timing of the introduction of gluten during weaning is also important. Recent studies show that if you introduce gluten in the first three months of your baby's life, you increase the risk of coeliac disease by up to five times. To reduce this risk you're advised to wait until your baby is at least 6 months old before you gradually introduce gluten-containing foods, and to continue to breastfeed while those foods are introduced.

I'm vegetarian or vegan

Being vegetarian can be a super-healthy way to eat, but sometimes by cutting out certain foods you can find that getting certain nutrients is harder. However, with careful planning you can get everything you need from a vegetarian or vegan diet, even when you're gluten-free. Look for foods that are naturally rich in nutrient sources or those where the manufacturers have kindly fortified them to give extra nutritional clout. The most common mineral deficiencies are iron and calcium, but good dairy and plant sources exist if you know where to look for them. These sources are shown in Table 6-2.

Table 6-2	Gluten-Free Sources of Iron and Calcium Suitable for Vegetarians and Vegans
*Sources of Iron**	*Sources of Calcium*
Fortified gluten-free breakfast cereals	Fortified gluten-free white bread and cereals, such as puffed rice (check the label)
Pulses and legumes Tofu and soybeans, TVP, eggs	Pulses, including baked beans and calcium-fortified soya milk and soya yogurt, tofu, milk, yogurt, and cheese
Dried fruits, such as apricots, figs, and prunes	Dried fruits, such as figs and apricots, calcium-fortified orange juice, some 'hard' bottled waters (check the label)
Nuts and seeds, especially cashews, mixed nuts and raisins, walnuts, and sesame seeds	Nuts and seeds, especially almonds, brazils, hazelnuts, walnuts, sesame seeds, and sunflower seeds
Dark green leafy vegetables, such as spinach, kale, and broccoli	Dark green leafy vegetables Orange juice with added calcium

To maximise your absorption of iron from plant foods, try to drink or eat vitamin C-containing foods, such as fruit juice, fruit, and vegetables, with your meal.

The most problematic vitamins for vegetarians and vegans are D and B12. Vitamin D is generally made by absorbing sunlight on the skin, but if you don't get out in the sun much you need an alternative source. You find very few natural vegetarian sources of vitamins D and B12, and so try to include some of the fortified foods shown in Table 6-3 or consider taking a daily supplement (double-check to ensure that they are also gluten-free).

Table 6-3	Gluten-Free Sources of Vitamins D and B12 Suitable for Vegetarians and Vegans	
Sources of Vitamin D	*Sources of Vitamin B12*
Fortified margarine	Fortified margarine
Fortified soya milk	Fortified soya milk
	Fortified textured vegetable protein
	Fortified yeast extract* and vegetable stock*

Generally gluten-free but you may want to double-check the label.

 Do seek the advice of your dietitian if you're bringing up your child on a gluten-free, vegetarian or vegan diet, or if you're a gluten-free vegetarian/vegan and thinking of having a baby. This can help put your mind at rest and ensure that you meet all the dietary requirements for both a healthy mum and baby.

I'm an active sportsperson

Being on a gluten-free diet need not be a barrier to performing well if you're an active sportsperson, no matter what sport you choose. Hayley Turner has coeliac disease. Hayley who we hear you saying? Well, actually she was horse racing's Lady Jockey of the Year in 2005 and the first woman to land the Apprentice Riders Championship in Britain, so she's pretty fit. A quick trawl through any gluten-free message board shows positive feedback from people with coeliac disease competing at a high level in everything from swimming to running to volley ball and tennis. The main concern for active sports people is getting enough gluten-free carbohydrate to fuel those active muscles. Eating carbs before, during, and after training or competition are essential to maintaining energy levels and speeding recovery after the event. This part is where all those gluten-free grains we outline in Chapter 4 come into their own. Think about basing your meals around brown rice, potatoes, corn, other gluten-free gains, or gluten-free pasta and pizza. (For more information check out the earlier section 'Weighing Up Carbohydrates: Introducing the Glycaemic Index and Glycaemic Load'.)

If you're very active, in your job, or in a sport or hobby, you're entitled to a higher monthly allowance of gluten-free prescribable items, such as pasta, bread, and crackers – do tell your doctor or dietitian to ensure that your increased needs are taken into account.

Refuelling after a training session or event is crucial for recovery. You may need to bring your own gluten-free snacks to eat after an event, such as bananas, gluten-free crackers, biscuits, or a sandwich. Most sports drinks and carb gels (carb-rich solutions that are absorbed quickly in the mouth to provide instant energy) are gluten-free, but some sport-designed meal replacement drinks and energy bars contain wheat and cost a fortune! You're better off eating real foods, but if you do buy them do check the labels first.

A gluten-free diet containing good quality protein and low-glycaemic-load carbs (that happen to be gluten-free) is the perfect diet for athletes of all types.

I'm an older person

As we get older, a poor diet can make us more susceptible to illness or affect our quality of life. If you're on a gluten-free diet, iron intake is especially important to prevent anaemia as you get older. Include rich natural sources of iron (red meat, offal, pulses, oily fish, eggs) or gluten-free products that are iron fortified (such as breakfast cereal) in your diet, along with vitamin C to help with absorption. Where possible, try to avoid having a cup of tea with your meal as the tannins in tea can impair iron absorption.

Getting enough calcium (especially from dairy foods) and vitamin D (to help absorb it) remains important as you get older for the prevention of osteoporosis. For people over 65, a specific recommended daily intake exists of 10 micrograms of vitamin D, because exposure to sunlight (the usual source of vitamin D) may be insufficient to make your own supply. Dietary vitamin D comes from meat, oily fish, evaporated milk, and margarine, but in our experience, you may be better off taking a supplement if you don't eat these foods regularly – your healthcare team can advise you further.

Folic acid can help to protect against age-related conditions such as heart disease and dementia, but because very few gluten-free cereals are fortified with folic acid, we recommend a daily supplement of about 200 micrograms.

Getting enough fibre to prevent constipation and diverticular disease can also be difficult on a gluten-free diet. Fruit, vegetables, pulses, and naturally gluten-free whole grains, such as brown rice, buckwheat, and millet, are all good fibre providers. Another way to increase your fibre is to choose products such as gluten-free muesli, gluten-free porridge, rice bran, and high-fibre, multigrain, gluten-free breads and crackers.

Don't forget that you need to drink plenty of fluid (at least 6–8 glasses a day – more in hot weather) to ensure that the fibre works. Drinks like water, squash, milk, fruit juice, tea, and coffee all count towards this total.

In the UK, a worryingly high number of older adults admitted to hospital from home are found to be undernourished. If you find shopping for, or preparing, meals hard you may benefit from receiving meals delivered to your home. Various systems for meal provision exist around the UK. This ranges from the local social service provision of hot meals on wheels to home deliveries of frozen foods that you can reheat when you need them from private companies. Several home delivery companies manufacture a range of meals and desserts that they guarantee to be free from gluten-containing ingredients and from contamination during manufacture.

The range of foods provided by Wiltshire Farm Foods is particularly impressive. For more information go to `www.wiltshirefarmfoods.com/search_ diet.asp`.

If you're unwell and can't easily manage to digest foods, milk-based supplement drinks can be a useful addition to your diet. You can buy these drinks in both sweet and savoury flavours and the majority are gluten-free. You can buy Build Up and Complan over the counter in supermarkets or pharmacies, and both (apart from 'Complan and Oats') are gluten-free. Other supplement drinks, such as Ensure and Fortisip, are also gluten-free, and can be obtained on prescription from your GP.

The sad fact of life is that the older you are, the more likely you are to have to pay a visit to hospital. If you do get admitted, you are very likely to be asked by the nurse or doctor admitting you whether you're on a special diet, and we're really glad to say that nowadays, most healthcare staff don't throw their hands up in horror if you say you're gluten-intolerant: Instead they reach calmly for the gluten-free hospital menu. Seriously, most hospitals can provide at least one gluten-free choice from the main menu, and even if they don't they're likely to have some frozen gluten-free meals in stock. Due to the speed of food ordering in most hospital systems (think of an oil tanker turning) you're probably wise to take some of your own foods in with you to cover the possibility of your first meal being delayed. If you know you're being admitted, ring the ward in advance. You can also bring in some gluten-free bread and biscuits for snacks in case the ward doesn't have any when you're first admitted.

I'm diabetic

If you have diabetes this means that you're that not producing or not respond-ing correctly to insulin, the hormone that converts carbohydrate from food into energy for use in your body. As a result, your sugar levels may have built up in your blood leading to a variety of symptoms. Of the two quite distinct types of diabetes, Type 1 diabetes generally occurs in children or younger adults, and is an autoimmune condition in which destruction to cells of the pancreas leads to a lack of insulin production. Type 2 diabetes tends to develop later in life and is due to a resistance to circulating insulin. Type 2 is more often related to being overweight or inactive.

Roughly 5 per cent of people with coeliac disease also have Type 1 diabetes, more than in the rest of the population. This occurrence is probably due to a shared genetic risk for both conditions. If you have both together, a gluten-free diet can help you control your blood sugar levels. People with coeliac disease have no increased risk of developing Type 2 diabetes, but the two conditions can occur side by side.

If you have either type of diabetes, you should aim to follow a healthy diet to keep your blood glucose levels as near to normal as possible and reduce the risk of other problems, such as heart disease. Eating the right types and amounts of fat, fibre, carbohydrate, and salt is especially important. For more information on a healthy gluten-free diet see the section 'Adopting a Healthy Approach to Gluten-Free Eating' earlier in this chapter. If you're trying to combine two dietary considerations, seek additional support from your dietitian.

I'm intolerant to lactose

Some people with coeliac disease can't digest the sugar (lactose) found in milk and suffer as a consequence from a range of rather unpleasant bowel symptoms, including diarrhoea and bloating when they drink certain milk products. This condition is usually only temporary and goes away when the villi in the small intestine recover on a gluten-free diet and are again able to produce the enzyme lactase that's needed to digest lactose. If you have a combined gluten and lactose intolerance you may benefit from cutting out dairy products and foods with hidden milk. The problem with this action, though, is that because milk and milk products are the main sources of cal-cium in the diet, your calcium intake is limited, with the associated risk of reducing your bone mineral density.

Even if you can't tolerate milk you may be able to manage yogurt or hard cheeses, such as mature cheddar, Parmesan, Emmenthal, or Gruyère, all of which are low in lactose as well as good sources of calcium. If not, think about including other sources of calcium (shown in Table 6-2) or canned oily fish (where you eat the bones).

We're delighted to see that some of the manufacturers of gluten-free mixes, breads, rolls, and even pizza bases have very helpfully fortified them with calcium up to a level three times above that found in normal bread – check the labels for suitable brands. Bear in mind, however, that as with all non-dairy sources of calcium, you do need to eat reasonable portions regularly to get an adequate intake. For many people with coeliac disease a calcium supplement may be useful to meet requirements.

Part III
Planning and Preparing: The Preludes to Cooking

'I just hope our prey has had the sense to keep a gluten-free diet.'

In this part . . .

We get you ready to cook your gluten-free meals. Hey, even if your idea of cooking is warming a frozen dinner (yes, frozen gluten-free meals are available!), you still need to plan what you're going to eat, buy it, and well, at least warm it up. Whether you cook to live or live to cook, meal planning, shopping, and preparing the food before you cook it present some unique considerations when you're gluten-free.

Here, we offer a nutritious approach to gluten-free eating so you can plan meals that are gluten-free and good for you. We help you create and maintain a gluten-free-friendly kitchen and offer recommendations for safely sharing the kitchen with gluten. Then it's off to the shops, where we offer several options for where and how to buy gluten-free foods without breaking the bank. As the final prelude to cooking, we offer tips and techniques that are unique to gluten-free cooking, and we help you work out how to make anything gluten-free, even without a recipe.

Chapter 7

Making Sense of Smart Gluten-Free Shopping

- -

In This Chapter

▶ Focusing on your objectives before heading to the shops

▶ Planning your meals so you know what ingredients to buy

▶ Choosing where to shop

▶ Getting gluten-free value for money

- -

Danna tells us that the first thing she did after her son Tyler was diagnosed with coeliac disease was to go shopping. No, not the head-for-shops-because-I'm-shattered-and-a-bit-of-retail-therapy-will-make-me-feel-better kind of shopping. She went food shopping.

Now keep in mind that this was way back in the 1990s – 1991 to be exact. The Internet didn't exist, she had no books on the subject, and no sources of information or support that she was aware of. So, off she went to the super-market, located the biscuit aisle, and began to read labels.

Was this true? No 'gluten' on the label anywhere! Finding foods without gluten was going to be a lot easier than she'd first thought.

Now we really have to defend her – she was shopping literally just hours after the diagnosis – and she wasn't thinking clearly. In addition, it was true that none of the biscuit wrappers had 'gluten' on the label and if you've been in a similar situation we can assure you that you're not alone.

The good news is that finding gluten-free products really *is* easier than you may think, and thanks to new labelling laws, increased manufacturer aware-ness, and the availability of comprehensive gluten-free food directories and product listings, it's getting easier all the time.

In this chapter, we start by helping you work out what you want to buy. Then we offer some guidance on where to shop, how to shop, and – importantly – how to avoid breaking the bank when buying gluten-free foods. We guide you down the right aisle to discovering important shopping tips that can help you save time, money, and frustration.

Knowing What You Want

One of the best things you can do to make shopping easier when you're enjoying a gluten-free lifestyle is to plan ahead. If you don't, especially at first, you can end up spending hours in the supermarket wandering in circles, trying to work out what to buy and worrying whether a product's gluten-free.

Planning meals ahead of time and making a shopping list saves you time and worry when you shop and can help ensure that the meals you're planning are both healthy and gluten-free.

Planning your meals

In our other lives, when we're not *For Dummies* authors, we follow the dictum 'plan your work, and work to your plan.' The same thing goes for meals, although 'plan your meals and eat them' isn't quite as catchy.

Most people think that planning meals sounds like a great idea, and they're able to pull it off once or twice. But more often, they're spontaneous and impulsive shoppers. They see something in the shop that looks particularly appealing (and because they're usually starving while they're shopping, *everything* looks good) so they toss it into their trolley. But planning meals ahead helps you focus on your objectives before you head to the shops.

When you're planning your meals, try not to think in terms of cutting out gluten, but instead think of how you can make substitutions. Consider the things you love to eat – with or without gluten – and build around those foods, making the substitutions you need to make to convert gluten-containing meals into gluten-free ones. (In Chapter 8 we explain how to make *anything* gluten-free with simple substitutions.)

We know that sitting down and making a meal plan isn't easy, but this approach can really pay off when you're pushed for time at the supermarket. You may find some of these tips helpful:

✔ **Encourage the whole family to eat gluten-free.** Even if some members of your family are gluten-eaters, make your life simpler by planning most of the family meals to be gluten-free. This planning isn't hard if you follow the approach of eating meat, fish, fruit, vegetables, and naturally gluten-free starchy staples (refer to Chapter 4 for more on these foods). Alternatively, if part of the meal contains gluten – for example, spaghetti bolognese – cook a separate portion of gluten-free pasta but serve up the gluten-free sauce to everyone.

✔ **Plan a few days' menus at once.** Look through recipe books (no, they don't have to be gluten-free ones) and at individual recipes for inspiration, keeping in mind the healthy guidelines we talk about in Chapter 6. Remember, the gluten-free diet is *not only* about rice, corn, and potatoes. In fact, the more variety, the better. Variety isn't just the spice of life; it's important from a nutritional standpoint.

✔ **Plan a marathon cooking day.** Designate one day as your day in the kitchen. With several gluten-free dishes already in mind, you can prepare several meals at once, freezing some, and saving yourself time cooking *and* cleaning up later.

✔ **Use foods where you can make tasty gluten-free leftovers.** If you're planning to cook a large roasting chicken for dinner one night (we just happen to have a tasty recipe for one in Chapter 12), you can count on leftovers for chicken stir-fry with rice the following night.

✔ **Plan meals you can cook in a slow cooker.** Slow cookers are great for complete one-course meals. And coming home to a house that smells like you've been cooking all day is so enticing!

Get the whole family to help with menu planning. Nothing is more frustrating than spending a weekend planning, shopping, and cooking only to hear moans and groans about how what used to be someone's favourite food is now considered 'yuck'. For that matter, enlist help with the cooking and washing up, too.

Making lists

Your spontaneity is exactly what food retailers and manufacturers are banking on. They want you to be impulsive, and that's why they tempt you with the naughty-but-nice foods with high profit margins situated at the ends of aisles and checkouts. How many times have you wandered around the supermarket thinking of delicious, healthy meals to make for the week, only to get home with dozens of bags of groceries, unable to remember what inspired you to buy them in the first place? Yes, us too.

At the risk of repeating ourselves, writing out shopping lists is really helpful. Not only do they remind you of foods and ingredients you need, but they also help prevent impulse shopping.

Keep a list of what you're running low on or what you need to buy next time you're at the supermarket. Make sure that the list is handy for everyone in the family to add to as well, so no one can complain that you 'forgot' a favourite food (when you weren't even aware that it was a favourite food). As you do your menu planning, add the ingredients you need for your week's worth of meals to the list.

Don't forget the snacks! Whether your idea of a snack is ice cream or dried fruit, snacks are an important part of your day. When you're making your shopping list, encourage your family members to add on their favourite snacks – preferably the healthy kind – so you don't have to hear, 'There's nothing to eat in the house!'

Deciding What to Buy

Obviously, the most important considerations for deciding what to buy are what do you like, what are you going to make, and is it gluten-free?

Remember that you have two kinds of gluten-free foods available: Those that companies make as specialty items and those that are naturally gluten-free. Several food directories or product listings are available, covering everything from gluten-free baby foods to ready meals. These are great because all the hard work has been done for you.

The Food and Drink Directory, published by Coeliac UK, is really the gluten-free bible – we find it an invaluable reference. Produced in printed form annually, the booklet is sent free to members of Coeliac UK each year. Non-members can also buy it for a small charge. It lists over 11,000 safe products verified to be gluten-free but is still small enough to fit into your pocket or handbag when you're shopping. The directory also covers the whole range of prescribable products and lists of own-label products from nine of the major supermarkets and can be updated monthly with any product changes (refer to Chapter 4).

If you're cross-checking items in a food directory or product listing you can do so as you make your shopping list or remember to bring it with you when you go shopping.

Checking out gluten-free specialty products

Some companies supply gluten-free specialty items that they specifically market to the gluten-free community. Most of the time, these products are foods – such as pasta, bread, crackers, biscuits, and flour – that normally have gluten in them but have been formulated to be gluten-free. (Take a peek at Chapter 4 for more on available specialty items.)

The specialty products are almost always labelled 'gluten-free', and so you don't have to question their safety as far as your dietary restrictions are concerned. The companies that make these products generally make several product lines and sell their foods by mail, online, or via food shops. Today you find that 'regular' supermarkets, not just health-food stores and pharmacies, are starting to carry more of these specialty items.

Don't forget that wheat-free doesn't mean gluten-free. If you see a package labelled 'wheat-free', the contents may still contain barley, rye, oats, or derivatives of those ingredients. Similarly, a gluten-free item may still say 'contains wheat' if it's made using Codex Standard wheat starch, which is safe for the majority of people with coeliac disease.

Remembering naturally gluten-free foods

Sometimes people think that the gluten-free lifestyle limits them to buying foods that say 'gluten-free' on the label. This notion is *so* untrue! Limiting yourself to those foods is restrictive, and it also means that you're overlooking lots of foods that are inherently – or naturally – gluten-free, some of which are the most nutritious of all. These foods contain no gluten, although the food industry doesn't necessarily market them as such. They include the obvious players – meat, poultry, fish, fruits, vegetables, and nuts – but they also include some products that you may believe have gluten in them, but don't.

Many manufactured and processed foods are inherently gluten-free and are listed as such in a food directory or product listing. Even some non-malted and organic breakfast cereals based on rice and corn are gluten-free but aren't labelled as such.

Asian foods – like rice wraps (circles of edible translucent rice paper made from rice starch, also known in some specialist shops as 'banh trang'), many Thai foods, and most fish or oyster sauces – are good examples of foods that are often inherently gluten-free (remember, though, that soy sauce usually contains wheat). Mexican and other international cuisines also offer a lot of naturally gluten-free foods. (Take a look at the later section 'International food shops'.)

Some of the easiest gluten-free foods to find are those without a label: meat, fish, fruit, vegetables, and so on. But many other foods are gluten-free and don't say so on the label. Read the list of ingredients, and if you don't see anything blatantly off-limits, cross-check with your food directory or product listing to confirm that the food is gluten-free. You may be surprised at how often you find products that you can safely enjoy.

If you wear reading glasses, take them with you to the shops. They're sure to come in handy for reading a food directory or making out all the ingredients if you're label-reading.

Asking for opinions

The last thing you want to do is spend loads of money on gluten-free specialty items only to find that they taste more like cardboard than cake. Because non-prescribable, gluten-free foods can be pricey, and because some are great and some are not so great, asking around and getting opinions from others who've tried them is more important than ever. Of course, opinions vary, and what one person loves, another may loathe, but opinions can be valuable, especially if you hear several of them.

If you want to hear opinions on products, you have a lot of options. Try some of these places:

- **Support groups:** If you attend support group meetings, ask the members whether they've ever tried a particular product or whether they have suggestions for, say, gluten-free birthday cake. Some groups even organise product tastings often sponsored by one of the manufacturing companies. You can get lots of helpful ideas (and freebies!) this way.

- **Exchanging online:** Posting questions and comments about gluten-free products can be valuable. You can subscribe to e-mail lists for people living a gluten-free lifestyle. A quick Internet search turns up several lists. In addition, www.celiac.com is a North American gluten-free diet support site that includes access to a helpful message board. Bear in mind that much of this information is of American origin and that some of the products or labelling regulations and ingredients may not be applicable in the UK.

Logging on to food blogs

You've probably heard of blogs, and maybe you've even added your tuppence worth. A blog is kind of like a real-time global conversation on the Internet. Short for _weblog_, a blog is a Web site where people can contribute opinions about a particular subject. The newest comments go on top, so you can have interactive conversations.

Food blogs are becoming popular, and before long gluten-free blogs are sure to become commonplace, too. Blogs can allow consumers to get the word out about shops that provide huge assortments of gluten-free products, gluten-free mixes that work and those that don't, restaurants that serve great gluten-free meals, and recipe suggestions. Exchanging product information is all about the continuing evolution of consumer power, and communication tools like blogs are likely to have a tremendous influence on how people shop for gluten-free products in the future.

- ✔ **Shoppers:** If you see people in a shop buying a gluten-free product you haven't tried before, ask whether they've tried it and whether they liked. At the same time, if you've tried a product and see someone looking at it, speak up.

- ✔ **Shop staff:** Sometimes the staff members, especially in a health-food shop, are very knowledgeable about the gluten-free products they stock. Ask them if they or other customers they know of have tried a particular product and whether they enjoyed it.

When you find products that you and your family love and have confirmed to be gluten-free, save the label or part of the packaging. File the labels in envelopes or a plastic wallet under sections labelled things like 'soup' and 'sweets'. Then bring the file with you to the shop so you can quickly spot the items again and rest easy, confident that you've picked up the product you like and that it's gluten-free.

Deciding Where to Shop

So you've decided what meals you want to prepare, you have at least some idea of what foods you want to buy, and you may have even written out a shopping list. Where do you go to buy all this stuff (some of which you may never have heard of before)? Well, for most of your shopping needs, you can go to any supermarket, because you're not as limited as you may think.

'Normal' supermarkets

You can do most of your shopping at 'normal' supermarkets. If you're surprised by this fact, don't be. Remember, we encourage you to eat mostly foods that are inherently gluten-free, and you can find those at your usual supermarket (or friendly, local, corner shops if you are lucky enough to still have one).

Obviously, these shops are more convenient and less expensive than health-food stores. But from a psychological standpoint, you have a couple of other, less-tangible reasons for shopping at a regular supermarket.

For instance, a gluten-free diet can seem restrictive and even daunting to some people, and some even find themselves feeling somewhat isolated by it (although hopefully not when they're finished with this book). Being forced to shop only at health-food stores or online confirms those feelings of isolation. Being able to shop at 'regular' supermarkets and buy the 'regular' brand-named foods that everyone else is buying is really liberating for people who feel this way.

If you have children on a gluten-free diet, considering the psychological impact of shopping at regular supermarkets is even more important. Kids want to be like all the other kids and eat branded foods (and junk foods) that all the other kids eat. And that's fine – feeling that way is perfectly normal. For most kids, fitting in with their peers is right up there with breathing.

Regular branded foods aside, many major supermarkets are starting to stock more gluten-free specialty items. If you have some favourite specialty products that you want your local shop to carry, don't hesitate to ask the manager whether they can stock them. How often you get a positive response may surprise you, and the manager may be surprised at how much interest customers have in the gluten-free products.

You may also be pleased to know that many of the regular supermarkets list the gluten-free products they sell, both name brand and own brand. Some of them provide the lists on their Web sites, and others offer the lists if you call their customer service numbers. A food directory, such as Coeliac UK's *The Food and Drink Directory*, also lists several major supermarkets own branded foods.

At first, the health-food aisles may seem to be the best bet for finding gluten-free foods. Not necessarily. Health-food aisles are full of product labels screaming 'wholegrain' or 'multigrain'. Lots of otherwise healthy foods are loaded with whole grains to provide fibre and other nutrients, and although the gluten-free diet sometimes allows whole grains like brown rice, millet, or quinoa, for instance, most of the whole grains in these products contain gluten.

Health-food sections do offer some benefits. The longer a food's ingredients list is, the less likely that it's gluten-free, and health-food aisles are good places to find items that have short ingredients lists. Read them carefully!

We're excited to see that the major supermarkets are starting to sell a larger variety of gluten-free specialty products in their health-food aisles. If your favourite shop stocks gluten-free products, tell the manager how much you appreciate the fact and even make suggestions for products the shop doesn't currently carry. Chances are, shop managers are 'testing' the gluten-free products, and your feedback may be valuable in making sure that the shops continue to stock them.

Online supermarket shopping

The majority of supermarkets now allow you to shop online and this can have a number of benefits for any shopper. For example, you can shop at your convenience, without interference, and allowing you to concentrate on the task in hand makes you less likely to be tempted by impulse buying. For a small charge the shopping can then delivered to your door, which takes the strain of having to cope with cumbersome bags.

However, online shopping also has some particular advantages for the gluten-free shopper. Many of the supermarkets have product information on the shopping Web site allowing you to see at a glance whether something contains gluten.

If you book your shopping slot in advance, you can always go back to your list before the shopping is delivered and add more foods to it as and when you need to. This can be helpful when you suddenly realise during the week that you're running low on a particular gluten-free food or ingredient.

Health-food shops

Most health-foods shops are well aware of the growing interest in gluten-free products, and they're stocking up to meet the increasing demand. You find a good range of gluten-free specialty items and lots of naturally gluten-free starchy foods; some health-food shops even have dedicated gluten-free sections. You can also find many suitable meats, fish, fruits, and vegetables (usually organic) that play such a big part in the gluten-free diet.

If you've not been to one before, health-food shops can be fun places to visit. Because they've become so popular, the range of goods they stock has expanded. Often they provide a huge array of exotic and gourmet health foods (many naturally gluten-free) to tempt your taste buds, along with animal- and environmentally-friendly cosmetics and household cleaning goods.

Farmers' markets

Coming soon to a town near you! Farmers' markets are popping up everywhere (not just next to farms), offering fresh produce, dairy goods, eggs, meat, fish, honey, nuts, and other (inherently gluten-free) items, often at prices below those of most supermarkets. The foods are ripe, organic is the rule rather than the exception, and you can often try before you buy because samples are widely available.

You also feel good knowing that you're supporting local farmers and the environment. The food is usually grown without pesticides and sold without unnecessary packaging. In addition, fruit and vegetables are usually grown locally and haven't been transported long distances, saving on fuel and pollution (food miles), and are considerably fresher.

International food shops

For an exotic shopping experience why not visit an Asian market or grocery store – the more authentic, the better – and discover a whole new world of gluten-free products. Don't forget the Thai and Indian aisles in normal supermarkets, too. Truly, the selection is amazing. Sauces, rice wraps, tapioca noodles, rice sweets, foods you've never heard of, and things that you may have wondered about for years – all gluten-free. Of course, they're not labelled as such, but that's okay. If the label is in English, you can see for yourself that gluten isn't in many of the foods. Asian manufacturers generally use very little wheat in their products.

Other international cuisines may surprise you as well. Mexican is just one of the many other cultures that use lots of inherently gluten-free ingredients in their cooking. If you allow it to, your gluten-free diet can open up a whole new food culture for you to explore without ever having to get out your passport.

Planning impulse purchases

High-powered psychologists have spent millions of pounds of retail industry money on studies that finally concluded with a shocking revelation: Shoppers are impulsive. Many supermarkets capitalise on your impulsivity by planning your impulsive purchases. 'Planned impulsivity' may at first seem to be a contradiction, but that's exactly what supermarkets are creating when they develop strategies for everything from stock placement to the muzak they play in the background.

Don't tell us you haven't fallen for the marketing. You're in the shop for just a few items ('I'll just use a basket'), and you walk out with a trolley full of things that you didn't even know you wanted. You're captivated by the free samples or the special 'buy one get one free' displays at the end of each aisle – which are there because the psychologists have done their research. And don't forget the fact that your children are the primary targets, because they tend to be quite influential when you make your impulsive purchases.

Rarely are these so-called *impulse* purchases directing you toward healthy foods, much less gluten-free ones. If you're having a hard time sticking to the diet, or if you're daunted by the tempting array of gluten-containing products out there, be aware of the efforts to snare you at the supermarkets, and have your guard up against impulsive gluten-containing purchases.

Specialty Web sites and product lists

If you prefer to do so, you can buy all your gluten-free shopping from the comfort of your favourite armchair, any time of the day or night – you can even shop in your dressing gown and slippers if you want. Make use of the great Web sites that specialise in selling gluten-free products, and within a few minutes you can place your order. Then, hey presto!, a couple of days later a big exciting food parcel arrives on your doorstep.

Most gluten-free specialty food manufacturers have Web sites, and so if you know a specific brand you want to buy, you can go to the site and see what they have to offer (you can find Web sites using a quick Google search).

Some sites allow you to select items with 'free from' combinations of ingredients so you can narrow down the products that are, for instance, gluten-free, milk-free, wheat-free, and soya-free. Some sites also provide details on each product, including shelf life, suitability for freezing, list of ingredients, nutritional information, and even suggestions for use to help you decide which ones to buy.

If you don't have a computer, many manufacturers have a customer phone number you can call, and some are happy to send you a gluten-free product list so that you can place your order by phone or fax.

If you're not using a food directory or product listing, another alternative is to print off an up-to-date safe and forbidden ingredients list from the Internet (try the Coeliac UK Web site at www.coeliac.co.uk) and take it with you when food shopping. Use it to cross-check ingredients on product labels to make sure that they're gluten-free.

Living Gluten-Free — Affordably

One of the most common complaints we hear about the gluten-free diet is that it's more expensive than buying standard food – but it doesn't need to be. Yes, we understand that a loaf of regular bread is less than half the cost of a loaf of gluten-free bread. And the fact that gluten-free crackers and bis-cuits are often smaller *and* twice the price of regular biscuits isn't lost on us. And yes, we know that you may pay more than your fair share in postage expenses for mail order items, too. But you have ways to save significant amounts of money when you're enjoying a gluten-free lifestyle. So before you take a second mortgage on your house to finance this diet, take note of these tips that can save you a lot.

Making the most of prescribable products

Once a diagnosis of coeliac disease (or dermatitis herpetiformis – DH for short) is confirmed a large range of gluten-free alternatives to your everyday staple foods are easily available to you on prescription from your GP. These items include bread, flour, crispbreads, crackers, biscuits, and pasta. The range in the UK is excellent and has greatly improved the ability of people with coeliac disease to follow a strict gluten-free diet. Getting these products on prescription may help you stick to your diet and is certainly cheaper than buying them individually. Prescription foods are intended for use only by the patient and are not for other family members. Chapter 4 tells you more about your entitlement to prescription foods.

Scaling back on specialties

Most of the extra expense incurred on a gluten-free diet is due to the high cost of special gluten-free items that are not available on prescription. We're not suggesting that you celebrate your birthday with rice cakes to save the expense of buying a gluten-free cake. You may need to have *some* non-prescription specialty items on hand, and cakes or special-occasion treats are definitely among them.

But if you find that you're spending far too much money to accommodate this diet, take a look at how many and what types of specialty items you buy. Gluten-free chocolate biscuits, cakes, pizzas, pies, pasties, and mince pies – they're pricey and you don't need lots of them. Most of the specialty items aren't that healthy, anyway – they're often high-fat, high-glycaemic-load foods (they raise your blood sugar quickly) that provide very little nutritional value. If you follow the more healthy approach to gluten-free eating that we outline in Chapter 6, you find very little room for these expensive indulgences.

Avoid buying specially labelled gluten-free items unnecessarily. For instance, if you're indulging your taste for chocolate, many of the normal brands that you can get at any sweet shop are suitable and far cheaper than chocolate bars specifically labelled as gluten-free. In fact, the confectionery section of Coeliac UK's *The Food and Drink Directory* stretches to over 20 pages (we know, we counted!).

Some other specialty items people buy are unnecessary. Gluten-free vanilla is a good example: All vanilla is gluten-free! You don't need to buy it as a specialty item. However, gluten-free items like baking powder and suet are useful as the normal product can contain gluten.

Over and above your gluten-free prescription, some specialty items may be important to have on hand for special occasions or treats, such as cakes, sweet biscuits, crumpets, muffins, or croissants. But in general, people buy more specialty items than they need, and these unnecessary extras can be what puts a burden on your budget.

Saving on postage

If you do buy specialty items by mail order, you can find ways to save on postage. For example, ask your local supermarket or health-food store to stock the product you want – that way the shop pays for the postage, not you.

If you're ordering online, order from a company that sells many different types of product. That way, you pay one postage charge for several different items. Buying products in small amounts from individual manufacturers can cost you a fortune in postage.

Developing good shopping habits

In addition to what we cover in this chapter, you can do other things to save time and money when you shop. For starters, try the following tips:

- **Don't shop when you're hungry.** If you shop on an empty stomach, you're more vulnerable to falling victim to impulse purchases.

- **Make a list.** Planning ahead before you go to the supermarket keeps you focused on the healthy and gluten-free foods you need, and means that you're less likely to buy things impulsively that you don't need.

- **Stock up when you can.** Buying non-perishable food in larger quantities is almost always cheaper if you can afford to do so and if you have somewhere to store the food.

- **Make the most of your freezer.** Remember that some gluten-free foods often have a short shelf life, so if you're going to stock up on fresh products, such as fresh bread, make sure that you've got room in your freezer.

- **Consider co-ops.** Co-ops aren't in all parts of the country, but if you have one nearby, they're a great way to save money. The idea is that a group of people form a cooperative, buy food in bulk, and then offer the food to others to buy. Usually anyone can become a member for a small charge (non-members can buy, too, but usually for a small fee). The focus is nearly always on healthy foods, including locally grown fruit and vegetables.

- **Dare to compare.** Always look at the unit price of a product (the price per 100 grams), not just the package price. Shops list unit prices on the price tags on the grocery shelves. The package price tells you only the cost of the entire item, whereas the unit price shows the cost per unit weight. This way, when you compare the price of one item to another, you're comparing like with like.

- **Check your receipt.** Sometimes shops do make mistakes. And on many occasions, believe it or not, those mistakes are not in your favour.

- **If possible, shop without your children.** Yes they're adorable, but they're enemy number one when you're trying to resist the impulsive shopping that the supermarkets are relying on. Kids are their primary target. Notice where all the sugar-coated cereals are located – right at eye-level for your 5-year-old. Supermarkets are counting on your kids to lure you into impulsive purchases of high-profit-margin treats like cereals and confectionery.

- **Buy own-label brands.** Lots of own-label or economy products are gluten-free. Some shops have lists of their gluten-free items available at the customer service desk or on the Internet.

Selecting supermarket own-brands

You can save money by buying supermarket own-label branded foods, especially from their economy ranges. Don't always assume that they're unsuitable for a gluten-free diet. These items are as clearly labelled as the major brands as to what they contain and are included in the supermarkets' own product listings available in-store or downloadable online.

Choosing fresh produce

Some people think that eating more fresh food is expensive. Not true. Fresh produce and meats do seem expensive – they can be! But many highly processed foods that are high in fat, sugar, and salt are relatively poor sources of other nutrients and so poor value for money.

When you buy fresh fruit and vegetables, choose what's currently in season. Sometimes, if you don't use foods within a few days, fresh produce isn't so fresh anymore. Select a mixture of ready to eat and not so ripe items to ripen later; thus avoiding waste. The cheapest way to buy fruit and vegetables is loose from your local greengrocer or street market. You can even consider growing your own. (Take a look at the earlier section 'Farmers' markets'.)

Eating in

Eating out at gluten-free restaurants or fast-food outlets is fun and easier to do than ever (head to Chapter 15 for more information). However, eating out on a regular basis can shrink your budget in no time. Eating at home not only guarantees that your meal is gluten-free, but also saves you money.

Planning and preparing home-cooked meals certainly takes time (we give some time-saving tips in Chapter 8), but saving money and benefiting from the peace of mind that your meals are healthy and gluten-free are well worth the effort.

Chapter 8

Cooking with Confidence: Tips and Techniques for the Gluten-Free Friendly Kitchen

In This Chapter

▶ Encouraging 'glutenous' and gluten-free foods to coexist in the kitchen

▶ Finding out how to make anything gluten-free

▶ Exploring how to cook with gluten-free grains

▶ Entering the wonderful world of gluten-free baking

*F*irst and foremost, this book helps you adjust to living a gluten-free lifestyle as simply and smoothly as possible. We go to great pains to make sure that the tips and recipes we give you for gluten-free foods follow the same line – unfussy, uncomplicated, and straight to the point. In this chapter, you find practical tips for keeping your gluten-free food from mixing with foods containing gluten, together with useful ingredients and cooking tips that let you eat the foods you want with confidence.

You don't need to be a Michelin star chef to cook this food – we're not Masterchefs and we don't expect you to be. In fact, we consider that if you bake something in your oven then the result is homemade. Therefore, by definition, using gluten-free mixes counts as homemade cooking!

Don't get us wrong. We like to cook – a lot. In fact, we love to cook. But we do it our way, adopting measuring terms such as *dollop*, *blob*, and *smattering*, which we use interchangeably. We guess that like us, you're pretty busy too, which can mean making use of convenient ingredients to adapt a recipe to your needs.

If you like the more technical approach, that's okay as well. The tips and techniques in this chapter apply to any preferred cooking style.

Sharing the Kitchen with Gluten

After you've worked hard to create a delicious, gluten-free meal, you wouldn't then proceed to garnish it with a dusting of wheat flour, would you? Of course not. Yet, sometimes the *way* you cook food can contaminate it as though you had done just that, and you may not be aware that you are contaminating your food.

Some people think that the only way to be 100 per cent gluten-free is to make the entire household and everyone in it gluten-free (take a look at Chapter 16 for the pros and cons of this idea). Not true. Certainly, doing so makes things easier – menu planning and cooking are simpler, and if the whole house is gluten-free, you don't have to worry about possible mix-ups or contamination. But is changing the whole family to a gluten-free lifestyle really practical, affordable, or realistic? Of course it isn't – rest assured that with a little knowledge and planning, if you choose to share your kitchen with gluten, you're going to be just fine.

When you're gluten-free, the kitchen needs a little extra attention. Keeping yourself safely gluten-free isn't hard, but you need to keep some special considerations in mind, especially if you don't live with other gluten-free eaters and your kitchen contains gluten. Some tips for avoiding glutenation (contamination with gluten) of gluten-free foods follow:

- ✔ **Use separate cooking utensils:** You can't turn a gluten-containing hamburger bun with a spatula and then turn a gluten-free burger. Well, you can, but then the second burger is no longer gluten-free. The same rule applies to tossing the pasta and stirring the sauce. Use separate utensils while you're cooking, and keep track of which one is which. You may find colour-coding them with tape helps you to keep a track of which utensil to use for gluten-free. Just because you don't see the gluten molecule jump from the food to the utensil doesn't mean it doesn't happen. Gluten is a tiny molecule, invisible to the naked eye, which is on the surface and the interior of foods, and so the slightest touch means it can be passed from food to utensil.

- ✔ **Use separate frying oil:** When you fry breaded products in oil, bits of the breadcrumbs or batter stay in the oil after you've finished frying. So if you fry gluten-containing foods in oil, don't use that same oil to fry your gluten-free foods. Fry the gluten-free foods first or use completely separate pans and fresh oil for the gluten-free foods.

  If you cook both glutenous and gluten-free foods in your frying pan (separately, not at the same time!), you need to be extra diligent when you're cleaning the pan to make sure that you get all the gluten out before using it for gluten-free use. If your frying pan isn't easy to clean thoroughly, you may want to consider having separate pans.

✔ **Gluten-free comes first:** If you're making two varieties of a meal – cheese on toast, for example – make the gluten-free one first. That way, the preparation surface, knives (always plural – see 'Negotiating spread-ables' later in this chapter), and pans stay uncontaminated. If you pre-pare the gluten-containing portion first, you need to wash the pan or baking sheet thoroughly before making the gluten-free cheese on toast or use an entirely separate pan.

✔ **Foil is your friend:** Using aluminium foil makes your life easier. Use it to cover baking sheets, separate different foods, and warm foods on, instead of placing them directly on to the oven rack. Foil is a great way to ensure that your gluten-free foods aren't being contaminated.

✔ **Vacuum sealers save time:** You may find that you're making more home-made foods than before, like gluten-free breads, biscuits, pizzas, and so on. Remember, homemade foods don't have preservatives in them (a good thing), and so they go off quickly (a bad thing). You can save time and money by making foods in larger quantities and then vacuum-sealing them so that they stay fresher for longer. Doing so is also convenient, because you can vacuum seal individual servings to pop them into a lunch box or grab them on the go. Vacuum sealers are now available from the kitchen section of most good department stores, such as Heals, Debenhams, and Lakeland.

✔ **Freeze it:** Remember, homemade foods don't have preservatives, so they don't stay fresh for as long. Freeze them for use later.

✔ **Use brightly coloured labels:** Because you're likely to have some left-overs that are gluten-free and some that aren't, consider using brightly coloured stickers or labels to identify storage containers so that you can easily tell which leftovers are gluten-free. This idea is especially helpful if you have babysitters or other people in the house who are likely to grab the wrong container.

Avoiding cross-contamination

When you're sharing a kitchen with gluten, it can contaminate your food in several ways. Crumbs have a habit of throwing themselves off gluten-containing breads and other foods, turning perfectly good gluten-free zones into danger zones in the blink of an eye.

Not only do crumbs fly, but also preparation surfaces, pots, pans, grills, and utensils can contaminate food, too. You know those tidy people who drive everyone nuts because they're compulsive about cleaning? Take a long hard look in the mirror and face reality, because that's you now. Cleanliness isn't an option anymore; it's crucial to maintaining a gluten-free lifestyle.

Clearing away crumbs

If you think bacteria are your biggest contamination problem in the kitchen, think again. In the gluten-free-friendly kitchen the humble breadcrumb is a major contamination risk. Crumbs can fly off bread like sparks in a fireworks display. We're not pointing the finger of crumb-contamination blame just on gluten-containing bread. More often than not, contamination comes from a simple lapse in kitchen caution – in other words, human error.

So here's the bottom line: When you work really hard to prepare a delicious gluten-free sandwich and then put it down on the work top in a pile of gluten-containing crumbs, you are literally eating a gluten-containing sandwich, and your efforts to find, buy, and stockpile gluten-free foods have been completely wasted. If you think a few crumbs don't matter, we urge you to read Chapters 2 and 5 until you do.

Even a few crumbs from gluten-containing breads or crackers can turn your gluten-free food into a harmful experience. Be diligent about cleaning crumbs, and remember the golden rule: When in doubt, leave it out. If you're not sure that your meal is uncontaminated, don't eat it.

So what about gluten-free crumbs? Do you have to be obsessive about wiping those up? Yes, if you're sharing your kitchen with gluten. Not for the sake of good hygiene as much as because you can't tell whether they're gluten-free by looking at them, and so you never know for sure whether you're putting gluten into your sandwich or not.

New rules for kitchen tools

You don't necessarily need to stock up on new pots, pans, and utensils, but you do need to pay attention to how you use the ones you have. Generally, if you clean your kitchen items well, you get the gluten off them. Nonstick surfaces that clean easily and thoroughly are especially safe.

Bear in mind a couple of exceptions. We recommend having separate colanders and pasta serving dishes and utensils if you're making both gluten-containing and gluten-free pastas in your kitchen. Clearly label one of each as being gluten-free only. Pasta tends to leave a residue that's sometimes tricky to get off. You don't want to drain gluten-free pasta in a colander that has remnants of the gluten-containing pasta on it. The same applies to the pasta servers.

Breadboards are another contamination culprit; avoid wooden breadboards (they're less hygienic anyway), stick to plastic boards, and clearly mark them 'GLUTEN-FREE' and 'GLUTEN'.

We also suggest buying separate pots, pans, or utensils if you have a favourite item and you just can't clean it well enough – a special cast iron pan, for instance. If you can see (or sense) that traces of gluten may remain on the surface and you don't want to replace the pan for one that cleans more thoroughly, just don't use it for your gluten-free cooking. We encourage you to mark your separate items well – one saying 'gluten-free' and the other saying 'gluten' – so that you don't get them mixed up.

Using a permanent marker or coloured tape may not be the latest trend in kitchen design, but this method can save you from being unsure and may even spare you health-threatening mix-ups. A big, bold 'GF ONLY' or 'GREEN FOR GLUTEN-FREE' on your gluten-free utensils can reduce the chance of inadvertently using the wrong kitchen items and contaminating your gluten-free foods.

Negotiating spreadables

To start, we need to define our highly technical term *spreadables*. Spreadables are the things that you spread, for example from jars or tubs, onto other things. You know – mayonnaise, butter, margarine, jam, marmalade, peanut butter, honey, yeast extract, and other things that usually fall into the condiment category. You can buy some condiments, such as honey, ketchup, pickle, mustard, and now even marmite, in squeezy bottles, which is great but most products still come in jars and tubs so you need to adopt a different approach when using them.

Most people dip their knives into the containers, scooping out some of the spreadable to spread onto their bread, cracker, scone, or other *spreadee* (the target for said spreadable). Then they scoop a little more and continue the process. Each time the knife goes from a gluten-containing spreadee back in the spreadable, gluten crumbs get a free ride into the container, contaminating the entire tub or jar. And you know what they say about one bad apple.

Use a spoon to dish out products from jars, dolloping them on to your plate or bread if they're fluid enough to do so (so you don't make contact with the bread), or use another separate spoon or knife to gentle remove the product. You must avoid putting any utensil that you use for spreading on your gluten-containing bread back into the jar or tub. Be prepared to get through a lot of cutlery (and washing up) this way!

That's why you need to be cautious when using condiments. But first, throw out all the contaminated tubs and jars you have. Keep all future tubs and jars gluten-free by using the multiple-cutlery method, or buy duplicate tubs and jars of the products that you use on a daily basis, marking them clearly for gluten-free use, and don't ever mix them up. For more on the damage even a small amount of gluten can do, refer to Chapter 2.

People frequently ask, 'Can I put the knife back into the spreadables if I used it to spread something onto gluten-free bread?' No. Because you end up with crumbs in the spreadables and you will always wonder whether those crumbs are the gluten kind or the gluten-free kind. Resist the temptation.

A tale of two toasters

Have you ever looked inside your toaster? Of course you have. What do you see? Crumbs. Lots of crumbs. If you're sharing a kitchen with gluten, some of those crumbs are probably of the gluten-containing variety. That means your gluten-free bread has lost its '-free' status.

Your safest option is to buy a second toaster, which may see extreme but that's really the only way to ensure that you're not getting gluten crumbs on your gluten-free toast. We've noticed that some of the larger supermarkets sell them very cheaply these days. If you don't have a second toaster, you can keep the toaster for gluten-free toast and use the grill for gluten-containing toast – but you need to make sure that everyone in the house knows the rules.

Gracious guests can lead to grief

Having too many cooks in the kitchen is bad enough, but when you're trying to keep your foods safely gluten-free and your visitors are especially 'helpful', maintaining a gluten-free zone can be more than a tiny bit stressful. Sweet Aunt Nellie's gracious offer to help butter the bread can have you diving to protect your pristine (and well-marked) tub of margarine because you haven't yet taught her to use the multiple-cutlery method. And as you rescue the margarine and quickly try to decide whether showing her to do so (and hovering over her so that she doesn't make a mistake) is easier than just buttering the bread yourself, at the same Uncle Bob is getting ready to flip the burgers – and the buns on the barbecue – with the same spatula! You see the problem?

If your visitors are occasional guests, give them safe tasks to keep them busy and let them lend a hand – something that doesn't put your gluten-free foods in peril. Get them to pour the drinks or lay the table. But if they're regular visitors who are sympathetic to your need for a gluten-free life, you probably need to invest the time to show them the method for keeping your containers free from contamination. Your spreadables are at risk! Your other options are to hide the tubs and jars and buy squeezables for their visit, or to buy separate containers and clearly mark which ones are gluten-free.

Storing foods separately for convenience

Generally, you don't need to have separate storage spaces for the gluten-containing and gluten-free foods, but you may want to for convenience purposes. After all, simply reaching up to the gluten-free section of your cupboard for a gluten-free flour mixture is easier than sorting through the shelves.

If you have children on a gluten-free diet and others in the family still eat gluten – or if some people in the home are just not likely to exercise the same caution as you – then having separate storage areas can be a very good idea.

Any gluten-free loved ones may be overwhelmed by seeing all the things they can't eat in the cupboard, even if the things they can eat actually outnumber the things they can't.

By separating gluten-containing and gluten-free foods in the cupboard, not only do you make quickly choosing from their safe shelves quite easy, but also the number of things the children can eat becomes more obvious to them. This method can be a big psychological boost in what can otherwise be a daunting experience. Nobody knows the people you live with as well as you – so this decision really needs to be yours.

Consider marking newly purchased gluten-free foods with a 'GF' as soon as you get home from the shops, so that the children have an easier time helping you put everything away in the right place.

Developing Creative Gluten-Free Thinking: Improvising in the Kitchen

We believe that if you give a person a recipe, you feed him or her for a meal; show that person how to make recipes gluten-free, and you feed him or her for a lifetime. We have an enormous amount of respect and admiration for the innovative cookbook authors out there, especially after writing the recipe section of this book. So if you love recipes, you may be delighted to know that this book includes 65 recipes and that you can choose from dozens of excellent gluten-free cookbooks available on the market written by professional cooks. Coeliac UK (www.coeliac.co.uk) produce some great books that we recommend in Chapter 5.

But we also believe in improvisation. Sometimes that means taking a recipe for something that normally has gluten in it and modifying the ingredients to be gluten-free: Other times, it entails throwing caution to the wind and doing without a recipe altogether.

No single ingredient is more important in gluten-free cooking than creativity. You may not always have ingredients to hand for making the gluten-free dish you want. You may not have a recipe handy for a meal that you've got in mind. You may think that you've no way to convert your old favourite standby into a gluten-free delight. Don't let any of those things stop you. Cooking gluten-free is actually easy if you improvise, explore alternatives, and stretch the boundaries of your creativity in the kitchen.

If you want to eat gluten-free, but still make some of your old favourite recipes, chances are that you're going to need to experiment with some new gluten-free ingredients. That may mean that not everything turns out perfectly first time – don't let this put you off. The more you play around and experiment with these new ingredients the quicker they become old friends. And like old friends, you get to know their personalities and quirky ways of behaving, as well as discover exactly how to handle them and keep them in their place!

Adapting any dish to be gluten-free

Quiz: You're standing in the queue at the supermarket, mindlessly perusing the magazines offering valuable, up-to-date, celebrity gossip and guaranteed ways to lose all your love handles in less than 10 minutes. Suddenly, the cover of your favourite cooking magazine catches your eye: A beautiful photo of (insert your favourite food here), glistening with – agh! – gluten! Do you:

A) Leave the supermarket in tears, feeling sorry for yourself as you try to improve your mood by eating yet another rice cake?

B) Buy the magazine as a reminder of a past life of gluten-gluttony?

C) Delight in knowing that because you or someone you love bought you this copy of _Living Gluten-Free For Dummies_, you can easily and confidently modify that recipe to be deliciously gluten-free?

The right answer is, of course, C. You can modify nearly any dish to be gluten-free. Some dishes are easier than others – baked goods are the toughest and so we deal with those last. You can try one of two ways when you're adapting a dish to be gluten-free: with a recipe or without.

Starting with a recipe

If you're following a recipe for something that's not gluten-free and you want to convert it, start by reviewing the list of ingredients the recipe calls for. Make a note of those that usually have gluten in them. Then, using the substitutions that we suggest throughout this chapter or some of your own, substitute gluten-free ingredients as necessary.

Generally, when you make substitutions, measurements convert equally – with the exception of flours, which we discuss in the section 'Substituting gluten-free flours'.

If you don't have the right substitutions, improvise. For instance, if a recipe calls for dipping something in flour before sautéing and you don't have any gluten-free flours, maybe you have a gluten-free mix that may work. Pancake mix, even bread mix, can work quite well as a substitute for a flour coating.

Cooking without a recipe

If you're not using a recipe, creativity once again prevails. What if you want to make your own chicken nuggets. You certainly don't need a recipe for that; just slice some chicken and think about what you want to coat it in before frying or baking. Put some of your favourite gluten-free crisps in a plastic bag, and crunch them up. Now you've got a coating!

At the risk of labouring the point, you have to develop your own creativity. The substitution ideas in this chapter are just that – ideas. Coming up with substitutions that work for your convenience, preference, and budget is up to you.

Using standby substitutions

To convert a recipe that usually contains gluten into one that's gluten-free, you need to make some simple substitutions. Generally, with the exception of the flours you use for making baked goods, the substitutions are simple – just swap one for the other. We cover flours for baked goods separately, in the later section 'Substituting gluten-free flours'.

- ✔ **Beer:** Some foods, especially battered, deep-fried foods, may call for beer in the recipe. You can use the gluten-free beers available online or try cider instead.

- ✔ **Binders:** A binder is just something that holds foodstuff together. Because gluten provides elasticity and stretch to baked goods, adding binders to foods that don't have gluten-containing flours in them is a good idea. Binders include xanthan gum, guar gum (check out the section 'Thickening with gluten-free flours and starches'), gelatin powder (which has the additional benefit of adding protein and moisture), and eggs.

- ✔ **Breadcrumbs:** No rocket science required here. Anyone who's ever eaten a piece of gluten-free bread (especially without toasting it) knows that breadcrumbs aren't hard to come by. You can buy gluten-free breadcrumbs from specialty stores or online, or alternatively make your own using any gluten-free bread: Put the bread in a plastic bag and rub it until you get crumbs or grate the bread on a cheese grater – although mind your fingers! By the way, the easiest way to make fine crumbs is to put dry crumbs into a food processor or chopper that's been thoroughly cleaned of any trace of gluten-containing foods. You can even toast the crumbs if you want added crunch or need dry breadcrumbs instead of fresh ones. Crushed gluten-free breakfast cereals work well in place of breadcrumbs, too. Also consider using mashed potato flakes or quinoa flakes.

- ✔ **Buns and rolls:** Consider using a lettuce wrap, corn tortilla, or of course, gluten-free bread. Many good gluten-free buns and rolls are available on prescription, including wholemeal and multigrain. Others can be bought online, in supermarkets, or from specialty shops.

- ✔ **Coatings:** If a recipe calls for some type of coating, you have several options. You can consider using any of the gluten-free flours we list later in this chapter, as well as any versatile gluten-free mix you have lying around, such as a mix for bread, pastry, cakes, or pancakes depending on whether the dish you are making is sweet or savoury. Cornmeal or cornflour with added seasonings gives an interesting texture, and crushed crisps (gluten-free, of course) also work well, although they can be high in fat so we don't suggest using them frequently. You may also want to try commercial brands of Cajun-style coatings, many of which are just corn-meal with some spices added – but of course, check the labels first.

✔ **'Cream of' soups:** Use a combination of chicken broth or stock and sour cream instead. Then add your preferred vegetables – mushroom, celery, potato, and so on – to complete the soup.

✔ **Croutons:** Homemade croutons are actually very easy to make. Most recipes for croutons suggest that you use stale bread, but we don't suggest this method for gluten-free bread, because you end up with crumbled crouton crumbs instead. Cut fresh gluten-free bread into bite-size cubes, brush them with a little oil, and bake in a hot oven. When cooked you can roll them in Parmesan cheese, spices, or any other flavourings you like. (Head to Chapter 11 for low-fat and alternative crouton substitutions.)

✔ **Fillers:** *Filler* is a highly technical culinary term for something that adds bulk. Generally not something you hope to see on a label, fillers aren't always a bad thing; they may be in homemade burgers or sausages, for example, where the recipe often calls for breadcrumbs, crushed crackers, and other filler-type materials to add, well, filling. Gluten-free bread or breadcrumbs are obvious substitutions here, but also consider left-over cornbread, mashed potato flakes, or even an unsweetened breakfast cereal that you've crushed up.

✔ **Flour:** Many recipes call for flour, usually to act as a thickener (see the suggested thickeners in this list). Consider using gluten-free flours such as rice flour, sweet rice flour (they're different), potato starch, sorghum flour, and gram flour.

✔ **Flour tortillas:** The obvious substitution here is corn tortillas. Some new gluten-free flour tortillas are on the market now, and you can find recipes for homemade tortillas online or in cookbooks. Other wrap substitutions include rice wraps (found in Asian supermarkets and featured in a few recipes in this book), or try stuffing iceberg lettuce leaves.

Making teriyaki sauce

The term *teriyaki* refers to a method of cooking, derived from the Japanese words *teri*, meaning *lustre*, and *yaki*, meaning *grill* (cleverly combined to form the word *teriyaki*). Traditional teriyaki dishes are marinated in the sauce and then grilled, creating a shiny *(teri)* glaze. Although you can substitute for it, the key ingredient in teriyaki sauce is *mirin*, a sweet Japanese rice wine for cooking.

✔ 120 ml gluten-free soy sauce

✔ 120 ml mirin (If you don't have mirin, use 120 ml of sake and 1 tablespoon of sugar)

✔ 3 tablespoons of sugar

In a small saucepan, mix together the soy sauce, mirin, and sugar. Heat on low heat for about 3 minutes then let the sauce cool. You can store teriyaki sauce in a clean bottle in the fridge.

✔ **Pie crust and pastry:** One of the easiest ways to make a sweet pie crust is to take your favourite cereal and smash it into tiny crumbs, add some butter (and sugar, if the cereal isn't sweet enough), and then press the mixture into the bottom of a pie pan. Some good gluten-free crackers and biscuits work well the same way. Some pie crusts are supposed to be cooked before adding the pie filling, and others aren't. The fact that the crust is gluten-free doesn't change whether you need to cook the crust before filling the pie. Also check out some of the gluten-free pastry mixes available on prescription, on the Internet, and in the free-from aisle of the supermarket.

✔ **Seafood sauce:** You can make your own 'seafood' sauce with just mayo and ketchup, both of which are gluten-free!

✔ **Soy sauce:** Most soy sauce has wheat in it (and the label clearly indicates wheat), but you can find brands that are wheat-free. (By the way, *tamari* – a thicker, Japanese soy sauce – is often but not always wheat-free, so check the label.) Use a wheat-free soy sauce or you may want to be adventurous and try an Asian sauce, such as fish sauce or oyster sauce. Most of these, but not all, are gluten-free (careful – the fish sauce is really fishy!).

✔ **Teriyaki:** Because most soy sauce has wheat in it, most teriyaki (which is made from soy sauce) does, too. A few brands of wheat-free teriyaki sauces are available, but don't be afraid to make your own (see our recipe in the 'Making teriyaki sauce' sidebar).

✔ **Thickeners:** Many recipes use flour as a thickener, but alternatives are available. For sweet things, try using a dry pudding or cake mix, gelatin or QuickJel. Arrowroot flour, agar, tapioca starch, and cornflour are also excellent thickeners. So is sweet rice flour, which comes from sticky or glutinous rice (despite the name, it really is gluten-free). And remember that cake mix you've had lying around. Not only do mixes thicken the recipe, but the sweet flavour is also a pleasant surprise. (You can find more information on using gluten-free thickeners in the section 'Thickening with gluten-free starches and flours'.)

Cooking with Wheat Alternatives

Most gluten-free cooking is pretty straightforward. You just substitute gluten-free ingredients for the gluten-containing ones, and you're pretty much set. The process is a little different for baked goods, as we explain in the later section 'Substituting gluten-free flours'. But most gluten-free cooking isn't that much different from normal cooking, especially if you follow the theme of this chapter and let your creativity take over.

Don't forget that if you have a diagnosis of coeliac disease or dermatitis herpetiformis (DH) you're entitled to a whole host of pre-prepared mixes on prescription.

Incorporating alternative gluten-free grains

Not only are the gluten-free grains and grain alternatives that we talk about in Chapter 4 super nutritious, they also add unique flavours and textures to your food. Generally, cooking them is just like cooking other grains, as you can see in Part III of this book and in cookbooks. But you need to be aware of a few things to perfect the art of using alternative gluten-free grains.

When cooking gluten-free grains as whole grains (as opposed to using them as a flour in baked goods), you find these alternative grains cook like most whole grains – just add to boiling water, reduce the heat, simmer for the recommended amount of time, and they're done. The grain-to-water proportion and cooking times are really the only things that vary. Table 8-1 shows approximate amounts of liquids and cooking time; you can modify them to suit your preferences.

Table 8-1	Cooking Alternative Grains	
Gluten-Free Grain (240 g)	*Water or Chicken Stock*	*Cooking Time*
Amaranth	120 ml	20–25 mins
Brown rice (long or short grain)	720 ml	40 mins
Buckwheat	480 ml	15–20 mins
Cornmeal	720 ml	5–10 mins
Millet	720 ml	35–45 mins
Quinoa	480 ml	15–20 mins
White rice	480 ml	15 mins
Wild rice	960 ml	45 mins

Quinoa, millet, amaranth, buckwheat, and the other alternative grains are great additions to soups, stuffing, and other foods. Some ideas for using alternative grains, whether you precook them or simply add them to the other ingredients, are as follows:

- **Snacks:** Using a little oil in a pan, you can pop amaranth grains on the stove like popcorn and eat them seasoned or plain.

- **Soups:** Use buckwheat, quinoa, or millet in soups instead of rice or noodles. No need to precook the grains first; just add them to the soup during cooking. Remember, they absorb liquid and double in volume. Whole amaranth grains are small, and may seem gritty in soups, although amaranth can work well to thicken soups if you use it in flour form.

✔ **Stuffing:** Use the larger alternative grains, such as cooked quinoa, millet, or buckwheat, instead of breadcrumbs and stuffing. Season the stuffing to your taste then stuff vegetables, poultry, or pork tenderloins.

Thickening with gluten-free starches and flours

People usually use starch-based thickeners, such as cornflour, arrowroot, and tapioca, to thicken their sauces and gravies. Starch thickeners give food a transparent, glistening sheen, which looks great for pie fillings and in glazes, but the thickeners don't always look quite right in gravy or sauce, and so knowing which ones to use is important.

To thicken with gluten-free starches, mix the starch with an equal amount of cold liquid (usually water) until it forms a paste. Then whisk the paste into the liquid you're trying to thicken. After you add the thickener to the liquid, cook it for at least 30 seconds or so to get rid of the starchy flavour. But be careful you don't overcook it – liquids thicken with these starches and may get thin again if you cook them too long or at too high of a temperature.

Some of these flours have the advantage of working well with foods that are acidic. Acidic foods include canned or fresh fruits, citrus fruits, tomatoes, and vinegar. Bananas, figs, avocados, and potatoes are examples of foods that aren't acidic (they're alkaline).

Take a look at your options for thickeners:

✔ **Arrowroot:** If you're looking for that shiny gloss for dessert sauces or glazes, arrowroot is a good bet. Use arrowroot if you're thickening an acidic liquid but not if you're using dairy products (it makes them slimy). Arrowroot has the most neutral taste of all the starch thickeners, so if you're worried that a thickener may change or mask the flavour of your dish, use arrowroot. You can freeze the sauces you make with arrowroot.

✔ **Cornflour:** Cornflour is the best choice for thickening dairy-based sauces, but don't use it for acidic foods. Cornflour isn't as shiny as tapioca or arrowroot. Don't use cornflour if you're freezing the sauce because the sauce goes spongy.

✔ **Potato starch:** Usually used to thicken soups and gravies, potato starch doesn't work well in liquids that you boil.

Potato flour and potato starch flour are different. Potato flour is very heavy and tastes very much like potatoes. Potato starch flour is very fine, with a bland taste, and great to mix with other flours for baking or use as a thickener for soups or gravies.

✔ **QuickJel:** This modified cornstarch works especially well for fruit pie fillings because it blends well with acidic ingredients, tolerates high temperatures, and doesn't cause pie fillings to 'weep' during storage. It also doesn't begin thickening until the liquid begins to cool, which allows the heat to be more evenly distributed.

✔ **Tapioca:** You can use pearl tapioca or tapioca granules to thicken puddings and pies, but they don't completely dissolve when you cook them, so you end up with tiny gelatinous balls. If you like the balls, you can also use instant tapioca to thicken soups, gravies, and stews. If you don't like them, you can get tapioca starch, which is already finely ground. Tapioca gives a glossy sheen and can tolerate prolonged cooking and freezing.

You can use any of the alternative grains to thicken sauces, gravies, stews, puddings, and so on. Depending on what you're making, you can use whole grains or flours as a thickener. You probably want to use flour instead of whole grain to thicken something like gravy, but whole grains add lots of nutrition and work well to thicken soups and stews.

When you're using alternative flours or starches as thickeners, substitution amounts are a little different. Instead of 1 tablespoon of all-purpose flour, use

✔ **Agar:** ½ tablespoon

✔ **Arrowroot:** 2 teaspoons

✔ **Cornflour:** ½ tablespoon

✔ **Gelatin powder:** ½ tablespoon

✔ **Rice flour (brown or white):** 1 tablespoon

✔ **Sweet potato flour:** 1 tablespoon

Trying Your Hand at Gluten-Free Baking

We aren't going to beat about the bush: Baking is the trickiest type of gluten-free cooking. But it's getting easier. Years ago, gluten-free baking produced bread like bricks and cakes that crumbled when you exposed them to air.

Gluten is what makes baked goods stretchy, elastic, and doughy. It also forms a support structure to hold the gases that expand during cooking, and to help bread or cake rise and become fluffy. Without gluten, baked foods tend to crumble excessively or be dense enough to double as a lethal weapon. Using xanthan gum and combining gluten-free flours are the keys to creating gluten-free baked goods that are just as good as the real thing.

Making use of ready made mixes

Swallowing your pride is a lot better than swallowing a dry lump doing its best to impersonate a biscuit, don't you think? Of course, cooking from scratch is terrific, and these days, especially with the help of the professionally written gluten-free cookbooks, the success rate is high (certainly higher than it was when Danna started on her self-taught-gluten-free-baking-from-scratch adventures in the early 1990s).

But you should consider using some of the incredible gluten-free mixes now available for pancakes, cakes, breads, biscuits, pizza crust, pastry, muffins, and just about anything else you can think of. Many of the mixes are so good these days that they rival even the best homemade gluten-containing foods. They're simple to make (get the kids to help!) and fill the house with that gorgeous smell of freshly baked treats.

Most of the mixes simply require you to add an egg or egg substitute, water or milk, and oil. Many of the companies are aware of multiple food intolerances and offer milk-free, egg-free, soya-free, and other allergen-free products. You can keep it simple or jazz it up, adding your favourite ingredients and accommodating other allergies and intolerances.

The most common complaint we hear about mixes is that they're expensive – and some of them they are, but don't forget that many are available on prescription if you have coeliac disease (or DH). When you consider that they're pretty much fail-proof, and you add up the cost of some of the specialty gluten-free baking ingredients like special flours and xanthan gum – not forgetting that you risk the possibility of failure when trying your hand at home-baking gluten-free treats, which may end up being fed to the dog – you realise that £3.00 per biscuit is pretty expensive dog food. So opting for the pre-prepared mix is good value.

Introducing xanthan gum: The star of the dough

Boasting unique properties that enhance the consistency of foods, *xanthan gum* is a key ingredient in successful gluten-free baking. Basically, xanthan gum holds particles of foods together, and it's the component in salad dressings, gravies, sauces, and ice creams that gives those foods a creamy, rich, smooth texture. Xanthan gum works well in gluten-free foods, and gluten-containing foods for that matter, providing essential stretch and elasticity qualities.

Here's a guide on how much xanthan gum to use for each cup of gluten-free flour:

- **Biscuits:** ¼ teaspoon
- **Bread:** 1 heaped teaspoon
- **Cakes:** ½ teaspoon
- **Muffins:** ¾ teaspoon
- **Pizza:** 2 teaspoons

We must warn you that xanthan gum is pricey. Some people use guar gum instead because it's cheaper. But be aware that guar gum is high in fibre content and can have a laxative and flatulent effect.

When you're making gluten-free dough, use nonstick loaf tins, baking sheets, and flan dishes; or be prepared to use lots of parchment, baking paper, wax paper, or aluminum foil. Gluten-free dough is especially sticky.

Substituting gluten-free flours

Several gluten-free flours work well for baking. But they don't always work in a one-to-one ratio. In other words, you can't just replace one 240 grams of all-purpose or wheat flour with 240 grams of potato starch – at least not for the best results.

You should play around with these substitutions to find the flavours and consistencies that you like best, but this list gives you a starting point for how you can use gluten-free flours.

Remember, each substitution is instead of *240 grams* of all-purpose flour:

- **Amaranth flour:** 220–240 grams
- **Arrowroot flour:** 220–240 grams
- **Buckwheat flour:** 210 grams
- **Cornflour:** 180 grams
- **Cornmeal:** 180 grams
- **Gram (chickpea) flour:** 180 grams
- **Millet flour:** 240 grams
- **Potato flour:** 120 grams

- **Potato starch:** 180 grams

- **Quinoa flour:** 240 grams

- **Rice flour (white or brown):** 220–240 grams

- **Sorghum:** 220–240 grams

- **Soya flour:** 180 grams

- **Sweet potato flour:** 240 grams

- **Sweet rice flour (glutinous or sticky rice flour; mochiko):** 210 grams

- **Tapioca flour or starch:** 240 grams

Combining your own gluten-free flour mixtures

One interesting discovery that professional cookbook authors stumbled across in the not-so-distant past is that if you mix a variety of flours together, they produce baked goods that have a better consistency and taste. The different combinations of gluten-free flour mixtures are endless – do some experimenting to find your favourite combinations.

If you're going to be doing a lot of baking, we suggest making up a large quantity of gluten-free flour mixture and storing it in a dark, dry place. That way you have it to hand whenever you want to bake. You can also buy many ready-mixed packets of combination gluten-free flours if you haven't got time to prepare your own mixtures.

Take a quick look through any gluten-free cookbook or visit gluten-free recipe sites on the Internet for dozens of variations on these flour mixtures. However, we give you three of the most popular basic mixes, which can be used as a one-to-one substitution for all-purpose flour. A good all round purpose flour is:

Bette Hagman's All-Purpose Gluten-Free Flour Mixture

- 2 parts white rice flour

- ⅔ part potato starch flour

- ⅓ part tapioca flour

Each type of gluten-free flour mixture has a unique taste and cooking properties. One of the more popular flour mixtures today is bean flour, which adds protein and texture. Here's a bean flour mixture:

Gluten-Free Bean Flour Mixture

- ✔ 1 part bean flour
- ✔ 1 part brown rice flour (or 1 part white rice flour)
- ✔ 1 part cornflour
- ✔ 1 part tapioca starch
- ✔ ¾ parts sweet rice flour

Carol Fenster has also developed a gluten-free flour mixture using sorghum and cornflour (she suggests using a small coffee or spice grinder to make the cornflour out of white cornmeal):

Carol Fenster's Cornflour Blend

- ✔ 1½ cups sorghum flour
- ✔ 1½ cups potato starch or cornflour
- ✔ 1 cup tapioca flour
- ✔ ½ cup cornmeal

Baking bread the gluten-free way

Those who have attempted the sometimes taste-defying feat of experimenting with gluten-free breads know that at times the word _bread_ is a euphemism for _brick_ and the word _edible_ is an overstatement. But never fear; help is here – whether you're a die-hard baker or a newbie to the kitchen, freshly baked, great-tasting, fabulous smelling, gluten-free bread is easier than ever to make.

Although some gluten-free breads do taste great these days, they still taste a little different from wheat-based breads. And why does that surprise people? That's like making an apple pie but using cherries instead of apples and being surprised that it doesn't have an apple flavour. Of course gluten-free bread doesn't taste exactly like wheat bread – it doesn't have _wheat_ in it!

Gluten-free breads tend to look a little different, too. In spite of great strides to make them fluffier and airier, they're still a little denser and turn out best if you make them in smaller loaves. They also don't rise as much, and so the tops are sometimes flat or even concave.

You may want to toast your gluten-free bread to give it a better consistency and make it less likely to crumble. Gluten-free bread is great for toasted sandwiches because the butter and grilling process gives it a crispy texture and seals the bread so that it doesn't crumble. Freshly cooked, part-baked gluten-free bread is probably the most palatable bread to eat untoasted.

Time-saving tips for the gluten-free cook

We know that we tend to have a *super positive* approach to the gluten-free lifestyle, but even we admit that being gluten-free sometimes takes more time and effort. That's why we thought you may appreciate some tips to save you time in your gluten-free cooking adventures.

✔ Make your gluten-free baking mixtures in advance, and double the recipe. Store them in large airtight containers in a cool, dry, dark place, and label them well (for example, 'GF bread mix' and 'GF baking mix'). Remember, though, not to add the yeast until baking day. Fresh yeast comes in amber-coloured (to protect it from the light), tightly sealed jars or individual packets to keep it as fresh as possible, which is best for baking.

✔ When you prepare a meal, try to ensure that as much of the meal as possible is gluten-free. If you have a mixed family — some members eat gluten and others are gluten-free — making most of the meal without gluten is easier for you. This practice also makes the gluten-free member feel more included.

✔ Save your gluten-free mistakes or stale bread, because one bad batch is another meal. If the bread didn't rise, the cake crumbled, and the biscuits fell apart, save the crumbs and use them for stuffings, casseroles, coatings, or breadcrumbs.

A few general bread-making tips are

✔ All the ingredients that you use, except water, should be at room temperature.

✔ The water that you mix the yeast with must be lukewarm. Too hot, and you kill the yeast. Too cold, and you don't activate it. Also, you should dissolve the yeast in the water before adding it to the rest of the ingredients.

✔ Adding extra protein in the form of egg, egg substitutes, dry milk powders, or cottage or ricotta cheese is important for helping the yeast to work properly.

✔ Vinegar, usually cider vinegar, helps the yeast ferment and promotes the flavour of the bread. Sometimes recipes call for lemon juice or a dough enhancer instead. These ingredients also act as preservatives.

✔ You should use small loaf tins for gluten-free bread to reduce drying out.

✔ Gluten-free bread tends to need to cook for longer, so cover your loaf with foil for the last 15 minutes to stop it from burning.

✔ Wait until the bread has cooled to room temperature before slicing it.

Given the choice of doing something by hand or using an efficient, easy-to-clean-made-for-the-job-tried-and-tested tool to do it, we're likely to opt for the tool. If you want to use a bread maker for your gluten-free breads, bear a few things in mind:

- ✔ Gluten-free bread needs only one kneading and one rising cycle. If you have a setting that allows you to do only one kneading and one rising, select it. Some bread makers now have special settings for gluten-free bread: Check with the manufacturer.

- ✔ You really shouldn't share your bread machine with gluten-containing recipes. Getting all the residue off the beaters, tin, and other parts is nearly impossible.

- ✔ If you haven't bought a machine yet, buy one with strong paddles, a strong motor, and a strong fan.

- ✔ If your bread turns out soggy, remove it a few minutes after baking, before the machine starts its 'keep warm' cycle.

- ✔ Keep dry ingredients separate from wet ingredients, and add them in the order that the machine's manufacturer recommends. Whisk together wet ingredients prior to mixing them with dry ingredients.

- ✔ A few minutes after the bread maker has started, use a rubber spatula to scrape the dough off the sides of the pan back into the dough.

If you're a glutton for punishment and choose to mix your dough by hand, consider the following tips:

- ✔ If you're following a recipe that calls for using a bread maker, double the amount of yeast and use a little more liquid (a couple of tablespoons).

- ✔ If you're following a recipe that calls for a bread maker and specifies using one teaspoon of unflavoured gelatin, leave it out.

Part IV
From Menus to Meals: Recipes for a Gluten-Free Lifestyle

'What have I told you about drinking the blood of coeliac disease sufferers, Count?'

In this part . . .

We give you gluten-free recipes. We feel compelled to come clean at this point and tell you that we're not Real Cookbook Authors, nor do we pretend to be on TV. But we *do* cook, and the recipes we're giving you are actual recipes that we use, and that we know work. When we cook, not only do we *de-glutenise* old favourites, but we also embrace traditional ingredients and preparations from various cuisines that are inherently gluten-free.

In this part, we bring you some of our favourite recipes: Some simple, some sophisticated – but all easy-to-prepare.

Chapter 9

First Things First: Beginning with Breakfast

In This Chapter

▶ Making the most of hectic mornings – quick and nutritious breakfasts

▶ Going to work on an egg – enjoying protein-packed egg dishes

▶ Starting off with smoothies

▶ Discovering quick gluten-free breakfast breads and cakes

▶ Bringing dinner to the breakfast table

*W*hen most people think of a typical breakfast, images of croissants, pancakes, toast, or muesli often come to mind. So what are those of us on the gluten-free diet supposed to do? Dig in, that's what! Yes, you can enjoy delicious traditional breakfast foods that may at first seem to be off-limits on the gluten-free diet.

If you don't have much time to prepare foods in the morning check out Coeliac UK's *The Food and Drink Directory* for gluten-free breakfast cereals that provide a quick grab 'n go breakfast. Many gluten-free breads and rolls are delicious toasted or even warmed in the oven.

If you've got more time, why not try one of our delicious recipes – not all these options are necessarily 'healthy' (some are higher in sugar and saturated fat) but alternating these recipes with healthy breakfasts, or healthier foods throughout the day, is what balance is all about.

Don't be afraid to think beyond the traditional breakfast fare. Smoothies are delicious and nutritious, and a plate of spicy peppers stuffed with egg and cheese can perk up any morning – or afternoon, for that matter. Use this chapter as inspiration for exploring alternatives to the old standby breakfast routines. When you start to think outside the breakfast box, you may discover a whole new world of wholesome gluten-free options to start your day off right.

Getting Your Day Off to a Gluten-Free Start

If mornings are rather chaotic in your house, taking the time to prepare a healthy, gluten-free breakfast may seem like a luxury you can't afford. But in reality, breakfast really is, as your mum probably told you, the most important meal of the day. Not only does breakfast help with weight management by stopping you snacking later on, but breakfast eaters also have a more positive attitude, and concentrate and perform better at work and school. Starting your day with a nutritious gluten-free breakfast has a beneficial impact on your entire day.

Breakfast is the first meal you eat after waking up – after you've 'fasted' for eight or more hours (hence the clever name!). Your body is literally starved of nutrition and in need of restoration to get going for the day ahead. Yet many people aren't hungry, or at least they think they aren't hungry – and most people are frantically rushing to get themselves or others out the door. Usually, a healthy breakfast is sacrificed in this whirlwind of chaos.

Reaching for grab 'n go starters

If you're limited for time, you still have plenty of nutritious gluten-free foods to choose from. The trick is to stock up on wholesome foods that are easy to eat and that you can take with you as you're running out the door. And the foods don't have to be traditional breakfast foods. Some suggestions include the following:

- Cartons of cottage cheese (with or without flavouring)

- Fresh or dried fruit or mini cans of fruit cocktails

- Gluten-free crackers with cheese slices

- Hard-boiled eggs (for extra flair, make them devilled)

- Homemade muesli (such as the gluten-free muesli recipe given in this chapter)

- Leftover gluten-free pizza

- Low-fat yogurt

Trail mix is a fancy way to describe a mixture of nuts, dried fruit, and other bite-sized munchies, and it makes a great portable breakfast! You can buy pre-made mixes, but be careful because some of the dried fruits (especially dates) are coated in oat flour, and some of the nuts have seasonings on them that may contain gluten – check the label first. Making your own selection using your favourite gluten-free ingredients is just as easy, and may include:

- Nuts (like walnuts, Brazils, hazelnuts, almonds, and cashews)

- Dry roasted peanuts (roast shelled nuts in a single layer in a shallow baking tray for 15 to 20 minutes at 180°C/350°F/Gas Mark 4. Stir once or twice during cooking and leave to cool before using)

- Dried fruit (like raisins, apricots, banana chips, and cranberries)

- Shaved coconut, diced dried papaya or pineapple, dried apple rings

- For a treat you can even mix in a few chocolate-covered raisins or peanuts

If you know you're going to be rushed in the morning, prepare a breakfast-to-go meal the night before. Pack trail mix, yogurt, an apple, and a small juice or water bottle into a lunch box and put it in the fridge. And don't forget a spoon for the yogurt!

🍑 Gluten-Free Muesli

Muesli is a great take-it-with-you breakfast food, but oats are still the number-one most controversial is-it-gluten-free-or-isn't-it food, and for now they're still on the forbidden list. That means most commercial muesli is a no-no. Several companies make gluten-free versions although none are available on prescription (check Coeliac UK's *The Food and Drink Directory*). The good news is that homemade gluten-free muesli is delicious, nutritious, and simple to make. In this recipe, we use dry roasted peanuts (see recipe above), but feel free to experiment by substituting any combination of nuts or seeds. Likewise, dried apricots, dates, and bananas work well in place of the raisins and dried cranberries. Many companies sell puffed rice and corn cereal, and you can also experiment with other gluten-free cereals, such as Barkat porridge oats, puffed buckwheat, puffed millet, Ener-G pure rice bran, or rice flakes – once again *The Food and Drink Directory* can guide you towards suitable choices.

Preparation time: *30 minutes*

Cooking time: *2 hours*

Makes: *12 servings*

80 grams/3 ounces gluten-free puffed rice cereal

80 grams/3 ounces gluten-free puffed corn cereal

60 grams/2 ounces gluten-free oat muesli

150 grams/5½ ounces dry roasted peanuts

2 teaspoons natural vanilla extract

120 millilitres/4 fluid ounces golden syrup

120 millilitres/4 fluid ounces honey (preferably runny)

60 millilitres/2 fluid ounces vegetable oil

75 grams/2½ ounces raisins

75 grams/2½ ounces dried cranberries

Vegetable or olive oil spray, for greasing the baking trays

1 Preheat the oven to 130°C/250°F/Gas Mark 2½.

2 In a large bowl, combine the puffed rice cereal, puffed corn cereal, oat muesli, and peanuts.

3 In a small saucepan, heat the vanilla extract, golden syrup, honey, and oil over a medium heat (it just needs to warm through so that it flows more easily; don't overheat it). Stir the mixture occasionally as it heats.

4 Pour the warm honey mixture over the dry ingredients, mixing well to ensure that everything gets coated.

5 Spray two large baking trays with the nonstick oil. Divide the mixture between the trays, spreading the mixture out evenly. Bake the granola for 2 hours, stirring every 15 minutes to stop the mixture from sticking.

6 Carefully add the raisins and cranberries to the hot cereal, folding them into the mixture so that they're well incorporated. Let the mixture cool to room temperature then serve, storing what you don't need.

Tip: *Homemade muesli tends to go stale quickly. Extend the life of your homemade version by using a vacuum-packing system to seal and store several individual-sized servings. If you're too late and the muesli mixture has already gone stale, use it to make muesli bars (see recipe in Chapter 14).*

Nutrient analysis per serving: Calories 287; Protein 5g; Carbohydrate 40g; Sugar 22g; Fat 12g; Saturated fat 1.5g; Fibre 1.5g; Sodium 30mg.

Power-starting your gluten-free day with protein

Protein really does pack a nutritional punch, working alongside carbohydrates to regulate blood-sugar levels and provide lots of slow-releasing energy throughout the day. By starting your day with a meal containing some protein, you're giving yourself a nutritional boost that can keep you going for hours.

Fortunately, high-protein foods are plentiful in the gluten-free diet. In fact, many of the foods found on 'traditional' breakfast menus that aren't gluten-free, such as croissants and toast, actually offer very little in the way of protein. In contrast, many foods that are inherently gluten-free, such as eggs and meat, are very high in protein.

From a gluten-free standpoint, whether your protein is from plant or animal sources really doesn't matter. Eggs are an obvious source of protein for breakfast (see the following section 'Introducing The Incredible, Edible Egg' for recipe ideas using eggs), but you can incorporate plenty of other protein sources into your first meal of the day:

- ✔ Bacon or ham slices
- ✔ Dairy products (low-fat milk, cheese, and yogurt)
- ✔ Lean sirloin or steak strips
- ✔ Nuts
- ✔ Protein shakes and smoothies (you can find recipe ideas under 'Smoothies for Starters')
- ✔ Turkey slices

Introducing the Incredible, Edible Egg

Eggs offer more value than many people realise. They're extremely nutritious, containing all the essential amino acids and several important vitamins and minerals. They're also convenient, inexpensive, easy to prepare, and easy to eat. Eating eggs rarely causes an allergic reaction, and they play an important role in a variety of recipes.

Have you ever wondered how to tell whether your eggs are raw or hard-boiled? Simply take 'em for a spin. A hard-boiled one spins freely, and a raw one doesn't. This happens because the hard-boiled one is solid, so everything spins in one direction all at once. The raw egg sloshes around and doesn't allow a fast spinning motion.

'Greece-y' Eggs

If you're in a Mediterranean-morning mood, try these 'Greece-y' eggs, which include sun-dried tomatoes, olives, and feta cheese. In no way greasy, this recipe is an especially low-fat version of Greek eggs because it uses only the egg whites. To see how to separate whites from yolks, go to Figure 9-1.

Tools: *Food processor, 10-centimetre (4-inch) ramekin or ovenproof bowl*

Preparation time: *10 minutes*

Cooking time: *15 minutes*

Makes: *2 servings*

120 millilitres/4 fluid ounces egg whites (separated from about 4 to 5 large free-range eggs)

30 grams/1 ounce sun-dried tomatoes (use the hydrated kind, not in oil)

Several large handfuls of fresh basil leaves

4 pitted Kalamata olives

1 teaspoon crushed garlic (about 1 clove)

25 grams/1 ounce feta cheese, crumbled

2 slices toasted gluten-free bread

Vegetable or olive oil spray, for greasing the ramekin

1 Spray a ramekin or bowl with olive oil. Place the ramekin in a large saucepan and fill the pan with cold water until the water level comes halfway up the sides of the ramekin.

2 Place the pan over a high heat. Mix the egg whites together then add to the ramekin. As soon as the water boils, turn the heat to low and cover the pot. Set an egg timer for 15 minutes.

3 While the eggs are cooking, combine the tomatoes, basil, olives, and garlic in a small food processor. Pulse the ingredients until finely minced. Stir in the feta cheese.

4 When the 15 minutes are up, check the eggs. The eggs are cooked when they're no longer runny. When the eggs are done, carefully remove the ramekin from the hot, simmering water.

5 Toast the bread. Spread two tablespoons of the basil-tomato-cheese mixture on each slice of toast.

6 Loosen the eggs from the dish with a knife and spoon half the eggs onto each piece of the toast. Decorate the eggs with the remaining basil-tomato-cheese mixture and serve.

3 WAYS TO SEPARATE AN EGG

1. CRACK THE EGG IN HALF, OVER A BOWL... ..AND PASS THE YOLK FROM 1 SHELL TO THE OTHER, ALLOWING THE WHITE TO GRADUALLY FALL INTO THE BOWL BELOW.

2. CRACK THE EGG AND BREAK THE EGG INTO YOUR CUPPED HAND HELD OVER A BOWL. GENTLY, RELAX FINGERS, ALLOWING THE WHITE TO SPILL THROUGH INTO THE BOWL BELOW.

3. USE AN EGG SEPARATOR! PLACE IT OVER A SMALL BOWL OR GLASS. CRACK THE EGG OPEN AND LET IT FALL INTO THE CENTRE.

THE WHITE WILL SLIP THROUGH THE SLOTS AND THE YOLK WILL STAY IN THE SEPARATOR.

Figure 9-1:
Separating
eggs.

Nutrient analysis per serving: Calories 185; Protein 9g; Carbohydrate 15g; Sugar 1g; Fat 10g; Saturated fat 2g; Fibre 0.5g; Sodium 556mg.

☺ Eggs in a Bread Basket

This recipe is a fun way to serve eggs and toast, especially if you have kids in the house. Because loaves of gluten-free bread tend to be smaller than other bread, you can lay two slices side by side, cutting shapes out of the touching edges to create the hole for the egg to go into.

Preparation time: *5 minutes*

Cooking time: *5 minutes*

Makes: *4 servings*

4 slices gluten-free bread

4 large free-range eggs

Butter, for spreading

1 Heat a griddle or large non-stick frying pan over a medium-high heat. While the pan is heating up, butter both sides of each slice of bread.

2 In the centre of each bread slice, cut out a circle about the size of an egg. You can use a knife to cut the circle, or use a biscuit cutter to make cute shapes. Retain the bread cut outs.

3 Make sure that the pan or griddle is hot enough by testing it with a drop of water; it sizzles when hot. When ready, place the bread – slices and cutouts – on the pan or griddle.

4 Fry for approximately 2 minutes or until the underside of the bread is golden brown, and then flip over each slice and cutout.

5 Carefully crack an egg into the hole in each slice of bread. You may find that the egg overspills on to the bread. That's okay.

6 After a further 2 minutes, when the second side of the bread is golden, flip over the slices to cook the other side of the eggs. When the eggs are cooked to your preferred firmness, serve the 'eggs in a basket' on plates, decorating them with the fried cutouts.

Nutrient analysis per serving: Calories 247; Protein 7g; Carbohydrate 12g; Sugar 0.5g; Fat 19g; Saturated fat 8g; Fibre 0.5g; Sodium 296mg.

Breakfast Quiche

'Real men' may not eat quiche, but gluten-free people can – with a few modifications, of course. The beauty of this dish is that with a few tricks, it's incredibly easy – and with a little creativity, it can be exceptionally nutritious. This dish is also easily adapted to suit vegetarians – just leave the meat out and add extra veg.

Preparation time: *15 minutes*

Cooking time: *45 minutes*

Makes: *4 servings*

180 grams/6½ ounces frozen hash browns, thawed

80 grams/3 ounces butter, melted

5 large free-range eggs

180 millilitres/6½ fluid ounces skimmed milk

200 grams/7 ounces cooked ham, diced

50 grams/2 ounces onion, diced

120 grams/4½ ounces Swiss cheese, grated

30 grams/1 ounce cheddar cheese, grated

30 grams/1 ounce mozzarella cheese, grated

Handful of fresh basil leaves, chopped

Freshly ground salt and pepper to taste

Vegetable or olive oil spray, for greasing the pie tin

1 Preheat the oven to 170°C/325°F/Gas Mark 3.

2 To prepare the crust, carefully break up the hash browns into small chunks and mix with the melted butter, making sure that the potatoes don't turn to mush.

3 Spray a 23-centimetre (9-inch) pie tin or quiche pan with non-stick oil spray. Press the potato-butter mixture evenly into the bottom and sides of the pan.

4 In a large mixing bowl, beat the eggs with an electric mixer for 2 minutes on low speed. Add the milk, ham, onion, the grated cheeses, basil, and season with salt and pepper. Stir until well mixed.

5 Pour the egg mixture into the potato crust, and bake for 45 minutes. To test whether the quiche is done, insert a knife in the centre. If it comes out clean, the quiche is ready.

Tip: *To add nutritional value and flavour, add your favourite combinations of any chopped up vegetables or meat.*

Nutrient analysis per serving: *Calories 600; Protein 32g; Carbohydrate 16g; Sugar 4g; Fat 45g; Saturated fat 24g; Fibre 1g; Sodium 1090mg.*

Discovering the Smoothie Way to Start the Day

Smoothies are a great way to start the day. These thick, smooth drinks use a base of fruit or fruit juice, milk, and yogurt or ice cream. No need for any fancy equipment – any blender, hand-blender, or even a cocktail shaker works. Not only are smoothies delicious and easy to whip up, but also you can sneak a lot of nutritious things into them without anyone knowing. Creamy, rich, refreshing, and energising, smoothies suit any taste and mood. The only thing limiting your options is your creativity. Perk up your smoothie with a winning combination of nutritional value, colour, and overall goodness by adding ripe fruit.

If you have bananas lying around that are a little too brown for your taste, or strawberries that are getting a bit mushy, pop them in a smoothie. Bananas and other fruits, especially when at the end of being aesthetically acceptable, sweeten up smoothies and add loads of nutritional value. Use frozen soft fruit if you can't buy fresh, and don't forget that you can freeze bananas, too.

⚇ Simple Fruit Smoothie

This recipe is the foundation from which all smoothies are born: Simple, delicious, and just waiting for you to enhance it with nutritious ingredients and a creative style all your own. This smoothie combines the sweetness of bananas and honey with the slight tartness of strawberry yogurt.

Tools: *Blender*

Preparation time: *4 minutes*

Makes: *3 glasses*

120 millilitres/4 fluid ounces skimmed milk

240 millilitres/8½ fluid ounces low-fat strawberry yogurt

2 ripe bananas

1 teaspoon honey (preferably runny)

60 grams/2½ ounces ice cubes

1 Place all the ingredients in a blender.

2 Mix until smooth, pour into glasses, and serve immediately.

Vary It! *Remember, you can make a smoothie countless ways – be creative, and use ingredients you have on hand, especially fruits that are past their best. Play with the portion sizes and types of ingredients to get the taste and nutritional value that suits you.*

Nutrient analysis per serving: *Calories 180; Protein 5g; Carbohydrate 32g; Sugar 30g; Fat 3.5g; Saturated fat 2g; Fibre 0.5g; Sodium 65mg.*

Chocolate Peanut Butter Smoothie

Fruit and berry smoothies are delicious and nutritious. But if you're in the mood for something with a little more substance – and, well, a few more calories – this chocolate peanut butter smoothie should go down a treat. Go ahead – live a little, and whip it up!

Tools: *Blender*

Preparation time: *4 minutes*

Makes: *2 glasses*

240 millilitres/8½ fluid ounces low-fat chocolate ice cream

60 millilitres/2 fluid ounces skimmed milk

2 tablespoons smooth peanut butter

1 ripe banana

60 grams/2½ ounces ice cubes

1 Place all the ingredients in a blender.

2 Mix until smooth, pour into glasses, and serve immediately.

Vary It! *We suggest chocolate ice cream in this recipe because, well, everything is better with chocolate. Feel free to experiment with different flavours of the ice cream. Almost any flavour works, but vanilla is sure to please.*

Nutrient analysis per serving: *Calories 459; Protein 11.5g; Carbohydrate 49g; Sugar 43g; Fat 24g; Saturated fat 11g; Fibre 3g; Sodium 175mg.*

Waking Up to the Smell of Baking: Hot Breakfast Ideas

Ah . . . few things get a morning off to a better start than waking up to the smell of fresh baking. Perhaps you think that you have to do without this experience on the gluten-free diet? Not a bit of it. This section proves that opportunities abound for those gooey breakfast foods that you feared were a thing of the past.

Many of the recipes for baked goods and quick breads call for a gluten-free flour mixture. You can use those available on prescription, buy a baking mix, or create your own. We give a list of recommended baking mixtures and recipes for how to make your own in Chapter 8.

○ Crêpes

The word *crêpe* is French for *pancake* and is derived from *crêper*, meaning 'to crisp'. Basically thin, crisp pancakes, crêpes are most delightful when filled with a variety of stuffings or smothered in garnishes or syrups. Although creating crêpe batter is simple, actually cooking crêpes can take a little practice. The technique starts with using the right kind of pan. You can buy pans made specifically for crêpes, but you really don't need one. Any flat-bottomed non-stick frying pan between 18 to 20 centimetres (7 to 8 inches) in diameter is fine. Make sure that the pan's non-stick and shallow with sloping sides.

Tools: *Crêpe pan or flat-bottomed non-stick frying pan*

Preparation time: *10 minutes*

Cooking time: *20 minutes*

Makes: *4 servings*

100 grams/3½ ounces gluten-free flour mixture	*Pinch of salt*
½ teaspoon xanthan gum	*30 grams/1 ounce butter, melted*
2 large free-range eggs, beaten	*Non-stick oil spray, for greasing the frying pan*
240 millilitres/8½ fluid ounces skimmed milk	

1 In a large mixing bowl, whisk together the flour mixture, xanthan gum, and eggs. Gradually add the milk, stirring to combine.

2 Add the salt and melted butter; beat the mixture until it's smooth. The consistency should be like that of cream. If it's too thick or runny, add a little flour or milk until you achieve the desired thickness.

3 Heat a pan over a medium-high heat. Check the pan's temperature is ready by sprinkling a drop of water on it. If the water sizzles and bounces, the pan is hot enough. Spray the pan liberally with the oil.

4 Pour just enough batter in the pan to be able to make a thin coating on the bottom of the pan. Lift the pan off the burner and quickly tilt the pan so that the batter sloshes from side-to-side, thinly covering the entire bottom.

5 Return the pan to the burner. When the crêpe is light brown on the bottom and firm on the top, after about 1 minute, gently loosen it with a spatula and flip it. Start checking the bottom of the crêpe when the sides become crispy and slightly loosen themselves from the pan. When both sides are light brown (the second side browns more quickly than the first), your crêpe is ready!

Tip: *Working out how to make crêpes is a matter of trial and error, and the pan temperature is important. The batter should cook as soon as it touches the pan but shouldn't sizzle. If your crêpes are thick or bubbly, turn down the heat or lift the pan off the burner for a while. If they stick or aren't browning or setting quickly enough, turn up the heat or return the pan to the hob.*

Vary It! *Dress to impress. Without toppings and fillings, crêpes are just, well, thin, crispy pancakes. The fun – and impressive way to wow your guests – is with the fillings and toppings. The key is, once again, creativity. You can choose to spread fillings on your crêpes then roll them up, or spread the filling and cover it with another crêpe, sandwich-style. You can make as many layers as you like, and even alternate fillings. Here are some ideas to get you started, which also work well with pancakes and waffles:*

    ✔ *Peaches 'n cream:* *Combine fresh, sliced peaches with cream cheese, sour cream, whipped cream, and brown sugar.*

    ✔ *Banana sundae:* *Not exactly on the Weight Watchers menu, this indulgence calls for using sliced bananas as a filling and then topping the crêpes with your favourite ice cream and sauce (caramel, butterscotch, chocolate, hot fudge, and so on). Top it off with whipped cream or even banana liqueur.*

    ✔ *Strawberry style:* *In a hurry? Mix a little strawberry jam with ricotta or cream cheese. You may want to sweeten it up with a dash of sugar or sugar substitute – and if you're feeling really wild and crazy, top the crêpe with fresh strawberries.*

    ✔ *Ready-to-spread toppings:* *Even quicker ideas for toppings include chocolate spread, icing sugar, or whipped cream.*

Nutrient analysis per serving (crêpes only, not fillings): *Calories 212; Protein 7g; Carbohydrate 23g; Sugar 6g; Fat 10g; Saturated fat 5g; Fibre 1g; Sodium 395mg.*

Crêpes Suzette

The most famous crêpe dish throughout the world is crêpes Suzette, often prepared in restaurants in full view of the guests. Served hot with a sauce of sugar, orange juice, and Grand Marnier, crêpes Suzette are usually topped with brandy and ignited for the pyro pleasure of everyone. In fact, the flames are all for show: Flaming the brandy doesn't change the flavour of the dish in any way because the alcohol is burnt off (shame!). (Our super-cautious editor insists that we warn you about the dangers of preparing flaming dishes, as the flame can be difficult to see and may still be present after you think it's extinguished. Now we have, and now you know.)

 *Coffee Cake*

We wonder why this recipe's called coffee cake when it contains no coffee, but coffee or no coffee, this cake is sure to get the family out of bed and down to the breakfast table in a hurry. And if they're anything like us, they're probably just after the cinnamon-sugar topping!

Preparation time: *10 minutes*

Cooking time: *25 minutes*

Makes: *6 servings*

For the cake:

60 millilitres/2 fluid ounces rapeseed oil

2 large free-range eggs, beaten

120 millilitres / 4 fluid ounces skimmed milk

150 grams/5½ ounces gluten-free flour mixture

1½ teaspoons xanthan gum

190 grams/6¾ ounces granulated sugar

2 teaspoons baking powder

For the topping:

100 grams/3½ ounces brown sugar

2 tablespoons gluten-free flour mixture

2 teaspoons ground cinnamon

45 grams/1¾ ounces butter, melted

Vegetable or olive oil spray, for greasing the cake tin

1 Preheat the oven to 190°C/375°F/Gas Mark 5.

2 In a large mixing bowl, combine the oil, eggs, and milk.

3 Sift together the flour mixture, xanthan gum, sugar, and baking powder. Add these dry ingredients to the egg mixture, and combine well.

4 Spray a 23-centimetre (9-inch) square cake tin with non-stick oil, and pour in the batter.

5 In a small bowl, create the cinnamon-sugar topping by mixing together the brown sugar, flour mixture, cinnamon, and melted butter. Spoon the topping mixture over the cake batter.

6 Place the cake on the middle shelf of the oven and bake for 25 minutes. Insert a cocktail stick in the centre of the cake to check whether it's done. If the stick comes out clean, the cake's ready. Allow to cool on a cake rack before slicing.

Nutrient analysis per serving: *Calories 470; Protein 5g; Carbohydrate 70g; Sugar 50g; Fat 19g; Saturated fat 6g; Fibre 1g; Sodium 487mg.*

⚘ French Toast

French toast makes us think of easy elegance, and it's ridiculously simple to make despite somehow boasting an air of sophistication, especially if you serve it with icing sugar and strawberries. Don't forget the golden syrup!

Preparation time: *5 minutes*

Cooking time: *6 minutes per slice*

Makes: *6 servings*

4 large free-range eggs

60 millilitres/2 fluid ounces skimmed milk

¼ teaspoon ground cinnamon (optional)

30 grams/1 ounce butter

6 slices gluten-free bread

1 In a medium bowl, combine the eggs, milk, and cinnamon (if desired). Beat the mixture with a whisk or fork until well blended.

2 Melt the butter in a large frying pan or griddle over a medium heat.

3 Dip each slice of bread in the egg mixture, coating the bread well on both sides.

4 Place the bread in the hot pan. Cook the bread until golden brown on both sides, about 3 minutes per side.

5 Serve the French toast warm, accompanied by your favourite topping.

Nutrient analysis per serving: *Calories 152; Protein 5g; Carbohydrate 13g; Sugar 1g; Fat 9g; Saturated fat 4g; Fibre 0.5g; Sodium 219mg.*

☺ Drop Pancakes

Pancakes have been cherished as a favourite breakfast staple around the world for centuries. You can also use this batter to make waffles – just follow the cooking instructions that come with your waffle iron. Dress up your waffles and pancakes by adding sliced bananas or chocolate chips to the batter, or top them with fresh fruit or whipped topping. Personally, we love pancakes and waffles because they soak up lots and lots of syrup.

Preparation time: *10 minutes*

Cooking time: *5 minutes per pancake*

Makes: *8 servings*

100 grams/3½ ounces gluten-free flour mixture	2 large free-range eggs, beaten
1 teaspoon xanthan gum	2 tablespoons vegetable oil
1 teaspoon baking powder	240 millilitres/8½ fluid ounces skimmed milk
Few drops of natural vanilla extract	Vegetable or olive oil spray, for greasing the frying pan

1 Heat a griddle or frying pan over a medium heat. Check whether the pan is hot enough by sprinkling a drop of water on the pan – if the water sizzles immediately, the pan's ready for use. Coat the pan lightly with the non-stick oil spray.

2 In a medium-size mixing bowl, combine the flour mixture, xanthan gum, and baking powder. Add the vanilla, eggs, oil, and milk. Stir the batter until well combined, using a whisk to remove lumps.

3 Use a large spoon to drop about two spoonfuls of batter onto the hot griddle or pan.

4 The pancake should begin to bubble after about 3 minutes. When it does, lift the pancake slightly with a spatula to see whether the underside is golden brown. If it is, flip the pancake over. Check occasionally to see if the pancake is browning. Usually, the pancake takes 2 to 3 minutes to become golden brown on the second side. Lift out of the pan with a spatula and serve on plates with your favourite toppings.

Tip: *Try using 'melted' berries for a healthy syrup option. Put fresh or frozen whole strawberries or blueberries in a saucepan with a little sugar, mash the berries slightly, and add a little water. Heat the mixture slowly until the sugar dissolves in the juice.*

Nutrient analysis per serving: *Calories 114; Protein 3.5g; Carbohydrate 12g; Sugar 3g; Fat 6g; Saturated fat 1g; Fibre 1g; Sodium 183mg.*

☙ Versatile Blueberry Muffins

Nothing makes you feel more like a 1950s American housewife than to call your kids to a breakfast of freshly baked muffins. You have lots of room for creativity here – hence the name *versatile* muffins.

Preparation time: *15 minutes*

Cooking time: *15 minutes*

Makes: *6 servings*

100 grams/3½ ounces gluten-free flour mixture

¼ teaspoon xanthan gum

50 grams/2 ounces granulated sugar

1 teaspoon baking powder

½ teaspoon ground cinnamon

2 teaspoons natural vanilla essence

2 large free-range eggs, beaten

1½ tablespoons vegetable oil

2 teaspoons skimmed milk

50 grams/2 ounces fresh blueberries

Paper muffin cases, for cooking

1 Preheat the oven to 180°C/350°F/Gas Mark 4.

2 In a large bowl, combine the flour mixture, xanthan gum, sugar, baking powder, and cinnamon. Add the vanilla, eggs, oil, and milk. Stir until all the batter is well mixed (using a whisk to remove lumps). Fold in the blueberries.

3 Pour the batter into a muffin tin lined with paper muffin cases.

4 Bake the muffins on the middle shelf for 20 to 25 minutes. Check to see if they're cooked by inserting a cocktail stick into the centre of a muffin. If the toothpick comes out without any batter on it (it may have blueberries on it), the muffins are done. Remove from the tin and leave to cool on a wire rack.

Vary It! *Instead of blueberries, consider using chunks of apples, banana, or other fruit. Add a dash of cinnamon, too.*

Nutrient analysis per serving: *Calories 158; Protein 3g; Carbohydrate 22g; Sugar 11g; Fat 6g; Saturated fat 1g; Fibre 0.5g; Sodium 209mg.*

Serving Up Dinner for Breakfast

Whether freshly prepared in the morning or left over from the night before, sometimes the best breakfast is dinner – after all, who says dinner has to be eaten after a certain hour?

☙ Chile Rellenos Casserole

Whether for breakfast, lunch, or dinner, chile rellenos is a great gluten-free meal that couldn't be much easier to make. When you eat these for breakfast, you're bound to have an *olé* kind of day. Poblano chillies are large dark green peppers abundant in Mexico where they're eaten in the same way that we eat sweet peppers. They're becoming more common in the UK but beware – they vary in strength, from mild to hot. Whatever their heat, they're delicious and full of flavour and we recommend casting aside your fear and trying one. Serve these rellenos with warm corn tortillas and salsa, topped with guacamole for a creamy, flavoursome touch (see Chapter 10 for our guacamole recipe).

Preparation time: *10 minutes*

Cooking time: *25 minutes*

Makes: *8 servings*

6 large free-range eggs

450 grams/1 pound cheddar cheese, grated

450 grams/1 pound mozzarella cheese, grated

8 poblano chillies

Freshly ground salt and pepper to taste

Vegetable or olive oil spray, for greasing the casserole dish

1 Preheat the oven to 180°C/350°F/Gas Mark 4. Spray a 23-by-33-centimetre (9-by-13-inch) casserole dish with non-stick oil.

2 Separate the egg whites from the yolks (use any of the methods shown in Figure 9-1). With an electric mixer on medium speed, whip the whites in a medium bowl until they're stiff. In a small bowl, beat the yolks with a fork or whisk until smooth. Fold the yolks into the whites. Add salt and pepper to taste.

3 Combine the cheeses.

4 Spread about ⅓ of the egg mixture on the bottom of the dish.

5 Split open the chillies, and layer them on top of the egg mixture. Then sprinkle a layer of cheese on top. Continue layering – egg, chillies, cheese – until all the ingredients are used. You should end up with about three layers of each ingredient, finishing with the egg mixture.

6 Bake the chile rellenos for 25 minutes or until golden brown. Cut into slices to serve.

Nutrient analysis per serving: Calories 320; Protein 20.5g; Carbohydrate 1g; Sugar 1g; Fat 25g; Saturated fat 15g; Fibre 0.5g; Sodium 506mg.

Chapter 10

Stylish Gluten-Free Starters

In This Chapter

▶ Preparing finger-licking gluten-free nibbles

▶ Rustling up relishes and spreads for gluten-free dipping

▶ Creating delicious fillings for gluten-free rice rolls and wraps

A really great get-together begins with a great-tasting starter whether you're at a casual gathering of friends and family or an elegant dinner party. Not only does a good starter whet the appetite, but it also whets the imagination, setting the stage for the meal to come.

But anticipation can quickly turn to disappointment for someone on the gluten-free diet, because more often than not, starters turn out to be one enormous glutenfest. And party planners perusing starter recipes for inspiration find that they're likely to contain flour, breadcrumbs, or a myriad of other gluten-containing ingredients, striking fear into hosts and hostesses everywhere: What can I serve that's impressive and gluten-free?

If you find yourself stumped for ideas, never fear: Gluten-free starters are here! Just don't blame us if everyone's too full for the main course.

Fashioning Finger-Lickin'-Good Finger Foods

People love to eat with their fingers. And as long as you're wearing jeans so you can wipe your hands off, what's the harm in dining with your digits? In this section, we bring you some of our favourite recipes that help get the party started with fun finger foods.

Triple Whammy Combo

This combination is our all-time favourite mix of finger lickin' appetisers. You can serve up this combo as a starter for guests, as nibbles to go with drinks, or as a light *al fresco* lunch. You can mix and match the fruits or vegetables to suit your taste but we urge you to try this combination first time round – we're pretty sure that once you've tasted our suggested combination of ingredients you aren't going to want to change a thing!

Parma ham with figs

Preparation: *30 minutes*

Chilling time: *10 minutes*

Makes: *4 servings of each dish*

12 small fresh figs

12 thin slices Parma ham

1 Using a sharp knife cut the figs into quarters lengthways, without cutting right through the skin at the base.

2 Gently pull the flesh of the fruit away from the skin, leaving the central part of the pulp still attached to the skin.

3 Stand the figs on a serving plate and drape the Parma ham between the figs. Keep refrigerated until ready to serve.

Nutrient analysis per serving: *Calories 166; Protein 16g; Carbohydrate 9g; Sugar 9g; Fat 7g; Saturated fat 2g; Fibre 1.6g; Sodium 1080mg.*

Stuffed avocados

2 ripe avocados

1 onion, peeled and chopped

2 tomatoes, chopped

2 hard-boiled eggs, shelled and chopped

100 grams/4 ounces cooked skinless chicken breast, chopped

2 tablespoons mayonnaise

1 Cut the avocados in half, remove the stones, scoop out a little of the flesh around the holes, and put into a small mixing bowl.

2 Add the remaining ingredients to the bowl and mix gently.

3 Pile the chicken mixture into the centre of each avocado half.

4 Refrigerate until ready to serve.

> **Nutrient analysis per serving:** *Calories 342; Protein 12g; Carbohydrate 4g; Sugar 4g; Fat 31g; Saturated fat 6g; Fibre 3.4g; Sodium 134mg.*

Asparagus cocktail

225 grams/8 ounces fresh asparagus

100 grams/4 ounces ham, diced

4 pineapple rings, canned or fresh

4 tablespoons mayonnaise

½ teaspoon brandy (optional)

2 tablespoons fresh lemon juice

Pinch of cayenne pepper

4 large iceberg lettuce leaves

1 Prepare the asparagus by cutting off any woody stems and rinsing under cold running water. Chop into 25-millimetre (1-inch) lengths then boil in water for 10 minutes or until just tender. Drain and cool.

2 Meanwhile, chop the pineapple rings and mix with the diced ham.

3 Add the asparagus to the ham and pineapple.

4 Divide the asparagus, ham, and pineapple mixture between each of the lettuce leaves.

5 In a bowl, mix the mayonnaise, brandy (if using), lemon juice, and cayenne pepper and spoon over the asparagus mixture.

6 Fold the leaves to make a parcel.

7 Serve immediately with the stuffed avocados and Parma ham with figs.

> **Nutrient analysis per serving:** *Calories 285; Protein 6g; Carbohydrate 6g; Sugar 6g; Fat 26g; Saturated fat 4g; Fibre 0.6g; Sodium 464mg.*

☙ Spicy Corn Fritters

This delicious dish uses polenta. Once considered a peasant food, polenta is an Italian cornmeal paste that's becoming quite trendy. You can find polenta at most supermarkets or health-food shops. For this starter, the polenta adds more than just flavour – it actually binds the corn balls together. You can find kaffir lime leaves in the Thai sections of Asian markets and some supermarkets.

Preparation time: *15 minutes*

Cooking time: *25 minutes*

Makes: *4 servings*

150 grams/5½ ounces sweetcorn (canned in water, drained)

2 fresh red chilies, seeded and finely chopped

1 teaspoon crushed garlic (about 2 cloves)

10 kaffir lime leaves, finely chopped

3 tablespoons chopped fresh coriander

2 large free-range eggs, beaten

110 grams/4 ounces ready made polenta

50 grams/1¾ ounces green beans, finely sliced

120 millilitres/4 fluid ounces rapeseed oil (for frying)

1 Place the sweetcorn, chillies, garlic, lime leaves, coriander, eggs, polenta, and green beans into a large bowl; mix them thoroughly. Use your hands to form balls about the size of golf balls. Put them on a plate.

2 Heat the oil in a wok, frying pan, or deep fryer on a high heat. You know that the oil is hot enough when you add a small drop of water into the oil and it pops. (Be careful, though: More than a drop, and it may spit and burn you.)

3 Turning the fritters occasionally, cook them in the oil until they're brown and crispy on the outside (about 7 minutes). Remove the fritters from the pan with a slotted spoon, and let them drain on kitchen roll before serving.

Nutrient analysis per serving: *Calories 302; Protein 5g; Carbohydrate 12g; Sugar 2g; Fat 26g; Saturated fat 5g; Fibre 1.1g; Sodium 38mg.*

Spicy Buffalo Wings

These savoury snacks are actually chicken wings, named *Buffalo* after the city in New York where they originated in 1964. Serve them with celery sticks and a salad dressing.

Preparation time: *5 minutes*

Cooking time: *10 minutes*

Makes: *2 dozen wings*

For the chicken:

150 grams/5½ ounces gluten-free flour mixture

1 teaspoon seasoned salt

24 fresh chicken wings (or defrosted if frozen)

Rapeseed oil, for frying

For the sauce:

120 millilitres/4 fluid ounces red wine vinegar

120 millilitres/4 fluid ounces runny honey

2 tablespoons black treacle

3 tablespoons tomato ketchup

3 tablespoons your favourite hot chilli sauce

Salt and pepper to taste

1 Put the flour mixture and 1 teaspoon of the seasoned salt in a large plastic bag, and shake the bag to mix. Add the wings (about five at a time) and shake the bag to coat them well.

2 Heat the oil over a medium-high heat in a heavy based frying pan. Fry the wings in about 5 centimetres (2 inches) of hot oil for approximately 5 minutes, until they're crispy on the outside. Break a wing open to make sure that the meat inside isn't pink. Drain the wings on kitchen roll.

3 Prepare the sauce by mixing the salt and pepper with the red wine vinegar, honey, treacle, ketchup, and hot sauce together in a medium bowl.

4 Dip the cooked wings in the mixture to coat them with the sauce.

Nutrient analysis per serving: *Calories 200; Protein 10g; Carbohydrate 16g; Sugar 6g; Fat 11g; Saturated fat 3g; Fibre 0.2g; Sodium 438mg.*

Helpful hints if you're relying on frying

Far from being one of the healthier modes of cooking, frying is, nonetheless, a common method for cooking many finger foods. Here are some important tips to help you create the perfect crunch:

✔ **Use oil you designate for gluten-free foods.** If you're preparing gluten-containing foods and gluten-free ones, make sure that you cook the gluten-free foods first or change the oil in between batches. Breadcrumbs and batters can contaminate the oil, turning your gluten-free goodie into an unwitting source of wheat.

✔ **Choose the right oil.** Some oils, like olive and sesame oil, aren't meant to be heated to the very high temperatures that deep-frying requires. Corn, rapeseed, and peanut oils are some of the best deep-frying oils, because they have a high smoking point. Find an oil that matches the flavour profile of the food you're cooking and turn down the heat if your oil begins to smoke, which

indicates the oil is degrading. Degrading oil can affect the flavour of the food.

✔ **Don't overload the basket.** If you're impatient, like we are, you may be tempted to 'hurry' the cooking process by cooking as much as you can at once. Overloading the basket can result in uneven cooking and may even cause the food to absorb extra oil.

✔ **Filter and clean often.** If the oil gets smoky or has debris in it, change it for new oil and start again. Clean your frying pans and deep-fat fryer regularly.

Once you've finished frying or deep-frying your favourite gluten-free goodies, you need to decide what to do with the used cooking oil. You can't just pour it down the sink; that's not only bad for the environment, but it's also bound to clog the pipes. After the oil has completely cooled, pour it into an empty can or jar with a lid. Seal the lid tightly and throw it in the bin. Keep empty cans and lids on hand to use for getting rid of used cooking oil

---

Indulging in Dips

Whether you're dipping vegetable crudités, crisps, or fried foods, a few good dips go a long way, and you can vary your repertoire of basic recipes to create exciting gluten-free graze-ables. Although many dips are inherently gluten-free, others require just a few tweaks here and there to make them safe for anyone avoiding gluten.

Double-dipping is *not* allowed, especially if some of the guests are eating gluten-containing foods. After people have dunked gobs of gluten into the dip, it's no longer gluten-free.

By the way, dips aren't just for dipping. Use them as fillings for hollowed veg or halved hard-boiled eggs, or spread them on crêpes (you can find a recipe in Chapter 9) or corn tortillas – you can roll the filling into a wrap and eat the whole thing as a tasty picnic snack or slice it into a stylish roulade.

✎ Artichoke and Spinach Dip

You aren't going to find this recipe in *Dieting For Dummies,* but it is gluten-free! Use this cheesy dip with corn tortilla chips, rice crackers, vegetable sticks, or deep-fried potato skins. Or if you have a favourite gluten-free bread, slice it thinly, toast it, and spread the artichoke and spinach dip on top.

Preparation time: *10 minutes*

Cooking time: *25 minutes*

Makes: *12 servings*

225 grams/8 ounces cream cheese

4 tablespoons mayonnaise

½ teaspoon crushed garlic (about 1 clove)

Handful of fresh basil leaves

Freshly ground salt and pepper to taste

100 grams/3½ ounces Parmesan cheese, grated

100 grams/3½ ounces Manchego cheese, grated

40 grams/1½ ounces mozzarella cheese, grated

400 grams/1 x 14 ounce jar artichoke hearts, drained and chopped

100 grams/3½ ounces canned spinach, drained and chopped

Non-stick oil spray, for greasing the dish

1 Preheat the oven to 180°C/350°F/Gas Mark 4. Let the cream cheese warm to room temperature.

2 In a large bowl, cream together the cream cheese, mayonnaise, garlic, basil, and salt and pepper. Setting aside a few teaspoons of each cheese to use as a topping, add the Parmesan, Manchego, and mozzarella cheeses. Mix until well blended.

3 Add the artichoke hearts and spinach, and mix again.

4 Spray an ovenproof serving dish with non-stick oil spray, pour in the dip, and top it with the cheese that was put aside in Step 2.

5 Bake the dip for about 25 minutes or until the top begins to brown and the cheese has melted. Serve the dip from the dish or spoon onto a platter with a selection of dippers.

Nutrient analysis per serving: Calories 213; Protein 8g; Carbohydrate 2g; Sugar 0.5g; Fat 19g; Saturated fat 10g; Fibre 0.1g; Sodium 501mg.

◔ *Guacamole*

Guacamole is an avocado-based dip that originated in Mexico. Most guacamole recipes start with fresh, peeled avocados and add lime (or lemon) juice, tomatoes, onions, coriander, garlic, and spices. The lime juice keeps the guacamole from turning brown when you expose it to the air. Leaving the avocado stone in the guacamole until just before serving also decreases browning. For this guacamole, feel free to kick it up a notch with your favourite hot chilli sauce.

Preparation time: *15 minutes*

Makes: *6 servings*

2 ripe avocados	*4 tablespoons fresh lime juice*
1 small-to-medium ripe tomato, diced	*2 teaspoons chopped coriander*
½ small red onion, chopped	*2 teaspoons Worcestershire sauce*
½ teaspoon finely cut jalapeño pepper	*Freshly ground salt and pepper to taste*

1 Peel the avocados, remove the flesh from the stones, and cut into cubes. Save the stones. (Check out Figure 10-1 if you're not sure how to remove the stone from an avocado.)

2 In a medium bowl, combine the avocado flesh, tomato, onion, jalapeño, lime juice, coriander, Worcestershire sauce, and salt and pepper.

3 Mix all the ingredients well, but keep the guacamole lumpy. Place the avocado stone in the dip, removing it just prior to serving.

Nutrient analysis per serving: *Calories 95; Protein 1g; Carbohydrate 1g; Sugar 1g; Fat 9g; Saturated fat 2g; Fibre 1.8g; Sodium 25mg.*

How to De-seed and Peel an Avocado

Figure 10-1:
De-stoning
an avocado.

Slice avocado in half lengthwise and pull apart.

Firmly strike the seed with a chef's knife.

Lift the seed out with a gentle twist of the knife.

GENTLY scoop out the meat with a spoon.

chop or slice according to your recipe.

Becoming an avocado aficionado

Avocados are one of nature's prepackaged wonder foods. Most people think they're a vegetable, but they're actually a fruit. Loaded with potassium (60 per cent more than bananas!) and good-for-you monounsaturated fat, avocados are virtually sodium- and saturated-fat-free. Some interesting avocado factoids follow:

✔ One avocado tree can produce about 120 avocados each year. That's about 25–30 kilograms of fruit.

✔ In many areas avocados grow all year-round.

✔ In Latin America, people wrap avocados and give them as wedding gifts.

✔ Some people claim avocados are an aphrodisiac.

✇ Mango Salsa

Salsas come in endless forms and flavours. Fresh mango salsa is versatile and easy to make. You can serve it as a dip or use it to dress up main courses, serving with grilled pork, chicken, or salmon. You can also use it to make fish tacos – just spoon this salsa over cooked fish and wrap the mixture in a corn tortilla.

Preparation time: *20 minutes*

Makes: *6 servings1 ripe mango, peeled, stoned, and diced*

½ medium red onion, finely chopped	2 tablespoons fresh coriander, chopped
1 jalapeño pepper, minced	4 tablespoons fresh lime juice
1 large tomato, diced	Freshly ground salt and pepper to taste

1 Combine the mango, onion, jalapeño, tomato, coriander lime juice, and salt and pepper in a bowl; mix until well-blended. Don't mix so hard that you mash the mango – the salsa should be chunky.

2 Chill the salsa for an hour or more to infuse the flavours.

Tip: See Figure 10-2 to see how to dice a mango. With that big seed in the middle, they aren't easy to work with.

Nutrient analysis per serving: Calories 26; Protein 0.8g; Carbohydrate 5.3g; Sugar 5.2g; Fat 0.2g; Saturated fat 0.0g; Fibre 1.1g; Sodium 0.025mg.

Simple but sexy spreads

The difference between a dip and a spread lies in its consistency. A dip is creamier, and so even a fragile dipper can withstand the pressure of a good dig through a dip. On the other hand, you usually serve a spread with spreading knives and load on to crackers or tortillas.

Today, several widely available varieties of rice, corn, and nut crackers make the perfect gluten-free crackers for spreads. Consider using these ideas to impress your guests but still have plenty of time left to enjoy your own party:

- **Brown sugar on baked brie:** Place a wedge or round of brie cheese on an ovenproof serving platter. Top the cheese with a layer (about 6 millimetres, ¼ inch, thick) of light brown sugar. Bake at 180°C/350°F/Gas Mark 4 for 8 minutes or until the inside of the cheese appears to be soft.

- **Crab cream cheese brick:** Set a brick of cream cheese on a serving platter. Drain a can of crab meat and spread the meat evenly over the top of the cream cheese. Drizzle a tasty, spicy sauce over the top (make a cool design if you feel so inclined).

- **Hummus:** Hummus is made from chickpeas and is flavoured with seasonings such as garlic and spices. Traditional hummus contains *tahini*, a sesame seed paste. Usually available at any large supermarket or health-food shop, hummus' consistency sits between a spread and a dip, and so it works well for either purpose.

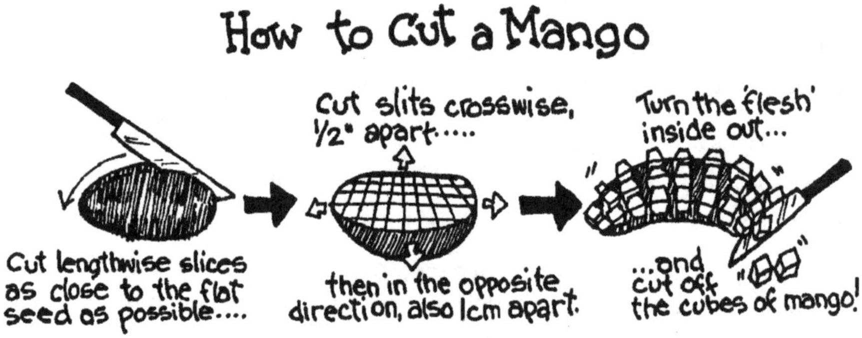

Figure 10-2: Dicing a mango.

How to Cut a Mango

Cut lengthwise slices as close to the flat seed as possible....

Cut slits crosswise, ½" apart.....

then in the opposite direction, also 1cm apart.

Turn the 'flesh' inside out...

...and cut off the cubes of mango!

⊙ *Homemade Tortilla Chips*

Corn tortilla chips, or *totopos* in Spanish, are great for scooping up salsas or dips. You can sprinkle them with a little grated cheese and serve them with other dishes, such as soups. Use corn tortillas that are a few days old; fresh tortillas don't crisp as well when you fry them.

Preparation time: *15 minutes*

Cooking time: *15 minutes*

Makes: *48 chips*

8 corn tortillas	*Salt*
1 tablespoon of rapeseed oil, for frying	

1 Cut each corn tortilla into six triangular wedges.

2 Pour the oil into a large, heavy based frying pan (or deep fryer) so that at least 13 millimetres (½ an inch) of oil is covering the bottom. You want enough oil in the pan so that both sides of the tortilla can cook at the same time. Place the pan over a medium-high heat.

3 Test the oil temperature by putting one tortilla wedge into the oil. If it bubbles and floats, the oil is hot enough. If not, discard that wedge and wait for the oil to heat some more.

4 Fry the tortilla wedges until golden brown (just a few moments). Use a slotted spoon or tongs to remove them from the oil then lay the chips out on sheets of kitchen roll to soak up any excess oil.

5 Sprinkle the tortilla wedges with salt, and serve.

Vary It! *To make lower-fat tortilla chips, bake fresh corn tortillas at 200°C/400°F / Gas Mark 6 for 8 to 10 minutes or until they're crispy. You can cut the tortillas into triangles before baking or break them into chips afterwards.*

Nutrient analysis per serving: Calories 158; Protein 2.3g; Carbohydrate 17.8g; Sugar 0.4g; Fat 8.6g; Saturated fat 1.2g; Fibre 2.5g; Sodium 0.05mg.

Getting to Grips with Wraps and Rolls

As one of today's most popular food trends, wraps offer never-ending possibilities for gluten-free dishes, many of which make great starters or main dishes. The only limits to what you can make into a wrap are your creativity and your sense of adventure. Use corn tortillas, crêpes, rice wraps, or lettuce for your wrapper, and then let your imagination run wild as you concoct clever, flavourful fillings depending on which wrapper you're using. (See Chapter 9 for a gluten-free crêpe recipe.)

A word of advice, though: You may want to skip the wraps on a first date or when you have the boss over for dinner. They're delicious but attempting to eat them doesn't always make the best impression: A serving of these finger foods usually turns into a fistful.

If you're having trouble deciding what to put in your wraps, we give you some recipes to impress all your guests in the following sections. But here are some ideas to get you started:

- **Caesar salad wrap:** Actually, any salad works well in a wrap, especially in a corn tortilla wrapper.

- **Fajita:** Fajitas are basically a Mexican blend of marinated meat and sautéed onions and peppers wrapped in a tortilla. Feel free to get creative, though, and use any meat or veg or bean combination you like. You generally serve the fillings separately from the tortillas so guests can load up their wraps themselves.

- **Fish wraps:** In California, these wraps are called 'fish tacos'. The taco or wrap is a corn tortilla stuffed with cooked fish. Add some 'Mango Salsa' from the recipe given earlier in this chapter, and you've got yourself a gourmet meal!

- **Leftovers wrap:** Seriously, every fridge on the planet has something in it that you can make into a wrap. Go for it. Mix. Blend. Be wild and crazy, and clean out the refrigerator at the same time.

- **Pulled pork wrap:** You can use a barbecue sauce, salsa, or flavoured mayonnaise to add more flavour to your pork pieces in this wrap. A corn tortilla or lettuce wrap works well with this combination.

- **Quesadilla:** A *quesadilla* is simply a folded tortilla – corn, for the gluten-free crowd – with melted cheese inside.

- **Spicy Southwest wrap:** If you're looking for a little zap in your wrap, spice it up with a Southwest flair. Wrap up any burrito or enchilada (parcels made from a folded tortilla) filling with lettuce or a corn tortilla.

Perfecting rice rolls

Rice rolls are a great type of wrap. Available in ethnic markets or the ethnic sections of larger supermarkets, rice paper wrappers come from a paste of ground rice and water, which are stamped into rounds and dried. When moistened, the brittle sheets of rice paper become flexible, making rice paper perfect for wraps. Rice paper wrappers can be tricky to use, but they're well worth the effort after you've mastered working with them.

Pre-made wrappers and bottled dipping sauces are readily available in Asian markets and the Asian section of most supermarkets. The secret to making great rice rolls is to use the freshest ingredients, moisten the rice paper wrappers until they're pliable but not too wet, and roll the bundles tightly. Try these tips and tricks:

1. **Soak 'em.**

   To make the rice paper wrappers pliable for folding, you need to soak them one at a time for about 4 to 5 seconds until they're soft. Although some people simply use hot water for soaking, others believe the key to making a rice wrap that's pliable but doesn't fall apart is in the mixture. If hot water makes your wrapper fall apart, try this for your soaking mixture:

   120 millilitres warm water

   25 grams sugar

   4 tablespoons cider vinegar

2. **Drain the wrappers on a flat surface.**

   You can use your hands to take the wrappers out of the water and lay them flat on a cutting board or plate. Don't put them on top of each other, though, or they stick together and you never get them apart. Pat them dry. Handling rice paper wrappers can be tricky, because they tend to stick to themselves. Be patient. With a few attempts, you can get the hang of handling them.

3. **Layer the ingredients in the wrapper.**

   Folding rice paper wrappers can be tricky: They're liable to stick to themselves or seem to rip in all the wrong places. To avoid ripping, don't overfill the softened wrappers. The easiest way to prevent tearing is to layer the filling mixture.

4. **Fold with finesse.**

   Check out Figure 10-3 to see how to fold these wraps.

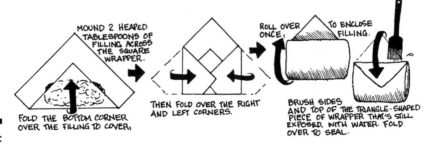

Figure 10-3:
Rolling and folding rice paper rolls.

MOUND 2 HEAPED TABLESPOONS OF FILLING ACROSS THE SQUARE WRAPPER.

FOLD THE BOTTOM CORNER OVER THE FILLING TO COVER,

THEN FOLD OVER THE RIGHT AND LEFT CORNERS.

ROLL OVER ONCE, TO ENCLOSE FILLING.

BRUSH SIDES AND TOP OF THE TRIANGLE-SHAPED PIECE OF WRAPPER THAT'S STILL EXPOSED, WITH WATER. FOLD OVER TO SEAL.

COVER THE SPRING ROLLS WITH A TOWEL TO PREVENT DRYING.

To give your rice wraps an extra special look, garnish them with a few sprigs of chives or spring onions poking out one end of each roll.

Vietnamese Rice Wraps, or Summer Rolls (Goi Cuon)

Get on a summer roll. Goi cuon (pronounced *goy koong*) is a fresh counterpart to the spring roll, which is fried. Summer rolls are delicious, nutritious, and gluten-free. You can make them with the rice paper wraps we talk about in the preceding section and fill them with raw vegetables, such as shredded iceberg lettuce, carrots, cucumber, spring onions, bean sprouts, mint, and basil. Add shiitake mushrooms and tofu for another variation. The meat inside these rolls can be cooked chicken, pork, prawns or fish.

Preparation time: *30 minutes*

Makes: *1 roll*

1 sheet of rice-paper wrapper

2 peeled and cooked prawns, cut lengthwise and sliced

3 iceberg lettuce leaves, washed and dried then torn to about the size of a deck of cards

3 fresh mint leaves

1 tablespoon bean sprouts

2 tablespoons rice vermicelli, soaked in warm water until soft

5 very thin slices of cooked pork

1 Soak a single rice wrapper in hot water or in a soaking mixture (see the numbered steps at the beginning of the 'Rice rolls' section) for 4 to 5 seconds. Drain the wrapper on a flat surface and pat dry.

2 Layer the ingredients in the rice wrapper: Prawns first, followed by the lettuce, mint, bean sprouts, vermicelli, and pork.

3 Fold the right side of the wrapper toward the centre then fold the short ends over the filling. Roll the wrapper gently – but firmly and tightly – toward the left until you form a neat, oblong bundle. Slice each roll in half at a slight diagonal.

Vary It! *For a vegetarian summer roll, substitute tofu for the prawns and pork.*

Tip: *This recipe makes one wrap. If you're going to make several wraps at once, you may want to gather the ingredients and separate them into bowls. You can refrigerate the ingredients for up to three hours before putting the wraps together.*

Nutrient analysis per serving: *Calories 143; Protein 12.3g; Carbohydrate 15.3g; Sugar 1g; Fat 3.6g; Saturated fat 1.2g; Fibre 0.8g; Sodium 1.2mg.*

Pork Spring Rolls

Although many spring rolls use a wheat-based wrapper, using rice wrappers works really well and makes a gluten-free version of this delicious treat. Because you fry spring rolls, they're not quite as healthy as the fresh summer rolls, but they're definitely delicious.

Preparation time: *30 minutes*

Cooking time: *10 minutes*

Makes: *8 servings*

8 rice paper wrappers

110 grams/4 ounces ground pork, cooked and drained

340 grams/12 ounces cabbage, shredded

3 carrots, shredded

75 grams/3 ounces onion, diced

1 teaspoon crushed garlic (about 2 cloves)

1 teaspoon minced fresh ginger

Freshly ground salt and pepper to taste

Corn oil, for frying

1 Soak the rice wrappers, one at a time, in hot water or in a soaking mixture (see the numbered steps at the beginning of the 'Rice rolls' section) for 4 to 5 seconds. Drain the wrappers on a flat surface and pat them dry.

2 In a large bowl, combine the pork, cabbage, carrots, onion, garlic, ginger, and salt and pepper.

3 Drop 2 tablespoons of the mixture into a softened wrapper. Fold the right side of the wrapper toward the centre. Fold the short ends over the filling. Roll the wrapper gently – but firmly and tightly – toward the left until you form a neat, oblong bundle. Place the rolls seam-side down onto wax or parchment paper until you're ready to cook them.

4 Heat the corn oil in a frying pan over high heat to about 350°C/650°F (check using a cooking thermometer). To test the oil's temperature, dip a corner of a roll into it. If the oil bubbles, it's ready. Fry the rolls two at a time in very hot oil until they're golden brown, for approximately 4 minutes.

5 Carefully remove the cooked rolls from the oil with a slotted spoon then place on to sheets of kitchen roll to drain.

Tip: You can freeze these rolls to use later. To reheat, bake them in a preheated oven at 190°C/375°F / Gas Mark 5 until warmed through, for about 10 minutes.

Tip: If the rice wrapper tears while you're preparing a roll, don't start all over again. Just use a second wrapper over the first one. You end up with a thicker skin, which you may prefer anyway.

Nutrient analysis per serving: Calories 227; Protein 4.5g; Carbohydrate 13.9g; Sugar 4.9g; Fat 17g; Saturated fat 2.8g; Fibre 2.3g; Sodium 0.3mg.

Exploring lettuce wraps

One of the coolest things about lettuce wraps – besides the cool, crisp palate-cleansing wrap itself – is the versatility they offer gluten-free diners. You can stuff lettuce wraps with any kind of meat, seafood, poultry, vegetables, beans, and cheese combinations.

Here are a few things to ensure that your lettuce wraps make an even bigger hit:

✔ **Use large, pliable leaves.** Consider iceberg and radicchio leaves or large spinach leaves. Core the lettuce and soak it in iced water for a couple of hours to help you remove the leaves off the head without tearing them.

✔ **Dry the lettuce before serving.** After you've removed the leaves, let them drain individually, and then lay them on some kitchen towel in the fridge for a couple of hours to make them crisp.

✔ **Serve the lettuce chilled.** Cold lettuce leaves make a great contrast to the warm innards you fill them with. Also, they hold together better when they're chilled; otherwise they tend to collapse into limp, lifeless leaves.

✔ **Use a variety of colours, textures, and flavours in the filling.** Ensure that your fillings have bold flavours, and varying texture and colour. Consider using flavourful ingredients like mustard, yogurt, plum sauce, hoisin sauce, and sesame oil in your fillings. When you're trying to decide what to serve, think about your stash of leftovers. They can usually inspire and delight you.

✔ **Make the fillings and sauces in advance.** Fillings are usually served chilled, and so make them in advance, which gives them time to refrigerate and you the chance to get on with preparing something else.

✔ **Let your guests assemble their own wraps.** People love to fill their own lettuce wraps, and so place the leaves and fillings where everyone can reach them.

Asian Pork Lettuce Wraps

The variety of lettuce wraps you can make is endless. This recipe follows one of the most basic approaches to lettuce wraps, featuring ground pork and an array of Asian flavours. You can also substitute minced or ground chicken for the pork. Serve the wraps with individual containers of peanut sauce or any type of gluten-free Asian dipping sauce.

Preparation time: *15 minutes*

Cooking time: *2 minutes*

Makes: *6 servings*

450 grams/1 pound cooked ground pork	*3 tablespoons grated carrot*
3 tablespoons rice vinegar	*100 grams/3½ ounces cooked rice vermicelli*
2 tablespoons gluten-free soy sauce	*Freshly ground salt and pepper to taste*
2 teaspoons sesame oil	*6 large chilled lettuce leaves*
2½ tablespoons chopped spring onions	

1 In a medium glass bowl, combine the cooked ground pork, rice vinegar, soy sauce, sesame oil, spring onions, carrot, and rice vermicelli. Season the ingredients with salt and pepper and mix well.

2 Cover the mixture and heat in a microwave oven on high for about 2 minutes, until the mixture is hot.

3 Serve the pork mixture in a bowl with a large serving spoon. On a separate platter, arrange a stack of chilled lettuce leaves (see the earlier section 'Exploring lettuce wraps' for why they should be chilled) so people can fill their own wraps.

Nutrient analysis per serving: Calories 211; Protein 29.8g; Carbohydrate 11.4g; Sugar 1.7g; Fat 9.6g; Saturated fat 3.2g; Fibre 0.4g; Sodium 1mg.

Chapter 11

Sensational Gluten-Free Soups, Salads, and Side Dishes

. . . .

In This Chapter

▶ Getting bowled over by delicious gluten-free soups

▶ Putting salads and dressings into a fresh perspective

▶ Stimulating your side dishes with mouthwatering gluten-free ideas

. . . .

Soups, salads, and side dishes can be just as important as the main meal itself. In fact, they can be the meal itself. But many soups are thickened with flour, salads are often dressed up and garnished with gluten-laden goodies, and side dishes are sometimes seasoned with sauces that make them unsuitable for people enjoying a gluten-free lifestyle.

So should you just forget about creamy soups, crunchy croutons, and rich, thick sauces or seasonings on your favourite side dishes? Are you stuck with boring salads of just lettuce and tomatoes? We don't think so. Are you limited to the old gluten-free standbys of rice, corn, and potatoes? No way. Stick with us, and you can whip up some scrumptious accompaniments to rival – or even serve as – the main course.

Creating a Storm in a Soup Cup

Soup has been a versatile and important part of people's diet for about 5,000 years. Soups can be hot, cold, thick, thin, creamy, chunky, sweet, savoury, elegant, or simple. You can create them from virtually anything in your cupboard, they're quick and cheap to make, and can help clear out your fridge of leftovers. Soups are comforting, satisfying, and nutritious.

Make no bones about it

The origin of the expression to 'make no bones about it' actually stems from eating soup. Today it means to speak frankly and directly – to have no difficulty or hesitation in saying what you want to say. But when a version of the phrase appeared in 1459, the author was making an analogy to soups that didn't contain bones; diners wouldn't hesitate to swallow their soup, because they didn't need to worry about eating around the bones.

However, commercial soups often contain flour, pasta, or other ingredients that make them taboo on a gluten-free diet. Fortunately, great-tasting gluten-free soups are easy to make, and even noodle-based soups are a breeze. And when you make soups yourself, they're generally more wholesome and you get to choose what goes in them, so you're bound to enjoy eating them even more.

Quinoa Vegetable Soup

This super-healthy soup suits just about anyone whatever their dietary requirements. As well as being gluten-free, it contains no dairy or egg and is even suitable for vegans. You're going to be amazed at how a recipe that's so 'free from' can taste so good!

Preparation time: *25 minutes*

Cooking time: *10 minutes*

Makes: *4 servings*

1 tablespoon vegetable oil
50 grams/2 ounces quinoa
1 carrot, peeled and diced
1 celery stick, diced
2 tablespoons finely chopped onion
½ green pepper, deseeded and diced

2 cloves garlic, peeled and crushed
960 millilitres/32 fluid ounces cold water
2 large tomatoes, finely chopped
50 grams/2 ounces cabbage, chopped
Freshly ground salt and pepper to taste

1 Heat the oil in a large saucepan, add the quinoa, carrot, celery, onion, pepper, and garlic and fry gently until golden.

2 Add the water, tomatoes, and cabbage. Stir and bring to the boil. Reduce the heat and simmer for 10 minutes.

3 Season with salt and pepper and serve hot.

Nutrient analysis per serving: *Calories 92; Protein 3g; Carbohydrate 12g; Sugar 6g; Fat 4g; Saturated fat 1g; Fibre 2g; Sodium 515mg.*

Faux Pho – Thai-Namese Prawn and Chicken Soup

This soup is our simplified version of a traditional Vietnamese noodle soup called pho. ('Faux pho' is supposed to be a play on words, except that the real pronunciation of the Vietnamese word is *fuh*. It may be a rather poor joke but we're sticking to it, so bear with us.) Today the soup is a worldwide favourite, with many variations. Our version has a Thai influence, with the fish sauce, ginger, and curry, but the rice noodles make it Vietnamese; hence the name 'Thai-Namese'.

Tools: *Heavy based pan with tight fitting lid*

Preparation time: *15 minutes*

Cooking time: *20 minutes*

Makes: *4 servings*

1 litre/1¾ pints chicken stock

227 millilitres/8 fluid ounces fish stock

2 tablespoons fish sauce

2 teaspoons crushed garlic (about 4 cloves)

2 teaspoons minced fresh ginger

¾ teaspoon red curry paste

225 grams/8 ounces fresh mushrooms, sliced

450 grams/1 pound large raw prawns, peeled

225 grams/8 ounces fresh chicken breasts, skinned and boned, cut into 25-millimetre (1-inch) cubes

65 grams/2½ ounces fresh mangetout, trimmed

Juice of 2 fresh limes

2 tablespoons granulated sugar

2 tablespoons spring onion tops, chopped

2 tablespoons chopped fresh coriander

400 grams/13½ ounces (usually 1 can) light coconut milk

700 grams/1½ pounds cooked rice noodles (slightly firm)

1 Combine the chicken stock, fish stock, fish sauce, garlic, ginger, and red curry paste together in a large casserole, stirring the ingredients with a whisk. Add the mushrooms, and bring the mixture to a boil over medium heat.

2 Reduce the heat and simmer the soup for 5 minutes. Add the prawns, chicken, and mangetout, and then bring the soup to the boil. Cover the soup, reduce the heat, and simmer for 5 minutes.

3 Stir in the lime juice, sugar, spring onion tops, coriander, and coconut milk. Cook the soup for 4 minutes or until it's thoroughly heated. Add the cooked rice noodles just before serving.

Nutrient analysis per serving: Calories 287; Protein 5g; Carbohydrate 40g; Sugar 22g; Fat 12g; Saturated fat 1.5g; Fibre 1.5g; Sodium 30mg.

Is chicken soup really nature's remedy for the common cold?

More than half of chicken soup sales in the UK take place during the cold and flu season. That's because many people believe that chicken soup has healing properties. Physician Moses Maimonides first proposed using chicken soup as a cold and asthma remedy in the 12th century, and scientists have studied the therapeutic properties of chicken soup extensively in recent decades. These studies indicate that scientific evidence supports this belief.

Most people agree that chicken soup has some positive effect on cold and flu symptoms, though they disagree about why. Some say that the steam helps clear up congestion. Others say that the blend of nutrients and vitamins in chicken soup slows the activity of certain white blood cells, reducing the pain and swelling that occurs when these cells fight infection; this temporarily relieves common cold and flu symptoms. And still others claim that the spices in the soup – garlic and pepper, for instance – thin the mucus and make breathing easier. Nearly all doctors agree that increasing fluid intake by eating the soup also relieves congestion.

Whether or not chicken soup really is a cure-all, it's delicious – and easy to make. Start from scratch, or use ready made gluten-free chicken stock (fresh or from a cube – check the label or *The Food and Drink Directory* for one that's gluten-free). Then add your favourite ingredients, like chunks of chicken, vegetables, beans, rice, and gluten-free noodles.

Many Thai ingredients are inherently gluten-free, although you do need to check the labels, especially in Westernised products. Fish sauce is a good example. Traditional fish sauce comes from fermented, salt-cured fish, and most fish sauce is just that – fish. But you may occasionally find a label that shows added wheat. Remember, you always need to read labels carefully. Authentic Asian products are labelled in English even if they've been imported.

Making Strides with Salads and Side Dishes

Most plain green salads are gluten-free – and of course, you can serve up steamed or boiled vegetables – but even hard-core veggie fans get tired of these options pretty quickly. In this section, we show you ways to dress up delicious and nutritious salads, and ideas for speedy satisfying dishes to make in a jiffy.

Some accompaniments fall somewhere between a salad and a side dish. These dishes aren't the simple salad variety; instead, they feature potatoes, pasta, rice, and other alternative salad ingredients.

Adding taste and texture to green leafy salads

Salads offer a great way to combine interesting grains, fruits, vegetables, and meats in one dish. Served on the side or as a complete meal, salads are nutritious and delicious, and they're especially great on a hot, summer's day, when they make a welcomed cool, quick dinner (without you having to resort to a bowl of cereal and milk).

Most of these salads start with a basic bed of greens or a variety of lettuce. Pre-washed salad leaf selections make life even simpler, but of course you can use any type of lettuce you want. Remember, the darker the leaf, the more nutritious the salad – watercress and spinach are vitamin-packed dark green leaves.

A few of our personal favourites include:

- ✔ **Caesar salad:** Chop up a head of romaine lettuce and add Caesar dressing. You can buy the dressing ready made or make your own following the easy recipe in this chapter. Remember to add freshly grated Parmesan cheese.

- ☞ **Cool as a cucumber salad:** In a medium-sized bowl, mix finely chopped cucumber (peeled and seeded) with plain yogurt, some finely diced spring onions, lemon juice, and black pepper. Spread it over a bed of green leaves and top with freshly chopped tomatoes.

- ✔ **Grilled garlic chicken salad:** In a small bowl, mix 3 to 4 tablespoons of Italian salad dressing with 2 teaspoons of crushed garlic and a dash of crushed red pepper flakes. Add slices of red pepper and mushrooms to the dressing, and toss to coat them. Fish the peppers and mushrooms out of the dressing, setting the remaining dressing aside, and grill them with your chicken. Place handfuls of salad greens on plates and top with the grilled vegetables and chicken. Drizzle over the remaining dressing.

- ✔ **Thai beef salad:** Start with a bed of greens and add 2 tablespoons of fresh mint leaves (torn into large pieces), half a cucumber (peeled and sliced), several thinly sliced pieces of grilled rump steak, 2 tablespoons chopped peanuts, and lime wedges (for garnish). Top the salad with an Asian salad dressing (see the one we give later in this section).

○ **Tomato and basil salad:** Over a bed of green salad leaves, add sliced steak tomatoes topped with a scattering of freshly torn basil leaves. If you fancy, add a slice of buffalo mozzarella. Then drizzle the salad with balsamic vinaigrette dressing.

○ **Warm beetroot salad:** In a large saucepan, cook some green beans in boiling water until tender (takes about 8 minutes). Add a jar of sliced beetroot (drained), and cook over medium heat until heated through. Drain the beans and the beetroot. Meanwhile, in a screw-top glass jar, combine about 3 tablespoons orange juice, 3 tablespoons extra-virgin olive oil, 1 tablespoon balsamic vinegar, 2 teaspoons crushed garlic, and a dash of white pepper. Shake the dressing well. Arrange some mixed greens on plates, place the beans and beetroot on top, and coat the veggies with the dressing.

Drizzling over dressings

Many commercially available salad dressings are gluten-free. People used to think that most salad dressings were unsuitable for those on a gluten-free diet, but that was because they thought vinegar wasn't allowed. Now that they know vinegar is okay, store shelves are loaded with ready to use options. But if you prefer to make your own dressings – because you enjoy doing so, you save money, and the result is fresher and healthier – the recipes in this section can get you started in the right direction.

No time for following complicated recipes? Check out these quick and easy dressings to add to your salads (simply adjust the amount of oil, vinegar, or lemon juice to achieve your desired consistency and taste):

✔ **Roasted red pepper vinaigrette:** Mix chopped roasted red peppers with white wine vinegar, crushed garlic, chopped flat-leaf parsley, extra-virgin olive oil, and salt and pepper.

✔ **Chickpea vinaigrette:** Mix coarsely mashed chickpeas with sherry vinegar, a good handful of finely chopped shallots, chives, and parsley, and combine with a few glugs of extra-virgin olive oil. Season to taste with freshly ground salt and pepper.

✔ **Lemon Parmesan dressing:** Mix fresh lemon juice and freshly grated Parmesan cheese with mayonnaise, crushed garlic, extra-virgin olive oil, and salt and pepper.

✔ **Pesto vinaigrette:** Mix a tablespoon of ready made pesto sauce with white wine vinegar, extra-virgin olive oil, and salt and pepper.

Don't fear the fat on salads

Most people are well aware that smothering their salads in fatty salad dressings turns a healthy meal into a high-fat, diet-sabotaging indulgence. So they opt for fat-free salad dressings in the belief that they're making a healthy choice. But a study published by the *American Journal of Clinical Nutrition* shows that people may be compromising the nutritional value of their salads by doing this, because some dietary fat is necessary for the absorption of nutrients from fruits and vegetables. In the study, people who ate salads with completely fat-free salad dressing absorbed far less of the helpful nutrients and vitamins from spinach, lettuce, tomatoes, and carrots than those who ate their salads with a salad dressing containing some fat.

Bear in mind, though, that you don't have to get the fat from your dressing, and you don't have to eat very much fat to help with the absorption of these important nutrients. Eating just a handful of nuts or a quarter of an avocado gives you enough dietary fat to help with absorption.

☜ Asian Salad Dressing

Most commercial Asian salad dressings use soy sauce, and they nearly all contain wheat. Asian salad dressing is easy to make yourself, though, and to keep it gluten-free, just use any type of gluten-free soy sauce. This dressing can also double as a marinade for meats or tofu.

Preparation time: *5 minutes*

Makes: *8 servings*

120 millilitres/4 fluid ounce rice vinegar

4 tablespoons gluten-free soy sauce

2 tablespoons water

1 teaspoon sesame oil

1 teaspoon toasted sesame seeds (simply dry roast them in a hot frying pan for a couple of minutes)

80 millilitres/2⅔ fluid ounces rapeseed oil

1 Combine the vinegar, soy sauce, water, sesame oil, and sesame seeds in a jar with a tight-fitting lid, and shake the mixture well.

2 Add the rapeseed oil and shake again.

Nutrient analysis per serving: Calories 101; Protein 0.3g; Carbohydrate 1g; Sugar 1g; Fat 11g; Saturated fat 1g; Fibre 0g; Sodium 535mg.

Caesar Salad Dressing

Everyone loves the dressing that accompanies Caesar salad, and you can make it in a number of ways. The real chefs prepare it at the table, gently mixing one ingredient at a time. Not us. We cheat. We make it in a blender or small food processor, and it takes less than 5 minutes to prepare. We haven't had a complaint yet.

Tools: *Blender or food processor*

Preparation time: *5 minutes*

Makes: *8 servings*

1 large free-range egg, beaten

120 millilitres/4 fluid ounces fresh lemon juice

120 millilitres/4 fluid ounces extra-virgin olive oil

2 teaspoons crushed garlic (about 4 cloves)

2 tablespoons gluten-free Worcestershire sauce

75 grams/3 ounces Parmesan cheese, freshly grated

56 grams/2½ ounce can anchovies

1 teaspoon freshly grated black pepper

1 Place the egg in a microwaveable dish and cover it with kitchen roll. Heat the egg in the microwave on high for 10 seconds. Alternatively cook the egg in a pan of boiling water until hard-boiled (approximately 8 minutes).

2 Combine the egg, lemon juice, olive oil, garlic, Worcestershire sauce, Parmesan, anchovies, and black pepper in a blender or small food processor, and process the dressing until smooth. If it's too runny, add a little Parmesan cheese. If it's too thick, add a little more lemon juice or olive oil.

Nutrient analysis per serving: Calories 202; Protein 6g; Carbohydrate 1g; Sugar 1g; Fat 19g; Saturated fat 4g; Fibre 0g; Sodium 400mg.

Creamy Green Anchovy Salad Dressing

This dressing is one of our all-time favourites. You can make a vegetarian version by leaving out the anchovies and adding a little salt instead. Alternatively, add a few chunks of avocado for a creamy twist. Use it on your favourite salad or greens. As the dressing is green and creamy, we especially like to serve on a colourful salad full of tomatoes; yellow, green, and red peppers; and avocados.

Tools: *Blender or food processor*

Preparation time: *5 minutes*

Makes: *8 servings*

450 millilitres/15 fluid ounces (1 large jar) mayonnaise

5 anchovy fillets, finely chopped

1 chopped spring onion

2 teaspoons freshly chopped parsley

2 teaspoons freshly chopped chives

1 tablespoon rice vinegar

1 teaspoon chopped fresh tarragon

2 teaspoons lemon juice

1 Mix the mayonnaise, anchovies, spring onion, parsley, chives, rice vinegar, tarragon, and lemon juice in a blender or food processor.

2 Process the mixture until the dressing is smooth. Refrigerate until you're ready to serve up the salad.

Nutrient analysis per serving: *Calories 411; Protein 2g; Carbohydrate 0g; Sugar 0g; Fat 45g; Saturated fat 7g; Fibre 0g; Sodium 209mg.*

Energising your salad

You can add many other foods to your salad to perk it up while also providing more nutrition:

✔ **Beans and legumes:** Try green beans, kidney beans, black beans, or chickpeas. Not only do they add flavour and provide you with slow-releasing low-GL energy (refer to Chapter 6 for more on low-GL foods), but they also add lots of fibre to your salad, too.

✔ **Cherry tomatoes:** Several varieties of cherry tomatoes are available. Sweet, juicy, and full of antioxidants, they come in all different colours and shapes.

✔ **Chopped ham or turkey:** A little less fatty than bacon, these meats add protein and flavour to a salad.

✔ **Crumbled bacon:** Of course, bacon adds some fat, but it also adds flavour.

✔ **Crumbled cheese:** Be creative – use a variety of types from feta to Parmesan and Manchego to mozzarella.

✔ **Fruit:** Grapes, pineapple, melon, kiwi – adding a handful of chopped fruit can liven up a salad to make a fresh and healthy treat.

✔ **Greens:** Iceberg lettuce is boring and relatively worthless nutritionally speaking. Consider using radicchio, romaine, kale, spinach, rocket, watercress, and other greens to increase the vitamin, mineral, and fibre content of your salad – not to mention flavour.

✔ **Herbs:** Adding a handful of whole or chopped fresh herbs can liven up your salad, provide you with extra vitamins, and introduce piquancy to your meal. Many pre-packaged, washed salad selections now include herbs in them.

✔ **Mushrooms:** Buy them already sliced to make preparing salads easier on yourself. They add lots of minerals and have a distinctive taste and texture.

✔ **Nuts and seeds:** Choose from a vast selection of fresh, unsalted nuts and seeds. They add nutrients, crunch, and flavour.

✔ **Olives:** Try black or green olives, or both, and add them whole or chopped so you can spread the flavour throughout your salad.

✔ **Onions:** Red onions and spring onions are two of the most popular varieties to include in salads. Onions and other crunchy white vegetables such as white cabbage and celeriac add nutrients, too.

✔ **Pak choi:** Pak choi (Chinese white cabbage) is loaded with nutrients, and is great on salads.

✔ **Radishes:** Not only do these add zip to your salad, but they provide potassium and vitamin C.

✔ **Raisins:** Also try similar dried fruit, such as dried cranberries.

✔ **Raw broccoli:** Ready prepared packs of broccoli make adding flavour and crunch easy. Broccoli is loaded with cancer-fighting antioxidants and calcium.

✔ **Shredded cabbage:** In the same family as broccoli, cabbage contains nutrients that are important for cancer prevention. Use red, white, and green varieties to add crunch, texture, and colour.

✔ **Sprouts:** Loaded with fibre and nutrients, sprouting beans and seeds are a great addition to any salad. And they're easy to grow yourself. See the 'Sprout 'em yourself' sidebar for tips on growing your own sprout garden.

Sprout 'em yourself

Sprouting seeds and beans are a great source of protein, fibre, and vitamins A, B, and C, as well as being loaded with antioxidants. In fact, a study at Johns Hopkins University in the USA found that broccoli sprouts actually have higher levels of cancer-fighting compounds than fresh broccoli.

You don't even need green fingers to grow sprouts – just invest in a few basic starter items, and you can watch your sprout garden grow.

You can grow sprouts in soil, just like any other plant, but most people grow them in jars. For that, you need the following:

- A large jar
- Cheesecloth or nylon netting
- An elastic band
- 1 tablespoon sprout seeds (alfalfa, radish, mung bean, or buckwheat are good sprout starters), available at nurseries or online
- Water

Here's what you do:

1. **Put one tablespoon seeds into the jar, cover the seeds with water, and tighten the cheesecloth or nylon netting over the jar opening with a rubber band.**

Let the seeds soak overnight.

2. **Drain the water from the jar through the cheesecloth. Leave the jar on a shelf in a cool, darkened place, in a cupboard, or under the kitchen sink.**

If you keep the jar in the dark, the sprouts grow white; if you expose the jar to light, the sprouts come out green.

3. **Rinse and drain the seeds once a day or more.**

This step is very important because the seeds need to be moist but not wet. If you don't rinse the seeds often enough, they may start to mould. If you notice a bad smell from your sprouting seeds, they've probably gone bad. Throw them away and start over again.

In less than a week, the sprouts should be ready to eat. To harvest them, just use scissors to cut the edible sprouts away from the roots, leaving what you don't need. The rest keep growing, and you can use them later.

Getting creative with croutons

Okay, we don't know about you, but we've got some pretty specific requirements when considering what makes a good crouton. After all, if you're going to indulge, you may as well do it right. Personally, our crouton criteria include crunch, flavour, and just a touch of decadence. For us, broccoli florets just don't cut it as a crouton; do they for you?

But croutons are usually made from bread and are therefore no good on the gluten-free diet. But don't worry – with a little creativity you can make all sorts of croutons. Try some of these ideas:

- **Barbecue crisps:** Crush these up on your salad. These crisps are a little lighter than tortilla chips, but they work well, too.

- **Deep-fried veggies:** Take your favourite vegetable – sweet potatoes work really well for this – and dredge them in any gluten-free flour mixture. Deep-fry until crispy and golden, and you've got yourself veggie croutons.

- **Gluten-free homemade croutons:** Use any gluten-free bread, cut the bread into cubes, and deep-fry. Then coat them with Parmesan and seasoning. If you want a lower-fat version, spread out the cubes on a baking tray and drizzle with extra-virgin olive oil. Season the bread with fresh herbs or seasoned salt and bake them in a moderate oven (160°C/325°F/ Gas Mark 3) for about 10 minutes until golden.

- **Polenta:** Polenta is a boiled cornmeal paste that you can buy ready made from supermarkets. Dice polenta into crouton-sized pieces and deep-fry it for a great salad topper.

- **Potato croutons:** Dice two potatoes and put the pieces on a baking tray coated with nonstick spray. Then drizzle the potatoes with oil and bake at 220°C/425°F/Gas Mark 7 for 30 minutes or until crisp and golden.

- **Potato skins:** Scoop the innards out of baked potatoes and save the skins. Deep-fry and season the skins with seasoned salt.

- **Tortilla chips:** Take any kind of gluten-free tortilla chip (even the flavoured kind) and crush them up for a quick and easy topping for soups and salads.

Making a Break from Traditional Side Dishes

Some people think that serving side dishes on the gluten-free diet is easy, and that's true to some extent. Rice, corn, and potatoes do serve as staple sides for most people new to the gluten-free lifestyle. But we say, 'Move over, mashed potatoes,' to make way for more provocative side dishes featuring interesting alternatives, such as quinoa, millet, and beans.

One of our favourite alternative grains is quinoa (pronounced *keen*-wa). Called an ancient food because it was once one of three staple foods of early South American civilisation, quinoa was then – and still is – known as the Mother Grain. Boasting nearly 20 per cent protein in some varieties, quinoa has more protein than any other grain. And it's a complete protein, with a good balance of all the essential amino acids. It's also high in fibre, vitamins, and minerals. We use it in recipes that use couscous (in place of couscous), tabbouleh, or just about any other grain. (Discover more about preparing quinoa in Chapter 8.)

☙ *Lemon Quinoa Crunch*

Crunchy, colourful, tangy, and nutritious, you can serve this dish at room temperature or cold (we prefer cold). This food makes a great stand-alone, side, or salad substitute. In fact, because quinoa contains all the amino acids that your body can't produce on its own, this grain can be the main dish. You may want to double the recipe, because the leftovers are fantastic – this dish gets better each day as the flavours infuse the grain.

Tools: *Fine sieve*

Preparation time: *15 minutes*

Makes: *6 servings*

For the dressing:

4 tablespoons fresh lime juice

¼ teaspoon white pepper

¼ teaspoon freshly ground black pepper

25 grams/1 ounce sliced marinated jalapeño pepper

¼ teaspoon coarse salt

60 millilitres/2 fluid ounces extra-virgin olive oil

For the quinoa:

700 millilitres/1½ pints cold water

360 grams/12¾ ounces quinoa

90 grams/3 ounces cucumber, peeled, seeded, and diced

135 grams/4¾ ounces fresh tomatoes, seeded and diced

120 grams/4½ ounces red pepper, sliced

40 grams/1½ ounces yellow pepper, sliced

25 grams/1 ounce spring onions, white part only, sliced

1 tablespoon chopped fresh parsley

1 tablespoon chopped fresh mint

Freshly ground salt and pepper to taste

1 Make the dressing by whisking together the lime juice, white pepper, black pepper, jalapeño, coarse salt, and olive oil. Set the mixture aside.

2 Place the quinoa in a fine sieve and rinse it under cold running water, rubbing your hands through it for a few minutes. Drain off any excess water.

3 In a large pot, pour in the water and add the quinoa. Bring the mixture to the boil, lower the heat, and simmer uncovered for about 10 to 15 minutes, or until the quinoa is barely tender, making sure not to overcook it. Carefully tip the quinoa into a sieve to drain thoroughly, and leave to cool. No need to rinse it.

4 Mix the quinoa in with the cucumber, tomato, red and yellow peppers, spring onions, parsley, mint, and vinaigrette. Add a little salt and pepper to taste (you don't need much, because this dish has plenty of flavour). Serve the dish at room temperature or cold.

Nutrient analysis per serving: Calories 294; Protein 9g; Carbohydrate 34g; Sugar 7g; Fat 13g; Saturated fat 2g; Fibre 1g; Sodium 174mg.

Rice Salad with Red Peppers, Chickpeas, Beans, and Feta

This dish is loaded with flavour, and it's already packed with nutrients, but to add extra goodness, try using brown rice instead of white.

Preparation time: *15 minutes*

Resting time: *1 hour*

Makes: *6 servings*

For the dressing:

120 millilitres/4 fluid ounces fresh lemon juice

2 teaspoons crushed garlic (about 4 cloves)

4 tablespoons extra-virgin olive oil

Freshly ground salt and pepper to taste

For the salad:

480 grams/1¼ pounds cooked brown or white rice, cooled to room temperature

400 grams/14 ounces (usually 1 can) chickpeas, drained and rinsed

150 grams/5½ ounces feta cheese, finely diced

2 tablespoons chopped fresh parsley

2 teaspoons chopped fresh dill

4 spring onions, washed, ends removed, thinly sliced

50 grams/2 ounces roasted red peppers (fresh or from a jar, drained of oil)

1 Make the dressing by whisking together the lemon juice, garlic, olive oil, and salt and pepper.

2 In a large serving bowl, combine the rice, chickpeas, feta cheese, parsley, dill, spring onions, and red peppers.

3 Pour the dressing over the rice mixture and mix well. Let it stand for at least an hour before serving. Serve at room temperature or chilled.

Nutrient analysis per serving: *Calories 354; Protein 12g; Carbohydrate 34g; Sugar 2g; Fat 19g; Saturated fat 5g; Fibre 3.5g; Sodium 654mg.*

Latin American Marinated Seafood (Ceviche)

Ceviche poses an imponderable question – is it cooked or not? *Ceviche*, sometimes spelled *seviche*, is a delicious Latin American seafood dish that people prepare by using an ancient method of 'cooking' that uses the acid from citrus juice instead of heat. The acid actually changes the protein structure in the fish, and you can watch the fish turn from translucent pink to opaque white. Ceviche is usually a mixture of chunks of raw fish, lemon and/or lime juice, chopped onion, crushed garlic, and chilli peppers. The fish cooks in the citrus while flavours blend into a spectacular dish that you can serve as a starter or even a main course.

Preparation time: *15 minutes plus 6 hours in the fridge*

Refrigeration time: *6 hours*

Makes: *8 servings*

1 kilograms/2¼ pounds fresh red snapper fillets, cut into 12-millimetre (½-inch) pieces	*2 teaspoons chopped fresh coriander*
40 grams/1½ ounces red onion, finely diced	*Dash of Tabasco sauce*
180 grams/6½ ounces fresh tomatoes, peeled, seeded, and chopped	*Pinch of ground cumin*
1 red chilli, seeded and finely diced	*120 millilitres/4 fluid ounces freshly squeezed lime juice*
1 teaspoon of salt	*120 millilitres/4 fluid ounces freshly squeezed lemon juice*

1 Place the fish, onion, tomatoes, chilli pepper, salt, coriander, Tabasco, and cumin in a glass or ceramic dish.

2 Pour over the lemon and lime juice, cover the dish in foil or cling film, and place in the fridge for at least 6 hours.

3 Stir the mixture frequently, ensuring that the citrus liquid covers the fish.

4 Serve the ceviche with heated tortillas and avocado slices or with tortilla chips for dipping.

Tip: *You can use prawns, scallops, or squid instead of or in addition to the fish. You can also use any type of fish you like – just make sure that it's firm, like red snapper or cod.*

Vary It! *Get creative and add diced fruit, such as mangos, and serve the ceviche rolled in a fresh, warm corn tortilla with lettuce and a little salsa, or with crisps for dipping.*

Nutrient analysis per serving: *Calories 121; Protein 25g; Carbohydrate 2g; Sugar 2g; Fat 2g; Saturated fat 0.5g; Fibre 0.3g; Sodium 400mg.*

☺ Sweet-Potato Potato Salad

You may have caught our comment about potatoes being an indulgence. But sweet potatoes (as opposed to 'regular' ones) are actually very nutritious, full of vitamins, and a valuable slow-releasing energy food. Try this simple and refreshing potato salad for a unique twist on an old favourite.

Preparation time: *15 minutes*

Cooking time: *20 minutes*

Refrigeration time: *2 hours*

Makes: *6 servings*

1 kilogram/2¼ pounds sweet potatoes, peeled and cooked

2 fresh green chillies, finely chopped

75 grams/3 ounces red pepper, chopped

2 teaspoons chopped coriander

Pinch of paprika

80 millilitres/5 tablespoons mayonnaise

1 Peel and dice the sweet potatoes. Steam them for 20 minutes, or until they're tender but not mushy.

2 In a large serving bowl, mix the sweet potatoes, green chilies, red pepper, coriander, paprika, and mayonnaise. Chill the potato salad for at least 2 hours; serve cold.

Nutrient analysis per serving: *Calories 240; Protein 2g; Carbohydrate 33g; Sugar 14g; Fat 11g; Saturated fat 2g; Fibre 4g; Sodium 90mg.*

Topping off the trusty spud

Baked potatoes are a staple side dish on the gluten-free diet. But seriously – do you think anyone ever gets a craving for a plain old baked potato with nothing on it? Not likely. Baked spud cry out for some serious support from the wonderful world of toppings. After all, if you're going to indulge (yes, we consider a potato a bit of an indulgence because it's a very high-glycaemic-index food; you can read more about the glycaemic index in Chapter 6), you may as well make it worth eating. Bottom line: An unadorned baked potato is too plain and simple unless you dress it up. Try these toppings:

- ✔ Bacon or ham pieces
- ✔ Barbecue sauce
- ✔ Broccoli florets
- ✔ Butter or margarine
- ✔ Caramelised onions
- ✔ Chilii
- ✔ Chopped chives
- ✔ Diced chicken
- ✔ Gluten-free soy sauce
- ✔ Grated cheese
- ✔ Guacamole or avocado slices
- ✔ Jalapeño peppers
- ✔ Ranch salad dressing (or any of the dressings in this chapter)
- ✔ Salsa
- ✔ Sour cream

Chapter 12

Mustering Up Mouth-Watering Gluten-Free Mains

*E*ating home-cooked meals is one of life's great pleasures. But today, many people are so busy that home cooking has become a luxury rather than an everyday event; and with the added restriction of cooking within the parameters of a gluten-free diet, you may find yourself stuck in a rut, preparing the same three or four dishes each week.

Well, forget plain roast chicken and boring old beef-burgers! You can make anything gluten-free, as long as you know how to make simple substitutions (yes really, check out Chapter 8).

Oh, and speaking of simple . . . bear in mind that we're not into complicated, lengthy recipes containing ingredients you've never heard of. We like to keep things simple – at least in the kitchen – but we love to eat, and taste is something we don't hold back on. In this chapter, we share a few of our favourite simple, but full on flavour, main courses – gluten-free style, of course.

Preparing Poultry with Pizzazz

You may not be making the most of poultry because you don't realise just how versatile a food it can be. Fresh poultry meat soak ups flavours from marinades, or try rubbing seasoning into your bird to create an array of flavours and taste experiences. In this section we provide some delicious gluten-free ways to bring the best out of your bird. White meat or dark? Breast or thigh? Skin or no skin? Don't underestimate the significance of these choices – to people with a preference, white meat versus dark is an entirely different bird.

Chicken is a great source of protein as well as niacin, vitamins B6 and B12, vitamin D, iron, and zinc. Skinless chicken is one of the lowest-fat meats you can eat. Although breast meat has the lowest fat content, even skinless dark meat is comparatively low in fat, and most of that is unsaturated – the healthy kind.

The darker meat of cooked chicken wings and legs (as opposed to the lighter meat from the breast) is dark because these fleshy areas contain more muscle tissue. The muscles in the chicken's legs and wings require more oxygen to function. *Myoglobin* is an iron-containing protein that transfers oxygen from the blood to the muscles, changing the colour of the meat – and providing you with more iron.

Spicy Chinese Poussin

Poussin (which are just young chickens) give the appearance of being fancy and ultra-gourmet, but they're actually simple to prepare and fairly inexpensive to buy. Marinating them enhances the flavour, but longer isn't necessarily better (see the later sidebar 'Merry marinades', which also tells you what kind of dish to use for marinating). Leaving your poussin soused for more than 8 hours is unnecessary, because the flavour doesn't really improve beyond that point.

You can usually find poussin in the fresh or frozen section with the other poultry. Plan on using half a poussin per person. This recipe uses hoisin sauce, oyster sauce, and Asian chilli sauce; you can buy them in the Asian food sections of supermarkets or health-food stores.

Preparation time: *15 minutes*

Refrigeration time: *30 minutes to 8 hours*

Cooking time: *20 minutes*

Makes: *8 servings*

2 teaspoons crushed garlic (about 3 cloves)

1 heaped tablespoon grated fresh ginger

3 spring onions, chopped

1 teaspoon chopped fresh coriander

180 millilitres/6½ fluid ounces fresh orange juice

4 tablespoons fresh lemon juice

4 tablespoons hoisin sauce

4 tablespoons oyster sauce

3 tablespoons sesame oil

1 tablespoon Asian chilli sauce

4 poussin, cut in half

1 Preheat the grill. If you're using a gas grill, heat it on high for 10 minutes then reduce the heat to medium.

2 In a small bowl, mix the garlic, ginger, spring onions, coriander, orange juice, lemon juice, hoisin sauce, oyster sauce, sesame oil, and chilli sauce. Set aside half of this mixture for basting the poussin; use the rest as a marinade in Step 4.

3 Place the poussin halves in a shallow dish or a sealable plastic bag, and add the marinade. Refrigerate the poussin for a minimum of 30 minutes and up to a maximum of 8 hours, turning occasionally.

4 Remove the poussin from the marinade, drain off any excess juice, and place the halves on to the grill pan under the heat (avoid placing them too close to the flame if using a gas grill; depending on the size of your grill you may need to cook the poussin in batches, keeping the cooked birds hot in a warmed oven). Cook for approximately 10 minutes each side, until the internal temperature is 160°C/320°F. You can measure this with an internal thermometer, or pierce the meat with a fork and the temperature is right when the juices run clear. Baste the poussin with the marinade you set aside in Step 2.

Vary It! *If you don't want to grill the poussin, you can roast them in a preheated oven at 220°C/425°F/Gas Mark 7 for 15 to 20 minutes until cooked.*

Tip: *To split poussin in half, use poultry shears to cut them through the breast and backbone (see Figure 12-1). Cut the backbone out and discard.*

Nutrient analysis per serving: *Calories 344; Protein 32g; Carbohydrate 7g; Sugar 4g; Fat 21g; Saturated fat 5g; Fibre 0.4g; Sodium 577mg.*

Figure 12-1:
Cutting a
poussin
in half.

Place the bird breast side up. Cut along the breast bone from cavity to neck end. Gently prise open.

Turn the hen over and cut along one side of the backbone. Cutting the bird in half.

Cut along the other side of the backbone to remove and discard.

discard

Chicken Nuggets

Chicken provides us with lots of great imponderables: Which came first, the chicken or the egg? Why did the chicken cross the road? Why does everything taste like chicken? Check out these interesting snippets of chicken trivia:

- Each year in the UK, consumers eat twice the amount of poultry as they do beef, and consumption continues to grow.

- In the UK, the average person eats approximately 24 kilograms (or 53 pounds) of chicken each year. The figure for turkey is 4.3 kilograms (or 10 pounds) per head – most of that is probably at Christmas time.

- The average hen lays 255 eggs per year and the average UK consumer eats 180 eggs per year.

- According to the Food Service Intelligence, chicken tikka masala should be the UK's national dish as it's the most frequently eaten meal nationwide. So we've got good news for gluten-intolerant curry lovers – we consulted *The Food and Drink Directory* from Coeliac UK and found a good range of gluten-free tikka masala sauces and marinades, and an even bigger range of ready made chicken tikka masala meals, including chilled, canned, and frozen dishes.

Herby Roast Chicken with Garlic

Few dishes are easier, more delicious, and more nutritious than roast chicken. However, with a few simple additions you can turn this dish into a fragrant, elegant affair. We like to stuff ours with any fresh herbs we have to hand in the kitchen or growing in the garden, but you can leave them out if you prefer. This dish is so good that you probably aren't going to have any leftovers, but if by chance you do, use them to add flavour to just about anything: salad, chicken soup, enchiladas, or stir-fry.

Preparation time: *10 minutes*

Cooking time: *1 hour, 15 minutes*

Makes: *4 servings*

40 grams/1½ ounces chopped onion

80 millilitres/3 fluid ounces fresh lemon juice

2 teaspoons crushed garlic (about 3 cloves)

2 tablespoons fresh rosemary, chopped (or any of your favourite herbs)

Freshly ground salt and pepper to taste

60 millilitres/2½ fluid ounces extra-virgin olive oil

45 millilitres/1½ fluid ounces sesame oil

1 large chicken, approximately 2 kilograms (4½ pounds)

1 Preheat the oven to 190°C/375° F/ Gas Mark 5.

2 In a small bowl, mix the onion, lemon juice, garlic, rosemary, salt and pepper, olive oil, and sesame oil.

3 Remove the giblets from the chicken and discard (or save them for another recipe). Rinse the cavity out with cool water and pat dry.

4 Spoon half the herb mixture into the chicken cavity. Use your hands to coat the inside of the chicken. Rub the rest of the mixture into the skin on the outside of the chicken until entirely covered, patting the chopped up onion and herbs onto the chicken as best you can.

5 Place the chicken in a roasting pan and cook for 1¼ hours, basting occasionally with the juices until the breast meat reaches 170°C/340°F (when tested with a cooking thermometer) or the juices run clear when you pierce the skin with a fork. Before carving, allow to rest for 10 minutes.

Tip: *Save the cooking juices from the chicken. Let them cool then skim the fat off the top. Pour the liquid into an ice tray and freeze. You can use the cubes for stock.*

Nutrient analysis per serving: *Calories 737; Protein 63g; Carbohydrate 1g; Sugar 1g; Fat 53g; Saturated fat 12g; Fibre 0.3g; Sodium 188mg.*

Skinless or skinful? It's not really so sinful

Although people often think that cooking chicken with the skin removed is healthier, it actually isn't. Caloriewise, the meat is the same whether you cook it with the skin on or off, and leaving it on actually helps the chicken retain moisture and intensifies the flavour. Of course, if you're keen to save calories, don't eat the skin after cooking. Just cook the chicken with it on and then – if you have the willpower – peel it off and throw it away. The good news? Chicken skin (unless seasoned or coated with gluten) is gluten-free, and so if you're into indulgences, go for it!

Some people like their chicken skin crispy and crunchy, others prefer a softer skin. The skin's consistency depends on how you cook the chicken. For a crunchy outside, cook the chicken at a very high oven temperature – 240°C / 475°F/Gas Mark 9 works well. After about 20 minutes, turn the oven down to 180°C/ 350°F/Gas Mark 4 degrees so that the meat can finish cooking before the skin burns. If you go this route, start the cooking process with the breast side down so that the legs and thighs get a head start. About halfway through, turn the chicken over so that the breast can brown. Lower oven temperatures don't make the outside crunchy, but the meat stays moist and tender.

Packing a punch with ginger

Ginger is often referred to as a root, but it's actually a *rhizome*, an underground stem. Commonly found in Indian and Asian dishes, it has a peppery, sweet flavour in its fresh, uncooked form. When dried, it gives a spicy kick. Ginger is also a stimulant for the circulatory system, and some cultures consider it an aphrodisiac. Add a few slices of fresh ginger to hot water for a refreshing, zesty pick-me-up tea.

Lemon Caper Chicken

We happen to love lemon, capers, and chicken, and so this dish is definitely one of our favourites, and it's easy to make, but looks like you've spent hours in the kitchen. The recipe calls for rice flour for dusting the chicken, but feel free to use any gluten-free flour or baking mix that you have available. (By the way, capers are a type of pickled flower bud – look for them near the pickles.)

Preparation time: *20 minutes*

Cooking time: *25 minutes*

Makes: *4 servings*

4 chicken breasts, boned and skinned

180 millilitres/6½ fluid ounces extra-virgin olive oil, for frying

40 grams/1½ ounces rice flour

Freshly ground salt and pepper to taste

For the sauce:

3 spring onions, chopped

1 teaspoon crushed garlic (about 2 cloves)

60 millilitres/2 fluid ounces chicken stock

120 millilitres/4 fluid ounces dry sherry

60 millilitres/2 fluid ounces freshly squeezed lemon juice

4 tablespoons capers, drained and rinsed

30 grams/1 ounce unsalted butter

1 Pound the chicken breasts to an even thickness – about 13 millimetres (½ inch) thick. If you don't have a meat tenderiser, you can use any other heavy, manageable object, like a heavy based frying pan.

2 Put enough olive oil into a large frying pan to coat the bottom of the pan (about 2 tablespoons). Heat the oil over medium-high heat.

3 Dredge the chicken breasts in flour seasoned with salt and pepper.

4 Fry the chicken breasts until brown; takes about 3 minutes on each side. If your pan isn't big enough, you may need to fry them in a couple of batches. Make sure that you have enough oil in the pan at all times (add another tablespoon of oil during cooking). Transfer the cooked chicken to a warm serving platter and cover with foil.

5 Wipe out the excess oil in the pan with kitchen roll, or use a clean pan. Reduce the heat to low and add the rest of the olive oil to the frying pan (you should have about 1 tablespoon left). Add the spring onion, garlic, chicken stock, sherry, lemon juice, and capers. Turn the heat up to medium-high and simmer until the liquid has reduced to half (about 5 minutes).

6 Tilt the pan so that the liquid pools on one side, and whisk in the butter until the sauce is smooth. Pour the sauce over the chicken breasts and serve immediately.

Nutrient analysis per serving: Calories 675; Protein 33g; Carbohydrate 9g; Sugar 1g; Fat 53g; Saturated fat 11g; Fibre 0.4g; Sodium 90mg.

Enjoying Meaty Mains

Yes, you can have your steak and eat it, too. And your pork and lamb and even venison – not to mention a number of other exotic and unusual meats, too. Even if you're trying to eat healthily, you can enjoy meat as part of a well-balanced gluten-free diet. Red meat does contain a fair amount of fat, but it's also a great source of protein, vitamins, and minerals. Just remember to eat it in moderation and to watch your portion size – an average serving of meat is about 100 grams or 3 ounces cooked (4 ounces before cooking), roughly the size of a pack of cards.

Buying beef

If you've ever stood at the meat counter wondering which of the huge variety of cuts on offer to choose, you're not alone. Adding to the confusion are the different names given for the same cuts and vague labels that confuse even the savviest of consumers. Don't fret because we give you some basic guidelines to help you make sense of enjoying the best of beef.

Beef grades

Prime, choice, and select grades of beef are descriptions of a cut's leanness and palatability and the age of the animal. *Select* cuts are leaner than *choice* cuts, and choice cuts are leaner than *prime* cuts. Select cuts look less marbled and aren't as tender or juicy as choice or prime cuts.

The aged meats you usually buy in fine restaurants are prime grades. You can find select and choice grades in the supermarket and in less expensive restaurants – but bear in mind that select cuts are the leanest. If you like the tenderness that comes with higher fat grades, you can work around the leanness of certain cuts with the use of marinades and simple cooking techniques.

Beef cuts

Beef is available in many different cuts, including steaks, roasts, brisket, stew meat, and ground beef. Tender cuts come from the ribs and loin, whereas tougher cuts come from the rump and shoulder (see Figure 12-2). Table 12-1 shows how some of the cuts compare nutritionally. The cuts at the top of the list give you the most protein per gram of fat.

Table 12-1 Nutritional Content of Cuts of Beef per 100 grams (Raw)

Cut Type	Grams Protein	Grams Fat	Energy (Kcals) Calories
Round	25.6	8.1	183.6
Flank	22.4	10.6	192.1
Sirloin	23.6	13.0	219.3
Chuck	23.2	20.2	282.2
Short Loin	19.7	19.8	262.6
Corned Beef Brisket	15.4	16.1	213.3
Beef Brisket	21.3	24.2	309.4
Ribs	18.6	25.1	306.1

Steak and Peanut Pepper Pasta

In this amazing dish, crunchy, colourful vegetables are mixed with some of your favourite gluten-free pasta served as a bed for thinly sliced steak covered in a spicy peanut sauce. Seriously, this dish is one of the most delicious, unique, and impressive (shhhh . . . it's really very easy) that we've ever made!

Tools: Blender

Preparation time: 25 minutes

Refrigeration time: 2 hours

Cooking time: 15 minutes

Makes: 4 servings

120 millilitres/4 fluid ounces rice wine vinegar

120 millilitres/4 fluid ounces extra-virgin olive oil

4 tablespoons gluten-free soy sauce

4 tablespoons smooth peanut butter

2 tablespoons chopped fresh coriander

1 teaspoon crushed garlic (about 2 cloves)

½ teaspoon cayenne pepper

450 grams/1 pound lean sirloin steak

115 grams/4 ounces fine gluten-free pasta

85 grams/3 ounces savoy cabbage, washed and shredded

85 grams/3 ounces pak choi, shredded

30 grams/1 ounce fresh spinach, washed and shredded

130 grams/4½ ounces carrots, cut into thin sticks

½ cucumber, thinly sliced (to garnish)

40 grams/1½ ounces unsalted peanuts, chopped (to garnish)

1 Preheat the grill. If you're using a gas grill, heat on high for 10 minutes, and then reduce the heat to medium-low.

2 Combine the vinegar, oil, soy sauce, peanut butter, coriander garlic, and cayenne pepper in a blender. Whiz the dressing until well-mixed.

3 Trim any fat from the meat. Place the steak in a shallow dish and pour about one-third of the peanut dressing over the meat. Cover and marinate the meat in the refrigerator for 2 hours, turning occasionally. Chill the remaining dressing.

4 Lift the meat out of the marinade and drain off any excess; discard the marinade as you don't need this anymore. Grill the steak until it's cooked to your preference, turning once halfway through. This should take about 8 to minutes, depending on the thickness of the meat and how well you like your steak cooked.

5 Cook the pasta according to the directions on the packet, making sure that they're *al dente* (slightly firm and not overcooked). Drain them and put to one side.

6 While the meat is still cooking, combine the cooked pasta, cabbage, pak choi, spinach, and carrots in a medium-sized mixing bowl. Add about half of the remaining dressing to the pasta-veggie mixture and stir until well-mixed.

7 When the meat is ready, slice it into thin slices across the grain. To assemble this dish, serve a portion of the pasta-veggie mixture on each plate. Add a few slices of meat on top of the pastas. Garnish the dish with a few slices of cucumber. Drizzle the remaining dressing over each plate, and sprinkle over up the peanuts.

Tip: Instead of shredding the veggies yourself, buy a pack of stir-fry mix, which includes broccoli, carrot, and cabbage. Use any combination of vegetables you like, as long as they're thinly shredded.

Nutrient analysis per serving: Calories 512; Protein 38g; Carbohydrate 27g; Sugar 7g; Fat 28g; Saturated fat 7g; Fibre 4.5g; Sodium 640mg.

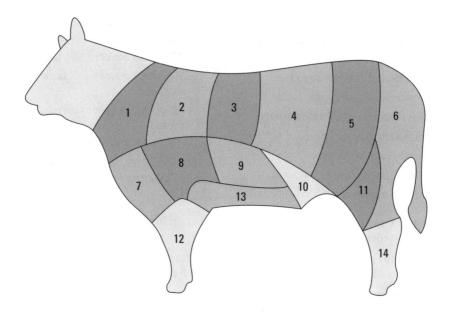

Figure 12-2:
Cuts of beef.

1. Neck
2. Chuckle & Blade
3. Fore Rib
4. Sirloin
5. Rump

6. Topside/Silverside
7. Clod
8. Thick Rib
9. Thin Rib
10. Thin Flank

11. Thick Flank
12. Shin
13. Brisket
14. Leg

Cooking with pork

Porky the pig's not so porky anymore. That's because farmers these days have changed their breeding and production methods to make the pork much leaner and healthier. In fact, if you cut all the fat off the edges and buy a lean piece of pork, the calorie and fat content is about the same as chicken. To see where most of the cuts of pork come from, see Figure 12-3.

Lean pork doesn't have fat to keep it moist, and so to avoid the meat getting tough and dry, not overcooking it is extremely important. Pork should be cooked to about 155 or 160°C (320°F).

You should let meat stand for about 10 to 15 minutes before you carve it. This is called a *resting period*, and it allows the juices to be redistributed so that your meat turns out moister. But the meat's temperature continues to rise about 5 to 10 degrees during this time, and so you need to stop cooking a little early to allow for this rise in temperature.

Here are a few ways you can tell if pork is done:

✔ **Use a thermometer.** Stick the thermometer into the thickest part of the cut. At 160°C (320°F), the meat's medium-done and safe to eat.

✔ **Prick it.** If you prick the meat with a fork, the juice that comes out should be clear, not pink.

✔ **Cut it open.** When you cut into the meat, it should be white.

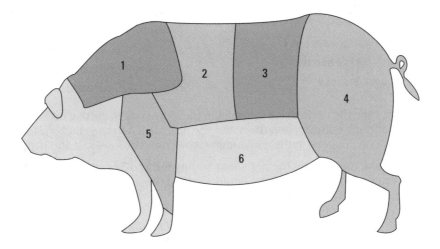

Figure 12-3:
Cuts of pork.

1. Spare rib
2. Fore loin or ribs
3. Hind loin

4. Leg
5. Shoulder
6. Brisket and flank

Shredded Pork

Occasionally, recipes for shredded pork call for flour. Flour certainly isn't necessary, as you can see from the recipe we use. This recipe is especially easy because you throw everything in a slow cooker and leave it to simmer magically into a delicious meal. Serve this dish with a serving of gluten-free pasta, using some of the leftover sauce to drizzle over the pasta.

Tools: *Slow cooker*

Preparation time: *15 minutes*

Cooking time: *4 to 5 hours*

Makes: *6 servings*

1 kilogram/2 pounds boneless shoulder of pork

120 millilitres/4 fluid ounces chicken stock

2 large onions, cut into quarters

4 jalapeño peppers, sliced

3 teaspoons crushed garlic (about 6 cloves)

2 teaspoons ground coriander

2 teaspoons ground cumin

2 teaspoons dried, crushed oregano

Freshly milled salt and pepper to taste

1 Trim any fat from the pork. Place the meat in the slow cooker, cutting off any bits of the pork that don't quite fit (pop them into the pot, too). Add the chicken stock, onions, jalapeño peppers, garlic, coriander, cumin, oregano, and salt and pepper.

2 Cover and cook the pork on the high-heat setting for 4 to 5 hours. Use a slotted spoon to remove the meat from the liquid; discard the liquid. When the meat cools, use two forks to shred it.

Tip: *You can use shredded pork to make a variety of meals. Dress it up with condiments and extras, such as sour cream, shredded lettuce, refried beans, olives, salsa, diced tomatoes, jalapeno peppers, spicy carrots, and guacamole, and use it for filling or serving with:*

- ✔ Burritos
- ✔ Enchiladas
- ✔ Fajitas
- ✔ Nachos

- ✔ Quesadillas
- ✔ Sandwiches
- ✔ Salads
- ✔ Tacos

Nutrient analysis per serving: *Calories 371; Protein 53g; Carbohydrate 5g; Sugar 3g; Fat 16g; Saturated fat 5g; Fibre 0.8g; Sodium 874mg.*

If you're watching your fat intake, pork loin is a good choice. Nearly as low in saturated fat as chicken breast meat, it's one of the leanest meats available.

Dining on Luscious Lamb

Even though lamb is considered to be a fatty meat, a lean leg joint can contain as little as 2.2 grams of fat if it's carefully trimmed. An average cut of lamb contains fractionally more saturated fat than unsaturated fat and is an important good source of iron, as are all red meats (see Figure 12-4 for the various cuts of lamb). People who have recently been advised to follow a gluten-free diet often have a low iron status because until diagnosis they haven't been able to absorb it well. The good news is that your gluten-free diet soon restores your ability to absorb nutrients just as well as everyone else, so enjoy!

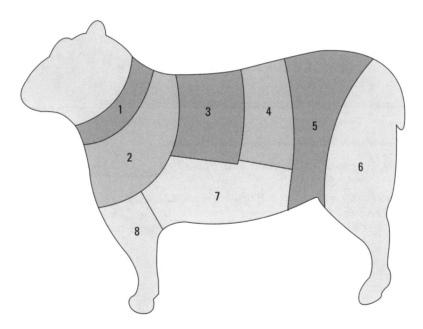

Figure 12-4:
Cuts of
lamb.

1. Scrag
2. Shoulder
3. Best end of neck
4. Loin
5. Chump
6. Leg
7. Breast
8. Fore shank

TIP

Merry marinades

Besides adding flavour, acidic marinades also tenderise foods. The enzymes in the acids break down the muscle and connective proteins in the meat, making the meat less tough. Some tips for marinating follow:

✔ Refrigerate meat to avoid the growth of harmful bacteria. The temperature at which you marinate doesn't affect the meat's tenderness. The enzymes break down proteins only at temperatures between 60°C/140°F and 80°C/175°F, so leaving the meat at room temperature serves no purpose.

✔ Poultry and fish can turn to mush or become tough if you marinate them too long. Poultry benefits when marinating for up to 4 hours, and about 30 minutes is a good amount of time to marinate seafood.

✔ Natural tenderisers include pineapple, figs, papaya, kiwi, mango, honeydew melon, wine, citrus, vinegar, tomato, yogurt, and buttermilk.

✔ Be careful with what kind of container you use for marinating. Never use aluminium containers – only glass, ceramic, stainless steel, or plastic. When you marinate in metals other than stainless steel, the metal and the acidic marinade produce a chemical reaction.

✔ Never reuse a marinade. If you're going to use some of the marinade for a sauce, take out the amount you need and set it aside before you marinate the meat or seafood. After you've marinated food in a marinade, throw the marinade away.

Lamb Coated in Spinach and Potato

This dish is a meal on its own, but for larger appetites it can be served with extra vegetables on the side. The cooking time leaves the lamb chops just a little pink in the middle but if you prefer your lamb well done, continue cooking for a further 5 minutes.

Preparation time: *30 minutes*

Cooking time: *15 minutes*

Makes: *4*

25 grams/1 ounce butter

4 tablespoons extra-virgin olive oil

8 lamb chops

175 grams/6 ounces fresh spinach (washed)

350 grams/12 ounces potato, peeled and grated

1 large free-range egg

1 onion, peeled and finely chopped

Freshly ground salt and pepper to taste

Pinch of grated nutmeg

1 Melt the butter and 1 tablespoon of the oil in a large frying pan. Add the lamb chops and lightly fry for 1 to 2 minutes. Remove from the pan and set aside.

2 Place the spinach in a large saucepan and sprinkle with a little water. Blanch for 3 minutes, drain, and finely chop.

3 In a tea towel, squeeze the potato to remove any excess moisture then place in a bowl and add the spinach, egg, onion, salt, pepper, and nutmeg and mix well.

4 Put the reserved lamb chops into the potato mixture and toss to make sure that each chop is coated.

5 Add the remaining oil to the pan and fry the chops for 5 to 8 minutes on each side or until golden brown. Remove from the pan and drain on kitchen paper. Serve immediately.

Nutrient analysis per serving: Calories 639; Protein 44g; Carbohydrate 16g; Sugar 2g; Fat 44g; Saturated fat 21g; Fibre 2.3g; Sodium 337mg.

Lamb Steaks with Thyme

This recipe is a real taste of spring. Thyme complements the sweetness of lamb perfectly to make this dish a great lunch served with salad or a more substantial meal with rice or potatoes and steamed green vegetables.

Preparation time: *30 minutes*

Cooking time: *10 minutes*

Makes: *4*

2 tablespoons extra-virgin olive oil

1 tablespoon fresh lemon juice

4 lamb steaks

Freshly ground salt and pepper to taste

Large sprig of fresh thyme

1 Combine the olive oil, lemon juice, salt and pepper, and rub both sides of each steak with the mixture.

2 Pull the leaves off the thyme sprig and scatter over the meat so that it sticks to both sides. Cover and refrigerate for 2 hours.

3 Preheat the grill to high. Grill the steaks for 5 to 10 minutes on each side according to taste and thickness.

4 Serve hot with your choice of side dishes.

Nutrient analysis per serving: Calories 323; Protein 28g; Carbohydrate 0g; Sugar 0g; Fat 23g; Saturated fat 7g; Fibre 0g; Sodium 268mg.

Diving into Seafood

Seafood has been an important source of protein and other nutrients in diets around the world since, well, people started eating. Fish and shellfish usually contain significant amounts of zinc, which studies show is important for thinking and memory.

Although many recipes call for coatings, breadcrumbs, or are served with pasta, which all ruin seafood for gluten-free types, you can easily modify the recipes to make them gluten-free, without losing any of their delicious taste.

People with dermatitis herpetiformis (DH – refer to Chapter 3 for details on DH) sometimes need to eliminate iodine from their diets as well as gluten. Iodine is commonly found in shellfish, among other things.

Tequila-Lime Prawns and Scallops

People usually eat this dish wrapped in flour tortillas – but you don't have to. Substitute corn tortillas for the wrap, or spoon the prawns and scallops over rice (preferably brown rice) or your favourite gluten-free pasta.

Preparation time: *2 minutes*

Cooking time: *10 minutes*

Makes: *4 servings*

450 grams/1 pounds medium-size prawns, cooked and peeled	*2 teaspoons hot chilli sauce*
225 grams/8 ounces raw scallops	*½ teaspoon ground cumin*
60 millilitres/2 fluid ounces fresh lime juice	*½ teaspoon dried oregano*
60 millilitres/2 fluid ounces fresh lemon juice	*1 large onion, sliced*
4 tablespoons chopped fresh coriander	*1 green pepper, cut into thin strips*
1 tablespoon extra-virgin olive oil	*1 red pepper, cut into thin strips*
4 tablespoons tequila	*1 tablespoon extra-virgin olive oil (for frying)*
2 teaspoons crushed garlic (about 4 cloves)	*4 lime wedges (to garnish)*

1 If your prawns or scallops are frozen, thaw and rinse them.

2 In a large glass, ceramic, or stainless steel mixing bowl, mix the lime juice, lemon juice, coriander, 1 tablespoon oil, tequila, garlic, hot sauce, cumin, and oregano. Add the prawns and scallops.

3 In a large frying pan over medium-high heat, cook the onion and green and red pepper slices in a tablespoon of oil until they begin to soften (about 4 minutes).

4 Add the prawn and scallop mixture to the frying pan, and bring everything to the boil. Cook and stir the mixture for about 3 minutes, until the liquid has reduced a little and the scallops are cooked.

5 Serve the seafood over rice, pasta, or in the wrap of your choice, and garnish with lime wedges.

Nutrient analysis per serving: Calories 465; Protein 40g; Carbohydrate 23g; Sugars 6g; Fat 10g; Saturated fat 2g; Fibre 2g; Sodium 1900mg.

Baked Lemon Fish

This delicious fish dish is high in protein and low in fat and carbs. You can use any mild, white fish fillet. Serve it on brown rice for extra fibre and nutrients.

Preparation time: *10 minutes*

Cooking time: *30 minutes*

Makes: *8 servings*

8 white fish fillets, boneless and skinned	*½ teaspoon paprika*
4 tablespoons fresh lemon juice	*2 tablespoons chopped fresh coriander*
45 grams/1¾ ounces butter, melted	*8 fresh orange slices*
½ teaspoon grated fresh ginger	*560 grams/20 ounces (usually 1 large can) crushed pineapple*
½ teaspoon crushed garlic (about 1 clove)	
½ teaspoon freshly ground black pepper	*Non-stick oil spray, for greasing the dishes*

1 Preheat the oven to 190°C/375°F/Gas Mark 5.

2 Using the non-stick oil spray, lightly grease two medium-sized baking dishes. Wash and pat dry the fish fillets, and lay them in a single layer in the baking dishes.

3 Mix the lemon juice, butter, ginger, garlic, black pepper, paprika, and coriander in a small bowl. Drizzle the lemon juice mixture over the fillets.

4 Place an orange slice over each fillet. Drain and discard about ¾ of the juice from the canned pineapple, and pour the crushed pineapple and remaining juice over the fillets.

5 Bake the fillets for about 20 to 30 minutes or until the fillets are opaque. Be careful not to overcook. Serve with brown rice.

Nutrient analysis per serving (with 100g brown rice): Calories 325; Protein 28g; Carbohydrate 37g; Sugar 8g; Fat 7g; Saturated fat 4g; Fibre 1.1g; Sodium 170mg.

Szechwan Scallops with Orange Peel

This simple Szechwan dish can impress anyone. If you're not a seafood lover, you can use chicken instead of scallops.

Preparation time: *1 hour 30 minutes*

Refrigeration time: *1 hour*

Cooking time: *15 minutes*

Makes: *6 servings*

1 large orange

450 grams/1 pound fresh scallops

2 tablespoons wheat-free soy sauce

2 tablespoons dry sherry

5 spring onions, cut into 25-millimetre (1-inch) pieces

½ teaspoon (or to taste) cayenne pepper

50 grams/2 ounces red pepper, sliced

1 teaspoon grated fresh ginger

1 tablespoon cornstarch

¾ teaspoon granulated sugar

120 millilitres/4 fluid ounces fresh orange juice

4 tablespoons extra-virgin olive oil

1 teaspoon dried chilli flakes

1 Preheat the oven to 110°C/225°F/Gas Mark ¼.

2 Use a vegetable peeler or sharp knife to cut the peel from the orange into 25-millimetre (1-inch) wide pieces, being careful not to cut into the pith (the white part of the peel). Cut the peel into 5-centimetre (2-inch) strips, and spread them out on a small baking tray. Bake them in the cool oven for about 30 minutes to dry them out.

3 In a medium-size bowl, mix the scallops, soy sauce, sherry, spring onions, cayenne, red pepper, chilli flakes, and ginger. Cover and refrigerate the mixture for an hour or so.

4 In a small bowl, mix the cornstarch, sugar, and orange juice. Cover and refrigerate this mixture for about an hour.

5 When you're almost ready to serve the meal, heat 2 tablespoons of the oil in a large frying pan over a medium heat. Stir-fry the orange peel until crisp and the edges are slightly browned for about 2 minutes. Drain the peel on kitchen roll.

6 Using the same frying pan, turn up the heat to high. Use the remaining oil to stir-fry the scallop mixture until the scallops are cooked through, approximately 5 minutes. Stir the orange-juice mixture prior to adding it to the scallops, and cook the mixture until the sauce has thickened slightly, stirring all the time, until it coats the scallops.

7 Spoon the scallop mixture onto a serving platter, and sprinkle with the orange peel.

Nutrient analysis per serving: Calories 176; Protein 13g; Carbohydrate 5g; Sugars 3g; Fat 11g; Saturated fat 2g; Fibre 0.3g; Sodium 450mg.

Exploring Vegetarian and Vegan Dishes

Typically, the vegetarian diet relies heavily on pasta, breads, couscous, various forms of wheat, and meat replacements – all of which are loaded with gluten. But plenty of dishes are naturally gluten-free and suitable for vegetarians and vegans; and you can easily convert plenty more to be gluten-free-friendly. Best of all, these vegetarian dishes are so delicious that even die-hard carnivores can't resist them.

◌ Fresh Harvest Penne

This recipe is an easy to prepare, complete vegetarian meal and a great way of using fresh vegetables. If you can't find gluten-free penne, use any type of gluten-free pasta.

Preparation time: *30 minutes*

Cooking time: *50 minutes*

Makes: *8 servings*

450 grams/1 pound (usually 1 packet) gluten-free penne (or any shape pasta)

2 tablespoons extra-virgin olive oil, for frying

½ medium red onion, finely chopped

100 grams/3½ ounces courgettes, thickly sliced

100 grams/3½ ounces yellow pepper, thickly sliced

1 tablespoon crushed garlic (about 6 cloves)

80 grams/3 ounces fresh aubergine, cut into 12-millimetre (½-inch) cubes

2 fresh medium-size tomatoes, chopped

2 tablespoons fresh basil, chopped

35 grams/1½ ounces vegetarian Parmesan cheese, freshly grated

1 Cook the pasta following the directions on the packet, being careful not to overcook it.

2 In a large frying pan, heat the olive oil over a medium heat. Add the onion, courgettes, and peppers to the pan, and sauté, stirring often, for about 5 minutes.

3 Add the garlic and aubergine to the pan, and continue stirring, frequently.

4 After about 5 minutes, when the aubergine begins to soften, reduce the heat and add the tomato. Continue stirring the mixture for 3 to 4 minutes.

5 Drain the pasta. In a large serving bowl, combine the pasta and vegetables, and sprinkle over the basil and Parmesan.

Nutrient analysis per serving: Calories 274; Protein 7g; Carbohydrate 48g; Sugar 4g; Fat 6g; Saturated fat 2g; Fibre 2g; Sodium 40mg.

☞ Vegan Lasagne

This dish is easy to make and a hit with guests, who may never guess that what they're eating is gluten-free. Be sure to double the recipe and freeze a pan of lasagne for later. When you're ready, take the frozen lasagne from the freezer, cover with baking foil, and place in a preheated oven (180°C/350°F/Gas Mark 4), cook for 1½ hours, removing the foil for the last 15 minutes of cooking to brown the top. This lasagne is even better eaten the following day as leftovers! If you prefer a vegetarian dish, you can substitute the soy cheese for cheeses that are suitable for vegetarians (they don't contain animal rennet – check the label first), such as a mixture of cream cheese, mozzarella, and Parmesan.

Preparation time: 15 minutes

Cooking time: 1 hour, 30 minutes

Makes: 10 servings

680 grams/24 ounces (usually 1 large jar) tomato sauce (passata)

2 teaspoons fresh basil, chopped

½ teaspoon onion powder

Freshly ground black pepper to taste

Freshly ground sea salt to taste

25 grams/1 ounce fresh spinach (washed and chopped)

65 grams/2½ ounces courgettes, diced

35 grams/1½ ounces black olives, sliced

20 grams/1 ounce mushrooms, sliced

40 grams/1½ ounces onion, chopped

1 tablespoon vegetable stock

225 grams/8 ounces soy based cream cheese

110 grams/4 ounces soy cheese, grated

285 grams/10 ounces (usually 1 packet) gluten-free lasagne sheet pasta, uncooked

Non-stick spray oil, for greasing

1 Preheat the oven to 190°C/350°F/Gas Mark 4.

2 In a medium bowl, mix together the tomato sauce, basil, onion powder, black pepper, and salt. Set the mixture aside.

3 Heat a large frying pan over a medium-high heat. Sauté the spinach, courgettes, olives, mushrooms, and onions in the vegetable stock for 4 minutes or until the onion starts to soften, being careful not to overcook. Set this mixture aside.

4 Spray a shallow 23-x-33-centimetre (9-x-13-inch) baking dish with non-stick oil. In the baking dish, layer the lasagne starting with one third of the sauce on the bottom of the dish, followed by a layer of uncooked lasagne sheets (just enough to cover the sauce). Mix the cheeses together and add half to cover the lasagne sheets, followed by half the vegetable mixture. Repeat this layering with another portion of the sauce, lasagne sheets, most of the remaining cheese, and the rest of the vegetables. Finish with the last third of sauce on the top.

5 Top the lasagne with a thin layer of cheese.

6 Cover the lasagne with aluminum foil and bake for 1 hour. Remove the foil and bake for a further 30 minutes or until the top is golden brown. Cool the lasagne for at least 15 minutes before cutting.

Tip : *Be creative with your choice of vegetables or alternative ingredients, such as adding roasted vegetables, lentils, or cannellini beans to the sauce.*

Tip: *If you prefer more flavour to your sauce, add a teaspoon of crushed garlic.*

Nutrient analysis per serving: *Calories 243; Protein 8g; Carbohydrate 32g; Sugar 8g; Fat 9g; Saturated fat 1g; Fibre 0.6g; Sodium 875mg.*

🍅 *Black Bean Veggie Burgers*

Gluten-free veggie burgers are hard to find – so why not make your own? This recipe uses black beans, but you can use a combination of any beans and even add grains such as millet and buckwheat. Wrap one of these burgers in a large iceberg lettuce leaf, top with salsa and guacamole, and you have a delicious, nutritious vegetarian meal.

Tools: *Food processor or blender*

Preparation time: *10 minutes*

Cooking time: *10 minutes*

Makes: *8 servings*

1.4 kilograms/3 pounds (usually 3 tins) black beans, drained and rinsed

40 grams/1½ ounces onion, chopped

75 grams/3 ounces red pepper, chopped

1 teaspoon cayenne pepper

1 teaspoon cumin

1 large free-range egg or equivalent vegan egg substitute

170 grams/6 ounces cooked quinoa

2 tablespoons fresh coriander, chopped

2 tablespoons extra-virgin olive oil

8 crisp, cold lettuce leaves

Salsa and guacamole (if desired)

1 Put the beans, onion, red pepper, cayenne, cumin, egg or egg substitute, quinoa, and coriander into a food processor or blender. Process the mixture until it forms a stiff consistency, but not too smooth that it doesn't contain any chunks.

2 Shape the mixture into eight rounds.

3 Heat 1 tablespoon of olive oil in a large frying pan over a medium heat. Add as many burgers to the pan as possible, and fry them for 2 minutes per side, turning once. Add the remaining tablespoon of oil and cook the remaining burgers.

4 Wrap each burger in a lettuce leaf, topping with salsa and guacamole.

Nutrient analysis per serving: *Calories 252; Protein 14g; Carbohydrate 37g; Sugars 7g; Fat 6g; Saturated fat 1g; Fibre 12.3g; Sodium 500mg.*

Cheese Enchiladas

You have to be careful with enchiladas, because many shop-bought or restaurant-prepared enchilada sauces have flour in them. You can dress up this quick and easy recipe with your favourite veg, other types of cheese, salsas, sour cream, or meat (such as the shredded pork from the recipe earlier in this chapter).

Preparation time: *25 minutes*

Cooking time: *1 hour*

Makes: *6 servings*

225 grams/8 ounces cheddar cheese, grated

225 grams mozzarella cheese, grated

½ teaspoon garlic powder

3 teaspoons cumin

3 tablespoons extra-virgin olive oil, for frying

1 small white onion, finely chopped

2 teaspoons crushed garlic (about 4 cloves)

1 litre/1¾ pints (usually 2½ cans) chopped tomatoes

2 tablespoons chilli powder

1 teaspoon oregano

2 tablespoons hot chilli sauce

12 corn tortillas

30 grams/1 ounce black olives, sliced

Non-stick spray oil, for greasing

1 Preheat the oven to 180°C/350°F/Gas Mark 4.

2 Combine the grated cheeses, garlic powder, and 2 teaspoons of cumin; set the mixture aside.

3 To make the enchilada sauce, heat 1 tablespoon of olive oil in a large frying pan over a medium-high heat. Add the chopped onion and garlic, and sauté until soft, for about 4 minutes. Add the tomato sauce, chilli powder, oregano, hot chilli sauce, and the remaining teaspoon of cumin. Cover the pan and simmer for about 30 minutes.

4 When the sauce is cooked, spray a 23-x-33-centimetre (9-x-13-inch) baking dish with oil, and pour approximately ⅔ of the sauce into it. Set aside the remaining enchilada sauce for Step 6.

5 In a small frying pan, heat the remaining 2 tablespoons of oil (or enough oil to generously cover the bottom of the pan) over a medium-high heat.

6 Briefly dip one corn tortilla into the hot oil to soften it (about 5 seconds), making sure that both sides get coated, and then dip it in the enchilada sauce, coating both sides. Lay the tortilla flat on a plate or cutting board, and sprinkle about ⅓ cup of the cheese mixture down the centre of the tortilla (lengthwise). Roll up the tortilla, and place it seam-side down into the baking dish.

7 Repeat Steps 5 and 6 for each enchilada, laying the enchiladas side by side in the baking dish. Pour the rest of the enchilada sauce over the rolled-up enchiladas, and sprinkle over any remaining cheese. Add the sliced black olives on top of the cheese.

8 Bake the enchiladas for 20 to 30 minutes, until the cheese melts and bubbles.

Nutrient analysis per serving: Calories 603; Protein 25g; Carbohydrate 54g; Sugar 6g; Fat 32g; Saturated fat 15g; Fibre 7.2g; Sodium 750mg.

Chapter 13

Enjoying Foods You Thought Were a Thing of the Past: Gluten-Free Pizza, Pasta, and Bread

In This Chapter

▶ Discovering how to make easy gluten-free pizza and tasty toppings

▶ Cooking tempting gluten-free pasta dishes

▶ Baking light and delicious bread

*B*eing gluten-free doesn't mean that you have to pine for pizza and back off from bread. In fact, some gluten-free versions of pizza and pasta – and yes, bread – are even better than the real thing.

You can choose to grind your own flours and press your own pasta, but you don't have to. These recipes are simple enough for a beginner to master, and they may even get those gluttons for gluten coming back for more.

Perfecting Your Pizza

When we first describe the gluten-free diet to people, they react with an emotion somewhere between disdain and horror. Very often when we're ringing the praises of the gluten-free lifestyle, people interrupt to ask, unable to hide the shock in their voices: 'You mean you can't eat pizza?'

The good news is that you *can* eat pizza. Maybe not the fast-food variety, but gluten-free pizza is delicious, nonetheless.

Touching base: The pizza foundation

The secret of a good pizza isn't in the sauce; the sauce is really just squashed tomatoes with herbs and spices. And it isn't in the toppings; those are just a euphemism for leftovers. No, the secret to any great pizza is undeniably in the base.

We believe in using mixes or even pre-made bases for our gluten-free pizzas, especially as these days they're so good. But this chapter is in the recipe section of this book, and our editors claim that simply saying 'take pre-made pizza base out of package' isn't good material. So we're including a delicious pizza base recipe that you can use when you have the time to indulge in recreating a little bit of Italy in your kitchen – and resist using one of those great-tasting gluten-free mixes or pre-made bases.

○ Gluten-Free Pizza Base

We like to double or even triple the recipe when making our pizza base. Prepare up to the end of stage 6 below, and then freeze the extra ones for another time. We love being able to pull a base out of the freezer, defrost for 10 minutes, top it, and pop it in the oven. Easy as pizza pie!

Tools: *Electric mixer or bread machine*

Preparation time: *30 minutes*

Rising time: *1 hour*

Cooking time: *25 minutes*

Makes: *One 43-centimetre (17-inch) or two 30-centimetre (12-inch) pizza bases (8 servings)*

150 grams/5½ ounces sorghum flour

150 grams/5½ ounces tapioca flour

75 grams/3 ounces bean flour (such as soybean)

80 grams/3 ounces rice flour

1 tablespoon xanthan gum

½ teaspoon salt

1 tablespoon active dry yeast (activated in warm water according to instructions on the packet)

1 tablespoon granulated sugar

⅓ teaspoon garlic salt

Pinch of dried oregano

60 millilitres/2½ fluid ounces milk, warmed

1 teaspoon cider vinegar

1 large free-range egg, beaten

2 tablespoons extra-virgin olive oil

A handful of rice, bean, tapioca, or sorghum flour, for dusting the board

1 In a large bowl, mix the sorghum flour, tapioca flour, bean flour, rice flour, xanthan gum, salt, activated yeast, sugar, garlic salt, and oregano. Then add the milk, vinegar, egg, and olive oil.

2 Use an electric mixer or bread machine to knead the mixture for about 3 minutes, until the dough is soft and thick. Roll the dough into a ball.

3 Dust a chopping board with a little rice, bean, tapioca, or sorghum flour. Using your hands or a rolling pin (dust with flour), flatten the dough on the board to your preferred thickness and shape of base (nothing says it has to be round). Add a little more flour if needed to keep the dough from sticking to the rolling pin and the chopping board.

4 Cover with a damp cloth and leave the dough to rise in a warm place for about 1 hour.

5 Preheat the oven to 220°C/425°F/Gas Mark 7.

6 Spread the dough onto a non-stick pizza pan. The diameter of the pizza depends on how thick you like to make your base. Use your fingers to pinch the edge and make a lip around the edge of the base.

7 Spread your choice of sauce and toppings evenly over the base, and bake the pizza in a preheated oven for 12 to 15 minutes or until the cheese has melted.

Nutrient analysis per serving (base only): Calories 189; Protein 9g; Carbohydrate 26 g; Sugar 4g; Fat 6g; Saturated fat 1g; Fibre 5g; Sodium 212mg.

Considering your toppings: Pizza sauces

We're going to let you into a couple of secrets. First, almost any commercial pizza sauce is gluten-free (of course, you still need to check the ingredients to be sure). Second, pizza sauce can be as simple as brushing on a little extra-virgin olive oil. If you like to be creative, feel free to come up with your own ideas. However, we offer a couple of simple recipes to get you started.

The passion for pizza has history

We know that pizza lovers everywhere can argue for hours about who cooks the best pizza and makes the best toppings. But pizza has evolved over the centuries – the credit for inventing pizza really goes to ancient Middle Eastern cultures that made flat, unleavened bread in mud ovens. Pizza took the form we're most familiar with in Naples, Italy, where peasants in the Middle Ages made a seasoned flatbread and covered it with cheese.

The mass appeal of the tomato-mozzarella cheese combination is thanks to a Neapolitan baker called Rafaele Esposito. In 1889, Esposito made a special pizza for the visiting King Umberto I and Queen Margherita. He decorated the pizza to look like the Italian flag, with red tomatoes, white mozzarella cheese, and green basil leaves as toppings. The pizza was a hit, and of course, naming the pizza after the queen didn't hurt its popularity; Pizza Margherita is still an Italian favourite.

Make use of bottled sauces and condiments that you already have in your kitchen as toppings for your pizza: gluten-free teriyaki sauce, Dijon mustard, hoisin sauce, taco sauce, ranch dressing, or barbecue sauce.

🍅 Tomato Herb Pizza Sauce

Traditionalists lean toward this type of a sauce, because, well, it's traditional.

Preparation time: *10 minutes*

Cooking time: *15 minutes*

Makes: *Enough for one 30-centimetre (12-inch) pizza*

2 tablespoons extra-virgin olive oil

1 teaspoon fresh garlic, crushed (about 2 cloves)

40 grams/1½ ounces onion, finely chopped

360 grams/12¾ ounces fresh tomatoes, chopped (or 1 can, including the juice)

1 teaspoon fresh oregano, chopped

2 tablespoons fresh basil leaves, chopped

Generous quantity of freshly ground salt and black pepper to taste

3 tablespoons tomato paste

1 In a medium saucepan, cook the onion and garlic in the olive oil over a medium-high heat until tender (about 3 minutes).

2 Add the tomatoes, oregano, basil, salt, and pepper to the pan, and continue cooking the sauce for a few more minutes.

3 Stir in the tomato paste. Reduce the heat to low and simmer the sauce for about 10 minutes.

Nutrient analysis per serving: Calories 49; Protein 1g; Carbohydrate 3g; Sugar 3g; Fat 4g; Saturated fat 1g; Fibre 1g; Sodium 141mg.

☙ Alfredo Sauce

This sauce is a great twist on an old favourite, and it makes a white pizza instead of a red one. The sauce is basically the same type of cheesy, creamy Alfredo sauce you use on pasta – in fact, if you're feeling adventurous, feel free to use it on your pasta!

Preparation time: 10 minutes

Cooking time: 5 minutes

Makes: Enough for one 30-centimetre (12-inch) pizza

60 grams/2½ ounces butter

3 cloves garlic, crushed

100 grams/4 ounces Parmesan cheese, grated

120 millilitres/4 fluid ounces double cream

Generous quantity of freshly ground salt and pepper

1 Melt the butter in a medium saucepan over a medium heat.

2 Add the garlic and sauté for 2 or 3 minutes, stirring constantly. While you're sautéing, sprinkle a little salt on the garlic, which brings out some of the moisture and prevents burning.

3 Stir in the Parmesan, cream, salt, and pepper. Heat the sauce for about 5 minutes, stirring constantly.

4 Remove the saucepan from the heat. Leave the sauce to cool for 5 minutes before spreading over the pizza base.

Nutrient analysis per serving: Calories 182; Protein 5g; Carbohydrate 1g; Sugar 1g; Fat 18g; Saturated fat 11g; Fibre 0g; Sodium 192mg.

Using a pizza stone

Using a pizza stone is the best way to get a crispy base, and avoid soggy pizza. To use a pizza stone, heat it in a hot oven (220°C / 425°F / Gas Mark 7) for about an hour before you want to cook your pizza. Then coat the stone with gluten-free flour and transfer the pizza base, complete with toppings, to the stone (if you're following a recipe that calls for letting the base rise, let it rise on a separate pan before moving it to the stone). Cook for about 10 to 15 minutes.

Important: Don't use oil on a pizza stone, because the high temperatures can cause the oil to catch on fire. *Equally as important:* If you cook gluten-containing pizzas and gluten-free pizzas, don't share stones; they can absorb the flour and contaminate your gluten-free pizza.

Going beyond the norm: Customising your pizza

For purists, adding anything to a pizza besides sauce and cheese is sacrilege. However, making your own pizza is a chance to flaunt your adventurous side, and so if you're a flaunter, read on.

Sauceless Inside-Out Seafood Pizza

Definitely not one for traditionalists, this 'sauceless inside-out' pizza is an Italy-meets-Hawaii creation that offers seafood and pizza lovers the best of both worlds.

Preparation time: *15 minutes*

Cooking time: *10 minutes*

Makes: *8 servings (two 30-centimetre (12-inch) pizzas)*

2 30-centimetre (12-inch) uncooked pizza bases (see the earlier 'Gluten-Free Pizza Base' recipe)

135 grams/4¾ ounces (usually 1 can) crab meat

130 grams/4½ ounces small cooked, peeled prawns

80 grams/3 ounces crushed pineapple (tinned)

35 grams/1½ ounces fresh mushrooms, sliced

100 grams/4 ounces pitted black olives, sliced

25 grams/1 ounce red pepper, sliced

120 grams/4½ ounces mozzarella cheese, grated

120 grams/4½ ounces cheddar cheese, grated

1 Preheat the oven to 230°C/450°F/Gas Mark 8.

2 Except for the cheeses, mix the ingredients together and divide the mixture evenly between the two pizza bases. Sprinkle each pizza with half of the grated mozzarella and half of the grated cheddar.

3 Bake the pizzas in the oven until the cheese is bubbly and starting to turn golden-brown. The pizzas should take between 10 and 15 minutes to cook.

Nutrient analysis per serving: *Calories 528; Protein 33g; Carbohydrate 55g; Sugar 9g; Fat 22g; Saturated fat 8g; Fibre 10g; Sodium 1241mg.*

Stuffed Pizza Pockets (Calzones)

Stuffed pizza pockets, or *calzones* as they're rightly known, have become increasingly popular with adults and children alike despite the fact that in many Central and South American countries the word *calzones* is Spanish slang for ladies' underwear! We have created our own gluten-free version using the 'Gluten-Free Pizza Base' recipe given earlier in this chapter. But you can use any gluten-free pizza dough recipe you like. Just make enough dough for two 30-centimetre (12-inch) pizzas (check out Chapter 8 for ideas on which flour mixes to use). Calzones are also great dipped in your favourite pasta sauce!

Preparation time: *40 minutes*

Cooking time: *40 minutes*

Makes: *4 servings*

1 quantity of Gluten-Free Pizza Base' dough, uncooked

120 grams/4½ ounces mozzarella cheese, grated

120 grams/4½ ounces cheddar cheese, grated

100 grams/3½ ounces pepperoni slices

40 grams/1½ ounces rice, sorghum, bean, or tapioca flour, for flouring the board

Olive oil spray, for greasing the baking tray

1 Preheat the oven to 190°C/375°F/Gas Mark 5.

2 Divide the dough into four equal parts, and roll each one into a ball. Place on a board or baking tray, cover the balls with damp kitchen roll, and leave the dough in a warm area for 20 minutes.

3 Dust a chopping board and rolling pin with gluten-free flour, and roll each dough ball out flat so that it's about 18 millimetres (¾ inch) thick. Trim the edges to make an oval shape.

4 Line a baking tray with foil, and spray it with oil. Place the ovals onto the foil-covered tray. Using your fingernail, a toothpick, or a knife, lightly cut a line across each oval, dividing it in half crosswise.

5 Put ¼ of the mozzarella, ¼ of the cheddar, and ¼ of the pepperoni on one of the halves of each oval, leaving about 12 millimetres (½ inch) of dough clear along the edges.

6 Fold over the other half of the dough (the half with nothing on it) so that it lies on top of the filling. Using your fingers, gently crimp the edges of the dough halves together.

7 Bake all four pockets in the oven for 35 to 40 minutes, until they begin to turn golden brown, or until melted cheese begins to ooze out.

Nutrient analysis per serving: *Calories 711; Protein 38g; Carbohydrate 53g; Sugar 8g; Fat 40g; Saturated fat 17g; Fibre 10g; Sodium 1227mg.*

MYOP (make your own pizza) parties

Rarely can an entire group agree on what should go on a pizza. So why not let everyone have exactly what they want by turning the event into a party? That's what an MYOP party is all about. Here's how you do it:

1. **Make several batches of gluten-free pizza dough.**

2. **Roll up balls that, when flattened, are each the right size for an individual-sized pizza (the balls should be about the size of a tennis ball).**

3. **Put out a selection of toppings – lots of them – in separate serving bowls.**

   Have some bowls of different sauces and others with different types of cheeses, pepperoni, mushrooms, pineapple, anchovies, and so on.

4. **Give each guest a dough ball and let him or her roll it out to the desired thickness.**

5. **Allow each guest to add sauce and their choice of toppings.**

6. **Bake the pizzas thoroughly until the cheese has melted and the crust is golden brown.**

Of course, MYOP parties are about the messiest type of party you can throw, with flour and dough flying. And you always have the ubiquitous show-off who just has to prove they can toss the dough like the real pizza-makers do. Be prepared to clean up afterwards. Remember that these parties always incite friendly-but-competitive cases of 'my pizza's going to be better than yours.' If you invite competitive friends, consider yourself forewarned!

⏾ Mexican Pizza

This version of Mexican pizza is vegetarian, but if you like meat, just add some cooked minced beef.

Preparation time: *20 minutes*

Cooking time: *25 minutes*

Makes: *6 servings*

2 30-centimetre (12-inch) pizza bases (see the Gluten-Free Pizza Base' recipe)

450 grams/16 ounces (usually 1 can) refried beans

2 large spring onions, thinly sliced

120 grams/4½ ounces cheddar cheese, grated

120 grams/4½ ounces mozzarella cheese, grated

50 grams/2 ounces pitted black olives, sliced

60 millilitres/2 fluid ounces sour cream

2 tablespoons fresh coriander, chopped

180 grams/6½ ounces fresh tomato, chopped

75 grams/3 ounces lettuce, shredded

25 grams/1 ounce jalapeño peppers, sliced

250 grams/9 ounces ready made salsa

1 Preheat the oven to 220°C/425°F/Gas Mark 7.

2 Bake the pizza bases for 8 minutes, or until they just begin to turn golden brown.

3 Divide all the ingredients in half. Spread half the refried beans on each crust. To make spreading the beans easier, mix in about 2 tablespoons of salsa to help thin the mixture if necessary.

4 Top each pizza with the spring onions, the grated cheeses, and black olives.

5 Bake the pizzas for 15 to 20 minutes or until the cheese begins to bubble.

6 Remove the pizzas from the oven and add half the sour cream, 1 tablespoon of coriander half of the tomato, lettuce, jalapeños, and salsa to each pizza.

Nutrient analysis per serving: Calories 866; Protein 44g; Carbohydrate 90g; Sugar 16g; Fat 40g; Saturated fat 13g; Fibre 19g; Sodium 1303mg.

Fulfilling a Passion for Pasta

Complaining about the taste of gluten-free pasta was once completely acceptable. They used to be gritty, heavy on the (insert flour flavour here) flavour, and they went from being *al dente* to mush in a millisecond.

But gluten-free pasta has come a long, long way. In fact, even the most discerning pasta aficionados appreciate the taste, texture, variety of shapes and sizes, nutritional value, and versatility of today's gluten-free pasta.

Although pasta can taste great served very simply with just a little extra-virgin olive oil or butter, you can also turn just about any traditional pasta recipe into a great gluten-free dish simply by using your favourite gluten-free variety. Or try our suggestions for something completely different.

Sweet and Tangy Noodles with Peanuts (Pad Thai)

Cheating with this dish is much easier than making it from scratch. You can buy pad thai kits, complete with noodles and sauce at many supermarkets and just about any Asian market. But if you're a purist and want to make the entire dish yourself, we show you how. Tamarind, which makes foods taste sour and is a natural preservative, is a critical ingredient in the sauce. Finding a replacement for tamarind is hard, and so stock up on this ingredient if you plan to do a lot of Thai cooking.

Tools: *Wok or large nonstick frying panlet*

Preparation time: *20 minutes*

Cooking time: *15 minutes*

Makes: *6 servings*

225 grams/8 ounces rice noodles, uncooked	*60 millilitres/2 fluid ounces fish sauce*
2 teaspoons tamarind concentrate	*50 grams/2 ounces granulated sugar*
2 tablespoons cold water	*1 tablespoon chopped chives*
2 teaspoons cooking oil	*110 grams/4 ounces roasted peanuts, crushed*
5 cloves garlic, finely chopped	
20 grams/1 ounce shallots, chopped	*100 grams/3½ ounces cooked peeled prawns*
125 grams/4½ ounces firm tofu, diced	*1 large free-range egg, beaten*
	80 grams/3 ounces fresh bean sprouts

1 Soak the rice noodles according to the directions on the packet so that they're pliable but not mushy. Mix the tamarind concentrate and the water to make a tamarind juice, and put aside for use in Step 3.

2 Heat the oil in a wok over a medium-high heat. When the oil's hot, add the garlic, shallots, and tofu. Stirring constantly, cook them until the garlic and shallots begin to turn opaque (about 5 minutes).

3 Add the tamarind juice (from Step 1), fish sauce, sugar, chives, and peanuts to the wok and stir-fry for 2 minutes, mixing the ingredients. Add the prawns and noodles, and stir-fry the mixture until the noodles are well coated with the sauce, about 2 minutes.

4 Scoop the noodle mixture to one side of the wok; slowly add the beaten egg to the other side, drizzling it into the hot wok to make a fine ribbon of cooked egg. Blend the egg and the noodle mixture together.

5 Add the bean sprouts, and cook the noodle dish for another 30 seconds or so.

Tip: A common garnish for pad thai is 40 grams (1½ ounces) uncooked bean sprouts, 2 to 3 tablespoons chopped chives, and 50 grams (2 ounces) coarsely ground roasted peanuts marinated in a tablespoon of lime juice, a teaspoon of tamarind concentrate, 2½ teaspoons of water, and a tablespoon of fish sauce. Sprinkle the mixture on to the cooked pad thai and place several lime segments and slices of cucumber around the serving platter.

Nutrient analysis per serving: Calories 394; Protein 19g; Carbohydrate 46g; Sugar 10g; Fat 15g; Saturated fat 2g; Fibre 2g; Sodium 703mg.

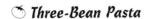 **Three-Bean Pasta**

This colourful, wholesome, and delicious dish is best served with tagliatelle, although you can use just about any gluten-free pasta you have to hand.

Preparation time: 20 minutes

Makes: 6 servings

450 grams/1 pound gluten-free tagliatelle, uncooked

425 grams/15 ounces (usually 1 can) kidney beans, drained and rinsed

425 grams/15 ounces (usually 1 can) chickpeas, drained and rinsed

110 grams/4 ounces fresh green beans, trimmed and rinsed

80 grams/3 ounces red onion, chopped

½ large red pepper, chopped

3 tablespoons Dijon mustard

3 tablespoons extra-virgin olive oil

3 tablespoons red wine vinegar

3 tablespoons fresh parsley, chopped

1 tablespoons fresh basil, chopped

1 Cook the pasta according to the directions on the packet, making sure that it's *al dente* (slightly firm). Drain and rinse under cold water.

2 In a large serving bowl, stir together the pasta, kidney beans, chickpeas, green beans, onion, red pepper, mustard, oil, vinegar, parsley, and basil. Stir the pasta well to mix the ingredients.

Nutrient analysis per serving: Calories 483; Protein 17g; Carbohydrate 83g; Sugar 5g; Fat 9g; Saturated fat 1g; Fibre 9g; Sodium 736mg.

Baking Fresh Bread

Gluten-free bread has a bad reputation. And for years, this reputation was well-deserved. But if any food deserves to win in the 'most improved' category in the gluten-free food world, it's definitely bread. Thanks to some dedicated experimental cooking, bread has evolved from being tasteless and brick-like to light, doughy, and tasty.

Best of all, the gluten-free cooks have done an incredible job of combining interesting, alternative flours that not only improve the flavour and texture but also add nutrients. Now that gluten-free bread actually tastes good, it's superior in many ways to gluten-containing processed white bread.

To give you a head start we have experimented and developed some simple bread recipes to share with you in this section. For some additional bread-making tips and tricks, refer to Chapter 8.

Of course, if you'd rather not buy and measure all the recipe ingredients that go into bread, don't bother. Lots of excellent bread mixes are available. Just pop a mix in your bread machine, add a few ingredients, and switch it on.

☺ Gluten-Free Flour Tortillas

We prefer tortillas made with corn to flour ones, but some people yearn for flour tortillas. This recipe is actually very good!

Preparation time: *30 minutes*

Cooking time: *20 minutes*

Makes: *6 servings*

320 grams/11¼ ounces gluten-free flour mixture

2 teaspoons xanthan gum

1 tablespoon granulated sugar

1 heaped teaspoon salt

1 teaspoon baking powder

30 grams/1 ounce margarine

240 millilitres/8½ fluid ounces warm water

1 Heat a heavy based frying pan over a medium heat.

2 In a large bowl, combine the flour mixture, xanthan gum, sugar, salt, and baking powder. Blend in the margarine using a knife.

3 Slowly add the warm water to the flour mixture, stirring after each addition, until the dough is smooth. Form the dough into balls, about the size of tennis balls.

4 Put the dough between two sheets of greaseproof paper. Using a rolling pin, flatten the dough balls, one at a time, until they're about 3 millimetres (⅛ inch) thick. They should be about 25 to 30 centimetres (10 to 12 inches) in diameter.

5 Remove the greaseproof paper. Cook the tortillas in the hot frying pan for about 45 seconds, or until the underside starts to develop brown flecks; the tortillas may begin to bubble. Turn each tortilla once. The second side cooks quickly, in about 20 seconds. Check the underside of each tortilla again to see if they've browned, which is when they're ready.

Nutrient analysis per serving: Calories 229; Protein 3g; Carbohydrate 45g; Sugar 7g; Fat 4g; Saturated fat 2g; Fibre 2g; Sodium 555mg.

'This is bread?'

Danna remembers her first experience with gluten-free bread. In fact, she remembers it vividly, like a bad nightmare that won't go away. Her then-toddler son had recently been diagnosed with coeliac disease, and she was more than just a little anxious about feeding him without poisoning him. This was, mind you, back in 1991 when gluten-free products were scarce.

She was relieved and ecstatic to discover, in the bowels of a freezer box at what was then the only health-food shop within a 50-mile radius, a loaf of gluten-free bread. Screeching with delight, right there in the store, she started to pull out a slice of the bread, exclaiming, 'Tyler, you can eat this!' But before the slice made it out of the flimsy plastic bag, the bread-like substance began to crumble . . . and then crumble some more. Somehow, she maintained her enthusiasm – albeit now waning – and bent down to her toddler son, eager to share with him the newfound treasure that was now nothing more than a fistful of dry, tasteless crumbs. 'Mummy', he said with sincere confusion, '*this* is *bread?*'

✎ Simple White Bread for Bread Machines

A loaf of simple white bread can go a long way. After all, everyone knows that bread is really just an instrument to allow you the pleasure of consuming butter without raising eyebrows. Simplify your life by substituting the same weight of a premixed gluten-free flour mixture in place of the flours in this recipe and use a bread machine to mix the dough and bake the bread. We like this particular recipe because the variety of flours enhances the taste, texture, and nutritional value.

Tools: *Bread machine*

Preparation time: *30 minutes*

Cooking time: *2 to 3½ hours (depending on your bread machine)*

Makes: *6 servings (one 1½ pound loaf)*

75 grams/3 ounces tapioca flour

40 grams/1½ ounces millet flour

80 grams/3 ounces sorghum flour

160 grams/5½ ounces white rice flour

160 grams/5½ ounces brown rice flour

1 large free-range egg, beaten

4 egg whites

1 tablespoon apple cider vinegar

60 millilitres/2½ ounces rapeseed oil

60 millilitres/2½ ounces honey (preferably runny)

480 millilitres/17 fluid ounces warm milk

45 millilitres/1¾ ounces butter

1 teaspoon gelatin

1 teaspoon salt

1 teaspoon xanthan gum

1 tablespoon active dry yeast (activated in warm water according to instructions on the packet)

1 Put all the ingredients into the bread machine in the order recommended by the manufacturer. Make sure that you add the yeast last, on top of all the other ingredients. Select the cycle for homemade breads. If your machine has the option of doing only one kneading and one rising cycle, choose that option (although letting the bread go through two kneadings doesn't hurt the bread).

2 After a few minutes of kneading, check on the dough. Scrape any excess flour off the sides of the tub back into the dough to mix thoroughly. Make sure that the consistency is just a little thicker than a cake batter: If it's too thick, add more milk; if it's too runny, add a little rice flour.

3 When the bread machine has completed its baking cycle, let the loaf cool for a few minutes before removing from the pan.

Nutrient analysis per serving: *Calories 481; Protein 14g; Carbohydrate 65g; Sugar 11g; Fat 19g; Saturated fat 6g; Fibre 4g; Sodium 508mg.*

Chapter 14

Getting Your (Gluten-Free) Just Desserts

In This Chapter

▶ Creating clever gluten-free decadent desserts

▶ Taking the biscuit with gluten-free sweet snacks

▶ Enjoying sweets and treats for the health-conscious

*O*nce the main course has been finished, everyone eagerly anticipates one thing – and it's not doing the dishes. Of course, we mean the dessert. If you think following the gluten-free lifestyle means having to deprive yourself of decadence and indulgence, this chapter surely proves you wrong.

If your idea of dessert is a bowl of sliced strawberries with a dollop of yogurt on top (for a splurge), that's cool. We've put together some health-conscious recipes in this chapter to satisfy your wholesome-and-healthy sweet tooth, as well as some recipes for delicious desserts that pack and travel well for when you're gluten-free and on the go. But if you're the more decadent type, you may be delighted to find recipes in this chapter for cakes, biscuits, fudge, and other gluten-free indulgences.

Daring to Be Decadent: Gluten-Free Indulgences

Yes, you can have your cake and eat it, too. As long as it's gluten-free! We're into indulgences; we mean, if you're going to live it up from time to time, you may as well really satisfy that craving and get it out of your system. Plenty of gluten-free desserts can satisfy your cravings, but these recipes are wickedly wonderful.

Making your own desserts

Close your eyes and think of the most delicious dessert you can imagine. Is it gluten-free? No? Well it can be – and here's how. Use mixes: Literally dozens of companies make absolutely incredible mixes for gluten-free baked goods. Using them can be a little pricier than baking from scratch, but some are available on prescription. However, take it from those of us who've made too many biscuits like bricks and cakes that didn't rise: Mixes are tried, tested, and – today, at least – absolutely delicious.

Dessert is the course that comes after the main course – of course. And in most cultures, dessert is comprised of sweet, decadent foods. But in many cultures, dessert isn't sweet at all but is simply a course consisting of very strong flavours, like cheese. The word comes from the Old French *desservir*, which means 'to clear the table.'

Flourless Chocolate Cake

One of the most incredible desserts on the planet, this flourless chocolate cake is rich, dense, moist, and surprisingly easy to prepare. It requires very few ingredients, none of which are difficult to obtain. Prepare to be amazed.

Tools: *23-centimetre (9-inch) loose-based or springform cake tin*

Preparation time: *30 minutes*

Cooking time: *50 minutes*

Makes: *8 servings*

227 grams/8 ounces unsalted butter	*6 large free-range eggs*
227 grams/8 ounces bittersweet chocolate, broken into pieces	*200 grams/7 ounces granulated sugar*
	Non-stick oil spray, for greasing the tin

1 Preheat the oven to 140°C/275°F/Gas Mark 1. Spray a 23-centimetre (9-inch) loose-based or springform cake tin with non-stick oil. If you don't know what a springform cake tin looks like, see Figure 14-1.

2 Put the butter and chocolate in a large bowl over a pan of hot water in a saucepan. Put the pan on a low heat and allow the chocolate and butter to melt. Alternatively, place in a microwaveable bowl and microwave the chocolate and butter in 10-second intervals until melted, stirring after each interval.

3 Separate the egg whites and egg yolks, putting the yolks and whites in separate small bowls. Whisk the yolks into the warm chocolate-butter mixture.

4 Whisk the egg whites (or beat them on low speed) for 3 minutes, and add the sugar. Continue to beat or whisk the egg whites until stiff and glossy, which should take about 3 minutes. Gently fold the stiffened egg whites into the chocolate mixture.

5 Pour the batter into the prepared pan, and smooth over the top of the batter with a spatula.

6 Bake the batter until the cake is set in the centre – for about 45 to 50 minutes. Let the cake cool for 15 minutes, and then remove from the tin.

Tip: Cover the cake in powdered sugar or cocoa powder, or drizzle with caramel sauce or chocolate sauce. If you're watching your waistline (yeah, right!), you may want to cover it in raspberries instead.

Nutrient analysis per serving: Calories 523; Protein 7g; Carbohydrate 42g; Sugar 42g; Fat 36g; Saturated fat 21g; Fibre 1g; Sodium 67mg.

Foolproof Peanut Butter Fudge

This incredible fudge is almost embarrassingly easy to make; it's foolproof. The hardest part of this recipe is being patient enough to wait until it's cooled before eating it.

Preparation time: *10 minutes*

Refrigeration time: *2 hours*

Makes: *8 servings*

500 grams/17½ ounces smooth peanut butter

397 grams/14 ounces (usually 1 can) sweetened condensed milk

2 teaspoons natural vanilla extract

Pinch of salt

1 Put the peanut butter into a medium-sized glass bowl, and add the condensed milk. Microwave the mixture on high for 3 minutes, making sure that it doesn't bubble over the sides of the bowl.

2 Stir the mixture to make sure that the peanut butter has melted and the mixture's smooth. Add the vanilla and salt, and mix well.

3 Line a 25-centimetre (10-inch) square pan with greaseproof paper, and pour in the fudge mixture. Refrigerate the fudge for 2 hours (if you can wait that long!). Cut into 7bf1/ 2-centimetre (3-inch) pieces to serve.

Nutrient analysis per serving: Calories 554; Protein 20g; Carbohydrate 34g; Sugar 30g; Fat 37g; Saturated fat 11g; Fibre 3g; Sodium 338mg.

Figure 14-1:
The cylinder of a springform cake tin unlatches, allowing the bottom to be removed.

Crustless Cherry Cheesecake

Really, the best part of the cheesecake is the innards, anyway. This crustless cherry cheesecake is rich and decadent – the perfect indulgence.

Preparation time: *10 minutes*

Cooking time: *20 to 30 minutes*

Cooling time: *30 minutes*

Makes: *8 servings*

227 grams/8 ounces (usually 1 packet) cream cheese, softened

100 grams/3½ ounces granulated sugar

2 large free-range eggs, beaten

2 tablespoons fresh lemon juice

1 teaspoon natural vanilla extract

25 grams/1 ounce gluten-free flour mixture

600 grams/21 ounces (usually 1 large can) cherry pie filling

1 spray can whipped cream

125 grams/4½ ounces fresh cherries (for garnish)

Non-stick oil spray, for greasing the dish

1 Preheat the oven to 180°C/350°F/Gas Mark 4.

2 Lightly grease a 23-x-33-centimetre (9-x-13-inch) casserole dish with the oil spray.

3 Combine the cream cheese, sugar, eggs, lemon juice, vanilla, and gluten-free flour mixture. Pour this mixture into the casserole dish, and bake for 20 to 30 minutes. The cheesecake is done when you insert a skewer in the centre and it comes out clean.

4 After the cheesecake cools for at least 30 minutes, spread the cherry pie filling over the top. Then spray on the whipped cream and garnish with the fresh cherries.

Nutrient analysis per serving: *Calories 324; Protein 3g; Carbohydrate 33g; Sugar 28g; Fat 20g; Saturated fat 12g; Fibre 1g; Sodium 148mg.*

Fashioning Gluten-Free Sweet Treats for On the Go

Some desserts are just meant for eating at home. This is fine if the get-together is at your house, but what if the party's somewhere else and the host asks you to bring a dessert? What can you bring to picnics? What packs and travels well for a sweet treat in the kids' lunchboxes? What if you just want a gluten-free sugar fix? We're glad you asked.

✆ Fruity Caramel Popcorn Balls

In keeping with the cereal-makes-good-desserts theme, this recipe also calls for any gluten-free puffed rice cereal.

Preparation time: *20 minutes*

Makes: *20 servings*

110 grams/4 ounces gluten-free puffed rice cereal

10 grams/½ ounce popped plain popcorn

75 grams/3 ounces peanuts

45 grams/1¾ ounces butter

60 grams/2½ ounces caramel sauce ice cream topping

1 In a large bowl, combine the cereal, popcorn, and peanuts.

2 In a small microwave-safe bowl, heat the butter and caramel topping on high for 1 minute, or until melted. Stir until smooth.

3 Pour the caramel mixture over the cereal mixture, and stir well to combine.

4 Spread the mixture onto greaseproof paper and leave to cool. When cool enough to touch safely, shape the caramel cereal into balls the size of a golf ball. Store the popcorn balls in an airtight container.

Nutrient analysis per serving: Calories 113; Protein 3g; Carbohydrate 11g; Sugar 4g; Fat 6g; Saturated fat 3g; Fibre 0.5g; Sodium 89mg.

☉ *Chocolate Marshmallow Bars*

Very few sweet snacks have withstood the test of time like marshmallow bars. But most cereals used to make those bars have gluten in them, and so they're usually unsuitable. Try this simple variation using Kellogg's Coco Pops. Although Kellogg do make gluten-containing cereals, Coco Pops are not considered at risk of contamination during production, and so are okay on a gluten-free diet.

Preparation time: *30 minutes*

Refrigeration time: *10 minutes*

Makes: *4 servings*

60 grams/2½ ounces margarine

284 grams/10 ounce (usually 1 packet) marshmallows

160 grams/5½ ounces Kellogg's Coco Pops

Non-stick oil spray, for greasing the dish

1 Spray a 23-by-33-centimetre (9-by-13-inch) pan or dish liberally with non-stick oil.

2 Put the margarine into a large saucepan to melt over a low heat. Add the marshmallows, and stirring constantly, cook until the marshmallows have completely melted and the mixture is smooth. Remove the pan from the heat.

3 Add the cereal, and mix well to coat the cereal thoroughly with the marshmallow mixture.

4 Spread the warm mixture into the greased pan. Using a spatula coated with non-stick spray, press the cereal mixture into an even layer.

5 Refrigerate the pan for 10 minutes and then cut the mixture into squares. If you prefer, you can put the squares back into the fridge to make them really cold.

Nutrient analysis per serving: Calories 479; Protein 5g; Carbohydrate 89g; Sugar 60g; Fat 12g; Saturated fat 4g; Fibre 0g; Sodium 300mg.

☺ Sweet Peanut Butter-Chocolate-Covered Cereal

These treats are sweet and crunchy, and they make a great snack to satisfy your sweet tooth. Usually, this recipe uses gluten-based cereals, but we've used a gluten-free puffed rice alternative and we dare you to notice the difference!

Preparation time: *20 minutes*

Refrigeration time: *30 minutes*

Makes: *12 servings*

180 grams/6½ ounces bittersweet chocolate, broken into squares

250 grams/8¾ ounces smooth peanut butter

120 grams/4½ ounces margarine

370 grams/13 ounces (usually 1 box) gluten-free puffed rice cereal

1 teaspoon natural vanilla extract

200 grams/7 ounces icing sugar

1 Combine the chocolate, peanut butter, and margarine in a medium-sized pan over a low-medium heat. Stir the ingredients constantly until they're melted and well mixed.

2 Pour the cereal into a very large bowl. Drizzle the chocolate mixture over the cereal, and mix well so that all the cereal is coated.

3 Put the icing sugar into a large plastic bag; add the cereal – a bagful at a time – and shake it to coat the cereal.

4 Spread the mixture out on to wax paper, separating the chunks of cereal to stop them from sticking together. Refrigerate the mixture for 30 minutes.

Nutrient analysis per serving: Calories 450; Protein 9g; Carbohydrate 53g; Sugar 29g; Fat 23g; Saturated fat 8g; Fibre 2g; Sodium 355mg.

☙ *Microwave Chocolate Chip Peanut Brittle*

Peanut brittle is a great eat-as-you-go snack. Break it into small pieces and convince yourself that it's not going to sabotage your diet because the pieces are tiny.

Preparation time: *20 minutes*

Cooling time: *1 hour*

Makes: *12 servings*

180 grams/6½ ounces bittersweet chocolate chips

200 grams/7 ounces granulated sugar

150 grams/5½ ounces golden syrup

220 grams/8 ounces salted peanuts

10 grams/½ ounce butter

1 teaspoon natural vanilla extract

1 teaspoon sodium bicarbonate

Non-stick oil spray, for greasing the trays

1 Spray two baking trays with non-stick oil. Spread half the chocolate chips on each baking tray.

2 Place the sugar and golden syrup into a large microwaveable bowl. Cover the bowl with kitchen roll, and microwave on high for 8 minutes. Stir the mixture, and then microwave it for a further 4 minutes. Watch to make sure that it doesn't bubble over.

3 Stir in the peanuts, and microwave for another 2 minutes. The mixture should be light brown in colour.

4 Add the butter and vanilla, blending well. Microwave the mixture on high for a further 1 minute. The peanuts should be lightly browned. Add the sodium bicarbonate and stir gently until the mixture is light and foamy.

5 Pour the mixture over the chocolate chips on the baking trays. Let the mixture cool for an hour. When cool, break into small pieces and store in an airtight container.

Nutrient analysis per serving: Calories 300; Protein 6g; Carbohydrate 35g; Sugar 35g; Fat 15g; Saturated fat 5g; Fibre 1g; Sodium 240mg.

○ Incredibly Easy Peanut Butter Cookies

By definition, a cookie can be any of a variety of flour-based sweet biscuits. We break all the rules with this recipe, because they contain no flour. Best of all, the cookies are incredibly easy – you only need four ingredients!

Preparation time: *5 minutes*

Cooking time: *20 minutes*

Makes: *24 cookies*

2 large free-range eggs	*200 grams/7 ounces granulated sugar*
258 grams/9 ounces chunky peanut butter	*Non-stick oil spray, for greasing the baking tray*

1 Preheat the oven to 180°C/350°F/Gas Mark 4. Lightly grease two baking trays with non-stick oil spray.

2 Beat the eggs in a medium-sized bowl. Stir the peanut butter and sugar into the eggs.

3 Drop dollops of dough from a spoon onto a baking tray about 5 centimetres (2 inches) apart. Use the back side of a fork to press them flat.

4 Bake the cookies for 10 to 12 minutes, or until the cookies spring back a little when you press them.

Nutrient analysis per serving: Calories 106; Protein 4g; Carbohydrate 9g; Sugar 9g; Fat 6g; Saturated fat 1g; Fibre 1g; Sodium 46mg.

Zebra Meringues

These delicious meringue biscuits are incredibly easy to make, but they give the impression that you've spent hours in the kitchen baking them.

Preparation time: *15 minutes*

Cooking time: *2 hours*

Makes: *40 meringues*

3 egg whites

Pinch of salt

Pinch of cream of tartar

100 grams/3½ ounces granulated sugar

1 teaspoon natural vanilla extract

180 grams/6½ ounces bittersweet chocolate, broken into chunks

Non-stick oil spray, for greasing the trays

1 Preheat the oven to 180°C/350°F/Gas Mark 4. Lightly grease two baking trays with non-stick oil spray.

2 Use an electric beater to beat the egg whites at high speed until they're foamy.

3 Add the salt and cream of tartar. Beat the whites until they form stiff peaks.

4 Add the sugar gradually, while beating. Then add the vanilla, beating it in.

5 Using a wooden spatula, fold in the chocolate.

6 Use a teaspoon to drop the meringue batter onto the greased baking trays; one teaspoon full for each meringue. Place the tray in the oven, and turn the oven off. Leave the cookies in the oven for approximately 2 hours. Remove and store in an airtight container.

Nutrient analysis per serving: Calories 34; Protein 1g; Carbohydrate 5g; Sugar 5g; Fat 1g; Saturated fat 1g; Fibre 1g; Sodium 28mg.

Being Sensible: Sweets for the Health-Conscious

'Healthy dessert'. Isn't that an oxymoron? For the most part, desserts can be like land mines in the Battle of the Bulge and the Hunt for Health, sabotaging even your strongest attempts to eat well. Most of the recipes we've seen for healthy desserts usually just make for unappetising, tasteless, no-substance affairs.

But you *can* satisfy without sabotage and still keep the dessert gluten-free. In fact, some of the recipes we offer in this section are downright good for you, and so you can enjoy them as part of a gluten-free, guilt-free, well-balanced diet.

Try sautéing fruits such as apples, pears, or bananas over a medium-high heat in sugar (or sucralose artificial sweetener, sold as Splenda) and water until they're caramelised a little. Doing so adds a caramel flavour without the fat of a caramel sauce.

⌔ *Grilled Banana Split*

You don't really have to grill the bananas, but they look good with the grill marks, and warming gives them a great texture.

Preparation time: *10 minutes*

Cooking time: *6 minutes*

Makes: *6 servings*

6 firm bananas, with skins intact

3 tablespoons honey (preferably runny)

1 litre (1¾ pint) tub low-fat vanilla frozen yogurt

2 tablespoons chocolate sauce

3 tablespoons reduced-fat spray whipped cream

1 Preheat the grill to a medium-high heat.

2 Don't peel the bananas! Cut each one in half lengthwise and then again in half widthwise so that you have four sections from each banana.

3 Brush honey on the flat sides of the bananas, and let them stand for about 5 minutes.

4 Put the flesh side of the bananas on the hot grill and cook them for about 3 minutes (until the bananas have grill marks). Turn them over and cook about 3 more minutes, until the peel begins to pull away easily. Make sure that the bananas don't slip through the grate.

5 Arrange four sections of banana in each bowl, and top with frozen yogurt, a drizzle of chocolate syrup, and whipped cream.

Nutrient analysis per serving: Calories 213; Protein 2g; Carbohydrate 37g; Sugar 35g; Fat 6g; Saturated fat 2g; Fibre 1g; Sodium 5mg.

☺ Blueberry Parfait

No need to peel, de-seed, core, dice, slice, or chop these berries. They're easy, delicious, and loaded with nutritional value. Blueberries are higher in antioxidants than many other fruits and vegetables, and they're also low in fat and calories, and high in fibre. Just one small serving provides about 20 per cent of your daily requirement of vitamin C. Fresh, frozen, canned, and dried blueberries are available all year long – but treat yourself to the sweet, fresh blueberries of summer, which are the best blueberries of all.

Preparation time: *30 minutes*

Freezing time: *2 hours*

Makes: *4 servings*

300 grams/10½ ounces blueberries

50 grams/2 ounces granulated sugar

2 tablespoons cornflour

60 millilitres/2 fluid ounces cold water

1 tablespoon fresh lemon juice

227 grams/8 ounces low-fat plain yogurt

330 grams/11½ ounces fresh strawberries, sliced

1 In a medium-size saucepan, stir together the blueberries and sugar.

2 In a small bowl, mix the cornflour and water together until the cornflour dissolves.

3 Add the cornflour-water mixture to the blueberries and sugar, and bring to the boil over a medium heat, stirring well. Let it boil for 1 minute. Stir in the lemon juice, and allow to cool.

4 Gently fold the yogurt into the cooled blueberry mixture, being careful not to crush the berries.

5 In four separate glass dishes, layer some of the blueberry mixture then some strawberries, and then the blueberry mixture again. Keep alternating layers until the dishes are full and you've used all the ingredients.

6 Freeze the parfaits for at least 2 hours. Take them out of the freezer 30 minutes before serving.

Tip: *Serve your favourite gluten-free biscuits with these parfaits.*

Nutrient analysis per serving: *Calories 151; Protein 4g; Carbohydrate 32g; Sugar 29g; Fat 1g; Saturated fat 0g; Fibre 3g; Sodium 49mg.*

⏱ *Muesli Bars*

Most muesli isn't gluten-free, and so use a commercially available gluten-free muesli or mix up a batch from the recipe we give in Chapter 9. Turn your muesli into a great gluten-free dessert with this recipe! This idea is a good way to use up muesli that's beginning to go stale.

Preparation time: *30 minutes*

Cooking time: *30 to 35 minutes*

Cooling time: *1 hour*

Makes: *4 servings*

250 grams/8¾ ounces gluten-free muesli

150 grams/5½ ounces chopped peanuts

60 grams/2½ ounces gluten-free flour mixture

75 grams/3 ounces raisins

1 large free-range egg, beaten

80 millilitres/3 fluid ounces honey (preferably runny)

80 millilitres/3 fluid ounces rapeseed oil

75 grams/3 ounces brown sugar

½ teaspoon ground cinnamon

Non-stick oil spray, for greasing the pan

1 Preheat the oven to 170°C/325°F/Gas Mark 3.

2 Line a 20-centimetre (8-inch) square pan with tin foil, and spray with non-stick oil.

3 In a medium-size mixing bowl, combine the muesli, peanuts, flour mixture, and raisins. Stir in the egg, honey, oil, brown sugar, and cinnamon. Press the mixture evenly into the pan.

4 Bake the muesli mixture for 30 to 35 minutes, or until lightly browned around the edges. Leave to cool for at least 1 hour.

5 Pull the foil out of the pan and flip the muesli mixture upside down so that you can peel away the foil. Cut the muesli mixture into 16 5-centimetre (2-inch) squares and store in an airtight container.

Nutrient analysis per serving: *Calories 883; Protein 20g; Carbohydrate 104g; Sugar 66g; Fat 44g; Saturated fat 6g; Fibre 7g; Sodium 358mg.*

Satisfy your sweet tooth with fabulous fruit

Humans do love their sweets. If you give a baby a spoonful of ice cream and one of sour cream, you don't need a team of researchers and a multimillion-pound, placebo-controlled, double-blind study to guess which brings a smile and which makes the baby grimace. We all need glucose – that's the sugar that powers the body. But you can make enough glucose from fruit, vegetables, and starchy carbohydrate foods. You also get the added benefit of vitamins, minerals, fibre, and antioxidants for far fewer calories than the 'empty calories' you find in sugary foods. So satisfy your sweet tooth, but try to do it with foods that pack a nutritional punch. Some ideas follow:

- **Chocolate hazelnut spread fruit dip:** Warm up chocolate hazelnut spread a little and dip fresh fruit in it.

- **Grapes and Chantilly style cream:** Combine reduced-fat sour cream, icing sugar, sucralose artificial sweetener (Splenda), and a dash of vanilla extract. Mix the cream with red, green, and black grapes.

- **Peaches 'n cream:** Place half a peach or pear in a dish and add a small scoop of vanilla frozen yogurt. Scatter with raspberries or strawberries.

- **Pudding:** If you use skimmed milk with a ready to mix pudding, for example a mousse, it's pretty good for you: Serve with bananas on top.

- **Strawberries and yogurt:** Slice strawberries and blend them with low-fat, flavoured yogurt. Top the mixture with artificial sweetener if you like a little extra sweetness.

- **Strawberry sweet and sour:** Dip fresh strawberries into reduced-fat sour cream and then into artificial sweetener or honey.

Remember: Fresh fruit is best for you when you store it properly. Don't refrigerate bananas and other tropical fruits. Melons don't need refrigeration until you cut them; store them in a separate bin, away from vegetables and meat.

Part V

Living – and Loving – the Gluten-Free Lifestyle

'Do......you.....serve.....gluten.....free
.....free....here?'

In this part . . .

We take a look at the social implications of living gluten-free, because getting out of the house is one of the most challenging practical aspects of living a gluten-free lifestyle. We give you the tools you need to enjoy eating at restaurants, travelling, and socialising – all while staying safely gluten-free – because your diet shouldn't ever stand in the way of your activities and adventures. We also discuss the unique emotional challenges that people face when embracing the gluten-free lifestyle and how to overcome those obstacles. Most of all, our goal in this part is to help you capture the essence of living – and *loving* – the gluten-free lifestyle.

Chapter 15

Getting Out and About: Gluten-Free Eating Away from Home

---

*F*or many people, following a gluten-free diet doesn't present their biggest challenge – the problem is managing that diet away from home. Even people who've been gluten-free for years sometimes find that eating out is difficult.

This book primarily focuses on the practicalities of shopping, cooking, modifying recipes, and keeping the kitchen gluten-free. But what happens when you have to rely on someone else doing that for you? When you eat out you don't have access to ingredients labels, you're limited to the dishes provided, and you have no idea whether the person who cooked the food knows how to avoid contaminating your meal with gluten.

Even so, we believe that eating out is an important part of life. Venturing outside to eat may require extra effort on your part. You may receive a meal that's contaminated with gluten and you may end up paying £20 for something that costs less than £5 to make at home. But is it still worth taking that risk? Absolutely. Living life in a bubble is for oxygen molecules, not humans.

The reality is that you can't always be at home in a crumb-free zone with cupboards stocked with your gluten-free favourites and toasters bearing the 'GF' stamp of approval. Whether you're out for lunch with clients, enjoying a romantic dinner for two, travelling for business, or touring the world for pleasure, you're sure to be eating out. And unless you want to miss out, you need to know how to cope with eating away from home. The good news is that with a bit of forward planning you can overcome most obstacles and accommodate your gluten-free lifestyle safely and comfortably.

Abiding by the Golden Rules of Eating Out Gluten-Free

Imagine that you've just arrived at the party of the year. You're feeling energised, looking fabulous, and eager to spend a great evening chatting with friends. And you're famished. You head for the buffet table and it's loaded with the most amazing spread, and then slowly you begin to realise that you can't eat any of it. Your mood plummets as fast as your panic rises, because you realise you're going to be there all night with nothing to eat.

In this section, we give you some basic rules of eating out gluten-free. These rules should prevent such a depressing scenario from happening, because you have no reason to let a little food (or lack of it) ruin a good time. Armed with these practical guidelines, your gluten-free social experiences can be as good as ever.

Relying on others to accommodate your diet

The office party is coming up in two months. Realising that food is obviously going to be provided, you arrange to meet the person planning the party, and you explain your dietary restrictions, right down to the sometimes intricate details of the gluten-free diet. She's making a good show of understanding you, nodding in the appropriate places, even adding an 'Oh, so you probably can't eat the bread rolls, am I right?' Great! She understands! Don't rely on it. And whatever you do, don't expect it. If she succeeds and you see gluten-free goodies on the table (in which case you'll be tempted to fiercely guard them, elbowing guests away, defending your territory and hissing, 'Those are for me! They're all I can eat!'), be gracious and appreciative. She didn't have to make the effort to meet your dietary needs, but she did.

Really, you shouldn't *expect* anyone to accommodate your gluten-free diet – no matter who they are. Even those closest to you – those you love most – are going to forget or make mistakes. Errors don't happen because they don't care. Often, the lack of gluten-free goodies is just an oversight, or sometimes people think that they understand the diet but they overlook some of the intricacies and what they thought is gluten-free is coated in breadcrumbs. Accept that you mustn't rely on anyone to accommodate your gluten-free dietary requirements.

Asking what's for dinner

Asking what's on the menu isn't rude, depending on how you go about it. When you're gluten-free and attending a dinner party, asking the host what's for dinner isn't going to put you on the social circuit blacklist. Of course, some ways of asking are ruder than others, so be tactful and simply ask, 'I have a dietary restriction and was wondering if it would be okay to ask you about what you're serving so I can plan accordingly.' People are generally receptive to discussing what they're planning for the menu, and may even ask for your input to be able to accommodate your diet as best they can.

Filling up before you go

You can't expect to see gluten-free goodies at the party, and so filling up before you go is a good idea. That way you're not ravenous and fixated on food, and you can enjoy the party for what it's really all about, which is fun and friends.

The biggest problem with this idea is that if you do arrive at a party only to find lots of gluten-free delights are on offer, you may be so thrilled that you want to make the most of them, even though you're not hungry.

BYOF: Bringing your own food

We're not suggesting that you walk into a formal soirée carrying bags of fast food, wafting the smell of fried food among guests in dinner jackets. That sort of grand entrance may not go down well with the hosts. The setting does, of course, determine the type of food you bring, whether you opt for taking some extra gluten-free bread or crackers or bringing your entire main course and dessert.

Don't worry that bringing your own food may offend the hosts. First, you can always discuss this option with them in advance. But if you don't, you can discreetly explain that you have a dietary restriction and rather than burden them with the details ('I know you've been busy getting ready for this party'), you thought that bringing a few things for yourself to eat would be easier. Say you hope they don't mind, ask where you should put your food containers, and state that when the time comes you're happy to serve them up yourself (to avoid contamination, but you don't have to tell your hosts that).

Biting your tongue

You've spoken to the hosts about their plans for the meal, and they've offered to make a few accommodations for you. You get to the party only to find nothing but filled filo pastries and deep-fried breadcrumb canapés. Do you:

A) Starve?

B) Starve, and shout at the hostess?

C) Starve, scream rude things at the hostess, and pick the innards out of the filo pastries (please don't, they're contaminated with gluten!)?

D) None of the above. You enjoy the party and relax. You weren't hungry anyway, because you filled up before you came out or bought something with you just in case?

The correct answer, of course, is D.

Enjoying good company

Whether you're at a nightclub, a dinner for 500, a restaurant enjoying an intimate dinner for two, a wedding, or a funeral – social gatherings are not about the food. They're about the occasion, the atmosphere, the ambiance, the people you're with . . . oh, and did we mention that you don't have to wash up?

However, we're not saying that social functions don't revolve around food. They do. Most societies use food as a focal point to draw people close during times of socialisation and celebration. But don't let going gluten-free mean that you miss out on the celebration itself and the reason that people are gathering in the first place.

Dining Out: Restaurant Realities and Rewards

Eating out at a terrific restaurant is priceless. Good company, nice ambience, respectful service, and delicious food combine to create an experience that's about far more than just the food.

Being on a gluten-free diet shouldn't stop you from having these experiences. Yes, eating out does involve some risk. You don't know for sure what ingredients are in your food, no matter how much you try to educate your waiting staff and chef. When they're busy, staff can (and do) make mistakes, and cross-contamination is always an issue. And by the law of averages, at least once in your gluten-free dining days, you're sure to receive a salad with croutons that you have to send back.

But with just a little extra forward planning and effort, you can help ensure that your meal is safely gluten-free, and you can enjoy gluten-free dining as one of life's more pleasurable social experiences.

We have some tips to make the most of your gluten-free dining experiences:

- **Phone ahead.** This advice is essential for giving your best shot at eating a gluten-free meal. Give details of your dietary requirements when making your table reservation or ring them separately if someone else has made the booking. Ask them what their policy is for catering for people on a gluten-free diet. Remember to avoid busy hours when you make your call; phoning after lunch is probably a good time to speak to the staff or head chef. Ask whether they can fax or e-mail you a menu. At the same time, you can fax or e-mail them a list of ingredients that you can and can't have. An obliging chef may even agree to make something entirely for you.

- **Express the seriousness of your condition to the serving staff and chef.** If you have to sound alarming, do so. One of the best ways to get their attention is to say, 'It's a bit like an allergy to peanuts.' You know it's not *really* like an allergy to peanuts, but it gets their attention.

- **Give them just enough information.** Not too much, not too little. You may have to look carefully at the waiting staff to see whether they really do understand what you're saying.

- **Don't be afraid to ask for what you want.** You're paying for the meal, and you should be able to enjoy it knowing that it's safe for you to eat. Gluten-free is not a fad diet – even small amounts of gluten can upset you. Don't ever feel like you're making an unnecessary fuss – your health is important.

✔ **Ask how the food is prepared.** The more you know about the preparation, the better decisions you can make when ordering. If they're using any ready made items, such as sauces, ask them to check the ingredients list.

✔ **Bring your own food.** By checking in advance you're likely to be able to bring your own bread or crackers to nibble on, and you may even be able to even bring items such as a gluten-free pizza base or portion of pasta for them to cook for you. Remember to offer suggestions for how to keep your food from becoming contaminated by the rest of the food in the restaurant. (For more information on specific ideas, see the later section 'Asking restaurants to cook the food you bring'.)

✔ **Send it back if it's not right.** Of course we're not suggesting that you're rude about returning your meal, but if they give you a salad with croutons on it, don't pick the croutons out and eat it. That's not safe! Politely say, 'Excuse me. I must have forgotten to mention that I can't have croutons on my salad. Do you mind bringing me a new one without them?' Don't make too much of a fuss. Just let them off the hook; even though you know that they know that you've already told them.

✔ **Remain pleasant and grateful.** If you're very demanding, you're going to put them on the defensive. When they accommodate your requests, be extremely grateful.

Choosing the restaurant

We may be stating the obvious, but if you choose an outlet that deals mainly with limited types of food you're setting yourself up for frustration and disappointment. Try to avoid restaurants that, by the very nature of their menus, aren't likely to have much (if anything) that's gluten-free.

Instead, go to restaurants that have a large and diverse menu selection, or choose a restaurant that's likely to have more gluten-free foods. Happy gluten-free dining starts with choosing restaurants that are likely to have gluten-free foods on the menu or foods that the kitchen staff can easily modify.

When dining at any restaurant, you have to check ingredients in specific dishes. And of course, food preparation is an issue (are they using the same spatula to turn the burgers and the buns?). Ask the staff to make your food in an uncontaminated manner or be prepared to eat somewhere where they do.

Finding fast food

One good thing about fast-food places is that they generally use standardised ingredients and follow standardised guidelines for food preparation. A call to their head offices can answer your questions about dedicated fryers, ingredients, and gluten-free items. For instance many offer fries, shakes, salads, ice creams, and sauces that are gluten-free. If you fancy a burger, make sure that it's 100 per cent meat with no cereal fillers and order it without the bun – even if you throw it away, the bun contaminates your dinner. Some fast-food places offer lettuce as a wrap instead of a bun, even when they don't advertise that they do so, and some are happy to put a burger inside a gluten-free roll if you provide one. Several fast-food chains even put their nutritional information and ingredients online. A range of suitable items from both Burger King and MacDonald's are listed in *The Food and Drink Directory* from Coeliac UK.

When you're ordering chips, make sure that they're not battered or coated in anything, and ask what other foods are fried in the same oil. You don't want to order fries that have been swimming with battered onion rings or something else that contaminates the oil with gluten. If you tend to eat at fast-food restaurants often, put any relevant information into a small file and keep it in your car. That way, when you're pulling into one of your favourite fast-food joints, you have a handy list of their gluten-free items.

Eating international

Many foods from international cuisines are naturally gluten-free. You need to work out which ones you like, and of those foods, which are inherently gluten-free. Then you can choose a restaurant of that variety and know what to order. Mexican, Thai, Vietnamese, and Indian cuisines are just a few that may offer gluten-free dishes. But, as with any meal, you need to make sure that the kitchen staff don't add flour to the sauce, and ask about the grains used in, for example, tortillas or noodles. Be careful – not all are going to be gluten-free, but they may be safe if they're corn or rice-based. Thai cooking uses fish sauce instead of soy sauce and so is generally gluten-free. Always be careful to double-check any ingredient that you're unsure of.

Be more wary of Chinese or Japanese restaurants as soy sauce is used in many, if not most, of their dishes, and soy sauce usually contains wheat. You can bring your own gluten-free soy sauce, but warn the cooks to be careful about contamination issues while they're preparing your food. Stir-fry restaurants and Pan Asian noodle bars are popping up all over the UK and, generally, they're happy to cook your dish to order in an individual wok. The rice and buckwheat noodles (soba) dishes are generally safe but some can be mixed with wheat flour – do ask before you order. As with other Asian restaurants, avoid contamination issues regarding soy sauce, but once again, you can bring your own. Most sushi, including the accompaniments such as seaweed, pickled vegetables, ginger, and wasabi, are usually gluten-free but beware of soy sauce glazes and 'imitation' crab, which contains wheat. Any sushi chef worth his or her salt can tell you what's in the ingredients they use. An alterative is sashimi, plain fish and steamed rice, which uses fewer sauces and is generally gluten-free.

International restaurants can be a real bonus to the gluten-free diner but always ask how the chefs prepare their traditional fare. Double-check doubtful ingredients and consider whether cross-contamination issues are likely to be a problem. Many international restaurants are more than happy to share the secrets of their national cuisine.

Other good bets

As a general rule, other types of restaurants that are a good bet include:

- **Soup and salad bars:** Not only do these chains usually offer lots of gluten-free items, but they also often have their ingredients handy so you can check soups and salad dressings to be certain. Sometimes, the ingredients are actually posted on placards in front of the item. If not, ask a member of staff whether they can provide you with a list of ingredients.

- **Barbecues:** Although you do have to check the sauces, many barbecues are good bets because they serve traditional fare, such as spare ribs, chicken, fish, corn-on-the-cob, jacket potatoes, and salad. You may prefer to bring your own sauces or dressings if you've been unable to check what's on offer. Politely ask the chef to clean the grill thoroughly before cooking your meal. Tell them that you have food allergies so they can keep your food separate from your neighbour's breaded chicken.

- **Cafés:** Ask for fresh cooked eggs and bacon and bring your own gluten-free bread (pop it in a toaster bag and they may even toast it for you). You can order tomatoes, mushrooms, hash browns, fruit, yogurt, and lots of other good gluten-free breakfast foods, too.

- **Steak and seafood:** These restaurants are likely to have steaks or burgers, seafood, salads (hold the croutons), baked potatoes or rice, chips, and ice cream for dessert.

Risky restaurants

You can get gluten-free meals at some of these restaurants, but in general, restaurants that aren't going to be a good bet include:

✔ **Bakeries:** We probably didn't need to point that out, did we? Even cakes like meringues and macaroons, which are inherently gluten-free, can become contaminated during cooking or storage.

✔ **Italian:** Most Italian restaurants serve many pasta, pizza, and breaded dishes. Some may (again, if you ask them nicely) add toppings to your own gluten-free pizza base if you bring one with you. Some Italian restaurants serve polenta, a cornmeal classic, risotto, and of course you can enjoy their wonderful (crouton-free) salads or a variety of grilled meat or fresh fish dishes.

When ordering any dish, you still need to remind the staff that even the presence of crumbs from gluten-containing foods can cause cross-contamination issues with baking trays, serving spoons, and pans.

✔ **Specialty coffee shops:** The trendy coffee shops you're familiar with offer foods and snacks, usually marketed as being wholesome or healthy. Unfortunately, what that usually means is that their muffins are bran muffins. Generally, other than yogurt, fruit, chocolate, or possibly fruit, nut, and seed bars, coffee shops offer very little in the way of gluten-free snacks.

✔ **Cajun food (served in the UK in some Mexican restaurants):** You can get blackened fish and other gluten-free foods at these restaurants, but be careful of contamination issues. Often, Cajun food is covered in breadcrumbs. And many gumbos and other Cajun dishes are often flavoured with a darkened roux sauce, which is made from flour. Some foods that appear to be okay, such as prawns, may be cooked in beer.

Letting someone else do the leg work

To take away some of the hard work of choosing a restaurant, Coeliac UK has developed a Web site called 'Gluten-free – on the go' (www.gluten-free-onthego.com).

The site guides you to gluten-friendly hotels, restaurants, pubs, fast-food outlets, and even coffee shops in the UK, and now even includes some in the US and mainland Europe. Venues listed cater especially for people on gluten-free diets. They have signed up to the gluten-free code of practice covering ingredients, preparation techniques, avoiding cross-contamination, staff training, and customer service. The site allows you to search geographically by region or town for venues. You can explore menus, price bands, directions, and contact details.

Call or e-mail these venues in advance to alert them to your arrival and be sure that they still provide gluten-free food – ownership can change suddenly.

Gluten-free menus

Close your eyes and imagine being at a beautiful restaurant with great company. The waitress says 'Hi, I'm Sarah. I'll be serving you today. Would you like to see the gluten-free menu?' Okay, you can open your eyes now, because we know how hard it is to read this book with them closed. Besides, this isn't a dream. It's a reality!

Today, some restaurants offer gluten-free menus – some of them are even online. You usually need to do your research in advance though. Alternatively, read the section 'Letting someone else do the leg work' for a pleasant surprise.

In the name of *For Dummies* research, we spent a couple of very happy hours surfing the 'Gluten-free – on the go' Web site and found over 140 entries for suitable establishments serving everything from English, French, Spanish, and Oriental, to specialist seafood and vegetarian establishments, right through to Afghan and Australian cuisines. We'd certainly go out of our way to dine at one of these venues.

The dedicated Web pages of the local branches of Coeliac UK contain up-to-dates listings of venues that cater for the gluten-free diet in your local area.

We were stunned by the enterprise and inventiveness of the gluten-free meals and desserts on offer at these dedicated gluten-free eating establishments. Fancy gluten-free chocolate almond torte or sticky toffee pudding anyone? We even spotted an ice cream parlour with gluten-free cones. And we especially warmed to the fish and chip shop that holds gluten-free fish and chip days, which are so popular that they've even started selling their gluten-free batter mix by mail order. Go to www.glu2go.co.uk for more information.

Making smart menu choices

Set yourself up for success. Choose menu items that are likely to be gluten-free or that the kitchen staff can easily modify to be gluten-free. Obviously, breaded and fried items aren't going to be your best choices, although sometimes cooks can use the same meat, season it with spices, and grill it instead.

So, do you order the fish in a beery batter? Not a good choice. The Chinese pork stir-fry with noodles? No. Fried chicken? Probably not. Grilled chicken? Quite possibly. Grilled fish? Steak? Very likely. Of course, you need to ask a few questions to be sure, but at least you're on the right track.

Ordering is a four-step process:

1. **Find the foods on the menu that are already likely to be gluten-free or appear that they can easily be modified to be gluten-free.**

2. **Choose the item(s) you want.**

3. **Ask about ingredients and food preparation methods.**

4. **Make sure that you've made your order clear and have offered suggestions for how to season and prepare your meal.**

Do a bit of research on food preparation. The more you know about how foods are usually prepared, the easier ordering is. For instance, you should know that some restaurants, especially Cajun food in Mexican restaurants, may cook seafood in beer. And the 'crab' you find in sushi is usually imitation, a mixture of fish and wheat flour.

Talking to the staff: Ask and ye shall receive

Our teenage kids hate being with us when we order food at a restaurant. All we have to do is hold up the menu and say to the waitress, 'Can we ask you a question?' and the kids start fidgeting, rolling their eyes, mumbling, 'Here we go. . .'. But what's wrong with getting what you want when you're paying for your food? (Certainly, our kids don't hesitate to put in their specific requests when we're the chefs!)

Getting the message over, nice and simple

Some companies produce discreet, durable 'dietary alert!' cards for people with specific dietary requirements. The card explains your dietary needs as a coeliac disease sufferer in simple, clear terms for you to show to waiting staff and chefs. You can carry the cards with you wherever and whenever you eat and present them to staff to explain your idiosyncratic dietary needs with the minimum of fuss.

This system can help avoid your message being 'corrupted' between the table and the kitchen and helps authenticate your request as a medical requirement rather than a 'fad diet'.

The range of cards available for sale includes an English dietary alert card for use while eating out in the UK or North America, alongside a range of cards for use abroad, which have been translated into French, German, Spanish, Italian, Bulgarian, Czech, Greek, Portuguese, Turkish, Arabic, Chinese, Japanese, Russian, and Thai (with new languages being released regularly)!

Don't be afraid to ask for what you want (even if your teenage kids are putting you off). People ask for special considerations at restaurants all the time, even when they don't have dietary restrictions. If you feel that the waiter or waitress doesn't understand you, ask to talk to the chef. Of course, be tactful about it. Asking for special considerations for your meal isn't rude – especially when your health depends on it. Many of today's chefs have an awareness of the gluten-free diet from catering college, and they love to put their skills and knowledge to work to please a customer.

For more information visit: www.dietarycard.co.uk or telephone 01506-635358.

Asking restaurants to cook the food you bring

Very occasionally, restaurants allow you to bring your own food into the restaurant, especially for a special occasion such as a birthday party. They may warm up the food or even cook it for you. If you do this, be aware of how they normally cook their food, because you probably need to ask them politely to watch out for some contamination concerns.

For instance, most pizza parlours use convection ovens that blow the flour all around. If you bring a pizza base and ask them to use their toppings and cook it, you have to be sure that their toppings aren't contaminated (they often are), and then you have to make sure that they wrap the pizza securely in tin foil before warming it in the oven – otherwise, your gluten-free pizza goes into a pizza oven that's blowing flour all over. The same goes for bringing a pre-made gluten-free pizza with you – make sure that it's wrapped carefully before asking the staff to warm it in their ovens.

If one person in a party brings his or her own meal, it's not usually a problem. Restaurants may not charge extra to warm or prepare an item you bring yourself, but you should ask in advance to be sure.

You may want to think about getting toaster bags for toasting your bread when you're away from home. The bags are great for making sure that your bread doesn't get contaminated when you're away from home. Just put your gluten-free bread in the bag, and anyone can put it in a toaster, toaster oven, or regular oven. Then just take your bread out, and you have perfectly uncontaminated gluten-free toast. The bags are washable and reusable, but you can just throw them away when you've finished with them.

Remembering the art of tipping

We don't take tipping lightly, because when people accommodate your gluten-free diet and give you the peace of mind that helps you experience the pleasure of dining out, you should express your gratitude. If they've done it with an eager-to-please attitude, showing your appreciation is even more important.

The number of people going gluten-free is escalating. Every waiter you talk to, every chef you inform, and every tip you leave improves the future for everyone going gluten-free today, tomorrow, and beyond. Tipping isn't as customary in the UK as in the US, but as general rule 10 to 15 per cent of the bill total is an acceptable tip.

Staying Gluten-Free when Travelling

Whether for business or pleasure, you don't have to limit or, worse yet, give up travelling because you're on a gluten-free diet. In fact, you may find some countries are more accommodating than you ever imagined. For instance, when you order a burger at McDonald's in some parts of Sweden or Finland, where coeliac disease is very common, they ask you whether you'd like that on a regular or gluten-free bun, and they even cook it on a separate gluten-free grill!

If you follow our guidelines given in the earlier section 'Abiding by the Golden Rules of Eating Out Gluten-Free', you're well-prepared for wherever your travels take you. And because travelling nearly always involves eating at restaurants, you should also pay particular attention to the advice in the preceding section on dining out. But to ensure a great gluten-free adventure, here are a few more things that you should know before you hit the road.

Researching your destination

Do yourself a favour and spend some time researching the area before you go on your trip. You can always find food shops or markets, restaurants, and fast-food places, all of which have at least some things you can eat. But you may do even better than that. National or local support groups and specific Internet discussion boards and chat sites may be able to steer you in the direction of gluten-free-friendly restaurants and shops (you can find more information about these in Chapter 5). Researching what's typically available in the area can tell you how much food to bring and how much you can get while you're there.

Knowing the boundaries when crossing borders

If you're travelling internationally, be aware of some special considerations. For instance, some countries don't allow you to bring in foods and some may understandably subject them to rather intense scrutiny at customs if your bags are searched. If that's the case, see whether you can send it ahead, or find out whether gluten-free products are available there, in which case you may not need to bring food with you.

Also be aware that different countries have different standards for what's allowed on the gluten-free diet. In Europe, for instance, we commonly use Codex Alimentarius wheat starch, which has the gluten removed, and products that contain it are labelled gluten-free. In the United States and Canada, however, Codex wheat starch isn't considered gluten-free. (Refer to Chapter 5 for more on the Codex Alimentarius.)

If, in doing your homework, you find health-food stores in the area of your destination, call ahead and ask what they sell in the way of gluten-free specialty items. You may be surprised to find that they have a huge array. If not, ask whether they would consider stocking a few items for you, and let them know when you're going to arrive.

Sprechen zie gluten? Speaking gluten-free in other countries

Knowing some key words in the language of the country you're visiting is important. For instance, 'flour' in Spanish is *harina*. But that can refer to cornflour or wheat flour, and so you have to distinguish further what you're talking about by saying *harina de maiz* (cornflour) or *harina de trigo* (wheat flour). Find out the words for *gluten*, *with*, *without*, *no*, and *allergy*. You can download free travel guides from www.coeliac.co.uk in Dutch, French, German, Greek, Italian, and Spanish. The online store also stocks a pocket sized multilingual phrase book boasting over 1200 phrases to help with international gluten-free (and other exclusion diets) travel.

Check out Table 15-1 for some key words in Spanish, French, and German.

Table 15-1	Terms for Explaining the Diet in Foreign Languages		
English Term	*Spanish*	*French*	*German*
I can	puedo	je peux	ich kann
I can't	no puedo	je ne peux pas	ich kann nicht

English Term	Spanish	French	German
(to) eat	comer	manger	essen
gluten	gluten	gluten	gluten
wheat	trigo	blé	weizen
flour	harina	farine	mehl
corn	maiz	maïs	mais
with	con	avec	mit
without	sin	sans	ohne
yes	sí	oui	ja
no	no	non	nein
allergy	alergia	allergie	allergie

Remember that each country has different regulations about what must be listed on the ingredients label. Some countries outside the EU aren't obliged to list items, such as wheat flour, if they only make up a small percentage of the product. A more reliable source of information may be a product listing of suitable foods produced by the coeliac support group for the country if it has one. Contact details can be found at: www.coeliachelp.me.uk.

Restaurant cards that explain the gluten-free diet are available in different languages; do a quick Internet search or try www.dietarycard.co.uk.

A useful guide dedicated to gluten-free eating out around the world is *Lets Eat Out – Your Passport to Living Gluten and Allergy Free Around the World* by Kim Koeller and Robert La France (R&R Publishing, 2005).

Choosing gluten-free-friendly accommodation

Where you stay can make your holiday a much more enjoyable experience. If possible, choose accommodation with some self-catering facilities. Even a small fridge and microwave can make your trip a lot easier. That way, you can go to a local supermarket and stock up on some essentials, like fruit, milk, popcorn, cold meats, and snack items. If you have a full kitchen at your disposal, you can prepare your own meals if you want to, sparing yourself the worry of eating at restaurants – not to mention the expense.

If you don't have a kitchen, try to find accommodation that has a restaurant attached or several restaurants nearby. You can call the hotel restaurant in advance and have the staff fax or e-mail you the menu so you can discuss items you may be able to enjoy. Some restaurants may even work with you to accommodate your dietary needs during your stay.

If your accommodation is near several national restaurant chains, you can look up their Web sites and see whether they have menus online. You may even be surprised to find an online gluten-free menu.

Packing your own provisions

You may want to bring your kitchen in your suitcase (everything but the kitchen sink!). Depending on where you're going and for how long, your kitchen-in-a-suitcase may include some of the following items:

- Baking mixes
- Biscuits
- Crackers and snack items
- Gluten-free cereals that may be hard to find
- Pans to make the baked goods
- Pasta
- Pizza bases
- Sliced bread
- Small toaster
- Toaster bags

With any luck, the food survives the trip and you arrive fully prepared to enjoy your gluten-free stay.

If you don't want to lug the whole kitchen and pantry with you, consider sending your foods ahead. Pack them up and send them in a box to your final destination or order them online and have them sent to where you're going. Hotels and self-catering apartments usually accept packages if you clearly mark the guest name and date of arrival on the box.

Getting there

As Robert Louis Stevenson once said, 'To travel hopefully is a better thing than to arrive.' Well, whether you're going by plane, train, car, or cruise ship, you need to consider the issue of eating on the journey itself in your gluten-free plans.

Flying high

Airports usually have fast-food restaurants, and so if you know which fast foods are gluten-free, you can always go there if you want or need to. Some of the kiosks and cafés sell yogurt, fruit, and salads, and some airports have large restaurant chains where you can order as you would in any other restaurant.

You may find that what they serve on the plane is limited in its gluten-free selections. Sitting for hours on a plane when you're starving, smelling everyone else's meal is pretty miserable. Some airlines allow you to pre-order a gluten-free meal when you book your seat (you need to do so well in advance). Others airlines only offer this service to their club or first class travellers. When you've notified them of your requirements, ring up again a couple of days before departure to check whether the order has been passed on. Once on board, make yourself known to the cabin crew to reduce the chances of your special meal going to someone else. Some airlines provide these meals brilliantly – we've seen delicious examples and we were once even served gluten-free rolls, individually packaged with all the ingredients clearly labelled!

Even if you've ordered a meal, bring some snacks just in case it doesn't turn up, or turns up consisting of soggy rice cakes and salad, or worse still, turns up looking delicious but isn't remotely close to being gluten-free. Taking extra rice cakes, gluten-free bread, rolls, or crackers is a good idea in case the meal is (as is very likely) low in carbohydrate. You may want to bring a small sachet of your own salad dressing or sauce to be safe.

As an alternative, or certainly on the 'no frills' airlines where very few snacks or sandwiches are suitable, you may want to bring your own food on board. Check whether you're allowed to carry foods on board as regulations can change from time to time. You may need to dispose of uneaten food before disembarking in your destination country as some have strict regulations about the importation of food items.

Cruising the high seas

Cruise lines are extremely good at accommodating dietary restrictions of any type. Most of the cruise lines we've looked into are very familiar with the gluten-free diet and even stock specialty items like gluten-free breads, pastas, crackers, biscuits, and cakes. They also offer lots of healthy fare, like fresh seafood, chicken, steaks, fruit, and vegetables.

If you're planning a cruise, call ahead and ask to speak to the executive chef for the line you're going to be on. Discuss the gluten-free diet with him or her – if the chef isn't familiar with the diet, fax or e-mail the guidelines and follow up with a phone call to discuss the specifics of what you want while you're on board, including contamination issues.

Let the train take the strain

If you're taking the train somewhere, your best bet is to bring your own food. Rail lines usually don't have any restrictions about bringing your own food, and so you can load up. The cafés or snack trolleys on trains rarely have much hot food that's gluten-free; instead, the cafés usually serve packaged sandwiches, filled croissants, muffins, pastries, and other not-even-close-to-being-gluten-free goodies. However, they may sell fruit and other suitable gluten-free snacks, such as crisps and nuts – take your food directory with you so you can check up. You don't want to derail your trip by starving the whole way.

Travelling near or far by car

Driving offers you the most flexibility, and so it's often the easiest way to travel, at least in terms of accommodating your gluten-free diet. (The traffic jams, or the kids fighting and asking 'Are we almost there?' the entire way, is another matter.) You can bring your own food, or stop off at a service station and cross-check in your directory, or drop into a fast-food outlet that you know sells suitable items.

Chapter 16

Raising Happy, Healthy, Gluten-Free Kids

*W*hen adults need or choose to adopt a gluten-free lifestyle, making all the necessary adjustments can be hard. However, when your kids need to be gluten-free, that's an entirely different matter. As the mum of a now healthy, happy coeliac son, nobody knows that better than Danna.

Her son Tyler was almost two when he was diagnosed with coeliac disease. That was back in 1991. (If you care to read their entire story, you can find it in Chapter 1.)

The abridged version is that he was sick, but the doctors didn't think so. They kept saying that nothing was wrong, even though he had severe diarrhoea, his tummy was growing distended, he was growing listless and lethargic, and his personality was changing before his parent's eyes.

Four paediatricians; a paediatric gastroenterologist; preliminary diagnoses of cystic fibrosis, cancer, or a blood disease; thousands of diarrhoea nappies; and nearly one year later, his parent's heard the bittersweet words that changed their lives forever: 'Your son has coeliac disease.' They were shocked, panicked, angry, sad, glad, confused, frustrated, and terrified to feed their own child. And that was all within the first 2.4 seconds of hearing those words.

We've packed this chapter with information to help you deal with your roller-coaster of emotions, the practicalities of having kids on the gluten-free diet, and the psychological impact this may have on your family; we even give you a glimpse into the wonderful world of Terrific Teenagers who are avoiding gluten.

Before you dive in, we feel compelled to give away the most important message of all (so much for teasing you into reading the whole chapter!): Getting the diagnosis is a *good* thing in your child's life and in yours. If you're having trouble believing us, read on.

Forging through the Feelings

Everything's different when your child's the one on the gluten-free diet: The feelings you have, the way you communicate about the diet, the resentment you feel toward parents who don't have to make special arrangements just to feed their child, the preparations you make to go anywhere, the way you shop, the foods you buy, the school lunches. The list of potential frustrations just goes on and on.

If you're a parent – or someone who loves a child as a parent would – and your child has to (for health reasons) adopt a strict, gluten-free diet, your emotions probably resemble a roller coaster. You know: up one minute, crashing the next, as in Figure 16-1. Just when you're feeling great about the diet, the lifestyle, and all the benefits that go along with it, you find out that a birthday party was held at school, and that your child was the only one without a slice of cake to take home. Your emotions go from flying high to a terminal-velocity free fall.

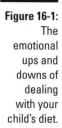

Figure 16-1: The emotional ups and downs of dealing with your child's diet.

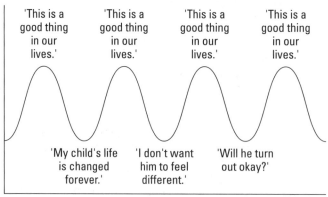

'This is a good thing in our lives.' 'This is a good thing in our lives.' 'This is a good thing in our lives.' 'This is a good thing in our lives.'

'My child's life is changed forever.' 'I don't want him to feel different.' 'Will he turn out okay?'

We talk in Chapter 17 about the emotional obstacles you may face when you switch to a gluten-free lifestyle. To quantify what the change feels like when your *child* has to go gluten-free, as opposed to you, take the magnitude of those emotions, multiply by 100, square that, and add an exponential factor of infinity, and you're getting close.

In addition to the emotions we talk about in Chapter 17, you face other worries – nagging concerns that distress you because your child's most affected. See whether some of the concerns in this section strike a familiar chord.

'My child's life is changed forever'

Yes, your child's life is changed forever. That's true. And forever seems like a really long time, doesn't it? What happened to those visions you have for your children – the perfect life, where things are easy and magical? Well, for one thing, with or without gluten, that's not the reality.

People forget to dream about the hardships their kids are going to face and how they're going to handle the difficulties in their lives. Yet, how your children handle adversity is one of the most important lessons they ever learn. This moment is a chance for them to find out at an early age how to turn adversity into advantage.

Furthermore, what you initially see as a difficulty may actually be a good thing in your child's life (and in yours). See the later section 'Focusing on the good things in life' for more information.

'I don't want my child to feel different'

You imagine your kids' lives as being smooth and painless, and part of that means fitting in. But kids are different in many ways, and although we're not playing down the importance of food and the part it plays in everything people do, your kids' differences are okay.

All children are different – some kids have blonde hair, others have red; some prefer cricket to ballet; some are in wheelchairs, others wear glasses. To pine away for your child's lost conformity is to send a signal that something about being different in this (gluten-free) way is *bad*. The last thing you want to do is send that message.

Parents worry that their kids aren't going to fit in or be accepted because of their 'different' diet, but kids can fit in regardless of what they're eating. Fitting in has much more to do with their attitude than anything else.

A kid's perspective

We asked Danna's son Tyler what he thinks about being a kid with coeliac disease, and he said that he thinks more about other things in his life – like friends, school, sports, and family – than about gluten. He knows the importance of being 100 per cent gluten-free and doesn't cheat. He's in control of what he eats and makes sure that when he's away from home he has access to gluten-free food. However, even though Tyler has been used to his gluten-free diet for a few years now, we thought his perspective was inspirational – in fact he sounded just like any other teenager we know! With a very few exceptions, his approach has been mirrored by most of the coeliac kids that we've come across in our careers, and in fact most of the exceptions are where parents have made the world revolve around coeliac disease rather than making coeliac disease fit in with their lives.

'Is my child going to turn out okay?'

All parents of gluten-intolerant or coeliac children are bound to ask this question. Just remind yourself that your child is going to be better than okay, because your child is healthy! But you may still agonise about the future when your child is first diagnosed.

The truth is that being gluten-free really doesn't have to be a big deal for your child, although getting kids involved with their gluten-free diet from the start is, we believe, crucial. We always maintain an optimistic yet realistic approach with families who are getting used to the idea that they have a child who needs to follow a gluten-free diet, and we find that's the best approach. We don't make false promises that everything is sure to be easy, but give plenty of practical advice to make the transition with the constant theme that above all, now that the family knows the problem, they can understand exactly how to manage the diet together so that their child grows up just fine.

'This is harder for me than it is for my child'

If you love a child the way a parent does (even if you're not the actual parent), you can comprehend the this-hurts-me-more-than-it-hurts-you phenomenon. Seeing a bloody knee or a broken heart truly causes pain – palpable pain – for the grown-ups who love that child.

Those of you who are agonising over the fact that your child has been diagnosed with a condition that requires a strict, lifelong, gluten-free diet may have trouble accepting this idea at first, but believe us: Dealing with the diagnosis is harder for you than it is for your child.

Your dreams for your child's future make you think that having to be gluten-free is hard – you envision your child skipping merrily down the road of life, not tripping over an obstacle like *food*, for goodness' sake. But kids don't have visions for the future like that. To a child, a vision of the future may take in the next netball game or next week's pocket money; it's far more near-sighted than your vision.

In most cases, kids are resilient. They accept what life dishes out, and they make the best of it. We think grown-ups should take note.

 If you don't believe that this diagnosis is harder on you than it is on your child, go up to several children and ask what they think about in their lives, and take notes. They're likely to mention things like 'football', 'my best friend', 'riding my horse', 'playtime', or any other number of answers. Go ahead – ask ten more kids. We're reasonably certain that you won't find any who answers 'my diet'. It's just really not a priority – nor should it be.

Focusing on the good things in life

Being gluten-free may be a good thing in your child's (and in your) life for a lot of reasons. We encourage you to make your own personal list to consult when you find yourself feeling frustrated or depressed, because the reality is that once in a while you're going to feel like that. A few ideas are listed here to get you started:

- ✔ **Your child has the key to better health.** Most people who have coeliac disease or gluten sensitivity never know what's wrong with them. They don't know that a dietary modification can fully restore their health, and so they continue to eat the very foods that make them ill.

- ✔ **Your child is less likely to develop associated conditions.** Your child has the advantage of being diagnosed early and going gluten-free at an early age. This means that his or her chances of developing associated conditions (refer to Chapter 2) are far lower than for someone diagnosed after years of being sick with gluten sensitivity or coeliac disease.

- ✔ **Your child is likely to become tolerant of other people's sensitivities.** In fact, he or she may be more tolerant in general.

- ✔ **Your child may have the opportunity to help someone else with gluten sensitivity or coeliac disease.** Remember, if 1,000 kids attend your child's school, about ten of them may have coeliac disease – and more may have a form of gluten sensitivity. This awareness and the opportunity to spread this knowledge can help improve other people's lives.

- ✔ **Your child may well find that controlling any other dietary issues, such as diabetes, is easier on the gluten-free diet.** This fact is true because your child is more diet-aware and more in control of what he or she is eating. But it's also true because, if done properly, the gluten-free diet can be extremely nutritious.

Talking to Your Kids about Being Gluten-Free

Whether your child is 18 months or 18 years old, now's the time to talk, and the entire family needs to be included. How you do this depends on your style, your internal family relationships, and your child's ability to understand the intricacies of the subject matter. Talking to your kids is step one towards making sure that they develop healthy attitudes and habits. Coeliac UK produce a fantastic booklet called *Me and My Tummy*, which gives some great tips on talking to children about coeliac disease and how to make parties, eating at school, and visiting friends as hassle free as possible.

Including the whole family

Even if your entire family doesn't choose to go gluten-free, having a gluten-free kid in the house affects everyone. All the family members need to know about your child's condition, the diet, and how to handle a variety of situations that may arise.

We're not suggesting that you organise an extended family reunion and include fifth cousins thrice removed. But you do need to include your immediate family in some type of discussion. Don't think that these talks need to take place all at once; discussion is an ongoing process, and you're going to be talking about the gluten-free lifestyle for months, if not years, to come.

Kids will be kids, and sibs will be sibs. Just because the brothers and sisters understand the diet, doesn't mean that they're always going to be kind. You may hear the typical taunting – you know, the 'I can eat this and you can't' type of thing. Treat this teasing the same way you treat any other act that you don't approve of between siblings. Don't let your feelings of frustration that your child has this condition make you overreact to unkind gestures. Quarrelling is quarrelling, and you should try to respond to it consistently.

Keeping the discussion upbeat

Everyone you talk to about the gluten-free lifestyle – and the conditions that require it – finds out how to feel about the gluten-free lifestyle from you. Is being gluten-free a bad thing in your life? A scary thing? A good thing? How you talk about it has a far greater impact than you may realise.

If you call a family meeting and gather somberly, you're going to scare your children right out of their pyjamas and cast an impression of doom and gloom. This conversation should be upbeat, lighthearted, and interactive – after all, becoming gluten-free is a good thing in everyone's life. If you can't remember why, go back to the preceding sections in this chapter or look at some of the thoughts in Chapter 18.

The most important person to stay upbeat around is your coeliac child. For the rest of their life, how they feel about being gluten-free depends on you and your attitudes. This is all new, and because they don't know how to feel they take their cue from you (granted, it's new to you, too, but you're the grown up). Give them the advantage of starting off upbeat and optimistic. If they are like most kids, they're going to take it from there and provide amazing strength and inspiration.

Don't make a huge fuss out of needing to be gluten-free. As huge as it may seem to you, chances are that this isn't going to be a huge deal in your child's life . . . unless you make it one.

Explaining the new lifestyle

The level of detail you get into about the condition depends on your child's age, maturity, and ability to understand this type of thing. In a nutshell, you want to provide your child with the 'why', 'what', and 'what now': Why they are gluten-free (to feel better); what gluten-free means; and what they can eat now that they're gluten-free. The latter is really the most important, because that's what matters most to your child.

Startled siblings

So you're sitting down to have a family discussion about Victoria's new gluten-free lifestyle, and before your very eyes, her sister, Mild-Mannered-Molly, turns into Bordering-on-Ballistic-Barbie. What's going on? You did your best to explain everything in a positive way. Why is she freaking out?

Don't be surprised if you see this type of reaction from other children in the family: Being scared, confused, and even a touch panicked is perfectly normal.

Siblings can be wondering all sorts of things: Is my sister poorly? Is she going to die? Am I going to catch it? If she has to eat horrible stuff, do I have to eat it too? (Correct answer is that *neither* of you has to eat horrible stuff!) Why does she gets special attention and I don't? What if she gets better stuff than I do? Why did this happen to our family? And, most importantly, are my friends going to think I'm weird because my sister eats different food?

Being aware that these reactions are typical can help you respond in a sympathetic, understanding way. Address the feelings you suspect the other children are having, even if they're not able to articulate their anxieties, and encourage them to tell you why the situation scares them. Before you know it, everyone can relax and you can have a more productive discussion.

Little ears are listening

When you're talking to other grown-ups about your child's diet and condition, bear in mind that your son or daughter may be tuning in to every word you're saying. They may seem distracted with toys or friends, and they may in fact be too busy to hear what you're saying. But kids have ears, and they know how to use 'em (unless, of course, you're asking them to do the washing up).

Are you apologising for the complexity of the diet? That can make your child feel like a victim.

Are you complaining about the restrictions? That may make them feel like a burden. Are you feeling sorry for yourself? Your child may then feel guilty for encumbering you with the challenges this lifestyle may present.

We're not saying don't vent your feelings – if you're frustrated, exhausted, or feeling overly burdened at the moment, that's fine, and having someone to confide in is therapeutic. Just make sure that little ears aren't listening.

Be patient, and don't try to rush explaining everything. Understanding and accepting may not happen all at once, but is more likely to be an ongoing process for you all.

Focusing on the benefits

Chances are that your child has had health issues that led to the need for a gluten-free diet, and so start the discussion with something positive like, 'You're going to feel *so* much better now that you're going to be eating gluten-free foods!'

Kids think in specifics. Drive the point home to them with something they can personally relate to, such as, 'You know how much your tummy's been hurting lately?' or 'You know how you've been feeling so tired lately?' – 'You aren't going to have that anymore now that you're gluten-free!' Specifics can help children understand exactly *what's* going to be better on the gluten-free diet.

Then, a few weeks into the lifestyle, remember to point out how much better they feel, thanks to the delicious gluten-free foods they're eating.

Using big words and good explanations

Don't underestimate what your kids can grasp. When explaining the diet to your child, use the 'big' words like gluten (spare them the carboxymethylcellulose, though, okay?). Even if your child has developmental or learning disabilities, use the proper terminology so that they can better communicate to others what's permissible to eat.

Of course, your child's not going to understand at first (did *you?*). Give examples they can understand – explain that 'gluten is in lots of the foods we used to eat, like bread, biscuits, and cereals', and then quickly let your child know that *lots* of wonderful things don't have gluten in them.

Offering gluten-free alternatives

Always focusing on what your child *can* eat is important. Anytime you or your child asks about or points out a food that's off-limits, try to point out something equally as scrumptious that's gluten-free.

Of course, you're not going to say, 'You can't have those cakes anymore, Oliver, but look here! You can eat all the broccoli your little heart desires!' That isn't going to win you any parent points, and little Oliver isn't likely to buy into this new lifestyle with much zest. Instead, you can accomplish three things at once here:

- ✔ Reward your child for grasping the diet
- ✔ Offer an alternative
- ✔ Reinforce that he or she can eat it *because* it's gluten-free

A couple of simple sentences do the trick: 'You're right, Oliver, you can't eat that cake. But you *can* have this one, instead, because it's gluten-free!'

 Always be prepared to do the Treat Trade. When your child wants to eat a treat that contains gluten, be ready to trade it for something equally as appealing – but of the gluten-free variety. Kids are relatively easily distracted, and if you have some delectable goodies waiting in the wings as a Treat Trade, you're sure to turn that frown upside down.

Reinforcing the idea that gluten makes your child feel poorly

Help your child to make the connection that gluten makes them feel poorly. You should use this in a couple of situations – first, whenever you talk about gluten: 'You're right, you can't eat that. It has gluten, and gluten makes you feel poorly.' This way, your child discovers that gluten is associated with feeling ill – and that's a very good thing. To state all this scientifically, the desire to cheat is inversely proportional to the realisation that gluten makes you ill, as shown in Figure 16-2. When you can chart something, it must be true, right?

The other occasion when you may want to point out the effects of gluten – and this is where a bit of prevarication comes in – is when your child doesn't feel well – for just about any reason. This strategy works best for younger kids, usually aged about 6 and under. And it only works if you really don't know exactly what's making your child feel bad – a tummy ache, for instance. You may know full well that the discomfort has nothing to do with gluten, but seize the opportunity to say, 'I'm sorry you don't feel well. We must have made a mistake, and you accidentally got some gluten. We'll have to be more careful next time.'

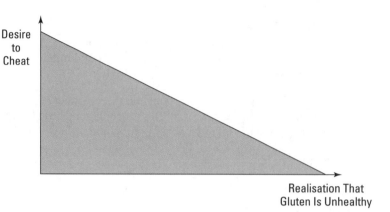

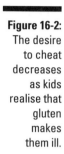

Figure 16-2:
The desire
to cheat
decreases
as kids
realise that
gluten
makes
them ill.

The chances that your child's going to sneak gluten (or even want it, for that matter) are inversely proportional to the clarity of this association between gluten and not feeling well.

Most likely, your child is trying really hard to stick to the diet. Make sure that they don't feel like they've done something wrong by making a mistake. Point out that we all make mistakes and that gluten can be hidden in all sorts of things. It just means that you have to be extra careful in the future.

When kids who have coeliac disease get tummy aches, you may jump to the conclusion that they feel ill because they got gluten, and find yourself agonising over the probable culprit. But remember, kids get tummy aches! They can be caused by all kinds of different things, but generally, they're a normal part of growing up. Being diligent about the diet is important as is working out what caused it when you see a gluten reaction. But sometimes tummy aches and other types of gastrointestinal distress are just normal parts of being a kid.

Handling your child's reaction

You can't predict how your child is going to respond when you first start talking to them about this new gluten-free lifestyle. The reaction depends on how you present the diet, and on your child's age, maturity, level of understanding, ability to express feelings, and of course, personality.

You probably realise that if your child shows anger, hostility, or other 'negative' emotions, you should be soothing, understanding, and supportive – those parental responses are natural.

Don't think, though, that the initial 'upset' reaction is going to stick, because it's most likely a fleeting response that, as time passes and your child becomes accustomed to the new lifestyle, evolves into a more positive outlook. Continue to remind of the benefits the child can look forward to now that their body is getting healthy by eating gluten-free foods.

Also, be prepared for little or no response. Appearing to be indifferent or apathetic is not unusual for kids. Don't read too much into it and assume this reaction is a 'cover up' for deep, disturbing thoughts – chances are, the response is an honest reaction to a somewhat confusing issue or to something that truly doesn't seem to matter much at the time.

Helping your child talk to others about the diet

Children needs to discover how to talk to other people – both adults and other kids – about the gluten-free lifestyle. They're going to be doing it for the rest of their lives, and the best time to start is the present. Of course, exactly what your child says and how they communicate it depends on age, personality, style, who they're talking to, and how comfortable they are talking about this type of thing.

Explaining what children can and can't have

Give your coeliac or gluten-intolerant child a phrase to use, even if they're too young to know what it means. Use something comprehensive that they can repeat to adults.

For instance, they can say, 'I can't eat gluten. That means I don't eat wheat, rye, barley, malt, and oats.' We know that definition isn't technically correct (malt is from barley, and oats are gluten-free but sometimes contaminated), but it tells adults what they need to know.

Maybe that phrase is too cumbersome; but if your child can handle the words, go with it. If not, find a phrase that's more age-appropriate or one that suits your child's personality. The idea behind the memorised 'sound bite' is that it covers a lot of situations with a relatively easy couple of sentences.

Of course, the more information children can add, the better. If your child can explain to people exactly what they can and can't eat, that's terrific – and if they can add the fact that gluten makes them feel poorly, that's even better. Before long, your child is going to decide what works best for them.

Educate your child to be open and conversant about being gluten-free. We're not suggesting that you and your child walk into a room, grab a microphone, clear your throats, and begin preaching about the gluten-free lifestyle. Nor do you want your child to feel automatically entitled to have people accommodate their diet. But informing people (especially those who may be involved in feeding your child) is important, and you can do this in a friendly, informative manner. You may find that your child becomes an effective awareness-spreading advocate before you know it.

Some kids feel more comfortable simplifying their explanation to something people can understand more easily, such as, 'I'm allergic to gluten,' or even 'I'm allergic to wheat.' Even though that explanation's not technically correct, sometimes it's easier. Just make sure that your kids know the *real* facts so they don't get confused later on.

Getting kids to say 'no thanks'

No matter how well children communicate the fact that they can't eat gluten, at some point a person, usually with the best of intentions, is sure to offer them something with gluten.

This situation can be really confusing to your child, especially if the well-meaning person is a loved one and is folding a biscuit into your child's hand and saying with a conspiratorial just-between-you-and-me wink, 'Don't tell Mummy and Daddy.' Nightmare! What's a gluten-free kid to do?

Explain to your child how and why this type of a situation may come up, and most importantly, how to handle it. Sometimes saying 'no thanks' or 'I appreciate it, but I can't eat that' is easy for a child. Other times, just accepting the treat and not eating it is easier and more conciliatory.

Even if your friends and family don't offering your child gluten, someone out there is sure to do so. You can spare your child disappointment and confusion if you help them deal with this type of situation before it comes up (and remember to take gluten-free treats with you when you are visiting friends and family, so you can do the Treat Trade in case you're accosted by well-intentioned folk!).

Deciding Whether the Whole Family Should Be Gluten-Free

Many people assume that because one child is gluten-free, the entire family should adopt the lifestyle. After all, wouldn't it be cruel to be feasting on doughnuts while your gluten-free child is choking on rice cakes? Yes, it would.

But having the entire family live gluten-free isn't always the right answer. You really have to weigh both sides of the issue and consider the practical and psychological issues.

The pros

Here are some advantages if everyone goes gluten-free:

- ✔ **You make only one version of each meal.** Rather than making a gluten-free version and a 'regular' version of some dishes at mealtime, you can make just one gluten-free version and be done with it.

- ✔ **You shop only for gluten-free foods.** You can pass the bread and cracker aisles altogether.

- ✔ **You cut out the risk of contamination in the kitchen.** (Check out Chapter 8.)

- ✔ **Your child doesn't feel different.** Being different is okay, but feeling the same is nice as well, especially when it comes to being family.

- ✔ **You can fill the cupboards with 'safe' foods.** You don't have to worry that you or your child accidentally grabs a gluten-laden snack, because you don't have any.

- ✔ **Your child isn't tempted to cheat.** At least not at home.

The cons

We're trying to offer both sides here, but if you sense that the cons list is a little weightier than the pros list, you're right. Ultimately, in our opinion, the cons outweigh the pros of having the entire family going gluten-free:

- ✔ **A gluten-free world is not reality.** Your child needs to understand that the rest of the world eats gluten. They're not doing it to ostracise or make your child feel bad, and no malicious or evil intentions are present. What better environment to find out that important lesson than in a loving, supportive home?

- ✔ **Your child doesn't find out how to make food choices.** Knowing how to choose which foods they can eat and which they can't is important for your child. If the cupboard's free of 'no-nos', your child doesn't need to decide and may become complacent about mindlessly grabbing food without giving a thought to whether it's gluten-free.

✔ **It can create resentment among other family members.** Siblings – even parents – can be a little bitter about having to give up bread and cakes if they don't have a health condition that requires it. They can direct that resentment toward your gluten-free child and that sets up an unhealthy family dynamic.

✔ **Your child isn't tempted to cheat.** Although this item also appears as a pro (it's really both a pro and a con), we believe that helping your child to discover how to resist the temptation (especially because gluten is practically everywhere) is better than never tempting them.

✔ **Eating a lot of specialty foods can be more expensive.** We're not advocating eating only specialty foods, but they have a place in the gluten-free lifestyle. Isn't it sensible to save the £4 pack of biscuits for the person who really needs them? The gluten-free foods on prescription are intended only for the person with coeliac disease and not for the whole family.

Middle ground

Sometimes a compromise is the best solution. See whether these ideas work for your family:

✔ **Make most meals gluten-free.** If you can make the majority of your meals gluten-free and still please everyone without using up your worth-their-weight-in-gold gluten-free specialty items, do so. This can make cooking and preparation easier, and everyone is able to enjoy the same meals.

✔ **Buy gluten-free condiments and staples.** Using gluten-free salad dressings, soy sauce, and other staple or condiment-type items makes life a lot easier on you – and you don't have to make separate stir-fries just because one of them has the gluten kind of soy sauce on it.

✔ **Enjoy the delicious gluten-free mixes.** Most of the gluten-free mixes these days for biscuits, cakes, and other baked goods are as good as the real thing. They're a little more expensive, maybe, but cost aside, you really have no reason to make separate batches of these things. Make one batch of the gluten-free kind and let the entire family enjoy.

Giving Your Child Control of the Diet

If your child doesn't take control of their diet, the diet controls them. No matter how young, your child needs to discover from day one to make decisions about what they can and can't eat – and the importance of not cheating, no matter how tempted.

From a psychological standpoint, not letting the gluten-free diet take centre-stage in your child's life is important – and that means they should be thinking of other things most of the time. But when the time comes to eat, they need to realise that making good choices is important. Food is something they need to pay close attention to.

A wise proverb says, 'Give a man a fish, and you feed him for a day. Teach him to fish, and you feed him for a lifetime.' Your kids need to choose foods they can eat for a lifetime. Giving your child control of the diet also creates bonuses for everyone:

- **Your child has confidence.** Even if you're not there, your child's able to eat safely and make healthy food choices.

- **You can relax.** You know that even if you're not there, your child is prepared to make good food choices. And if you are there, you don't have to be doing all the decision-making.

- **Your child is discovering the importance of healthy eating.** How many kids read food labels or give even a first thought (much less a second) to what they're putting in their mouths? Your child is finding out how to be conscious of nutrition at an early age, which is a valuable lifelong lesson.

Working together to make good choices

When we say to give your child control, we're not suggesting that you let them make all the decisions alone – like everything else in life, children need a little guidance, especially at first. You can do lots of things together to help kids find out how to make good food choices.

- **Read labels together.** Even if your child is too young to read, pretend. Hold the ingredients label where you can both see it, and go through the ingredients out loud, one by one (just like when you're tired and reading them bedtime stories, you can skip the superfluous stuff). Point to the words, and when you come to pertinent ones, like *wheat*, remind them, 'No. This one has gluten in it.' And then, because you're well-conditioned to quickly point to the alternative, follow up with, 'Let's try *this* one,' and grab something you know is gluten-free.

- **Make a game out of it.** When you're reading labels or talking about foods, see who can decide which one is gluten-free (or not) first. (Note to those of you competitive types: Let 'em win a few.)

- **Encourage your child to telephone food manufacturers.** (This works best if your child is old enough to talk!) After they've seen you query food ingredients a few times, let your child make the calls. Sometimes being on another extension so you can take over is a good idea.

✔ **Get your child to plan the occasional meal.** Not only does this give them a chance to practice working out what's gluten-free and what isn't, but also you know they're actually going to eat everything that's served. So what if their menu consists of chips, rice, sweets, and gluten-free macaroni and cheese? Go with it. Remember, for that meal at least, your child's in control and this exercise is primarily to get them to think gluten-free, and not to demonstrate their knowledge of a healthy, balanced diet.

✔ **Allow your children to pack their own lunch.** If it's not perfectly nutritionally balanced, make some suggestions and see whether they'll add the nutritious stuff you want. If not, go with it. One unbalanced meal isn't going to kill them – but it does let them know that they can choose foods that are gluten-free (and tasty!).

✔ **Let your child help with the cooking.** Kids *love* to cook, even though it usually ends up being far more work than if they don't help. Discovering how to cook at an early age is important for all children, especially for those who are going to require some specially prepared foods for the rest of their lives.

Trusting kids when you're not there

Letting g-g-g-g-go is one of the hardest things parents ever do; yet it's your job as a parent. On a daily basis, you're preparing your children for life so you can eventually set them free. If you do your job well, you can relax knowing that they have all the tools they need to make decisions that lead to safe, happy, healthy lives.

The idea behind giving your kids control of their diet is that they need to know how to feed themselves, because you aren't always going to be there, and that's true for all kids. You don't have much of a problem giving them control of certain things – toilet training, washing their hands, and switching on the computer. But when it comes to choosing foods, trusting that they're going to make safe choices is hard – particularly when some foods can make them really ill!

You'll know when the time is right and you can actually relax knowing that your children are making safe food choices. That time is most likely to come long before you expect it, and you should be prepared for it to arrive before *you're* ready.

Your children are going to make mistakes. But bear in mind that mistakes aren't going to kill or permanently harm them, and with any luck the error causes some discomfort so that they realise the importance of being more attentive next time.

Getting Out with the Gluten-Free Gang

Living life in an overprotected environment is not healthy. Your child's life shouldn't be restricted just because of a restricted diet!

Really, getting out and about with gluten-free kids isn't much different from the way gluten-free adults do it: You follow the same golden rules of gluten-free eating out and travelling, and ordering at restaurants isn't very different, except that you may be ordering from a kids' menu instead of an adult one. We cover all these things in detail in Chapter 15, and so for the most part, if you master the general ideas of that chapter, you're going to do great getting out and about with the kids.

We do have a few suggestions that are specific to getting out with gluten-free kids:

- **Let your children order for themselves.** At first this idea may be cumbersome, because they're likely to order chicken nuggets or spaghetti, assuming that they eat the gluten-free kind at home. Don't worry about taking a long time or bothering the waiter. Discovering how to order at a restaurant is really important for children, an important part of the living gluten-free process.

- **Don't be shy.** Some kids are mortified when adults 'make a scene' (asking a question) at a restaurant. All you have to do is say, 'Can I ask you about this menu item. . .' and the eyes start rolling, the 'Oh no, here she goes, it's sooooo embarrassing' comments start spewing forth. Ignore your kids and ask anyway. If they don't ask, you need to.

- **Consider taking along a gluten-free dessert for your child.** You can't assume the desserts at a restaurant are gluten-free, and so just in case they don't have any, bring your own or go somewhere else for dessert.

Leaving Your Gluten-Free Kids in the Care of Others

Leaving your kids with other people is scary enough, even when your kids don't have dietary limitations that can make them ill. But trusting someone else to feed your gluten-free child safely? Are you insane? Letting go of a little parental control can be frightening, but spending time apart is an important part of growing up for kids and parents.

Trusting your kids with friends, family, and sitters

The most important thing you can do to ensure that your kids are in good hands from a gluten-free standpoint is to educate the people caring for your child. If you suspect they don't fully understand the diet, work harder to make sure that they do or find a new carer.

When you leave your child in someone else's care, try to take or leave prepared food as often as you can, and clearly mark on containers that the food is gluten-free. That prevents any mix-up between your child's food and someone else's.

Sending your children to school

Because they're away at school for several hours at a time, day after day, sending your gluten-free kids to school is one of the biggest challenges you face. Some important tips follow:

- ✔ **Educate your teachers, school nurse, school cook, and head teacher.** In fact, educate as much of the staff as possible. In this way, not only are the staff members better prepared to deal with your child's diet, but also the chances are that they have other kids at the school who need to be gluten-free and don't know it yet. You may have an enormous positive impact on those kids as well!

- ✔ **Give the teacher a stash of treats for your child.** Nothing's worse than finding out at the end of the day that it was a friend's birthday and your child ate nothing while the other kids smeared cakes all over their faces. Bring bags of fun-sized gluten-free treat packages that the teacher can store in a special place for your child in case of a surprise party or an event that involves treats. (Head to Chapter 14 for some great gluten-free sweet treat recipes.)

- ✔ **Be aware of craft time.** Play dough has gluten in it, and although kids aren't *supposed* to eat it, show us one kid who can resist. We know we couldn't! Other crafts involve gluten-containing cereals, and those activities often become a matter of 'one for the necklace, one for me . . . one for the necklace, one for me.' Make sure that the teacher and your child pay attention at craft time.

- ✔ **Work with the catering team.** Teachers can help you find contact information. Being given the opportunity to buy lunch from the school canteen even once a week may be a big deal to your child. Most caterers are willing to work with you to find ways in which your child can eat at least one meal each week. Somehow, standing in that dinner queue is cool!

Party time!

Parties are supposed to be all about fun! But to parents, parties sometimes seem like they're all about food. Apparently, a new law has been drawn up that requires all children's parties to be held at pizza or fast-food restaurants. For a few pounds per child, parents can host a party that lasts all of about an hour, and stuff the kids with pizza, burgers, and cake. So what about those pizza, burgers and cake? Do you let party time turn to pouty time? No, of course you don't. Try some of these ideas:

✔ **Make sure that your child eats before going to the party.** If your child's full, they aren't going to be thinking about food, and missing out isn't such a big deal.

✔ **If you know that the only food served has gluten, bring your own.** If possible, bring something close to what they're serving – gluten-free pizza, for instance.

✔ **If the party is at a restaurant that may have gluten-free food available, ask the host ahead of time whether you can order separately.** This request isn't the least bit rude, and your host is probably happy to help you with the details.

✔ **If it's your child's party, serve gluten-free foods.** This notion may sound like a no-brainer, but it's not. *Don't*, however, try to serve gluten-free pizza or something else that may cause that one kid (you know which one I'm talking about) to spit it five feet and ask, 'What *is* this?' Serve hot dogs or hamburgers, and maybe do sundaes that kids can build themselves for dessert.

✔ **Beware of the Eating Exchange.** Swapping food in school lunches is very serious business. Kids get right down to it, swapping an egg sandwich for chocolate biscuits (*not* a fair trade). Talk to your child about the importance of not trading food – even if someone else's food looks okay, it may not be (not to mention the fact that your kid's just going to give away those £4 gluten-free biscuits you bought). Ask the lunchtime supervisors to be on the lookout and make sure that your child doesn't participate in the Eating Exchange.

For a manual that thoroughly covers everything – snack and lunch ideas, talking with school staff, and managing all kinds of child-related situations – we suggest you read *Information for Parents and Carers* produced by Coeliac UK, and available for mail order from www.coeliac.org.uk, and check out the whole section on the Web site devoted to kids – both are excellent resources.

Guiding Your Gluten-Free Teenagers

You can't push a teenager any more than you can push a rope. By the time your kids are teenagers, the best you can do is hope that you've laid a good foundation and are still able to guide them in the direction you think they should go.

If your teenager is newly diagnosed, the teen years can be a scary time for them. They're already going through many changes, and adopting a gluten-free lifestyle is one change that they may think casts them way beyond being different and into the realm of being a real freak.

If your teenager has been diagnosed, even if that diagnosis happened years ago, you may see your child evolve from one who was very accepting and easygoing about the diet into one who fights it and may even cheat from time to time.

All these responses are normal, if *any* definition of the word 'normal' applies to teenagers. You should handle these reactions with patience, understanding, and communication on both sides.

Noticing changing symptoms

Now you see 'em, now you don't; sometimes children's symptoms seem to do a disappearing act during their teenage years – usually referred to as a *honeymoon period.* For some teenagers, the symptoms do go away – at least temporarily. At this point, they may be tempted to devour a pizza. They think that because they don't feel symptoms, they're going to be okay. Not true! In fact, the whole thing is just an illusion (like some of the other things that take place during the teenage years!). Although your kids may not *feel* the effects, the gluten still does damage.

For other teenagers, the symptoms don't really go away but evolve into those traits more characteristic in adults – headaches, fatigue, and depression, for example. These teenagers, too, sometimes think that their symptoms have disappeared, because what they used to associate with eating gluten – diarrhoea, for instance – is no longer their typical reaction. They may not realise the headaches they get, or other symptoms, are also signs of their gluten intolerance.

Understanding why teenagers may cheat on the diet

We cover the topic of cheating and being tempted to cheat on the gluten-free diet in Chapter 17. But teenagers are different animals, and they sometimes cheat or want to cheat for different reasons. Really, by the time kids become teenagers, parents can't stop them from putting something in their mouths. But knowing why they want to cheat, so that you can be sympathetic and have an open discussion with them, may help.

No longer is their desire simply a matter of 'I want it, so I think I'll eat it.' With teenagers, they may want to eat gluten because of the following:

- **Peer pressure:** At no time in their lives is peer pressure greater than when kids are teenagers. Even if their friends aren't pushing them to eat gluten (they don't usually do that), your teenager may just *want* to be like everyone else and be tempted to cheat on the diet.

   Kids love to proclaim how they want to be unique, but they really don't want to be different, and this diet may make them feel different. Don't be surprised if your teenager orders a burger with a bun just to be like their mates.

- **Rebellion:** Your teenager may be tempted to eat gluten as a way of being rebellious. Even if they don't tell you about the incident, they may sub-consciously be exerting their control: A type of 'I'll show you who's in control' behaviour.

- **Curiosity:** A child who's curious about what gluten tastes like may actually have more restraint than a curious teenager. Even if your teenager's been diligent about following the diet for years, they're most likely to succumb in the teenage years.

- **Weight control:** Many teenagers work out that if they eat gluten, they aren't absorbing all the available calories. Sadly, some intentionally cheat on the diet in an effort to lose weight.

Watch for signs of eating disorders in your kids. Sometimes they become obsessed with their restrictions and take them too far – or they use gluten as a means of losing weight. Address this issue immediately, as eating disorders are extremely serious issues.

So, what do you do about your cheating teenager? The best you can do is to have a two-way conversation. Try to find out why your child cheated and what the consequences were, if any. Educate your child about what's happen-ing to their body and remind them that even if they don't *feel* the effects of gluten, those effects are still doing tremendous harm to their body.

Helping teenagers after they move out

One of the hardest things for teenagers to handle, especially if they're new to the gluten-free lifestyle, is moving out. Being on their own actually isn't quite as difficult as if they move into college or university halls, where a meal plan and a lack of transport can limit them to the food in the dining halls. Whatever the case, make sure that your child fully understands the diet and can choose foods that are healthy and gluten-free.

If your child lives on campus and has to eat in dining halls, get them to contact the catering manager to discuss their dietary needs. Many of the available foods are already gluten-free – and many aren't. They may need to bring their own soy sauce, for instance, or otherwise modify what they're eating.

Having access to a fridge and even a full kitchen is helpful. Work with housing or residential services to make sure that your child has access at least to a microwave and refrigerator so they can store foods that have been bought at the supermarket. Student lounges in halls often have a microwave and/or fridge that students have access to if they can't have one in their room. Coming up with snacks and menus that your child can make in the microwave (even gluten-free pasta!) is relatively easy.

Check the hall's policies before buying a mini-refrigerator or microwave. Some halls that allow these appliances have size and power restrictions.

Food parcels are sometimes the next-best thing to being there. Think about sending some gluten-free goodies from time to time.

Chapter 17

Beating the Gluten-Free Blues: Overcoming Emotional Obstacles

---

In This Chapter

▶ Coping when things don't feel so great

▶ Confronting and coming to terms with denial

▶ Dealing with dietary lapses

▶ Looking at the big picture

▶ Staying on track

Maybe we're just not looking hard enough, but we haven't seen many bestsellers in the bookshops with titles like *How To Cope When Things Are Going Really, Really Well For You*. No, you really need the most help when you're facing life's challenges. And some people feel that the gluten-free lifestyle is one big challenge. Some of that has to do with why they're going gluten-free in the first place.

People who embark on a gluten-free lifestyle usually do so for one of two reasons:

▶ **They've chosen to.** They haven't been diagnosed with any medical conditions, or if they have been tested, their tests came back negative. But they suspect that they're going to feel better on a gluten-free diet. Or maybe they just want to support a loved one who's going gluten-free.

▶ **They have to.** They've been diagnosed with a medical condition that requires it.

Guess which group of people has the easiest time from a psychological perspective. Spot on! When you choose to do something, you're starting off with a huge emotional advantage. Not only are you mentally prepared for the challenge, but also you're welcoming the changes to come.

On the other hand, when someone tells you that you have to do something (those going gluten-free for the second reason), you're likely to have a harder time with it. (Think back to your childhood when you were just getting ready to clean your room voluntarily and then your mum yelled, 'Don't forget to clean your room!' Talk about a motivation drain.) Add in the unique social and practical challenges that arise when you're living a gluten-free lifestyle, and some people find themselves dealing with all sorts of complex emotional issues.

Okay, so some people have accused us of being overly optimistic when considering the virtues of a gluten-free lifestyle. But we're not unrealistic – don't forget, we've been involved with this lifestyle for a very long time, and believe us, we've witnessed our share of the emotional challenges it can bring on. The best idea is to find out how to identify those challenges and obstacles and overcome them.

The key thing to remember is this: Deal with it; don't dwell on it. You can be mad, sad, uncomfortable, fed up, or ready to scream with frustration. That's okay. All those reactions and emotions, and the others we talk about in this chapter, are perfectly normal when someone has told you to change your entire life. But allowing yourself to get bogged down with the negativity and difficulty of the situation is easy, and these feelings may begin to consume you. Allow yourself the time to experience the difficult emotions, and then move on.

In this chapter we discuss a range of different ways in which you can break out of the negativity and see things in a more positive light. Yes, for some people this change is a difficult transition in life . . . but ultimately, you're going to be better for it.

Recognising Common Emotional Struggles

The reasons why living gluten-free can be difficult from an emotional standpoint are vast:

> ✔ **Social activities revolve around food.** Now, because you don't eat gluten, you may feel isolated, or you may be afraid to participate in these social functions because you think you can't eat anything. (If you're struggling with eating away from home, read Chapter 15.)

- **People you love don't understand.** In Chapter 15, we also talk about how to discuss the lifestyle with others. But sometimes, no matter how much you say or don't say, some people, many of whom are your closest friends or family, just don't grasp the importance of your situation.

- **People may think you're crazy.** When you try to explain the gluten-free diet to some people, or when they watch you stumble through one of your first experiences ordering at a restaurant, they may think that you have an eating disorder, or are outlandishly high-maintenance, picky, or crazy.

- **'Comfort food' is called that for a reason.** Weight-management lectures aside, for better or for worse, many people find eating to be a stress-reliever. When your food options are limited, eating can be disconcerting and create anxiety.

- **Some people don't cope well with even the smallest of changes.** For those people, something that involves changing their entire lifestyle can be really disruptive.

- **You're losing control in your life.** You're hereby 'sentenced' to a life of dietary restrictions. Wow. How's that for taking control away? You've been eating since you were a baby and choosing your own foods not long after that, and now someone's going to tell you what you can and can't eat? It's difficult sometimes.

- **The problem seems so permanent.** Oh, wait. That's because it is. And that doesn't help someone feeling 'put upon' by the restrictions.

- **You feel like you're on an island.** If you do, you better hope that the island's large, because millions of people are going gluten-free. But we digress. The gluten-free lifestyle seems isolating to some people; they even feel ostracised. If you're feeling like that, read on, because this chapter helps you to realise that you have control over those feelings and that you don't have to be isolated or feel like you're alone.

In this section, we talk about some of the common emotions that people experience when they hear they have to go gluten-free. You may notice that the issues people face look a lot like reactions you may see in people who've experienced a trauma. That's not so surprising, because for some people, being told they need to change their entire way of eating *can* be traumatic and stressful.

Total shock and panic

If you've ever seen a teenage girl who can't find her mobile phone, you've seen panic. For some people, changing to a gluten-free lifestyle is far worse than that.

On one hand, it all seems so sudden. You're in the doctor's surgery talking about your bowel movements and blood tests, and the next thing you know, you're labelled with a condition you've probably never heard of that changes the way you eat for the rest of your life. Yet in some ways, it's not sudden at all. The chances are that you've been having health problems for years. And now it has a name: and a treatment. Both of which can stun you.

You what? That's about all you can think or say. You're numb – you're in shock. The good news (let's see, some good news has got to be here somewhere – okay, here it is) is that by definition, you get this shocked feeling only once. (Have you ever tried to shock someone figuratively twice with the same news? Few people are that gullible.)

Have you ever had fingers that were so cold they were nearly frozen? They're numb at that point, aren't they? But when they begin to thaw, they throb and feel like you've just run them through a paper shredder. That's almost how you can feel when sheer shock turns to pure panic. That's when the reality of the words 'diet for life' begins to sink in, and you start to panic. What are you going to eat? How are you going do it? Where can you find special foods? Can you do it?

Rest assured that these feelings are normal, and they do pass. You will soon work out what you can eat, and your panic subsides as you become more comfortable with the diet, which begins on day one. The learning curve is steeper for some than others, but you *will* adapt, and the panic will wear off.

Anger and frustration

The shock and panic have subsided, and you're beginning to feel more comfortable with what you can and can't eat. But something's eating away at you. You realise you're angry. Peeved. Fuming and agonisingly frustrated!

Who or what you're angry with doesn't matter – some people in this situation are angry at their parents for giving them a 'defective' gene; others are annoyed with themselves for passing the gene on to their kids; some are furious at their partner for not being more understanding; most are irritated by the major cereal manufacturers who feel that a Universal Cereal Manufacturer's Law exists that means they must put malt flavouring in every cereal they make; and a few take it out on a more divine being for 'thinking up' this stupid condition.

The bottom line is, you're furious and that's making you stressed. Anger is a healthy emotion, and discovering how to deal with it is one of the most valuable lessons you can take on board in life. Taking your anger out on those closest to you is tempting, especially if they're adding to the frustration by being less-than-understanding about your new lifestyle. If you need help dealing with your anger, ask for it. Whatever you do don't lash out, especially at the people closest to you, because they're not to blame, and they can be immensely supportive when you need it most.

Grief and despair

Are you grieving? Do you feel like you've lost your best friend? In a way, you may have. Food, your control over what you eat, and even the simple act of putting food into your mouth can soothe you and bring you comfort. When you're forced to give up your favourite foods (if they weren't your favourites before, they're sure to be after you give them up!), the change can make you feel sad and nostalgic. Furthermore, some people feel that they're the only ones who have this problem, which can intensify feelings of isolation or loneliness.

If your child is going gluten-free, those feelings of grief can magnify. You dreamed that your children's lives were going to be carefree and ideal; having to deal with dietary restrictions that prevent them from eating what seem to be staples in a child's diet isn't usually part of your plan.

Some people reach a point of desperation or despair. They find the diet to be cumbersome and difficult, and they keep making mistakes. Then they decide that if they can't do this right, they may as well not do it at all, and they give up.

Grief and despair are normal emotions, but don't give in to them. You're going to get over your feelings of sadness and loneliness, and this lifestyle doesn't have to be in the least bit isolating or depriving. As for doing it right, give it your very best effort – truly 100 per cent – and you're sure to succeed. Dealing with a mistake from time to time is better than giving up and not trying at all.

Loss and deprivation

You may feel several of kinds of loss when someone tells you that you have to go gluten-free. You obviously lose some of your favourite foods – and what about the social situations that go hand-in-hand with them? You miss the takeaway pizza and beer during the football or Granny's famous sponge cake where everyone fights over the last piece. And what about the great nibbles – all of which are heavily skewed toward the gluten-containing variety – that you normally put out when the girls come around for the evening. (Okay, we'll stop with the reminders now.)

Many of your favourite foods, in the form you currently know them, are a thing of the past. At first the social situations may not seem the same without them – and they aren't totally the same. They're the same but different, and that's all right. Remember when you attend these events that they're not really about the food – they're about the socialising. Also remember to bring yourself foods that you love – and follow the golden rules of going out gluten-free that we cover in Chapter 15.

Another sense of loss people feel is that of convenience. These days food is prewashed, precut, prepeeled, precooked, prepackaged, pre-resealed, practically pre-eaten, premetabolised, and stored as fat around your waist before you ever get it home from the store. Convenience foods come as a complete snack or meal, in various combinations to please any palate. Yes, these foods are convenient – and sometimes, when you grab them off the shelf of the fresh produce section, they're even good for you and gluten-free. But many of them, for you, are a thing of the past.

So, yes, many people do suffer from a loss of convenience. Your days of calling for pizza delivery are behind you, at least until the big pizza companies begin offering gluten-free pizza. No longer do you race through the supermarket mindlessly grabbing products off the shelves because they look good or they're on special offer.

Okay, so giving up gluten isn't as convenient – and you miss your old favourites. We give you that – you can feel a sense of loss. But look what you've gained. Your health! The gluten-free diet is your key to better health, and that's priceless.

Sadness and depression

Occasionally, people get so overwhelmed with the whole concept of their medical condition and the gluten-free diet that they feel an impending doom, and experience depression to a certain degree.

Be aware that depression is a symptom that you may experience if you eat gluten despite your intolerance: Is the depression due to accidental (or intentional) gluten ingestion, or is it a lingering emotional discomfort from the pre-diagnosis days? Some people, before they're diagnosed (and some even afterwards), are accused of making up their problems, or they're told that the symptoms are all in their head. These accusations can be so hurtful and frustrating that they cause the person to go into a state of depression.

People with coeliac disease have a higher incidence of depression, and other neurological problems. We talk more about how gluten affects behaviour in Chapter 2.

In addition, of course, you also feel the restrictions, grief, sense of loss, anger, and the other reactions we discuss in this chapter. All these emotions can lead to depression.

Unfortunately, depression caused by illness can result in a vicious cycle. The physical symptoms lead to suffering and depression, and then the depression makes the physical symptoms worse. Furthermore, depression can weaken the immune system and can affect your heart. Another reason to turn that frown upside down: People with depression are four times more likely to have a heart attack than those without.

If you're feeling depressed, make sure that your diet is 100 per cent gluten-free so you know that what you're feeling isn't a symptom of gluten ingestion. Also consider therapy of some type, whether that's confiding in friends or seeking professional help. Your GP is a good place to start or try Mind, the charity for better mental health, which has a wealth of information online at `www.mind.org.uk` and a really helpful phone line: 0845-7660163.

If you feel your case of the blues isn't serious and you want to try to work it out on your own, see whether these activities help:

- **Exercising:** When you exercise, your brain produces endorphins, and those chemicals create a natural high. Exercise also helps you get rid of stress hormones that build up in the body and wreak all sorts of physical and emotional havoc.

- **Eating well:** And that means, besides eating a healthy diet, staying strict about your gluten-free diet. Eating gluten exacerbates the physical and mental symptoms you may experience, and if you're gluten intolerant, gluten robs you of the important nutrients that are supposed to energise you and make you feel good. Stay away from the high-glycaemic-index foods we talk about in Chapter 6, because those mess up your blood-sugar levels and affect your moods.

- **Avoiding alcohol:** Booze is bad news for people suffering from depression. Alcohol is a depressant, and so by definition, it brings you down – it also interrupts your sleep patterns, which are important for feeling your best.

- **Relaxing (whether you want to or not):** Chilling out is hard sometimes, we know! But relaxation (even if you force it) is important to maintaining your mental health. Sometimes you may forget to take care of yourself, but doing so is crucial – otherwise you aren't able to help anyone.

- **Doing something nice for others:** We've all heard the expression 'you only get back what you give', and many people believe that the amount of happiness you feel is directly proportional to the happiness you bring to others. Have you ever been feeling down and done something nice for someone else? Not feeling better when you make someone's day is practically impossible.

Dealing with Denial

Denial isn't just a river in Egypt. Denial comes in all sizes and shapes – some types affect you, other types affect those around you, but nearly everyone living gluten-free goes through it to some extent.

When you're the one in denial

When you hear that you have to give up gluten for health reasons, deciding to run, not walk, to the nearest sand pit to start digging a hole for your head is quite common – this reaction is a form of denial. You go through several phases of denial.

Immediate Denial

Your doctor: You have coeliac disease and you need to eliminate all gluten from your diet starting immediately.

You: Gluten? You mean like sugar?

Your doctor: No, I mean like pizza, bread, and beer.

You: Surely you can't be serious.

Your doctor: I am serious, and don't call me Shirley.

Okay, so this isn't the time to joke, even if it is with classic lines from the movie *Airplane!* But the initial reaction is a common one: I can't have that condition; I've never even heard of it; I'm too fat to have that; I'm too old to have it; I'm too (insert whatever adjective supports your denial) to have that.

You can deny till the cows come home (where *were* they, anyway?), but that doesn't help your health much. What does help is getting on track as fast as you can, because you have improved health to look forward to.

Denial farther down the road

Another type of denial settles in after you've been gluten-free for a while and you're feeling great. In fact, you feel so good that you start to think maybe nothing was really wrong with you, and you can't really remember ever feeling too bad.

Of course, this moment is about the time that the reality starts to set in that you're following this diet for the rest of your life, and you're tempted to cheat – but surely it's not cheating if you don't really need to be gluten-free now, is it? So begins the battle in your brain, where good and evil don't see eye to eye.

The good half of your brain is telling you, 'Mmmmm, this is the most delicious gluten-free cracker I've ever had!' But the demon-in-denial side is saying, 'No way am I sitting through another football match eating rice cakes and sipping white wine while the other guys are plowing through pizza and guzzling beer. Besides, I don't have an intolerance . . . come on, just one slice of pizza won't hurt. . . .'.

Get away from that pizza box. This phase is a period of ambivalence, in which you're hoping beyond hope that you don't really have to give up gluten and are 'proving' it to yourself by ignoring your conscience.

Acceptance

The biggest problem with denial is that it justifies eating gluten. When you have this fake epiphany, 'realising' that you don't need to be gluten-free, you're tempted to run, not walk, to the nearest bakery. Resist the temptation. If you've been gluten-free for a while, yes, you feel great, but that's because of the diet, not in spite of it. The danger in testing your little theory is that you may not have any reaction when you do, and then you're likely to jump to the obvious (by which we mean 'desired') conclusion that you never needed to eliminate gluten in the first place.

If you're still not sure that you really should be gluten-free, here are some steps that you can take to help clarify things for you:

- ✔ **Get properly tested.** Denial is one of the most compelling arguments in favour of proper testing. Flick to Chapter 2 for more information about testing.

- ✔ **Realise that 'negative' tests don't always mean you're free to become a glutton for gluten.** Wheat allergy tests don't pick up coeliac disease; coeliac tests can be falsely negative. Testing techniques have changed over the years, and maybe your tests were done long ago. Problems with gluten can develop at any point, and so just because you were negative once doesn't mean you're going to be negative again. And finally, some people are negative on all the tests, yet their health improves dramatically on a gluten-free diet and we still don't quite know why.

- ✔ **Get another opinion.** If you're particularly stubborn, you may even want to get a third opinion. Remember when Dad said no, and you went and asked Mum? Well, if they both say no, you may want to admit defeat.

- ✔ **Talk to others who've been there, done it, and got the gluten-free T-shirt.** Most people have gone through denial in one form or another. Talk to other people who've been diagnosed with a coeliac disease – your local clinic or coeliac support group is a good place to start. They probably give you that smug smile with the yep-you've-got-a-classic-case-of-denial look on their faces, because they've been there before. You don't really need to hear much more.

> ✔ **Take notes.** Write down your symptoms, how you feel when you eat certain foods, and the symptoms of gluten intolerance or coeliac disease. Do you see a correlation? When you eat certain foods, do you notice that some of the symptoms you have are similar to some of the symptoms of the condition? Hmmmm. . . .

When others are in denial

The most common type of denial that other members of your family can exhibit occurs when they themselves have all the symptoms but refuse to admit it. Why is it so hard for relatives to believe that they may have this? Problems with gluten, after all, run in the family, and family members often have classic symptoms. Why is it so hard for friends? Gluten intolerance of one type or another is a common condition – yet often they say, 'I don't have that'. The bottom line is that they don't want to have it.

Conditions that require you to be gluten-free, such as coeliac disease, have a unique common denominator: People don't always believe what you're telling them about your condition or the fact that a gluten-free diet may fully restore health. They also don't always understand how strict you really need to be in sticking to the diet.

On more than one occasion we've been accused of being neurotic about the need to avoid all sources of gluten: making sure that food is gluten-free. Doctors have told Danna that she's going 'overboard' because she checks the ingredients of tiny pills. And she's heard more than her fair share of waiters muttering something about her being high maintenance as they walk away from serving her.

Handling the people in your life who refuse to believe you about your condition is difficult, as is dealing with those who refuse to accept that they may also have an intolerance to gluten. The best you can do is work hard to educate them. You have no way to force people into testing or trying the diet, which is sad – because those steps may dramatically improve their health.

Getting Back on Track when You're Feeling Derailed

Even we admit that some difficult emotional challenges arise when you go gluten-free. You may be making a monumental change in your lifestyle! But overcoming those challenges and getting back on track to enjoying life and all it has to offer – far beyond food – are important.

Regaining control

If you don't take control of this diet, the diet controls you. Part of the reason you sometimes feel out of control when you're told to go gluten-free is because you're afraid. Afraid of making mistakes. Afraid of believing inaccurate information. Afraid of letting go of your habits and favourite foods. Afraid you're going to feel deprived. Afraid of being different. Afraid of trying new foods. Afraid of an entirely new lifestyle.

The only way to get beyond the fear is to try new things. Be creative – explore new foods – tantalise your taste buds with all the gluten-free goodies you can think of. Arm yourself with accurate information. Be prepared when you're out and about. Taking control of the diet – and giving your kids control of theirs – is key to living and loving the gluten-free lifestyle.

If you're finding that all your favourite comfort foods are now on the forbidden list, realise that those old comfort foods were probably *dis*comfort foods that actually made you feel bad because they contain gluten. Choose new favourites, but try to avoid the pitfall of undermining weight management efforts by turning to food for comfort.

Getting beyond scary words with heavy implications

Many people embarking upon a gluten-free lifestyle hear some rather scary words being bandied around. Words like *disease*, *chronic*, *restrictions*, *lifelong*, *malabsorption*, *intestinal damage*, and *intolerance* are usually the catalysts for going gluten-free.

Although you can easily be somewhat stunned by the heavy implications of these words, looking beyond them is important. Thinking more about the fact that your health's going to improve, and you're going to feel better and have more energy, can help shift your perspective in a more optimistic direction.

Focusing on what you can eat

When the only food you can eat is gluten-free, every menu item begins to look like a croissant. Wanting what you can't have is the essence of human nature. Tell someone that they can't juggle flaming torches and they're likely to have a sudden urge to do so.

Feeling a bit grumpy? You may have dieter's depression

People who are on a diet of any kind usually feel a 'high' in the beginning, while they're still ultra-motivated and passionate about their commitment. But then, usually around the second or third week, something commonly called *dieter's depression* sets in, and making the right food choices becomes harder. Dieters in this stage aren't much fun to be around. Usually, they're feeling resentful and emotionally deprived, especially if food was a source of comfort for them.

Also, low levels of the hormone serotonin can lead to depression, and the brain needs carbs to produce serotonin. Sometimes when people go gluten-free, they cut their carb level significantly and become depressed as a result. If you think you may be falling into a dieter's depression, first make sure that you're getting good carbs from fruits and vegetables as well as gluten-free cereals. If you find that cooking steamed garden favourites like broccoli and courgettes is too time consuming, you may want to opt for grab-'n-go fruits and vegetables like apples, carrots, and mangetout. All are an excellent source of slow-releasing carbohydrate, full of antioxidant vitamins, and have other health benefits, too. Then finish reading this chapter, which gives you lots of tips for lifting your spirits and focusing on the positive.

Believe us, we know how depriving this lifestyle can be. After all, we've had to compromise, eating gluten-free dinners with nothing but lemon caper chicken, steak and peanut pepper pasta, and scallops with orange; boring side dishes, including sweet potato salad, lemon quinoa, and Vietnamese rice wraps; and tedious desserts, such as cherry cheesecake and blueberry parfait. Depriving, indeed. For more deprivations, turn to the recipes in Chapters 9 to 14 of this book.

If you're feeling deprived, please don't let our sarcasm offend you. Imagining that your selections are limited (they're limited but not limit*ing*) and pining away for freshly baked baguettes is a perfectly normal feeling. Reading the menu and feeling like the only thing you can order is a salad is also normal – or staring into your cupboard and seeing only oatcakes.

We look to vegetarians as role models for how you can improve your perspective. They revel in their diets, usually celebrating their meat-free lifestyle without feeling compromised, because they adopt an innovative approach to keeping their diet healthy and well-balanced.

Focus on what you can eat, rather than what you can't. The list of things you can eat is much longer than the list of things you can't, and if you don't believe us, start writing. Make a list of all the things you can eat – that should keep you busy for a while!

One of the quickest ways to make a particular food take centre stage in your life is to ban it, because human nature is to want what you can't have. For many people, putting gluten on the banned list makes them want it even more. So if you're feeling deprived, indulge yourself! Not with gluten, of course, but with your favourite gluten-free treat. A splurge from time to time can remind you of lots of delicious things you can eat and help take your mind off the things you can't.

Deflecting the temptation to be annoyed or offended

When dealing with your dietary restrictions, you're likely to encounter people who appear unconcerned, uninterested, thoughtless, and sometimes even downright rude. From time to time you may feel hurt and even feel ostracised. Occasionally, you find that people do care but forget to make allowance for you or just miss the point and serve foods you can't eat.

Bear in mind that as you embark upon this new lifestyle, you're probably gaining an entirely new respect for food and a heightened awareness of what having dietary restrictions feels like. And you're probably much more aware of other people's restrictions and sensitivities.

Meanwhile, the rest of the world remains in the dark about the intricacies of the gluten-free lifestyle and may actually be insensitive enough to suggest you join them for dinner – at your (former) favourite pizza place.

Don't be annoyed or offended. People are busy and sometimes so focused on their own fast-paced lives that they can't possibly remember to accommodate yours. Most of the time they're not being rude or thoughtless (okay, sometimes they are); they're just unaware. Be glad that they asked you to dinner, and bring something you can eat, order the salad, or suggest a different restaurant. Save the negative energy for something that really matters – like your next-door neighbour who feels compelled to practise the drums at midnight.

Faking optimism

We're not big fans of people who fake it. Fake people try to be something they're not, usually in an attempt to impress others, and that doesn't go down well with us.

On the other hand, faking optimism is an entirely different thing. This technique is when you pretend to yourself that you feel good about something that you really don't feel good about at all. Before you know it, you really do feel better about it. That's the amazing power of mind over matter!

Faking optimism is easier for some people than others, because everyone falls on different parts of the Optimism Spectrum to start with. Wherever you fall doesn't really matter, though, you can fake optimism and have it affect your overall outlook in a positive way.

Start by thinking of all the reasons why the gluten-free lifestyle is a good thing (visit Chapter 18 if you need some help). Maybe you've improved your focus on nutrition; perhaps you're benefiting from spending more time with the family eating home-cooked meals; maybe you're appreciating the improved health you're experiencing as a result of the diet; or perhaps you've helped someone else in the family discover the key to better health, too.

Write out your list to convince (or remind) yourself that adopting this lifestyle is a wonderful thing in your life. Get excited about it – tell your friends and family how great you feel and why. Before you know it, you've convinced yourself and you aren't faking anymore.

Spreading attitudes – they're contagious

Attitudes can spread like wildfire but bad attitudes spread the quickest.

If you're unhappy about having to adopt a gluten-free lifestyle and haven't found the tips in this chapter helpful for reducing your anxiety, at least don't spread your misery around to other unwitting victims. Most people aren't all that familiar with gluten, the gluten-free lifestyle, and the medical conditions that benefit from it. You may well be the first person to tell them about gluten-free living, and so try to be positive.

If you feel compelled to moan about the foods you miss or express excessive feelings of deprivation and despair, people feel sad and sorry for your 'misfortune'. Do you really want their pity? Instead, when talking to others, try to portray living gluten-free as a great lifestyle and a healthy way to live, so that others can feel that way, too.

You can grieve for the foods you can't eat anymore, or you can rejoice in your new-found health and strength.

Redefining Who You Are

If your doctor has diagnosed you with gluten intolerance or coeliac disease, you may feel different. You are different from other people – and that's okay. We're all different. Some have an interest in sports, others a head for numbers. We readily acknowledge and accept that we're different in those types of things, but sometimes we don't like to be different with the gluten-free diet. Yes, your diet is different – but in the big picture, your restrictions are no different from those of people, such as vegans or people with peanut allergies, who have other dietary restrictions.

You're different from other people – but you're not different from who you were before your diagnosis. Your lifestyle is different, but you're not.

Sometimes people let their condition define who they are. Try not to do this. Is having this condition a disappointment? Maybe – maybe not (we hope after you finish this book you don't think so!). But maybe you're fed up about it, and that's okay.

What you're not is a victim, a martyr, or an invalid. In fact, you're on the road to recovery and amazing health. Lots of people have some kind of adversity in their lives, and they deal with it – you can, too.

If you're having trouble dealing with the gluten-free lifestyle from an emotional or psychological standpoint, step back and take a look at the bigger picture. Why are you giving up gluten in the first place? Probably because each and every molecule of gluten has compromised your health.

Force yourself to remember that the gluten-free diet is key to improving your health, and focus on the great thing you're doing for your body by being gluten-free. Check out these extra tips to help you beat the blues:

- ✔ **Psych yourself up.** Change your perspective on why you eat, what you eat, and how you eat. Remember, you're supposed to eat to live, not the other way around.

- ✔ **Think outside the box.** Getting stuck in food ruts, eating the same basic meals day after day, week after week, is easy. Explore new foods, find new favourites, and be creative in finding new ways to tantalise your taste buds.

- ✔ **Remember, the diet gets easier with time.** If the gluten-free lifestyle seems difficult to you from an emotional or practical standpoint, realising that it gets easier with time can help. If you accept and adapt to it, we hope you'll come to love it!

So you're on a diet. That makes you unique?

You can't eat certain things. If you do, you have to deal with physical consequences. Your selections on a menu may be limited, you have to be careful about what you eat when you're in social situations, and you can't always eat what everyone else is eating. Your diet is restricted, and it's a pain in the neck. So what's so different about you? You sound like you're on a diet. That makes you unique? We think not!

You can go on a diet for lots of reasons. People usually think of going on diets to lose weight, but some are on special diets to gain weight (much to the annoyance of those trying to lose). Others are on special diets because they have high blood pressure, high cholesterol, heart disease, food allergies, diabetes, or kidney failure. For health or religious reasons, some people choose to avoid meat or foods that contain certain additives. Athletes in training often have special diets, and pregnant or lactating women sometimes choose to modify their diets to optimise their baby's health. Those of us on a gluten-free diet tend to think of it as being different from other diets – but in many ways, it's not different at all!

✔ **Seek help.** Whether help comes from family members, support groups, friends, or counsellors, sometimes others can help make the transition easier.

✔ **Avoid negative people and influences.** Basically, rid your life of the negative. If the gluten-free way of life is a struggle for you, the last thing you need is a malicious friend or relative sabotaging your efforts.

✔ **Recommit yourself.** Sometimes you need to reaffirm your commitment by remembering why you're living gluten-free.

Resisting the Temptation to Cheat

Sometimes we feel as if a million and one diets exist out there: low-fat, high-protein, low-carb, low-calorie, low-glycaemic, and everything in between. The thing they all have in common is that people cheat on them, and that's a fact. People cheat on diets.

But you can't cheat on this diet, especially if you have coeliac disease. No, not even a little. Approaches such as 'everything in moderation' and 'a little isn't going to hurt you' don't apply if you have gluten intolerance or coeliac disease.

Resisting the temptation to cheat starts with understanding why you want to cheat.

Realising why you want to cheat

You may want to eat forbidden glutenous goods for many reasons, and if you hope to resist the temptation, working out what's driving your desire is important. Some of the more common triggers that may tempt you to cheat on the gluten-free diet are:

- ✔ **The food is just too good to resist.** We realise that this isn't a particularly profound insight as to why they do it, but most people who indulge in a food that's not on their diet do so because it's just too yummy to say no.

- ✔ **Just this once.** Not a good plan. 'Just this once' is the start of a slippery slope to a diet becoming long-forgotten.

- ✔ **You want to fit in.** If everyone else were jumping off a cliff, would you? (Bungee jumpers aren't allowed to answer that.) In reality, other people probably aren't paying much attention to what you're eating anyway. Social situations are about the company, the conversation, and the ambience. Yes, they're about the food as well, but people aren't paying attention to what *you're* eating.

- ✔ **You turn to the food for comfort eating.** In difficult times, people sometimes turn to certain foods. If a gluten-containing food is your comfort food, a weak moment may send you straight to the food that you think consoles you – even though you know it isn't going to make you feel better.

- ✔ **It's a special occasion.** Try again. This excuse may work for other diets, but not this one. Eating even a little bit of gluten may turn your social affair into a dreaded nightmare. No occasion is worth compromising your health, and furthermore, special occasions are about the *occasion*, not the food.

- ✔ **You're bored by the diet.** If all you're eating is rice cakes and celery, we don't blame you. Live it up, get creative, and try new things. Use this book as a guide to work out exactly what you *can* eat, and then challenge yourself to try something new. If you need a little inspiration, check out Chapter 8, which offers ideas for getting creative in the kitchen and finding out how to make anything gluten-free.

- ✔ **A little gluten isn't going to hurt.** Yes it is. If you plan to use this excuse, we urge you to read Chapters 2 and 3.

- ✔ **The diet's too hard.** Hey, this is a *For Dummies* book, remember? This book is supposed to make it really easy to work out what you can and can't eat, and how to live (and love!) the lifestyle. Sometimes changing your perspective isn't easy, we give you that. But you *can* do it, and between your friends, family, books like this, and the helpful resources listed in Chapter 5, you've got plenty of support.

✔ **Someone's sabotaging your diet.** People really do this; in fact, it's common! Usually, they're not aware that they're doing it, and they all do it for different reasons. Sometimes people sabotage because they're jealous that you're getting healthier than they are. Sometimes they do it because they don't 'believe' you need to be on the diet (see the earlier section 'When others are in denial'). Other times, people do it because they don't want to have to follow the clean-kitchen rules or have to put the effort into preparing gluten-free foods. Don't succumb to sabotage efforts. Instead, try to find someone who seems particularly supportive of your gluten-free lifestyle, and ask for help. People *love* to help, and they get tremendous satisfaction out of lending a shoulder, an ear, or a hand.

✔ **You think you've already blown the diet so much that it doesn't matter anymore.** Not true. Today can be the first day of the rest of your gluten-free life.

Although these are powerful factors in enticing you to go for the gluten, overcoming the temptation is important. Sometimes the key to saying no is taking a look at the consequences.

You choose to cheat – or not – because you have full control over what you put in your mouth. When you cheat on the gluten-free diet, you're cheating yourself out of better health.

Assessing the consequences

One of the most difficult parts about looking at the consequences of your actions is that if they're not immediate and drastic, you sometimes feel that they don't matter. People who are dieting to lose weight often don't notice any consequences from a setback or two because they don't see the extra centimetres jump back onto their waistlines when they eat a bowl of ice cream – and for that matter, they may never gain the weight back, because for them, a high-calorie indulgence from time to time may be okay.

If you have gluten intolerance or coeliac disease, though, the consequences can have serious adverse effects on your health, and if you cheat chronically, those effects can be cumulative. In fact, you may be setting yourself up to develop conditions like osteoporosis, anaemia, thyroid disease, and lots of other conditions that we're betting aren't worth eating that chocolate digestive. For a friendly reminder of how much damage you can be doing when you cheat, head to Chapters 2 and 3.

Overcoming temptation

After you discover why you want to cheat and you remind yourself of the consequences, you have to take the final step and just say no. Here are a few things you can do to make saying no a little easier:

✔ **Indulge in your favourite gluten-free goodie.** If you're craving a piece of shortbread, eat it – the gluten-free kind, of course. Just about anything that has gluten in it has a gluten-free counterpart these days. If you prefer to grab a (gluten-free) chocolate bar, that's fine, too. If you're tempted to eat something with gluten, try to find something else that satisfies you just as much but still keeps you on track with your gluten-free lifestyle.

✔ **Reward yourself when you resist.** If you've been challenged by temptation and successfully overcome it, give yourself a treat. It doesn't have to be food – maybe buy yourself something special or do something nice for yourself. Doing so can reinforce your strength and commitment to the lifestyle.

✔ **Simplify what you need to do.** If the diet seems too much effort, perhaps you're trying to do too much and need to go back to the basics. When your menu plans are overwhelming, cut something out so that you don't have so much to think about. If you don't understand the diet, read parts of this book again, particularly Chapters 4 and 5. You may also want to seek out some of the resources in Chapter 5.

✔ **Make your lifestyle a priority.** This change is about you – your health and your future. If you find this lifestyle too difficult because of your work commitments, think about changing your work pattern. If you have negative people in your life who seem to sabotage your efforts, avoid them if you can. If something's not working in your life, change it. Being gluten-free is about more than a diet; it's about a lifestyle, and should be a high priority.

Part VI
The Part of Tens

'When did you first notice the bloating,
Mr Snellthorpe?'

In this part . . .

We summarise some of the many benefits of being gluten-free in Chapter 18. Chapter 19 lists tips to help you come to terms with, and come to love, the gluten-free lifestyle. In Chapter 20, we introduce you to the wonderful organisation known as Coeliac UK, and give you some of the many compelling reasons why you should join it.

Chapter 18

Ten Benefits of Being Gluten-Free

*H*ow about these benefits: no more diarrhoea, no more headaches, no more fatigue, no more depression, and no more irritable bowel syndrome? (You can read more about how these conditions may benefit from a gluten-free diet in Chapter 2.) If you're going gluten-free because you have some form of gluten intolerance, coeliac disease, or dermatitis herpetiformis (DH), we don't need to tell you how lousy you can feel – and the key to not feeling lousy is being gluten-free. For you, the benefits are obvious.

You Know How to Improve Your Health

We always get over excited and end up telling the punch line halfway through a joke. Here we go again, giving you the very *best* benefit of being gluten-free right out of the starting gate: You, unlike many people, have the key to better health – a gluten-free diet.

This idea is especially true if you've been diagnosed with gluten intolerance or coeliac disease; most people who shouldn't eat gluten aren't so lucky. They don't even know that they have a problem with gluten, and so they have no clue what's making them feel so ill. They try various unscientific tests that tell them to start cutting out milk, eggs, or some other potential allergens needlessly, at the same time missing out on important nutrients. You, on the other hand, know exactly what's making you ill – gluten because you've been checked out properly – and you can eliminate it from your diet, enjoying fully restored health.

Your Health Improves Right Away

If you have coeliac disease, gluten damages your intestinal tract. The minute you go gluten-free, your body starts healing, you begin to absorb nutrients again, and before you know it, you're feeling so great that you can't even remember how awful you used to feel. Whether you've been unwell for years, days, or never even seemed to feel any effects from gluten, your body can begin healing immediately, and that means your health can improve, too.

Your Diet Can Be Super Healthy

You can adopt the gluten-free diet in several ways. You can just cut out gluten and forget about the rest of your diet, or you can fit a gluten-free diet into an otherwise healthy diet. A diet that's almost automatically gluten-free and very healthy is based on the cave dweller's *Paleolithic diet*, which consists of eating meat, poultry, fish, seafood, fruit, vegetables, berries, nuts, ancient alternative 'grains', and other foods that your body was designed to eat – all of which are naturally gluten-free. Follow this form of a gluten-free diet, and you may look and feel better and live longer. You can find more information on this approach by flipping to Chapter 6. Watch out, though, because many of the Paleolithic diets that you find on the Internet tend to focus on the fad end of the diet scale and aren't always written by people like us, who understand the risks of faddy diets.

You Can Never Develop Coeliac Disease

You need three things to develop coeliac disease: the genetic predisposition, an environmental trigger of some kind (a virus, surgery, trauma, pregnancy, or emotional distress, for example), and a diet that includes gluten. If you're not eating gluten, you can't develop coeliac disease!

You May Be Less Likely to Develop Associated Autoimmune Diseases

Many autoimmune diseases go hand in hand, meaning that if you develop one, you're likely to develop another. If you have coeliac disease and you continue to eat gluten, your chances of developing associated autoimmune diseases increase over time. Some studies have shown that the sooner you cut gluten out of your diet, the lower your risk of developing other conditions (to find out more about related conditions, check out Chapter 2).

You Can Restore Your Nutrient Status to Optimal Levels

Many people with coeliac disease and gluten intolerance can also be seriously lacking in some nutrients. This deficit may occur because their condition has affected their ability to absorb their nutrients or because their diet is woefully restricted: They may have excluded different foods that they suspected made them ill.

Either way, once you're following the right restriction diet – in your case the gluten-free diet – your gut begins to heal straight away and in turn your ability to absorb nutrients gets a boost. You can also eat a more varied and complete diet because you now know the culprit, and so you can start to reintroduce all those other healthy gluten-free foods you were previously avoiding.

You Can Avoid Complications

People suffering from coeliac disease, who are undiagnosed or don't follow a strict gluten-free diet, are prone to develop complications, such as osteoporosis, bowel cancer, or fertility problems.

Malignant complications are the most serious type, but once you've followed the gluten-free diet for 3 to 5 years the risk is reduced right back to that of people who haven't got coeliac disease or even heard of it.

The risk of osteoporosis is increased in people who are diagnosed late in life due to long-term malabsorption of calcium. Being aware of this risk and taking action means that you're more likely to avoid complications of osteoporosis, such as fracture.

The risk of infertility and adverse events of pregnancy are increased in undiagnosed coeliac disease, but again the risks are reduced following diagnosis and a gluten-free diet.

Your Weight Can Be Easier to Manage

When you go gluten-free the nutritious way (dip into Chapter 6), you eat a varied diet with good quality protein and low-glycaemic-index foods. Eating these types of foods helps stabilise the 'I'm hungry' and 'I'm full' hormones so that you don't always feel hungry; this diet also causes your body to use the stored fat (read 'love handles' or 'saddlebags') as energy.

Sometimes when people go gluten-free, they hunt down specialty gluten-free products like biscuits, cakes, pizza basis, breads, rolls, and pasta. These foods can be really useful and many may be available to you on prescription, but they're not always so good at managing your hunger. Eating plenty of foods that are naturally gluten-free is also important. If you eat a balanced diet containing both naturally gluten-free diet and special gluten-free products, you help your body to function the way it's supposed to, decrease your hunger pangs, and make managing your weight much easier.

You're More Aware of Nutrition

Now that you're gluten-free, you're much more knowledgeable about nutrition than most people. For one thing, you read labels. You know that processed foods usually have multisyllabic ingredients (with lots of x's and y's in them). You, unlike the other people in the supermarket, know that malt usually comes from barley, maltodextrin doesn't contain malt, and glucose isn't the same as gluten (if you're thinking, 'Isn't it?' please read Chapter 3). Hopefully, you've even experienced the joys of quinoa, millet, and other alternative grains that many people have never heard of, and you know that they're nutritional powerhouses compared to some cereal grains.

Your Blood-Sugar Levels May Stabilise

If you're following the gluten-free diet in a nutritious way, as we outline in Chapter 6, you're essentially eating low-glycaemic-index foods that help stabilise your blood-sugar levels. Many wheat-based products are high-glycaemic and quickly turn to sugar in your bloodstream and cause your insulin levels to spike and then drop quickly. Energy levels and even moods can follow this yo-yo pattern: Not only is that unhealthy, but also getting a rush of energy only to crash and burn quickly is no fun. A naturally gluten-free diet helps stabilise your blood-sugar levels and gives you sustained energy throughout the day. If you have diabetes, you can benefit greatly from this approach when you're trying to control your blood sugar.

Chapter 19

Ten Tips to Help You (Or Your Child) Love the Gluten-Free Lifestyle

The transition from gluten-glutton to 'gluten-free is good for me' is harder for some people than others. Discovering how to live gluten-free is one thing; finding out how to *love* living gluten-free is sometimes quite another. You can be getting along just fine with the gluten-free lifestyle, and then for some reason life seems to turn into one big gluten-fest and resisting your gluten-eating friends, who seem to be taunting you with gluten galore, becomes even harder.

Focus on What You Can Eat

Staring into a cupboard to see nothing but gluten is really easy. Sometimes you may seem to find more gluten around you than the air you breathe. It's true – gluten is everywhere – yet the reality is that the list of things you can eat is a lot longer than the list of things you can't. You just have to shift your thinking a bit. Instead of thinking about the foods you can't have anymore, focus on the foods you can eat, and put a special emphasis on those that you especially enjoy. If you're feeling a little restricted or deprived, treat yourself to your favourite gluten-free indulgences. Try to think outside the box and explore foods you may not otherwise have tried, or work out how to make your favourite glutenous meal into a gluten-free zone (Chapter 8 helps you get creative in the kitchen). Before you know it, you realise that the gluten-free lifestyle may have its restrictions, but it's definitely not restrictive.

Expand Your Culinary Horizons with Alternative Grains

A bold, gluten-free world exists out there, filled with foods that most people have never heard of: quinoa, amaranth, sago, millet, buckwheat, and corn-flour top the list of our favourites. Don't underestimate your children's willingness to try new foods. Even if they're reluctant to experiment at first, they usually make the leap and find out how to broaden their horizons. Whether your palate is conditioned to enjoy bland and tasteless foods or foods exploding with flavour, you can experience a vast range of unique and exceptionally nutritious foods.

Enjoy Some International Flair

Lots of cultures use naturally gluten-free ingredients in their cooking. Many Asian cuisines, including Thai and Vietnamese, are often gluten-free, as are many Mexican and Indian dishes. Do some research on the Internet to find out what ingredients a particular culture uses, or explore cookbooks including recipes from around the world. You can work out how to cook foods from those cultures or venture out to restaurants to enjoy new gluten-free taste experiences – globally!

Take Control of the Diet

Whether you're 2 or 102, if you're going gluten-free, you need to take control of the diet. The diet can suddenly control things such as what you eat, when and where you eat, with whom you eat, and even how you eat. But remember that you're in control. You decide what you're going to eat, when you're going to eat, and with whom. Planning ahead helps – we talk about menu planning and shopping in Chapter 7 – and making sure that something's always available for you when you're hungry is important. We cover the golden rules of going out gluten-free in Chapter 15, because part of being in control of the diet is being able to get out and about and know that you're able to eat safely when you're not at home.

If your child's on the gluten-free diet, start giving him or her control from day one, no matter how young. People vastly underestimate children's ability to understand the diet and why being strict about following it is so important. Check out Chapter 16 for more about bringing up happy, healthy, gluten-free kids.

Eat to Live, Don't Live to Eat

Your body is designed to use food as fuel, not as a comforter or soul mate. Of course, food has become a huge part of society and interpersonal relationships, and by definition, social functions often revolve around food. But that doesn't mean food *is* the social function, or that you have to eat the food that's on offer. Food tastes good, and having a full stomach often feels good. But food serves a greater purpose, and you should treat it as a fuel, not an emotional crutch.

Remember: You're Different. So What?

People talk about wanting to be unique, and yet cringe when they're afraid they may stand out from the crowd. The bottom line is that everyone is different, even when people try to look the same. If you're on the gluten-free diet, your bread may look a little different, and you may sometimes appear to be a little demanding at a restaurant. So what? Many people ask to 'customise' their meal from what's on the menu. Vegetarians have to avoid a huge portion of the buffet table. Some people don't like chicken, others can't tolerate milk, and some can even die if they eat foods to which they are severely allergic. Lots of people have different diets and lifestyles. Yours happens to be healthy, delicious, and the key to your better health.

Go Ahead – Enjoy a (Gluten-Free) Splurge

If you put too many restrictions on yourself when trying to maintain a healthy, gluten-free lifestyle, you may just find yourself getting bored and frustrated, and start to feel deprived. Give yourself a break. Indulge from time to time in your favourite gluten-free extravagance, whether it happens to be a sweet treat or a baked potato loaded with sour cream and butter. Finding and maintaining a good balance is as important a part of a gluten-free lifestyle as any other healthy diet.

Tune In to the Benefits

When you tune in and remind yourself of the benefits of being gluten-free (refer to Chapter 18), that step reinforces your thinking as to *why* you're living a gluten-free lifestyle. If you think that writing down all the good things about being gluten-free may be helpful, do it. Stick the list on the fridge, if you want a daily reminder, or keep a list in a diary on your desk. Maybe you want to challenge yourself to add an item to the list each day or week. When you focus on the reasons why being gluten-free is a good thing in your life, you can gain a new or renewed appreciation for the lifestyle itself.

Turn Away from Temptation

Avoid putting yourself in tempting situations where possible, saving your strength for when you have no choice in the matter. You're not doing yourself any favours if you surround yourself with tidbits of temptation, whether at work, at home, or in social situations. You probably shouldn't take that job at the bakery. Don't think you're building character by holding a slice of pizza to your nose and taking a big whiff. And yes, you may want to think twice about entering that pie-eating contest. Enough gluten exists in this world without setting yourself up for temptation and frustration – so when you can, make it easy for yourself.

Deal with It; Don't Dwell on It

If you're angry, sad, grief-stricken, confused, frustrated, agitated, and down-right ticked off about having to live without gluten, that's okay. Lots of people experience those feelings, especially if they're forced to embark upon an entirely new – and sometimes very different – lifestyle. But deal with those feelings, and move on. Tell your friends, family, and support groups, share with them how you're feeling, and let them try to help you work through the feelings. If you need professional help, get it. Not wallowing in the negativity of your circumstances is important, or your thoughts may intensify and can even end up causing other physical and emotional problems.

Chapter 20

Ten Reasons to Join Coeliac UK

. . . .

In This Chapter

▶ Discovering a source of medical and dietary information you can trust

▶ Getting hold of useful and practical leaflets

▶ Tapping into a nationwide support network

▶ Supporting research into gluten intolerance

. . . .

Coeliac UK is the only charity in the UK for people with gluten intolerance. It was founded in 1968 and today has more than 70,000 members, with about 650 new members joining every month! Becoming a member is free if you've been medically diagnosed with coeliac disease or dermatitis herpetiformis (DH), or if you are the parent of a child with coeliac disease. When you register, Coeliac UK requests the name and location of the hospital or GP surgery where you were diagnosed and the method of diagnosis. If you're gluten intolerant, but haven't been medically diagnosed with coeliac disease, you can still make good use of Coeliac UK for advice and support via the Web site and telephone helpline. If you haven't yet discovered Coeliac UK for yourself, this chapter contains the ten best reasons for doing so.

Accessing Updated Medical Info

Coeliac UK is a source of expert medical advice about the symptoms, diagnosis, and ongoing health care you can expect if you have gluten intolerance. This information is especially helpful if you're struggling to come to terms with being gluten-free or with managing your condition. The Web site (www.coeliac.co.uk) is a good place to start, accessible to members and non-members alike. The section 'Coeliac Disease – Frequently Asked Questions' is a mine of useful facts. If you can't find the answer to a medical question, or if you want more detailed advice, as a member you can call the free helpline (0870-4448804) manned by a dedicated diet and health team. Alternatively, you can complete the contact form on the 'Contact Us' page. If you've got spare time, the site contains a fascinating history of the discovery of the cause of coeliac disease and the evolution of treatment.

Sourcing Dietary Advice You Can Trust

With so much information (and *mis*information) about the gluten-free diet available, you may have difficulty knowing where to turn for independent and reliable dietary information. We hope you find this book to be a good source but we are also huge fans of the dietary support on offer from Coeliac UK. If you are new to gluten-free living you may want to order the packs from their online shop entitled *Getting Started*. This sets you off to a flying start with leaflets on what you can eat, a gluten-free checklist, and hints and tips on shopping for gluten-free food. A second pack, *Gluten-free Living*, includes leaflets on cooking, healthy balanced eating, and tips for vegetarians. The Web site also has pages of useful dietary advice on everything from food labelling to recipes you can download. The helpline can link you to expert dietitians who are available to answer your food and drink queries on 0870-4448804.

Foraging for Safe Foods

Each year Coeliac UK produces the gluten-free bible, *The Food and Drink Directory*, containing over 11,000 safe gluten-free foods, each one researched and checked by Coeliac UK. The directory also contains a handy list of all products available on prescription in the UK. The booklet is sent free to members or you can buy it from their online shop. Make sure that you always use an up-to-date version because manufacturers have an annoying habit of changing the ingredients in their products. Monthly updates can be accessed via the Web site or e-mailed to you. They can also be sourced on BBC2 Ceefax, via a telephone hotline, or even via good old Royal Mail (if you send a self-addressed envelope to Coeliac UK).

Managing the Diet Away from Home

When newly diagnosed with coeliac disease, you may feel as if eating out is never going to be the same again. Even if you've been managing okay for a while you may feel like you need more inspiration. Well, the Coeliac UK Web site is the place to find it. The site is packed with pages of advice to help you cope with eating away from home and the dedicated Web pages of the local branches of Coeliac UK contain up-to-date listings of venues that can cater for the gluten-free diet in your local area. You can download free phrase guides, available in several languages, and order books that make managing your gluten intolerance on holiday just as easy. You can also follow a link to the Web site www.gluten-free-onthego.com, also run by Coeliac UK, which contains several gluten-free restaurant and accommodation listings to take the work out of finding somewhere that understands your dietary needs.

Finding Family-Friendly Facts

For parents with young children on a gluten-free diet, Coeliac UK can provide practical, family-friendly advice from experts. If you're having a particular problem, the chances are that someone else has found a solution to it. A good start is to order the *Parents' and Carers Pack* from Coeliac UK. It covers things such as: beginning playgroup, starting school, packed lunches, prescriptions for children, and even a template letter to give to the school to help them understand gluten intolerance. The Web site also has a section dedicated entirely to child-friendly information: weaning your baby, children's party ideas, guidelines for school cookery classes, and fun recipes for kids. Coeliac UK even produce a special children's storybook, *Me and My Tummy*, which can help you explain gluten intolerance to a young child.

Shopping Sensationally

The Coeliac UK online shop has a whole section of great recipe books covering everything from home baking to dinner party entertaining, the sale of which helps to raise funds to support the organisation. We have also discovered a page on the Web site with direct links to the Web sites of a whole range of manufacturers and retailers. From these you can order a range of gluten-free products or services, ranging from beer and sausages, right through to a range of meals that can be delivered directly to you door. Ordering can be online or by phone direct from the comfort of your armchair. How convenient is that?

Seeking Support

Support is one of the most important things in helping you to follow a gluten-free lifestyle long term. We are great believers in seeking support wherever you can. Coeliac UK coordinates a network of 100 voluntary groups around the UK and can put you in touch with your local support group. These groups provide help to newly diagnosed people locally and offer a chance to meet and talk to other people with coeliac disease. They also support existing members and run educational or fun events and fund-raising activities. Details of groups can be found on the Web site or by ringing the helpline. Knowing that you're not alone is great.

Keeping Up with the Gluten-Free News

Getting stuck in a rut on any diet is all too easy – cooking the same old meals, buying the same old foods – and the gluten-free lifestyle is no exception. Finding new recipes or products (including prescribable items) that are gluten-free is very useful. Coeliac UK has two publications to help you do just that. *Crossed Grain* – sent out free of charge three times a year to all members – is a lively, vibrant magazine packed full of practical advice and inspirational features written by experts. If you're a non-member you can still order copies from the online shop. *eXG* is a free monthly online newsletter containing the news, medical updates, new cooking products, and *The Food and Drink Directory* updates. You can sign up for it via the Coeliac UK Web site.

Supporting Good Healthcare

Coeliac UK works with various members of healthcare teams in hospitals and primary care, facilitating good management of members, and improving diagnosis and treatment. The organisation also liaises with the food manufacturing and food service sectors to raise awareness of coeliac disease and influence food labelling and availability of gluten-free food inside the home and out. Finally, Coeliac UK also works with the media to get coverage of coeliac disease, and to raise awareness among the general public and government to get coeliac disease high on the political agenda.

Aiding Research

Coeliac UK funds are used not only to subsidise free membership but also to support cutting-edge medical research into all aspects of coeliac disease and dermatitis herpetiformis (DH) including diagnosis, prevention, and treatment. One such project currently running that caught our eye aims to identify which fragments of gluten cause coeliac disease with the ultimate hope of discovering a form of gluten that's non-toxic to people with coeliac disease. Full details and updates on all ongoing research project are covered in a consumer-friendly fashion in the online newsletter *eXG*.

Coeliac UK is not government funded, but relies on donations, sales of products, and fundraising. Coeliac UK can be contacted by post at: Suites A–D Octagon Court, High Wycombe, Buckinghamshire, HP11 2HS, UK, via the helpline on 0870-4448804, or by visiting www.coeliac.co.uk.

The registered charity number is 1048167.

Index

• **X** •

• **Z** •

Notes

FOR DUMMIES®

Do Anything. Just Add Dummies

PROPERTY

UK editions

978-0-7645-7027-8

978-0-470-02921-3

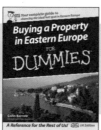

978-0-7645-7047-6

PERSONAL FINANCE

978-0-7645-7023-0

978-0-470-51510-5

978-0-470-05815-2

BUSINESS

978-0-7645-7018-6

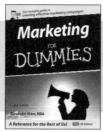

978-0-7645-7056-8

978-0-7645-7026-1

Answering Tough Interview
Questions For Dummies
(978-0-470-01903-0)

Arthritis For Dummies
(978-0-470-02582-6)

Being the Best Man
For Dummies
(978-0-470-02657-1)

British History
For Dummies
(978-0-470-03536-8)

Building Self-Confidence
For Dummies
(978-0-470-01669-5)

Buying a Home on a Budget
For Dummies
(978-0-7645-7035-3)

Children's Health
For Dummies
(978-0-470-02735-6)

Cognitive Behavioural Therapy
For Dummies
(978-0-470-01838-5)

Cricket For Dummies
(978-0-470-03454-5)

CVs For Dummies
(978-0-7645-7017-9)

Detox For Dummies
(978-0-470-01908-5)

Diabetes For Dummies
(978-0-470-05810-7)

Divorce For Dummies
(978-0-7645-7030-8)

DJing For Dummies
(978-0-470-03275-6)

eBay.co.uk For Dummies
(978-0-7645-7059-9)

English Grammar For Dummies
(978-0-470-05752-0)

Gardening For Dummies
(978-0-470-01843-9)

Genealogy Online
For Dummies
(978-0-7645-7061-2)

Green Living For Dummies
(978-0-470-06038-4)

Hypnotherapy For Dummies
(978-0-470-01930-6)

Life Coaching For Dummies
(978-0-470-03135-3)

Neuro-linguistic Programming
For Dummies
(978-0-7645-7028-5)

Nutrition For Dummies
(978-0-7645-7058-2)

Parenting For Dummies
(978-0-470-02714-1)

Pregnancy For Dummies
(978-0-7645-7042-1)

Rugby Union For Dummies
(978-0-470-03537-5)

Self Build and Renovation For
Dummies
(978-0-470-02586-4)

Starting a Business on
eBay.co.uk For Dummies
(978-0-470-02666-3)

Starting and Running an Online
Business For Dummies
(978-0-470-05768-1)

The GL Diet For Dummies
(978-0-470-02753-0)

The Romans For Dummies
(978-0-470-03077-6)

Thyroid For Dummies
(978-0-470-03172-8)

UK Law and Your Rights
For Dummies
(978-0-470-02796-7)

Writing a Novel & Getting
Published For Dummies
(978-0-470-05910-4)

Available wherever books are sold. For more information or to order direct go to www.wiley.com or call 0800 243407 (Non UK call +44 1243 843296)

FOR DUMMIES®

Do Anything. Just Add Dummies

HOBBIES

Poker
978-0-7645-5232-8

Sewing
978-0-7645-6847-3

Drawing
978-0-7645-5476-6

Also available:

Art For Dummies
(978-0-7645-5104-8)

Aromatherapy For Dummies
(978-0-7645-5171-0)

Bridge For Dummies
(978-0-471-92426-5)

Card Games For Dummies
(978-0-7645-9910-1)

Chess For Dummies
(978-0-7645-8404-6)

Improving Your Memory
For Dummies
(978-0-7645-5435-3)

Massage For Dummies
(978-0-7645-5172-7)

Meditation For Dummies
(978-0-471-77774-8)

Photography For Dummies
(978-0-7645-4116-2)

Quilting For Dummies
(978-0-7645-9799-2)

EDUCATION

Cooking Basics
978-0-7645-7206-7

The Koran
978-0-7645-5581-7

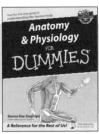

Anatomy & Physiology
978-0-7645-5422-3

Also available:

Algebra For Dummies
(978-0-7645-5325-7)

Algebra II For Dummies
(978-0-471-77581-2)

Astronomy For Dummies
(978-0-7645-8465-7)

Buddhism For Dummies
(978-0-7645-5359-2)

Calculus For Dummies
(978-0-7645-2498-1)

Forensics For Dummies
(978-0-7645-5580-0)

Islam For Dummies
(978-0-7645-5503-9)

Philosophy For Dummies
(978-0-7645-5153-6)

Religion For Dummies
(978-0-7645-5264-9)

Trigonometry For Dummies
(978-0-7645-6903-6)

PETS

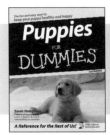

Puppies
978-0-470-03717-1

Dog Training
978-0-7645-8418-3

Cats
978-0-7645-5275-5

Also available:

Labrador Retrievers
For Dummies
(978-0-7645-5281-6)

Aquariums For Dummies
(978-0-7645-5156-7)

Birds For Dummies
(978-0-7645-5139-0)

Dogs For Dummies
(978-0-7645-5274-8)

Ferrets For Dummies
(978-0-7645-5259-5)

Golden Retrievers
For Dummies
(978-0-7645-5267-0)

Horses For Dummies
(978-0-7645-9797-8)

Jack Russell Terriers
For Dummies
(978-0-7645-5268-7)

Puppies Raising & Training
Diary For Dummies
(978-0-7645-0876-9)

Available wherever books are sold. For more information or to order direct go to www.wiley.com or call 0800 243407 (Non UK call +44 1243 843296)